THE LATEST BOOK IN THE MOST EFFECTIVE, BEST-SELLING MARKETING SERIES OF ALL TIME

"Ask almost any successful entrepreneur what the best book is for building a small business, and one of Levinson's titles will surely come up...The best-selling classic, *Guerrilla Marketing,* has helped to revolutionize marketing. This is more than a book. It's a winning edge."
THE ENTREPRENEUR'S BUSINESS SUCCESS GUIDE

"It effectively lays out the many options for small companies that can't afford to hire an advertising or PR agency and, more important, that want to conduct their own marketing."
INC. MAGAZINE

"Slam dunk!"
JULIE LOPRESTI, ADVERTISING MANAGER, PACIFIC BELL

"No one knows how to use the weapons of the trade better than industry expert Jay Levinson."
ENTREPRENEUR MAGAZINE

"A veritable plum pudding of marketing techniques and secrets."
LOS ANGELES TIMES

"I just finished reading *Guerrilla Marketing.* Wow! I learned more about marketing from this book in a week than I did during my five years in college, and I was a marketing major!"
ROBERT POPE

"*Guerrilla Marketing Excellence* has taught me more than I ever knew about marketing. In fact, I have just rewrtitten every ad for our business, reshaping each one to meet guerrilla specs."
MURRAY CANN

"I've used *Guerrilla Marketing* as my business bible for the last three years. Since first reading it I have almost quadrupled my business."
DAVID COBABE

"In case you didn't know, *Guerrilla Marketing* is the best selling marketing book in the world. It's easy to see why...Levinson has a unique way of illuminating the obvious, in terms than anyone can understand."
JEFF McNEAL, *ON-HOLD MARKETING QUARTERLY*

"No matter what business you're in, *Guerrilla Marketing,* the bible of lively, low-cost marketing tips, is invaluable. Levinson provides real-world strategies, including how to make contact with potential customers and close the sale. The book is better than ever"
JANE APPLEGATE, COLUMNIST, *LOS ANGELES TIMES*

"Your books on guerrilla marketing have become my bibles! I owe so much to the information contained in them. I have recommended them to many people and have given them as Christmas presents!"
WENDY MIDDLETON, GO SECRETARY DIRECT

"Jay Conrad Levinson wrote the book that made 'guerrilla marketing' an office-hold word. Keep it on your shelf and reread it from time to time."
ELAINE FLOYD, *ADVERTISING FROM THE DESKTOP*

"Jay Conrad Levinson...the guru of guerrilla marketing...has a knack for showing us how to get the most out of marketing. Levinson has...business strategies that work for the 90s."
AMERICAN BOOKSELLER MAGAZINE

"Jay is one of the foremost marketing experts in the world."
CENTEX BUSINESS EXPO

"Resourceful, penny-wise marketing techniques."
KIRKUS REVIEWS

"A source of inspiration for many independent entrepreneurs."
BOOKLIST

"Actually, every book by Levinson is worth reading."
JANE APPLEGATE, *SUCCEEDING IN SMALL BUSINESS*

"When it comes to marketing, the best-selling *Guerrilla Marketing* is my choice."
LINDA CASE, *HIT THE BOOKS*

THE
GUERRILLA
MARKETING HANDBOOK

THE
GUERRILLA
MARKETING HANDBOOK

Jay Conrad Levinson and Seth Godin

Houghton Mifflin Company
Boston   New York

The Golden Mailbox, by Ted Nicholas
©1992 by Dearborn Financial Publishing, Inc. Published by Enterprise•Dearborn, a
division of Dearborn Publishing Group, Inc./Chicago. All rights reserved.

For information about permission to reproduce selections
from this book, write to Permissions, Houghton Mifflin Company,
215 Park Avenue South, New York, New York 10003.

CIP data is available.

ISBN 0-395-70013-2

For information about this and other Houghton Mifflin trade and reference
books and multimedia products, visit The Bookstore at Houghton Mifflin
on the World Wide Web at http://www.hmco.com/trade/.

Printed in the United States of America
RMT 10 9 8 7 6 5 4

ACKNOWLEDGMENTS

This book is dedicated to my coauthor, Seth Godin, who was one of the original guerrillas, an early fan of guerrilla marketing, and had the whole idea for a valuable sourcebook that would enable wannabe guerrillas to become real-life guerrillas. Seth did the lion's share of work—research, coddling, creating, computing, word processing—and was an ideal partner. His wife, Helene, and new son, Alexander, are very lucky. So am I.

Jay Conrad Levinson
GMINTL@aol.com

In fact, this book wouldn't have happened without the input and effort of a number of extraordinary people. Steve Lewers, our editor at Houghton Mifflin, has been a tremendous asset to the Guerrilla series for years. He put Jay and me together, and shepherded this book through almost a year of writing and production. His masterful editing was above and beyond the call of duty.

Julie Maner did most of the heavy lifting on this book. Every word, every picture, every sidebar, and every resource passed through her computer on the way to the printer. Her talent, patience, and effort were boundless.

We were lucky enough to receive insight and opinions from dozens of guerrillas around the country. Mark O'Halloran, Ivan Levinson, Alan Schlenker, Jim Dornbos, and Herschell Gordon Lewis were generous in their feedback and support. *How* magazine gave us access to their talented subscriber base. Thanks to Lori Kozlove for helping us navigate through their organization.

Megan O'Connor and Lisa DiMona painted countless bananas with camouflage paint, and the rest of the SGP staff—Jen Gniady, Carol Markowitz, Karen Watts, Robin Dellabough, Amy Winger, and Bruce Cato joined them in contributing ideas. Houghton copyeditor Lisa Sacks cleaned up our text, and Alan Andres, Kristin Robbins, and Debbie Applefield helped the book reach the market. Thanks also to Ann Gallager for our "in your face" cover.

Through the years I've had the pleasure of meeting thousands of guerrillas and learning from most of them. Special thanks to David Seuss for his example and to Bill Godin and Lenore Godin for the ethical thread that is so essential to effective guerrilla practice. Of course, most of the thanks goes to Jay, who responded to the corporate mania of the '80s by codifying the most essential elements of marketing into what is still the best marketing book ever written: *Guerrilla Marketing*. Without that book, I'd probably be working in some investment bank, making a lot of money and being miserable all the time. The afternoon I spent with Jay in 1983 changed my life forever. Thanks, Jay.

This book is dedicated to my wife, Helene, who never stops believing in my journey.

Seth Godin
seth@sgp.com

CONTENTS

A cornucopia of advice, insight, wisdom, concepts, resources, examples, checklists, and good ideas.

THE DIFFERENCE BETWEEN A GUERRILLA AND AN ORDINARY MARKETER

An ordinary marketer sells to markets. She buys ads on television, sponsors the Olympics, and buys magazine schedules, all in the hope of seducing a demographic.

A guerrilla marketer sells to individuals. She wants to sell her product one person at a time. Her marketing is personal, handmade, and ranks high on impact.

An ordinary marketer is pleased with a 2% response on junk mail. He floods your mailbox with catalogs and letters, hoping that one out of fifty of you will respond. With 3,000,000 letters mailed, that's not bad.

A guerrilla marketer shoots for a 15% response on targeted personal mail. He handwrites the envelope, uses pretty stamps, or delivers the package in a gorilla suit. With 100 letters mailed, 15 new customers is pretty good.

PART I: CHOOSING YOUR MARKETING TOOLS

73 low-cost, high-impact ways to send your marketing message

TRADITIONAL ADVERTISING

MINI-MEDIA

TARGETED MEDIA

PART II: RESOURCES

An ordinary marketer budgets by calendar quarter and drops a product that doesn't respond. It's too expensive to put another $5,000,000 into selling a loser product.

A guerrilla marketer is patient. She thinks a year at a time and is willing to take her time, reaching one customer after another until business is booming.

An ordinary marketer plays it safe. Doing what worked before is the strategy that gets her promoted.

A guerrilla marketer has nothing to lose. Every marketing outlet, from late night TV to magnetic business cards to a jelly bean sweepstakes, is fair game.

Ordinary marketers think that the guerrilla marketers are only at tiny companies located in garages.

Guerrilla marketers know that Guerrilla Marketing techniques work in any setting, from AT&T to Johnny's Pizza.

Ordinary marketers wear three-piece suits.

Guerrilla marketers wear bathing suits — in Aruba, after they've made all their money.

Guerrilla marketers have more fun!

INTRODUCTION

If you don't have a plan, how will you know when you get there? The single greatest mistake most entrepreneurs make is embarking on a business venture without a written plan.

This section outlines the most important elements in making a plan, then highlights one of the most successful guerrilla marketers ever.

HOW TO USE THIS BOOK

! *We've left plenty of room to write in the margins. Use this area as a workbook to help you plan and execute your guerrilla marketing campaign.*

IS THIS BOOK FOR YOU?

At first glance, most of the techniques described in the *Guerrilla Marketing Handbook* seem tailor-made for the small businessman, and many of them are.

But if you're the president of a $30 million company, or the V.P. of marketing at Macy's, or the receptionist at a Wall Street investment bank, this book is for you, too. Guerrilla marketing isn't a bunch of gimmicks used by little companies run out of someone's basement. It's an attitude.

The guerrilla attitude has been used with success by companies in every industry and of every size. Regional railroads have used it to double their profits, nationwide phone companies have increased their subscriber base, and, yes, even landscapers have used it to quadruple their profits.

This book is divided into three sections:

➤ **Tactics and Strategies: Creating a Plan That Works**
In this section, we'll cover the nuts and bolts of determining what benefit you offer consumers, budgeting for success, determining a media plan, and choosing from the many weapons available to you. We focus on positioning and basic marketing strategy, helping you avoid the dangerous pitfalls that snare so many marketers.

➤ **The Guerrilla Marketing Arsenal**
From magazine advertising to blimps, from envelope stuffers to a killer logo, we cover the entire range of guerrilla techniques. Browse through this section to find the tools that are most appropriate to your business. In each section, you'll find a handy glossary that helps you talk like a pro, and each entry includes names and phone numbers for quick follow-through.

➤ **The Appendix**
This section is filled with contact names and numbers of the top media outlets around the country. You'll also find details on rate cards and CPM (cost per thousand) for various advertising vehicles. Finally, there are our top 50 recommended books for the guerrilla marketer.

OUR GUARANTEE

There isn't a company in America or an employee working at one of those companies that won't benefit from the lessons outlined in this book. And to put our money where our mouth is, here's our guarantee:

Read the *Guerrilla Marketing Handbook*. Try at least five of the techniques described herein. If you don't earn back at least 50 times the cost of this book, we will gladly refund your money. Just send us your store receipt along with a list of what you tried and the materials you used, and we'll send you back every penny you paid for this book. Send to: SGP, Box 321, Dobbs Ferry, NY 10522.

WE'D LIKE TO HEAR FROM YOU

Like all true guerrillas, we love to hear from our customers. Please drop us a line with advice, feedback, requests for new books, whatever. You can reach Jay and Seth by e-mail at:
GMINTL@aol.com and seth@sgp.com

If you're not using electronic mail yet, our regular mail address is:
SGP, Box 321, Dobbs Ferry, NY 10522.

To subscribe to *The Guerrilla Marketing Newsletter*, by Jay Levinson, send a check for $49 to GMI, Box 1336, Mill Valley, CA 94942—or use your credit card by calling (800) 748-6444 or e-mailing GMINTL@aol.com. If you're not 100% satisfied with the newsletter, send back your first issue and Jay will return your $49 plus $2 extra just for trying it.

CREATING A PLAN

Understanding the Guerrilla Manifesto and the idea of positioning, and creating a seven-step foolproof marketing plan.

If you're reading this book, it's probably because you've got a product or service that you want to sell. Guerrilla marketing can be used to sell just about anything, from $100,000 cars to massages. You can use these techniques to market yourself when you're looking for a job, or to market your skills as a tattoo artist.

About fifteen years ago, classical brand marketing reached its peak. The idea behind brand marketing was simple: Buy a slate of advertising in national media, run ads, and wait for people to come to the store and buy your product. Classical brand marketing turned Kool Aid into a $600 million business, built Procter & Gamble into a money machine, and even worked for service businesses like American Express and MCI.

All of sudden, all of these Fortune 500 companies, together with hundreds of thousands of smaller businesses, have changed course completely and embraced guerrilla marketing. Why now? There are many reasons, including increased skepticism among consumers, increased competition, and a fragmentation of the mass media. The giants have learned what many small companies knew all along—guerrilla marketing is the best (sometimes the only) way to build your business.

THE GUERRILLA'S MANIFESTO

In order to sell a product or a service, a company must establish a relationship with the consumer. It must build trust and rapport. It must understand the customer's needs, and it must provide a product that delivers the promised benefits.

Smart marketers use every technique available to gain a foothold in the consumer's mind. With guerrilla marketing, the focus changes from the *volume* of advertising to the *impact* of the message. The guerrilla would rather reach ten people with a message that works than 100 people with one that doesn't.

The guerrilla is obsessed with benefits. Whenever offering a product or service, she focuses on how it will benefit the consumer and builds everything—the product, the delivery, the marketing—around that benefit.

The guerrilla understands positioning. She knows that challenging the market leader on his turf is foolish—an invitation to disaster. Instead, the guerrilla maneuvers *around* the leader, repositioning him to her advantage. Every self-respecting guerrilla can recite the position of her product or service in one or two sentences.

The guerrilla is a cheapskate. She knows that every dollar allocated to marketing is essential, and she doesn't plan to waste a penny. But she's not foolish. When necessary, she hires the best designers, media planners, and experts in the business—she realizes that the best is often the cheapest in the end.

Most of all, the guerrilla is committed. She understands that marketing doesn't work overnight. By setting a goal and sticking to it, the guerrilla has an easier time of dealing with the inevitable setbacks that occur. The guerrilla knows that path to marketing success is filled with failed marketers who gave up just a little too soon.

THREE REASONS WHY MARKETERS FAIL

➤ **Lack of Commitment**

If you don't believe in your product, or if you're not consistent and regular in the way you promote it, the odds of succeeding go way down. The primary function of the marketing plan is to ensure that you have the resources and the wherewithal to do what it takes to make your product work.

➤ **Lack of a Clear Benefit**

It seems so obvious, but few marketers understand that you must SELL SOMETHING PEOPLE WANT. Without getting close to your customer, doing the research, and looking hard at what you have to offer, you're unlikely to stumble onto a hit. Too often, companies look at their skills or their factory and invent a new product or service that will be easy for them to make. That's the last reason to offer a product. Customers don't care about your skills or inventory. They want to know what's in it for them.

➤ **Poor Positioning**

Sometimes there is no position available in a crowded or depressed market (we'd argue that starting a large overnight delivery company, for instance, probably isn't that smart). But markets where there are no positions available are few and far between. More often, marketers make the mistake of going up against a market leader on his own turf. As the marketing plan takes you through the positioning segment, pay careful attention. The best product and the best execution won't help if a market leader is selling the same benefit in the same way for half the price.

WHY YOU NEED A MARKETING PLAN

Why is a marketing plan so important? Very few businesses have an accounting plan or a manufacturing plan, so why the focus on marketing?

! BENEFITS
■ EXERCISE
Choose a branded product that you and your family use—toothpaste, luxury car, perfume, clothing, etc. Then make an honest list of the benefits that the product offers. You'll probably be surprised at how little these benefits have to do with the actual utility of the product.

———————————
———————————
———————————
———————————
———————————
———————————
———————————
———————————

Unlike most other aspects of your business, marketing involves unquantifiable risks. There's just no way to know how your ad is going to pull, how many people will come to your grand opening, or what sort of word of mouth you'll be able to generate.

One way to deal with this uncertainty is to ignore it. Many businesses blindly plod along, investing money in marketing when business is good, cutting back when sales go down. (Does that sound as silly to you as it does to us?) When an ad campaign doesn't pull right away, they kill it quickly. When it works well, they soon tire of it and move on to something new.

The guerrilla understands that a marketing plan is the first key to success. Zig Ziglar tells the story of the airplane pilot who takes off on a flight from Dallas to New York, gets blown a little off course, and returns to the airport and starts again. Obviously, very few flights would get to their destinations if pilots were this shaky in their ability to deal with setbacks. The secret of a marketing plan is that it will enable you to see your ultimate goal with clarity, making minor setbacks and failures along the way unimportant. Just as important, a plan helps you communicate your vision to employees, ad agencies and investors. When completed, your plan will outline seven critical elements in your approach to marketing.

THE SEVEN CRITICAL ELEMENTS OF YOUR MARKETING PLAN

1. The benefit to consumers

2. Your positioning in the marketplace: What business are you in?

3. Your target market

4. Your advertising strategy and positioning

5. Your budget

6. The tools and techniques you'll use to reach your audience

7. A month-by-month implementation timetable

A SEVEN-STEP PLAN

In this section we'll take you through each of these steps and help you create your own plan. Feel free to make notes in the *Handbook*—it will help you clarify your thinking and ensure that you keep a permanent record of what you're going to do.

STEP 1: THE BENEFIT TO CONSUMERS

The only products or services that succeed are those that offer a benefit to consumers that is greater than their cost. If necessary, write that on a big sign and post it over your desk. It is the obvious but often overlooked key to marketing.

Marketers frequently confuse features and benefits. Features are elements of a product that deliver a benefit. A quick look at the following table will help you remember the difference:

Feature	Benefit
Airbags	Lowered risk of serious injury
Large type	Ease of reading
Digital recording	Hiss-free listening
Soft leather sneakers	More comfortable walking
Mercedes Benz logo	Increased self-esteem based on status

Think about the last time you went to buy a new car. You probably thought about what you wanted: safety for your family, low operating costs, lots of room for the kids, etc. It's not too hard to translate these benefits into features: airbags, good gas mileage, an extra-large trunk, etc. But it's the benefit, not the feature, that sells the car.

But what do people want? In our rapidly evolving consumer-based society, understanding the answer to this question can unlock the potential of your marketing campaign. As soon as you can distinguish between wants and basic needs, as soon as you understand how to talk directly to the consumer's psyche, you can begin to establish your role in their life.

Most Americans have everything they need to survive. They have enough food to eat and a place to sleep. Most marketers are no longer concerned about satisfying these basic needs. Instead, they're focusing on consumers' wants and desires. Here's a partial sampling of what people want:
➤ To be safe
➤ To be happy
➤ To have fun
➤ To eat delicious foods
➤ To be attractive

!Is your business a commodity?
It's easy to fall into the trap of believing that the only reason people buy from you is price. After all, your competitors offer virtually the same product. The problem is that commodities—salt, sugar, and airline seats, to name a few—are notorious for low profits.

You can transform virtually any commodity into a branded product by focusing on your customer and delivering exactly what they want. King Arthur created a branded flour, Nucor makes branded steel, Evian even turned ordinary water into a product people will pay a premium for.

➤ To be successful

➤ To like themselves

➤ To be liked by other people

➤ To protect their family and friends

➤ To be free from pain

Here's a list of best-selling products. All of them sell for many times their manufacturing cost, which means that customers are paying for more than the products themselves. See if you can determine which of the key desires these products position themselves to satisfy.

➤ Coca-Cola

➤ Master locks

➤ Volvo cars

➤ Marlboro cigarettes

➤ Hostess Twinkies

➤ American Express cards

Mastering the list of what people want and communicating the benefits of your product are crucial steps in understanding marketing. No successful guerrilla would build a marketing plan without keeping these desires in mind.

STEP 2: WHAT BUSINESS ARE YOU IN?

You'd be amazed how much easier it is to succeed when you create a product or service that people really want. Some examples:

➤ Musicals and plays open and close on Broadway all the time. Marketers struggle to fill the seats and keep the theaters (barely) afloat. Ricky Jay, a closeup magician, opened on the edge of the Broadway theater district on February 10th. By February 15th, every seat at every show was sold out. He added four more weeks of shows in March. Those tickets sold out in six hours. The reason has not got that much to do with marketing tools and everything to do with benefits—Ricky Jay was offering a small segment of people exactly what they wanted.

➤ Federal Express was the first company to offer overnight service to virtually everywhere in the country at an affordable rate. Once people tried Fedex, they were hooked. It wasn't that hard to persuade first-time customers that overnight delivery was a service they couldn't live without. Again, the bene-fit here is so obvious, so tangible, that Fedex doesn't have to spend much time persuading business customers to send stuff overnight.

➤ Southwest Airlines opened service to a number of cities that already had quite a few major airlines, including American and United. Yet their flights were quickly booked. People liked the low fares, the friendly people, and the excellent service.

What do these successes have in common? In each case the marketers identified a genuine need on the part of customers to use their service. They offered a clear and distinct benefit, and positioned themselves to reach consumers with a personal message about how their lives would be better once they used this product or service.

Critics tell us that this is too obvious. "Of course," they say, "you should offer a product that people want." Maybe the fact that this is so obvious explains why so many people ignore it. Take a look at the movie flops in the video store, or the expensive failures in the supermarket. Fingos breakfast cereal was launched with a $32 million marketing campaign. After first year sales stalled at $22 million, the marketers gave up. While the idea behind the cereal seemed appealing, it just wasn't something consumers were willing to pay for.

The hard part is figuring out what sort of product or service people are going to line up for. When Microsoft creates a new word processor, they go through more than 10,000 hours of consumer testing, surveys, and feedback. You can be sure that the products they make appeal to a wide range of computer users. On the other hand, most businesses don't even bother to ask their best customers for ideas for new products.

If you're not Microsoft, how can you introduce a product and maximize the chances that it will succeed? A little planning can go a long way. Let's start the process.

First, write down the product or service you offer or plan to offer:

_____

_____

_____

Don't be shy. Write directly in the book—it's more permanent that way. Be as specific as possible. Don't say, "a grocery store." Say, "a gourmet grocery store stocking 10,000 items, located in the swank village of Williamsville."

List the features that your product will offer that are different from or better than your competitors':

Domino's Pizza is a great example of how understanding your customers' desires can help grow a business. Most pizza lovers agree that Domino's is not the best pizza you can buy. But it is the fastest and most convenient. By staying close to his customers, Tom Monaghan understood that college students (his original market) wanted fast and easy food, not necessarily gourmet quality. Many competitors have been stymied trying to offer a better pizza instead of a pizza that gave customers what they wanted.

Remember, if you think you can differentiate your business on price, you're probably mistaken. Customers are far more frequently motivated by service, speed, quality, or other non-monetary attributes.

_____

_____

_____

Now identify the benefits of using your product. How will you make the user's life better? Remember, list benefits, not features.

_____

_____

_____

Take a look at the benefits you've listed. Are they substantially better than your competition? If not, what will compel consumers to switch?

STEP 3: WHO'S THE PRODUCT FOR?

Once you've established the benefits of your product, you've implicitly identified a target market. A fishing lure, for example, that is guaranteed not to prick your finger, is probably not aimed at infants or vegetarians—it's for anglers. Now segment your market even further. Exactly who wants and needs your product?

_____

_____

_____

_____

If you said "everyone," try again. There are very few products that appeal to everyone. Usually that's shorthand for "no one really wants this product a lot, everyone wants it a little." Use the space below to identify exactly who wants your product the most. Talk about their age, income, shoe size, race, musical taste, height—whatever differentiates your market. Can you identify what magazines they read? What TV shows they watch?

_____

_____

_____

_____

If you're having trouble identifying a market, it may be time to start again. But this time, work backward. Start with the market first, then create a product especially for that market. For example, you might discover that widowed women over 70, living in south Florida, have trouble getting their prescriptions filled. Solving this problem would create an obvious benefit.

Once you've identified your target market, it's time to test your thinking. You'll need to find a dozen or so members of your target market and assemble them for a focus group. This is a decidedly unscientific way to get feedback on your ideas, but a lot better than nothing.

Invite the focus group out to dinner or to your office for coffee. Sit them in a comfortable room and start asking questions. Ask them about what they use now to achieve the benefits you're offering. Ask them what they like about the product or service—and what they don't like. Find out how much they pay for the benefit you're offering. Let them talk. Best of all, let them disagree with each other.

You don't have to run a focus group in person. If your market is scattered, try using an on-line computer service or a mail-in survey to get feedback. If it turns out that you've completely misjudged your market (a likely scenario), then you'll have to go back to step one and try again.

After you've worked your way through this process (and it may take a few tries) you will know the benefits you're offering to your target market. Turn this knowledge into a one- or two-sentence marketing statement that makes it clear what you have to offer and to whom you are offering it. For example:

➤ Hard Manufacturing offers reliable, hassle-free hospital cribs to pediatric nurses at major hospitals.

➤ Boston Chicken offers healthy, delicious, homemade-tasting chicken meals to busy families.

➤ Marlboro cigarettes offer a feeling of ruggedness and freedom to urban youth around the world searching for the American dream.

➤ Dr. Johnson offers pain-free dentistry (that children might even find fun) in the 10070 zip code.

Notice that in each case you can clearly visualize the audience—in some cases, like Dr. Johnson or Hard Manufacturing, you could even buy a mailing list of every possible customer. This precision is critical in reaching your market.

! *IMPORTANT*
■ *Remember that a focus group doesn't present a statistically significant sample. If 9 out of 12 people in the focus group independently endorse your product, it doesn't mean you're guaranteed to succeed. This isn't a survey. Instead, it is a chance for you to hear your customers' wants and desires in their own words.*

UNDERSTANDING POSITIONING

Before you go any further, take a minute to understand how the competition affects your ability to offer your benefit to your target market. One of the best marketing books of the 1980s was *Positioning: The Battle for Your Mind* by Trout & Reis (published by Warner Books). This book is a must-read for every guerrilla.

With so many products on the market (and thousands more being introduced every year) and the countless advertisements that promote them, consumers have become virtually immune to traditional marketing tactics. They just don't have enough room in their brains to store every piece of information about every product. Instead, they either categorize a product or ignore it.

The concept behind positioning is simple: Find a hole and fill it. People pick one or two attributes to associate with a product, then file that information away. When they need those attributes, the product comes to mind.

Here's an example: If you could rent any car made, what car would you choose to pick up an important visiting executive at the airport? Most people would say a Mercedes, a Cadillac, possibly a Lexus. Why? Because those products have been positioned as expensive, impressive executive sedans. While they also go fast, hold an entire family, and offer safety, first and foremost they've been positioned as status cars. The "status" position has been filled by these cars. If you decide to market a product that competes with these cars, you're going to have to throw one of them out of the prospect's mind. You may find that it's easier to invent your own position than fight an industry leader for his spot.

What car would you use to drive a carpool of six kids to nursery school? Most yuppie parents would instantly pick a Volvo. While it's a safe car, there's nothing that specifically makes it a parent's car except for the advertising done to position it. The brilliance behind Volvo's position campaign is that they repositioned a fairly boring Swedish car into the darling of well-heeled parents. Without changing one thing about the car, Volvo was able to find a 'hole' in the market—safe cars for families—and fill it with their own product.

7-Up used a guerrilla marketing technique to outposition Coke. While Coke's marketing budget was many times larger, 7-Up was able to turn their bigness against them. How? By calling themselves the UnCola, they told consumers "We're not Coke." For those who want to be different, 7-Up provided an easy way to stand out from the crowd. The more Coke advertised, the more they helped 7-Up. 7-Up has never challenged Coke as the market leader in the overall soft drink market, but by inventing their own market (soft drinks that are not Coke) they became a market leader in a smaller, but still profitable realm.

The single biggest reason that guerrillas fail is that they're unable to find a niche. They open a dry cleaner, or a gardening service, or a hairdresser that is not positioned any differently than their competitors. If you're just like the other guy but the other guy got there first, you've got quite a challenge on your hands.

Plotting your position and the position of your competitors takes a little imagination, but it's worth it. Let's look at the market for toothpaste for some simple examples.

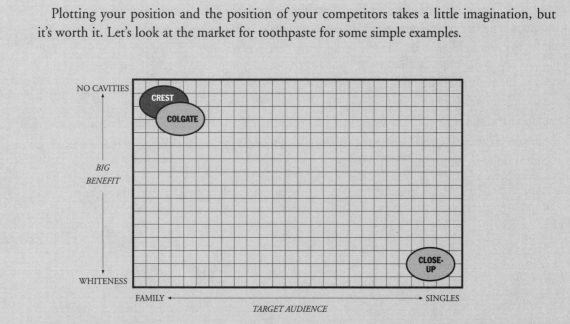

When Close-Up was introduced, the major brands of toothpaste were all fighting for one position—the family toothpaste that fights cavities. Close-Up was brilliantly positioned as a toothpaste for single young adults, who care about sex a lot more than cavities.

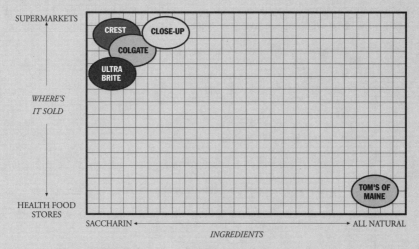

When Tom's of Maine decided to introduce a toothpaste, they drew a different map. Instead of using cavities and sex appeal as axes, they used two other surprising choices:

Tom's of Maine chose to reposition on the basis of where the product was sold and what it contained. They established a niche for healthy toothpaste.

By redefining the competition, Tom's *eliminated* its competition. For more than five years,

Tom's has been the only national brand that is all natural. A consumer shopping at a health food store had essentially one choice when selecting a toothpaste: Tom's.

In virtually every market, there is an opportunity to reposition the competition and create your own niche. Use this positioning process to discover where your competition is, and how you can outposition them to find a niche.

➤ List the brands that are competing for your consumer. Be broad. For example, if you're in the pretzel business, your competitors include potato chips, carrot sticks, and beef jerky, in addition to other pretzel manufacturers.

_____

_____

_____

_____

_____

_____

➤ Next to each brand, outline that product's position—who it is tailored for, how it is different from its competitors.

➤ Use this grid to plot each relevant product or brand. The bottom axis can contain one variable, like price, or quality, or service, or some other differentiation. The other axis grids a different variable (see the example for toothpaste).

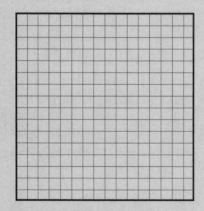

➤ Find a niche. Fill it. If you can't find a niche, don't expect customers to find you, unless you have enough money to bring them in the door in head-to-head competition with your entrenched competitors.

➤ Describe your proposed niche. You should be able to do it in one short phrase or sentence. Some examples:

The most expensive hairdresser in Milwaukee.

The best customer service of any supermarket in town.

The lowest-priced gym.

The restaurant with the best-looking waiters.

The world's leading manufacturer of hospital cribs.

Your niche:

_____

_____

Finding the right position for your company only works if you back it up. You have to follow up with conviction and sell your position. Every aspect of your marketing plan should reflect the special niche you fill. Your position is your character—express it!

The Body Shop retail chain positioned itself as an environmentally friendly cosmetics company dedicated to helping people find "wellness," not "glitz and glamour." They pack their products in environmentally friendly containers, stress health and well-being in their advertising, and design their stores in cool, earthy colors, all in an attempt to back up their position in the marketplace.

After the enormous fat content of Chinese food became a news story, many restaurants saw their business plummet—some by as much as 50%. One enterprising guerrilla decided to reposition his restaurant.

Overnight, Hunan Garden Szechuan Restaurant became Cafe 19 Chinese Health Food Restaurant. The owner didn't change the menu—he already had a dozen fat-free steamed dishes on the menu. He didn't change the decor either. Just the sign.

By repositioning the restaurant as a health food establishment he was able to increase his sales. In fact, he increased them to a level greater than before the fat controversy. Of course, it wouldn't have worked if there weren't steamed dishes available. The lesson is simple: Once people thought about his restaurant a different way, they were more likely to patronize it. The healthy dishes were there all along, he just needed to focus on them.

Keep in mind that positioning without substance never works in the long run. When computers became the hottest consumer electronic a few years ago, Smith-Corona tried to persuade consumers that their word processor was just as good and just as complicated—a big mistake. Only when they went back to the basics and stressed the simplicity of their product did sales rebound.

K Swiss had a difficult problem. A small marketer of tennis sneakers, they were dwarfed by the giants in the industry. Realizing that they had no chance of out marketing Nike or Reebok, K Swiss abandoned plans for celebrity endorsements and thousands of models, and decided to create the un-Nike—a sneaker for people who wanted to look good, get plenty of support for their feet, and not deal with gimmicks or fads.

- *Product: Tennis sneakers*

- *Target market: Upper-middle-class occasional athletes*

- *Competition: Nike, Reebok, Adidas, Converse*

- *Product's benefit: You will look better and feel better in the classic K Swiss design.*

- *How is it differentiated from the competition: Most of the competition features gimmicks–lights, pumps, and celebrity endorsements. K Swiss uses a 25-year-old, classic, all-white design, with a focus on perfomance, not frills.*

STEP 4: YOUR ADVERTISING STRATEGY AND POSITIONING

Now that you have positioned your competitors and your product, you're ready to create your Advertising Strategy Sheet.

➤ Product or Service

_____

_____

_____

➤ Target market

_____

_____

_____

➤ Competition

_____

_____

_____

_____

➤ Product's benefit

_____

_____

_____

➤How is it differentiated from the competition (outline your position and theirs)?

_____

_____

➤ If the reader gets one idea out of the ad, what should it be?

_____

_____

_____

➤ What action should the reader take after reading the ad?

_____

_____

Now you've positioned your product, established the benefits, come up with the competition's positioning, and designed a strategy. Time to crunch some numbers.

STEP 5: COMPUTING A BUDGET

Many entrepreneurs wonder why they need a marketing budget. They figure they'll run a few ads and as business comes in, run some more. This myopic thinking almost always leads to disappointment. Every business has a natural rhythm, levels of sales and marketing that are self-sustaining. If you don't do enough marketing, you whither. Do too much and you waste marketing dollars or generate more business than you can handle.

The first step in creating a marketing budget is determining what percentage of sales you'll be able to devote to marketing. A good rule of thumb is 10%, but some businesses (like perfume or cigarettes) require more. If your business is regional, ask a successful non-competitor in a different region to share his data with you, or you can call the trade association for your industry to get the inside scoop.

Whatever is standard in your field, plan to increase that number by a few percentage points. Leaders often spend more on marketing, and it helps them grow. Under no circumstances should you create a marketing plan that is built around spending a smaller percentage of sales than your competition.

Now you need to guess. How much are you going to sell next year? There are lots of ways to do this calculation, ranging from market share to shelf space to astrology. We won't spend a lot of time on it here.

Come up with a range of potential first-year sales. For example, a dentist just starting out might compute it this way:

- *If you get one thing out of the ad, what should it be?* If you demand comfort and performance, as opposed to gimmicks and peer acceptance, K Swiss is the sneaker for you.

- *Action to take:* Go to the local Athlete's Foot and ask for a pair by name.

! RULE OF THUMB

Take the Value of a Customer number (see next page) and triple it if you want to include the word of mouth factor as well.

. . . .

TEN THINGS A GUERRILLA SHOULDN'T DO

- *Run a nationwide ad campaign without testing it.*

- *Be less than 100% truthful with customers.*

- *Refuse to fix a customer's problem because of store policy.*

- *Pull an ad campaign while it is still producing.*

- *Ignore customer mail and phone calls.*

- *Focus on only mass media.*

- *Spend a dollar without having a marketing plan.*

- *Hesitate when asked to describe her marketing position in two sentences.*

- *Be afraid to fail.*

. . . .

Average fee per patient: $60

Possible patients per day: 10

Expected patients per day: 3 to 6

Yearly income (200 days): $36,000 to $66,000

As you can see, there's enough of a range here for the dentist to make a rough guess of her income without having to commit to too much marketing money.

WHAT'S A CUSTOMER WORTH?

Take a minute to determine a critical marketing statistic: What's the value of each customer over his or her lifetime? Write it down, post it over your desk, share it with your employees.

Why is this statistic so important? Because it helps you determine how much you might be willing to spend to acquire a new customer. And, just as important, it forces you to realize how much it costs you to lose a customer once you've got him.

Stew Leonard, the most successful independent grocer of all time, used this analysis frequently. He figured that the average customer would shop with him for seven or eight years before moving out of the neighborhood. With a monthly food bill of $250, that worked out to $3,000 a year in sales, or $21,000 over the course of seven years. With a gross margin of about 10%, that means that a customer was worth $2,100 to him (that's without factoring in word of mouth—a dissatisfied customer can spread enough ill will to keep ten others from ever setting foot in your store.) Once Stew realized that each and every customer was worth more than $2,000, he was a lot more willing to replace a box of rotten strawberries or run an extra ad or service—cheap tools if they helped maintain that cash flow.

Federal Express is another company that focuses on the value of a customer. If a mid-size company sends 30 packages a week (at $25 each), that's $750 a week, or $18,750. If a customer gets angry over a $25 shipment and switches his business to a competitor, Federal Express loses thousands and thousands of dollars. That's why every Federal Express supervisor is authorized to grant a $100 refund on the spot, no questions asked, for any delayed shipment. $100 is a small price to pay to keep an $18,750-a-year customer.

To compute the value of a customer, answer these simple questions:
➤ If you continue to provide acceptable service and quality, how long will the customer patronize your business?

➤ How much will the customer buy in the average year (make sure you include sales increases due to growth on your part or the customer's)?

➤ What's your gross margin?

This number should be engraved on your forehead and you should share it with all your employees. It will help you focus on the critical elements of building your business.

Using 10% of projected sales, our dentist figures that she has $3,600 to $6,600 to spend on marketing. Do some analysis and come up with your own range of projected sales and then take a percentage. Remember, some businesses need a greater investment (especially at first) while others are able to do just fine with less (for example, a gypsum mill can probably get by with less than 1% invested.)

STEP 6: CHOOSING YOUR TOOLS

Once you've determined your budget, it's time to read Section Two of this book. Look through each tool and decide if it is a cost-effective way to reach your target market. As you find each tool that appeals to you, write it down here.

TOOL	COST PER USE	MONTHLY FREQUENCY	MONTHLY COST

STEP 7: IMPLEMENTING A MONTH-BY-MONTH MARKETING TIMETABLE

Once you've ranked the tools that appeal to you, fill in this grid to determine your media plan:

TOOL	JAN	FEB	MAR	APR	MAY	JUN	JUL	AUG	SEP	OCT	NOV	DEC

TOOL	COST PER USE	MONTHLY FREQUENCY	MONTHLY COST

TOOL	JAN	FEB	MAR	APR	MAY	JUN	JUL	AUG	SEP	OCT	NOV	DEC

Here are two extra charts to use when creating alternate plans.

GUERRILLA CHECKLIST

Before spending a dollar on media, ask yourself these questions to be sure you're ready to start:

1. What benefit do you offer the consumer?

_____

_____

_____

_____

2. Exactly who is your consumer? Be specific.

_____

_____

_____

_____

3. What is your position relative to your competitors?

_____

_____

_____

_____

4. What barriers exist to keep others from stealing your market share?

_____

_____

_____

_____

5. How will you (personally) communicate with your customers?

_____

_____

_____

_____

6. How will you measure the response of your promotions?

_____

_____

_____

7. Do you have sufficient inventory and manpower to deal with increased demand?

_____

_____

_____

8. Have you worked through the non-media tools to ensure that you've established the framework for a successful media campaign?

_____

_____

_____

_____

9. What is your month-by-month media plan? Have you planned for enough frequency with your target market? Do you have enough money budgeted to support the plan even if initial sales are weak?

_____

_____

_____

_____

_____

_____

(Attach a copy of your marketing plan here)

10. Does your media meet your tactical and strategic goals, or is it just pretty?

_____

_____

_____

_____

ESTABLISHED BUSINESSES: TAKE A GUERRILLA AUDIT

If your company already exists, audit your company's position. Make a simple questionnaire and send it to your employees, asking the following:

➤ Who is our target customer?

_____

➤ What benefits do we offer that our competition doesn't?

_____

_____

➤ If you could use just two sentences to describe what our business stands for, what would they be?

_____

_____

_____

You may be surprised at the answers. Once you've checked in with your employees, call a few of your customers on the phone (you do have their numbers handy, don't you?) and ask them the same questions. Place a stack of comment cards on your counter and encourage people who come into your store to fill one out.

If your business is new there's still one step that you can take in this audit: Show your new advertising to some strangers. Ask them the same three questions:

➤ Who is our target customer?

_____

➤ What benefits do we offer that our competition doesn't?

_____

_____

➤ If you could use just two sentences to describe what our business stands for, what would they be?

_____

_____

If any person you ask can't answer these questions after reading your ad, think twice (maybe three times) before spending a penny running it.

CASE STUDY: THE GUERRILLA PSYCHOTHERAPIST

Donna is a newly licensed psychotherapist trying to build a practice on New York's swanky Park Avenue. Realizing that the market is quite crowded, she understands that just putting out a shingle is an unlikely way to attract new business. But in her words, "I can't really go out and put up a billboard." Donna decided to segment her market. She needed a specialty and chose new mothers. Why? First, because as a new mother herself, she was aware of the stresses and joys of motherhood and felt she had something to offer. But just as important, she understood that by focusing on a small market, she could quickly position herself as a market leader and generate the word of mouth that is so critical in a business like psychotherapy.

Having established her target market, her positioning, and the benefit to her customers, Donna called a list broker and bought a list of 500 women who lived within ten blocks of her office and were scheduled to have a baby within the next six weeks. (These lists are created by list companies, who pay gynecologists for the names of their expectant patients. *Parents* magazine and others rely on these lists for promotions.)

Once she had the list, Donna wrote a personalized letter to each mother, timed to arrive two weeks after each baby was born. The letter outlined some of the feelings that Donna had gone through when she had her baby nine months earlier, and then described her credentials and how she might be able to help a mother who was having trouble coping.

She offered a free play date, on which the new mothers could come to her office and meet other new moms, and share stories and experiences. This session was totally unpressured and gave moms a chance to meet her without any stigma.

The envelopes were hand addressed, hand stamped, and mailed in batches. Donna actually tried three different letters, each taking a slightly different tack. She also put two different hourly rates in her letters—and carefully recorded which of the six letters each person got.

Over the next two months, Donna received 40 phone calls from her letter; 25 women came to a get acquainted session, and 3 became patients, generating $7,200 in fees over the course of a year. More important, she started the process of generating word of mouth, and discovered a marketing method that she could use every three months if she needed it.

GUERRILLA MARKETER OF THE YEAR

Jordan's Furniture
Boston, MA

More than a thousand businesses around the country entered our inaugural competition for America's top guerrilla marketer. The competition was tough—there is definitely an impressive group of innovative, successful guerrillas operating out there. But as we sized up the success stories, one company emerged from the pack in terms of creativity, customer-sensitivity, perseverance, guts, and profitability.

Jordan's Furniture, located near Boston, MA, is our choice for Guerrilla Marketer of the Year. As you'll discover from many sidebars about them sprinkled throughout this book, Jordan's has fearlessly tried almost every guerrilla weapon—and made most of them work. They stand as living proof that guerrilla techniques can radically increase the size and profitability of a business (and help you have more fun, too).

When Barry and Eliot Tatleman took over Jordan's Furniture in early 1973, the single store in Waltham, MA, had eight employees and annual sales of about $500,000. Last year, sales at the three Jordan's locations stood at an incredible $100,000,000 a year. That's an increase of 20,000% in just over 20 years, or an average 1,000% growth per year!

How did they do it? Not by mortgaging their houses to buy expensive advertising. In fact, over the years, they have spent less than half the industry average on their advertising. But they do it so well that most Bostonians and Southern New Hampshirites have become convinced there is really only one furniture store in town.

Every marketing move they make seems bold, deliberate, and definitely "guerrilla." Their ads are targeted and efficient—and the brothers are smart about the radio time they buy, always maximizing their advertising dollars. Their message is repeated over and over. Their stores offer a staggering array of innovative customer-service courtesies. (For instance, customers who pick up furniture get a free car wash. If you come by on Sunday afternoon you can watch the ball game in amazing comfort while your spouse shops. Customers enjoy riding the $3 million amusement park ride in back of the store. The list is almost endless.)

An average furniture store turns its inventory over three times a year. That means the average piece of furniture sits unsold for about four months. At Jordan's, a piece of furniture is lucky to last a month (they turn eleven times a year). This inventory turn leads to huge sales per square foot (about $790), which in turn generates huge profits and keeps their advertising war chest full.

Barry and Eliot rely on more than gimmicks to keep their furniture behemoth humming. "Our customers know we stand behind our products. We have one of the best reputations in the industry with the Better Business Bureau," says Barry.

They do more than just play fair with their customers. Each salesperson is empowered to make decisions, so no one passes the buck at Jordan's.

Jordan's leaves no guerrilla marketing stone unturned—their efforts are intense, effective, and filled with panache. In total, they offer a challenge and a model for all aspiring guerrillas. Congratulations and thank you!

Nominate your business for next year's Guerrilla Marketer of the Year. Send us examples of your brochures, ads, and fliers. Send us photos of your store— whatever. Address your nonreturnable nomination to: Guerrilla Marketer of the Year, Box 321, Dobbs Ferry, NY 10522.

AN INTERVIEW WITH BARRY AND ELIOT

➤ **Is there a philosophy behind Jordan's?**
We have always done what we do because we believed it was right, not because we were focused on profits...and it has worked. We believe in servicing the customer. It sounds kind of sappy, but we believe it, our people believe it, and we do it.

➤ **How important is price to your success?**
The public has to feel it is getting value along with service. One is not enough—you have to have both. Pricing is an important spoke in the wheel, but it needs to be kept in line with the other spokes.

➤ **Do you write your own stuff?**
Yes. We get ideas from everywhere—our people, current events, things we read, concerns of the public.

We had a third brother—Milt—who passed away a year ago. He did not work in the business day-to-day, but he was extremely involved in our creative process. He was a wonderful sounding board for ideas and we miss his creative genius. He used to say that he had created Barry and Eliot because he was the one who talked us into going on the radio more than twenty years ago.

Our customers have gotten so wrapped up on our commercials that we get hundreds of letters—many of them with ideas—each month! It's great to know that they feel they are part of the process.

➤ **What was the most effective promotion you've ever done, and why?**

I'm not sure you would call it a promotion, but "MOM," our Motion Odyssey Movie, would definitely be our most effective initiative. We call "MOM" a win-win-win. Our customers win because it's such fun and they expect fun in our store; the business wins because "MOM" brings new people into the store; and the community wins because we give all the profits from "MOM" to charity (over $300,000 to date).

The power of our advertising still amazes us. Every time we open a new store, the pent-up demand and the credibility that we have built up are so great that we actually have to get on the radio and tell people *not* to come down for awhile. Our store openings created two of the worst traffic jams ever seen in the area!

➤ **Do you still prefer radio? Why?**

We have a very soft spot in our hearts for radio, but we don't necessarily prefer radio over every other medium. It depends on who your customer is. We do feel that whichever medium you select, you need to do it right and dominate it. We have selected radio and television and they work for us.

➤ **Is training new employees a challenge?**

It's easy to "Jordanize" fresh new employees. The bigger challenge to training new employees is keeping employees that have been with you a long time motivated. We spend the most time working on the growth, training, motivation, and teamwork of our existing staff.

➤ **How have you handled your growth?**

We recognize that growth can present more problems than stagnation. We work very hard at trying to be ready for it. Sometimes we're caught short and business increases too rapidly. At those times, the burdens on each employee increase. It's critical to our success that we recognize and appreciate how hard our team works—especially at high-stress times.

➤ **What's next for Jordan's?**

It's never been our dream to be the biggest—only the best. We're looking to add a fourth store in the near future that will be bigger, better, and more innovative. We would like to bring the shopping experience to an even higher level and to have our displays and entertainment offer a greater level of excitement.

This is the Snack Attack Emporiyum in MOM where Jordan's features Spaceballs—the ice cream of the future. All profits from the Snack Attack, the T-shirt sales, and the MOM ride are donated to charity.

Even the dog sitting on the curb next to Barry and Eliot in this diorama gets in on the act. He moves his head and wags his tail and is a favorite with the kids. The real Barry (right) and Eliot (left) are shown above.

Jordan's thinks of each customer as a guest (above). They also put a fact tag on each piece of furniture that explains the manufacturer, the construction, warranties, sizes, care instructions, etc. (below). Jordan's asks each manufacturer to sign off on the information to ensure accuracy. According to Barry and Eliot, "Giving customers honest information is critical to everything we do."

ADVERTISING

ADVERTISING FOR GUERRILLAS

If when you think of advertising, you think of the boring mass of dishwasher detergent, toilet paper, and sneaker ads you watch on television every night, then you aren't thinking like a guerrilla. Guerrilla advertising is more focused, more personal, and in the long run more effective than the advertising methods used by most traditional mass marketers.

In this section we'll show you how to use advertising to build your business one customer at a time—the goal of every guerrilla marketer. From television to Yellow Pages and outdoor advertising, you'll learn how to focus on your target market and garner more profits for every advertising dollar that you spend.

ADVERTISING BASICS

Guerrillas use advertising dollars wisely. Make your advertising as cost effective and targeted as possible.

Advertising is the heart of most guerrilla marketing plans. There are countless advertising books, including the recently published *Guerrilla Advertising*. Rather than covering all that ground again, we'll just focus on some of the critical elements. Here are the cardinal rules of advertising.

RULE #1: ONE-SHOT ADS (ALMOST) NEVER WORK

Research shows that the average American sees more than 30,000 ads per year. On average, only one out of nine well-designed ads is ever seen by the targeted consumer. We also know that an ad needs to be seen at least three times before it makes enough impact to spur action. Quick calculation: You need to put your ad in front of your target consumer twenty-seven times before it makes a difference.

If you don't have a long-term commitment to advertise, don't advertise. If you decide to advertise, plan to run the same ad, in the same media, often enough to reach your target consumer countless times. Of course, there are examples of one-shot ads that capture the nation's attention. But there are also examples of people who won the lottery the first time they bought a ticket. You can try, but don't bet the mortgage money.

Soon after your ad comes out, you'll get tired of it. Soon after that, your family, friends and coworkers will get tired of it. Ignore them. Don't change your ad until your accountant gets tired of it.

RULE #2: QUALITY COUNTS

Compared to the cost of placing an ad, the cost of creating an ad is a bargain. In fact, you can usually get your ads made for free by an ad agency (see below). One mistake that many guerrillas (large and small) make is running mysterious, ineffective, or just plain bad advertising. Watch any sitcom. Odds are that at least half the ads you'll see during the program don't satisfy any objectives and are designed to be entertaining, not effective.

Don't start the process with what the ad looks like, or by writing a catchy slogan. Start at the beginning by deciding what your advertising goals are. The Strategic Advertising Form on the next page lets you and your company decide what you want your ad to do *before* you start creating it. Don't allow anyone to show you ads without first telling you how well the advertising satisfies the entries on the Strategic Advertising Form.

STRATEGIC ADVERTISING FORM

➤ Product or service

_____

_____

_____

➤ Target market

_____

_____

➤ Competition (name names)

_____

_____

➤ Product's benefit (unique selling proposition)

_____

_____

_____

➤How is it differentiated from the competition (outline your position and theirs)?

_____

_____

_____

_____

➤ If the reader gets one idea out of the ad, what should it be?

_____

_____

➤ What action should the reader take after reading the ad?

_____

_____

By filling in the form above, you will identify the primary message you want your advertising to convey as well as the market you want your advertising to reach. Shouldn't you know what you want your advertising to accomplish BEFORE you advertise?

Absolut Vodka was unknown twenty years ago. Michael Roux, head of Carillon Imports, hired TBWA Advertising and they created one of the most profitable guerrilla ad campaigns of all time.

What made it a guerrilla campaign?

- It was consistent. They used (and continue to use) the same look and feel and positioning and benefit for more than a decade. While traditional marketers prefer *consistency*, guerrilla marketers insist *on it*.

- It was focused. Absolut used targeted magazine advertising, which allowed them to carefully choose the audience they were addressing.

- It was positioned. By using young contemporary artists as leverage, Absolut established themselves as the hip, intelligent alternative to existing vodkas. They invented their own category and they owned it.

The fact that Absolut's budget wasn't tiny (it was dwarfed by the competition, but it was still millions of dollars) has nothing to do with their tactics: 100% guerrilla.

ETHICAL ADVERTISING GUIDELINES

This is a partial list of advertising guidelines suggested by the Direct Marketing Association. The entire list of guidelines is published in the DMA's *Guidelines for Ethical Business Practice*. While designed primarily for direct marketers, the guidelines listed here apply just as well to all advertisers. It is impossible to build a business on deceit—the guerrilla never cuts corners when communcating to the public.

➤ **Honesty**

All offers should be clear, honest, and complete so that the consumer may know the exact nature of what is being offered, the price, the terms of payment (including all extra charges), and the commitment involved in the placing of an order. Before publication of an offer, direct marketers should be prepared to substantiate any claims or offers made. Advertisements or specific claims that are untrue, misleading, deceptive, fraudulent, or unjustly disparaging of competitors should not be used.

➤ **Disparagement**

Disparagement of any person or group on grounds such as race, color, religion, national origin, sex, marital status, or age is unacceptable.

➤ **Advertising to Children**

Offers suitable for adults only should not be made to children.

➤ **Photographs and Art Work**

Photographs, illustrations, artwork, and the situations they represent should be accurate portrayals and current reproductions of the products, services, or other subjects in all particulars.

➤ **Sponsor and Intent**

All direct marketing contacts should disclose the name of the sponsor and each purpose of the contact. No one should make offers or solicitations in the guise of research or a survey when the real intent is to sell products or services or to raise funds.

➤ **Identity of Seller**

Every offer and shipment should sufficiently identify the name and street address of the direct marketer so that the consumer may contact the individual or company by mail or phone.

➤ **Solicitation in the Guise of an Invoice**

Offers that are likely to be mistaken for bills or invoices or notices from public utilities or governmental agencies should not be used.

➤ **Use of the Word "Free" and Other Similar Representations**

A product or service which is offered without cost or obligation to the recipient may be described as "free." If a product or service is offered as "free," for a nominal cost, or at a greatly reduced price, and/or if the offer requires the recipient to purchase some other product or service, all terms and conditions should be clearly and conspicuously disclosed, in close conjunction with the use of the term "free" or other similar phrase.

When the term "free" is used or other similar representations are made (for example, 2-for-1, half-price or 1-cent offers), the product or service required to be purchased should not have been increased in price or decreased in quality or quantity.

ADVERTISING RESOURCES

Adweek
Published by BPI
1515 Broadway • New York, NY 10036 • (212) 536-5336

Provides seminars for anyone involved in creating, placing, or buying advertising around the country through their Media School. A valuable resource for anyone responsible for advertising placement or design. Call (215) 649-0704 for information.

Advertising Age
Circulation Department • 965 E. Jefferson Ave. • Detroit, MI 48207
(800) 678-9595

Do-It-Yourself Advertising
by Fred E. Hahn • Published by John Wiley & Sons

This book covers all the basics. Topics covered include newspaper and magazine advertisements, brochures, catalogs, direct mail, publicity, telemarketing, and trade shows.

Advertising and Marketing Checklists
by Ron Kaatz • Published by NTC Business Books

How to Make Your Advertising Twice as Effective at Half the Cost
by Herschell Gordon Lewis • Published by Bonus Books, Inc.

How to Make Your Advertising Make Money
by John Caples • Published by Prentice Hall

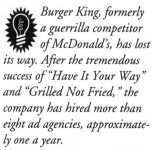

Burger King, formerly a guerrilla competitor of McDonald's, has lost its way. After the tremendous success of "Have It Your Way" and "Grilled Not Fried," the company has hired more than eight ad agencies, approximately one a year.

In spite of the success of their original campaigns, Burger King began to focus on short-term promotional advertising (to build store traffic) instead of long-term positioning and brand building. As soon as they lost patience and went for the quick hit, they were doomed.

ADVERTISING TERMS YOU SHOULD KNOW

ACCOUNT EXECUTIVES—employed by ad agencies, they try to represent the interests of the client, the firm, the art director, and the copywriter simultaneously.

BINGO CARDS—those little cards that advertisers insert in magazines that allow readers to circle numbers to request more information. Most magazines that accept bingo cards will supply the names and addresses of respondents to advertisers at no charge.

CPM—cost per thousand. This is the cost of an ad divided by the circulation of the magazine. For example, a $30,000 ad in a magazine reaching 1,000 people has a cpm of $30.

COLUMN INCHES—an ad one inch high and one column wide is exactly one column inch in size.

DEMOGRAPHICS—the population and makeup of your audience. The people who read *Seventeen* obviously are a different demographic mix than those who read *Modern Maturity*.

4X—four times. The number preceding the X indicates how often you'll commit to running your ad over the next year. You get a discount for running your ad frequently.

MEDIA KIT—provided by publications and other media, these expensively produced packages contain rate and demographic information for an advertiser. Study these to get a sense of what you're buying.

REACH & FREQUENCY—two critical measurements in designing a media plan. Reach is the number of different people you impact with an ad campaign. Frequency is the number of times you hit the average person with your ad campaign.

REMNANT SPACE—print publications are printed in signatures (usually groups of 8, 16, or 32 pages), and you can't have an odd number of pages. If there's leftover space at press time, that remnant space has to be filled with something. It's usually sold to advertisers at a discount.

RUN OF STATION—broadcast advertising without a guaranteed run-time. Radio stations and cable stations will often offer a discount for ads that they have the option to run whenever they have room, rather than at a certain time.

COMMISSION—most mainstream advertising media automatically grant recognized advertising agencies a 15% commission on all ads placed.

A photograph gives the ad instant credibility.

The Ultimate Tax Shelter For <u>ALL</u> Incomes

by Ted Nicholas

Tax experts are calling a small, privately-owned corporation "the ultimate tax shelter."

Because government has recognized the important role of small business in our country, there are numerous laws favoring corporation owners. With the help of my book, anyone — from any income bracket — can take advantage of this readily available tax shelter.

Anyone Can Incorporate

Small, unincorporated businesses, enjoyable hobbies, part-time businesses, even existing jobs can be set up as full-fledged corporations. I've written HOW TO FORM YOUR OUR CORPORATION WITHOUT A LAWYER FOR UNDER $75, to show you the simplest, fastest and least expensive way to incorporate.

If you're intrigued with the thought of running your own corporation, even on a part-time basis, but don't have a specific idea in mind, I believe my book can stimulate you to action. It's important to remember that you don't need to have a big operation or business to benefit. Ninety-eight percent of businesses in the U.S. are small — often just one person working out of his home.

How You Benefit

Your initial investment can vary from zero to a few hundred or a few thousand dollars. I know it can be done because at age 22, with no capital, credit or experience, I incorporated my first company — a candy manufacturing concern and raised $96,000. From that starting point, grew a chain of 30 stores. You, too, can go as far as your determination and imagination will take you.

When you incorporate, you limit personal liability to your investment in the business. Your home, furniture, and car are not at risk. You can raise capital by borrowing or selling stock and still keep control of your business. You can put

aside up to 25 percent of your income tax free into lucrative retirement, pension, and profit-sharing plans. Your own corporation enables you to maintain continuity and facilitate transfer of ownership. Many tax free fringe benefits can be arranged, such as the deductible health and life insurance programs. Medical and dental expenses for both you and every member of your family can become tax deductible to your corporation. If you wish, you may set up a non-profit corporation or foundation. You can even draw a salary while helping your favorite charity. If you prefer maximum privacy, you may operate anonymously under a pen name you can record for one dollar.

Startling Facts Revealed

Lawyers charge substantial fees for incorporation when often they prefer not to and I'll explain why. You'll discover why two-thirds of the New York and American Stock Exchange companies incorporate in Delaware — the state most friendly to corporations. You'll learn how you can have the same benefits as the largest corporations.

You'll be able to hold all corporate offices: President, Vice-President, and Secretary, if you wish.

What Readers Say

"I was quoted a legal fee of $1,000 each for three corporations I wanted to form. This book saved me almost $3,000!"
— *Joanne Strickland, Wilmington, DE*

"This book succeeds . . . because it fills a real need."
— *PUBLISHER'S WEEKLY*

"Please accept my many thanks for a great book and "Do It Yourself Kit" for the little guy to be able to incorporate without all the hassles and added expenses that normally transpire."
— *John Silvestri, Coral Springs, FL*

Free Bonus

As a bonus for ordering my book, HOW TO FORM YOUR OWN CORPORATION WITHOUT A LAWYER FOR

UNDER $75, I'll send you absolutely free THE INCOME PLAN. This portfolio of valuable information which normally sells for $19.95 shows you how to convert almost any job into your own corporation. You could increase your take-home pay by up to 31 percent without an increase in salary. Employers will also save time and money on payroll records and withholding taxes.

My Personal Guarantee

If you are not completely satisfied with my book, return it undamaged within 30 days, and your money will be promptly refunded. And even if you do return it, THE INCOME PORTFOLIO is yours to keep.

Ted Nicholas

Save $300 to $1500

You'll save from $300 to $1500 simply by using the convenient tear-out forms included in my book. Everything you need is there: certificates of incorporation, minutes, by-laws, and complete instructions.

In a hurry? Orders may be faxed to Nicholas Direct, Inc. 302-529-7567 or mail coupon below.

Mail To:
Nicholas Direct, Inc. Dept.
1000 Oakfield Lane,
Wilmington, DE 19810

Please mail ____ copies of HOW TO FORM YOUR OWN CORPORATION WITHOUT A LAWYER FOR UNDER $75 by Ted Nicholas @ $19.95 plus a $2.95 postage and handling fee. It is my understanding if I am not completely satisfied with the book, I may return it within 30 days of receipt for a prompt refund and keep the Income Portfolio, normally $19.95, for my trouble.

☐ I enclosed my check for $19.95 + $2.95 Shipping & Handling

☐ Charge my ☐ Visa ☐ Mastercard ☐ AmEx

_____ exp. date _____

Signature _____
My name is _____
I live at _____
City _____ State ___ Zip Code ___

Fax credit card orders to:
1-302-529-7567

© Nicholas Direct, Inc. 1992

If coupon is missing, send orders to Nicholas Direct, Inc. 1000 Oakfield Lane, Wilmington, DE 19810

Over 200,000 copies of my first book were sold using this successful space ad.

The dotted line on the coupon encourages the reader to clip and mail.

Testimonials are the most powerful element in this ad.

Heavy copy works, and here's proof! Ted Nicholas sold over 200,000 copies of his book with this display ad.

Source: *The Golden Mailbox* by Ted Nicholas

AD AGENCIES

Find the right agency for you—and hire them for the right reasons.

ADVERTISING AGENCIES

If you're doing more than $50,000 a year in advertising, you should seriously consider hiring a full-service agency (and if you're running any ads at all, you should be using a designer or an art director).

In general, ad agencies are paid by the media, not by you. Therefore, the astute guerrilla will find the best, most aggressive agency he can find. Many agencies are willing to take on small clients if the ads they create will help improve their visibility and win awards. And since you're a guerrilla, you're an ideal partner for an aggressive agency. Just make sure that the awards are being won for effectiveness, not flash.

There are two good ways to find an agency. The first is quite simple: look for ads you feel do a great job, call the advertiser, and find out which agency did them.

If your account is larger—perhaps $600,000 a year or more in ads—you might consider hiring a selection agency. These consultants will contact a number of agencies on your behalf, set up review meetings and help you choose one.

If you are determined to find an agency on your own, order *Adweek's Agency Directory*. It's an annual volume that contains information about thousands of advertising agencies throughout the country. Call (800) 468-2395 to order a copy. One other source you can use is the *Standard Directory of Advertising Agencies* published annually by the National Register Publishing Company. It is available at your local business library.

ADVERTISING SELECTION AGENCIES

Many of the firms listed below have specialties. Some focus on a particular geographic area, while others specialize in one or more industries. When contacting one of these firms, quiz them on their past clients, their rates, and their focus. Start by calling the ones closest to you. You can also use the Yellow Pages to broaden this list.

Advertising Agency Register
155 E. 55th St., Suite 6A • New York, NY 10022 • (212) 644-0790

Advertising Agency Search Service
30 E. Huron, Suite 1910 • Chicago, IL 60611 • (312) 649-1148

Bismark Corp.
30 Bismark Way • Dennis, MA 02638 • (508) 385-6889

The Canaan Parish Group
Ogden Rd. • New Canaan, CT 06840 • (203) 972-2859

Dorward & Associates
150 Grand Ave., 2nd Floor • Oakland • CA 94612 • (510) 452-0587

EBJ Management Consultants
7229 S. Janmar Circle • Dallas, TX 75230 • (214) 361-1427

W.E. Hooper & Associates
Box 107 • Gibson Island, MD 21056 • (410) 437-1196

Jones-Lundin Associates
625 N. Michigan Ave., Suite 500 • Chicago, IL 60611 • (312) 751-3470

Morgan, Anderson & Co.
136 W. 24th St. • New York, NY 10011 • (212) 741-0777

New England Consulting Group
55 Green Farms Rd. • Westport, CT 06880 • (203) 226-9200

Pile & Company
535 Boylston. • Boston, MA 02116 • (617) 267-5000

Richard Roth Associates
73 Cross Ridge Rd. • Chappaqua, NY 10514 • (914) 238-9206

Wanamaker Associates
3060 Peachtree Rd., Suite 1430 • Atlanta, GA 30305 • (404) 233-3029

10 QUESTIONS TO ASK YOURSELF BEFORE HIRING AN AD AGENCY

➤ What's our time frame—are we looking for long-term market share results or quick promotion?

➤ Does our agency need a media-buying capability or will we handle that separately?

➤ Do we want to pay our agency a flat fee or a percentage of our budget?

➤ Are we looking for a particular campaign or for a company?

➤ How important is it to have regular access to the head of the agency we choose?

➤ Which medium do we need our agency to handle?

➤ Do we need our agency to handle existing projects only or new product launches as well?

➤ Does it matter if our agency is conveniently located?

➤ Do we want a company with a particular philosophy or one that is willing to work with the philosophy of its clients?

➤ Who do we want in charge?

EVALUATE EACH AGENCY BY ASKING YOURSELF THE FOLLOWING:

➤ Do they understand our company's objectives?

➤ Do they care about our company's objectives?

➤ Do they have the necessary credentials and experience?

➤ Do they have an interest in and knowledge of our business?

➤ Do they have a knowledge of our competitive situation?

➤ Do they present sound marketing strategies?

➤ Do they present clear, creative solutions?

➤ Do they have good internal resources?

➤ Can we work together?

Source: adapted from Small Business Reports, *August, 1991*

FORMING YOUR OWN IN-HOUSE ADVERTISING AGENCY

Media outlets traditionally pay agencies a 15% commission for placing ads with them. That 15% is figured in to the price of the advertising, so they don't care whether they pay it to you or to an agency. So, you can save 15% on all the advertising you place in traditional media like magazines, newspapers, and even television. If your ad budget is small and you don't need the services of an ad agency, this 15% rebate can make a big difference to your bottom line.

Simply print up some letterhead and insertion orders for your new agency. There's no need to fib—if you'd like, you can just append the words *In-house Agency* after the name of your company. When placing an ad, request the "standard 15% agency commission" and most advertisers will grant it (note:

When advertising first began, newspapers would pay independent sales reps a 15% commission. In exchange, they sold the ad and typeset it for the advertiser.

As advertising became more complicated, the commission arrangement remained. With few exceptions, ad agencies make their money from the media, not from the client. If you don't use an ad agency, you can take advantage of this arrangement by starting your own agency.

don't expect a commission if you're cutting a special deal on remnant space or per inquiry ads, or if you need help with layout and typesetting.) You can usually get a commission on classified advertising as well.

If you are granted the commission, it's considered tacky to delay payment—you should plan on submitting payment with the insertion order.

ADVERTISING AGENCY RESOURCES

American Association of Advertising Agencies
666 Third Ave. • New York, NY 10017 • (212) 682-2500
Trade Association

Association of Direct Marketing Agencies
c/o Cohn & Wells • 350 Hudson St. • New York, NY 10014
(212) 886-4400
A great resource if you are looking for an agency that specializes in managing direct marketing campaigns

Adweek Agency Directory
Published by *Adweek* Magazine
Circulation Department • P.O. Box 2006 • Lakewood, NJ 08701
(800) 468-2395

Standard Directory of Advertising Agencies
Published by National Register Publishing Company
Available at most business libraries

TIPS FOR ADS IN NEWSPAPERS AND MAGAZINES

The most common form of advertising used by small businesses.

By far, the number one use of small business marketing money is newspaper display advertising. Newspapers combine local access with near universal impact. They also offer a high degree of flexibility in that you can decide to run an ad or make changes in it up to a couple of days before the ad runs. It's also a medium that is easy to test and gives the guerrilla the consistency and repetition that make an ad campaign successful.

There are far more newspapers in your region than you ever imagined—in addition to big city papers, there are regional papers, Pennysavers, ethnic papers, and more. Determine which ones overlap your market the best and then test an ad in as many of them as you can.

Use coupons in your ads. Have each coupon make a different offer, and request in the ad that the customer bring the coupon when coming to your place of business, or mention the coupon when calling you. By measuring the responses, you'll soon see which newspapers—and which coupons—work the best for you.

BASICS

THE ADVERTISING GOLDEN RULE: REPETITION

Design and copywriting are crucial to the success of your advertising, but always remember that repetition is the key. For every three advertisements viewed, the average consumer will ignore two. It takes an average consumer nine exposures to an ad before the ad is readily remembered. Thus, a specific ad should be run **at least 27 times** *in media directed toward a specific consumer niche before the ad is changed.*

ADVERTISING DESIGN

Don't underestimate the importance of your ad's appearance. Far more people will see your ad than will see you or your place of business, so their opinion of your business will be shaped by your ad. Don't let the newspaper people design your ad, and don't let them write the copy. If they do, it will end up looking and sounding like all the other ads in the paper. Your competition is not just the other people in your business, but everybody who advertises.

You're out there vying for the reader's attention with banks, airlines, car dealers, cigarette companies, soft-drink companies, and who knows what else, so give your ad a distinct style. Hire a top-rate graphic designer to establish the look for your ad. Later, you can ask the paper to follow the design guidelines set down by your art director. But at first you need a graphic designer who can create an advertising identity that conforms to your marketing plan. You won't win customers by boring them into buying. You have to create an image, and a good-looking ad helps immeasurably. (Actually, the difference is measurable, because all guerrillas test their ads!)

What size ad should you buy? If it doesn't cost a fortune, a full-page ad is certainly the best way to attract attention. But you won't want to pay for a weekly full-page ad and, fortunately, the consistency of your advertising is much more important than its size. A half-page ad costs about half as much, but can have nearly the same impact as a full-page ad, especially if you run it regularly.

Before planning your ad campaign, call the paper and request a media kit. It'll give you all the display advertising rates. Newspapers charge for advertising by the column inch. There are fourteen lines per inch, so if the newspaper charges $1 per line, you pay $14 per inch. If you want your ad to be fifteen inches high and three columns wide, you multiply $14 by fifteen (fifteen inches), coming out with $210. Now multiply the $210 by three (three columns), and your total cost is $630. Do some calculating before you call the newspaper to place your advertising. That way you will already have a good idea of when and how often you want to advertise.

WHAT ARE THE BEST DAYS TO RUN YOUR ADS?

➤ Run ads on days your store is open. A simple rule, but often overlooked.

➤ Target your market. Monday's sports section is a male magnet. The food section usually runs on Wednesdays. The entertainment section on Fridays is an obvious spot to advertise bars and even home electronics.

➤ Papers charge a premium for Sundays, since readership is highest on that day. Test a Sunday ad to be sure that the premium translates into more sales.

If you have a truly good ad—one that tells all the features and benefits of your offering—consider making multiple reprints and using them as circulars, customer handouts, mailing pieces, or interior signs. 47th Street Photo, the electronics mecca in New York, has someone standing outside the store handing out its ads all day. You can be sure that more than one customer has walked into the store because something interesting was in that flyer.

If your ad is visually appealing, you can also have it made into a promotional

for an extra dollar. People are encouraged to sit and listen, and the salespeople are surprisingly helpful.

While his prices are among the lowest in town, he focuses on a few loss leaders to really build traffic. While most stores are selling blank audio tape for $3 each, he's selling the same premium tape for 89 cents. No limit.

From that one room on Main Street in Buffalo, The Stereo Advantage now fills an entire car dealership, with a dozen other branches around the country, scores of phone operators, and more than 1,000 accounts. He creates loyal customers, and they tell their friends, generating considerable word of mouth.

Tony positioned his business as a different type of stereo store, and customers responded.

*In case you're interested, an incus is the middle part of the inner ear—pretty clever, huh?

poster. Posters (see *Posters*) cost very little, and can create more excitement in your store.

The real value in newspaper advertising comes from realizing that many people newspaper-shop before going out to purchase a product. In order to reach those people, you must target your advertising to them right at the moment they are making the decision about where to shop. If your product is aimed at a particular group, such as businesspeople, consider running your ad in a business paper rather than a metropolitan paper. If your offering is geared to discount hunters, run it in a shopper-oriented paper. A final newspaper marketing plan usually calls for ads in a number of papers.

TIPS FOR SUCCESSFUL NEWSPAPER ADVERTISING

➤ Make sure you have a strong headline. If the headline doesn't grab 'em, the rest of the ad won't either.

➤ Emphasize the word FREE and repeat it when possible.

➤ Show a picture of your product or service in action.

➤ Include testimonials.

➤ Make an offer. You need to ask the reader to act in some manner. Add a sense of urgency to your offer by making it valid for a limited time or limited quantity. Get those sales now!

➤ Put a border around your ad. Borders help small ads act like big ones.

➤ Try adding a color to your ad. Red, blue, and brown work well. You can't do this with tiny ads, but some newspapers allow color in their larger ads.

➤ Test several types of ads and offers in different publications until you have the optimum ad, offer, and size. Then run the ad with confidence over and over and over again. But don't get lazy—keep testing alternatives.

➤ Don't change your ad because your friends and family are sick and tired of looking at it. You will get tired of your ad a long time before your prospects will. Repetition and reinforcement are the keys to successful newspaper advertising.

➤ Do everything in your power to get your ad placed in the front section of the newspaper on the right-hand page, above the fold. Merely asking isn't enough. Insist.

➤ Don't be afraid to use lengthy copy. It's been statistically proven time and time again that ads with more copy draw better than those with less. You

Before advertising in any newspaper or magazine, call the advertising department and ask them to send you a media kit. They'll send it for free. The kit will tell you everything you need to know to advertise, including who reads the publication, how many copies are distributed, and to what locations.

want to give the reader as much of the story about your product or service as possible. Tell a story that will compel them to buy.

➤ Say something timely in your ad. People read papers for news, so your message should tie in with the news when it can.

➤ Always include an address and a phone number so people know where to find you. Don't make the mistake of putting your address only on the coupon part of your ad. If you use a coupon, have your address appear on it and outside of it so that when the coupon gets clipped, your address still appears.

People will make the decision to read or ignore your newspaper or magazine ad primarily because of your headline. If the rest of your ad is a winner, but the headline is a loser, you are making a major marketing blunder. Here are several hints for writing headlines.

HEADLINE TIPS

➤ Your headline must either convey a benefit or intrigue the reader into wanting to read more.

➤ Speak directly to one reader, not a group. Make your headline personal and immediate.

➤ Write your headline in news style. Use words that have an announcement quality such as "Announcing" or "New."

➤ Put a date in your headline if it adds to the timeliness of your message.

➤ Feature the price—if you're proud of it—in your headline. It need not be a low price for the ad to succeed.

➤ Announce a free offer.

➤ Start to tell a story with your headline. Stories are one of the best techniques you can use to engage the reader. Of course, you want to tell a success story.

➤ Use your headline to instruct. Begin it with "How to," "Why," "Which," "You," or "This."

➤ Use a testimonial-style headline.

➤ Create a sense of urgency with your headline. "Act Now" usually does the trick.

MAGAZINE ADVERTISING

Magazine advertising has been the linchpin for many a successful small business. The single most important reason people patronize one business over another is confidence. And magazine advertisements breed confidence by instilling familiarity and giving credibility. A properly produced magazine ad gives a small business more credibility than any other mass marketing medium.

Consumer confidence will not necessarily be gained from one exposure to your magazine ad. If you're going to rely on magazine ads, plan on a schedule that runs your ad again and again.

Magazines also offer you a great opportunity to test your advertising campaign. Take advantage of the split runs offered by many magazines. Send two ads to the publication. Vary your headline or your offer. Code each ad for response so you'll be able to tell which of the two ads pulls better. The magazine will run one ad in half the issues, the other ad in the rest.

For example, a manufacturer of exercise equipment once ran a split ad with a coupon. One headline said "Strengthen Your Wrists For Better Golf!" and the other said "Strengthen Your Wrists In Only 2 Minutes A Day!" By putting a different department number on each coupon, the advertiser was able to measure which ad drew better. Incidentally, the ad selling stronger wrists in 2 minutes a day attracted a better response.

DESIGN TIPS

➤ Use upper- and lowercase letters. ALL CAPS ARE HARD TO READ.

➤ Avoid using reverse type anywhere in your ad.

➤ Sans serif type should be used only in headlines and subheads.

➤ Stick with one typeface for headlines and one for body copy.

➤ Make sure your typeface is large enough.

➤ Don't put dots around your coupon. Use dashes instead.

➤ Include a photo of your product.

Source: The Golden Mailbox *by Ted Nicholas*

20 Things You Can Do To Make Your Company Grow.

In the '80s it was easy. Most industrial companies grew without any special effort. A super-charged economy is like that. Of course, those that did plan and promote their business did uncommonly well. They enjoyed growth rates of at least double their competitors. And they're the ones still breaking growth records today.

What did they do and how did they do it? You'll learn all the answers in an extraordinary new booklet. It's based on our direct experience and observations in working with thousands of Thomas Register advertisers in hundreds of industries.

We've singled out 20 of the most effective strategies that these industrial companies are using. Strategies that you too can use to grow.

For your free copy of "20 Things You Can Do To Make Your Company Grow", just contact us at the address below.

Thomas Register of American Manufacturers
Attn: Barbara T. Hanson
One Penn Plaza, New York, New York 10119
Fax-(212) 290-7206 Phone-(212) 290-7225

☐ **SEND ME** your free booklet—
"20 Things You Can Do To Make Your Company Grow."

☐ **ALSO** tell me more about Thomas Register and how it has helped industrial companies like mine grow.

Name

Title

Company Name

Address

City   State   Zip
(   )
Phone

Principal products/services   B

Thomas Register of American Manufacturers

Reader Service # 124

You don't have to be flashy to be effective. This ad for the Thomas Register *has a good headline, a free booklet offer, and a cut-out reply card to inspire action.*

ADVERTISING RULES OF THUMB

➤ A two-page spread attracts about 25% more readership than a one-page ad.

➤ A half-page ad is about two-thirds as effective as a full page ad.

➤ A full-page color ad attracts about 40% more readers than a black and white one.

➤ Multipage ads attract more readers than single pages or spreads, but not in direct proportion to the number of pages involved.

➤ Position in the front or back of the magazine (except for the covers) does not matter.

➤ Readership does not drop off when an ad is rerun several times in a magazine.

➤ Photographs are more effective than drawings.

➤ Illustrations showing the product in use are better than static product illustrations.

➤ Ads with people in them typically have a higher response rate than those without.

Source: Starch Research, as reported in Business Rules of Thumb

JUDGING THE EFFECTIVENESS OF YOUR ADVERTISING

➤ Does the headline communicate a clear, compelling benefit?

➤ Does the subheadline elaborate on the benefit and increase reader interest?

➤ Does the first paragraph of the body copy expand on the headline and quickly get to the point?

➤ Do the subheadlines break up the copy and add visual interest?

➤ Are the paragraphs short for easy reading?

➤ Have I made the reader a compelling offer that's hard to refuse?

➤ Is ordering information complete and easy to understand?

➤ Is the vocabulary I'm using a good match for my readers?

➤ Can I use a guarantee to add credibility?

➤ Is the copy lively enough to keep the reader with me?

➤ Is my copy free of cutesy, coy, or flowery language?

➤ Am I always answering the reader's crucial question, "What can your product or service do for me?"

Source: Ivan Levison, publisher of The Levison Letter.

ADVERTISING RESOURCES

There are so many great books and periodicals that have been written about print advertising that we couldn't list them all. Take a look at the bibliography at the back of the book for some of our favorites.

One businessman placed a full-page ad in Newsweek *one time. After the ad ran, he asked customers where they had heard of his company. At the end of a week, only five people claimed to have seen his ad. At the end of a month, that number climbed to eighteen people. After a full year, sixty-three people said they had first heard of the company through that same ad in* Newsweek. *Hundreds more probably saw the ad too, but didn't speak up—not a bad response considering the ad probably only cost $500.*

Even better, the businessman turned the ad into an attention-getting poster.

This is a before and after critique of a magazine ad by Ivan Levison. Notice the effective headline, free offer, and prominence of the 800-number, product, and reply coupon on the right.

Source: Ivan Levison, author of *The Levison Letter*.

Driving next to a big rig can be more than a little intimidating. But there's a way around that. It's called Neon. And it's *Automobile Magazine's* "Automobile of the Year."

We pushed Neon's wheels out to the corners and moved the leading edge of the windshield forward to give it the remarkable stability that comes with an aerodynamic, cab-forward design.

We also gave it a four-wheel independent suspension. Special tires developed with Formula One racing technology. And plenty of passing power in

Hi.

the form of a responsive, 132 horsepower, sixteen-valve engine. Because while we wanted you to like the new Neon...we didn't want you to be blown away.

neon

$8,975 FOR STARTERS. $12,500 NICELY LOADED.
ONLY FROM DODGE AND PLYMOUTH
1-800-NEW NEON

OFFICIAL SPONSOR OF THE 1994
U.S. OLYMPIC TEAM   36 USC 380

MSRPs exclude tax & destination charge.

Always wear your seat belt.

This magazine ad is part of one of the best positioning campaigns we've come across in years. It's obvious from this ad that the Neon is a cute, fun, and affordable car. Remind you of anything? How about the Volkswagen Bug?

SMALL ADS

Small size, big impact.

When you think of advertising, do TV commercials or full-page ads immediately spring to mind? Too bad, because small display ads are often more effective and more profitable for the guerrilla. We define these ads as one column wide (about two inches) and as small as two to five inches tall.

FOUR SECRETS TO CREATING SUCCESSFUL SMALL ADS

➤ **Run Them in the Right Publication**
If the magazine or newspaper doesn't run many ads like yours, it's probably because they don't work. You'll do much better in a magazine where there are lots of little ads.

➤ **Make Sure Your Ad Makes Your Product Obvious**
You only have a microsecond to grab attention, so use a graphic or an obvious headline to outline the benefit you offer.

➤ **Use a Border**
This will make your ad seem far bigger.

➤ **Make it Easy to Respond**
Note that our example ads stress an 800 number or an address.

➤ **Be Consistent**
Run the ad for a long, long time. It may take three or six or nine issues before someone is comfortable enough with your ad to respond to it.

Small ads are usually the most likely candidates for running on a remnant basis. Because they're so small, they can fit into nooks and crannies. If you offer the publisher of a magazine a year-long contract, with instructions to run the ad on a space-available basis, you may be able to save money.

The New Yorker is a great idea factory for guerrillas using small ads. These ads are expensive, but have generated huge results. One furniture maker, Thomas Moser, has built a multi-million-dollar business around his small ads.

When running your ad, don't forget to test several versions. The bottom line is to find out which ad works, and then use it over and over again.

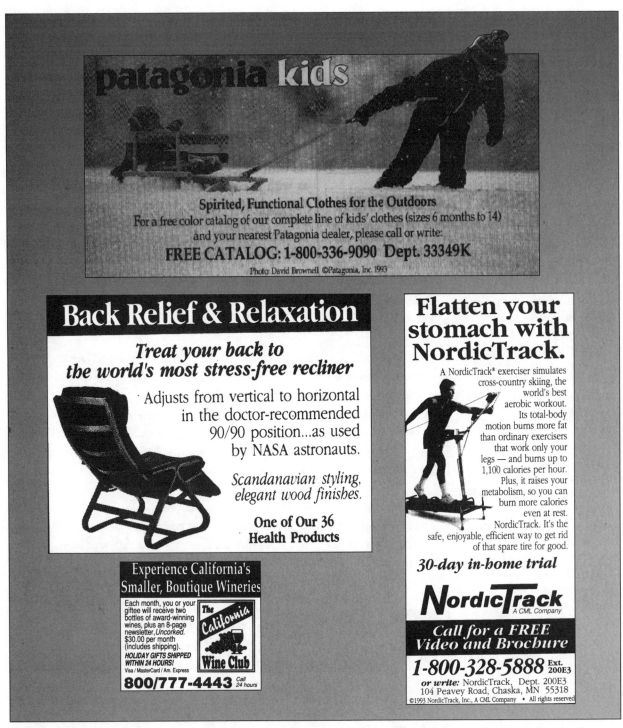

patagonia kids

Spirited, Functional Clothes for the Outdoors

For a free color catalog of our complete line of kids' clothes (sizes 6 months to 14)
and your nearest Patagonia dealer, please call or write:

FREE CATALOG: 1-800-336-9090 Dept. 33349K

Photo: David Brownell ©Patagonia, Inc. 1993

Back Relief & Relaxation

Treat your back to the world's most stress-free recliner

Adjusts from vertical to horizontal
in the doctor-recommended
90/90 position...as used
by NASA astronauts.

*Scandanavian styling,
elegant wood finishes.*

**One of Our 36
Health Products**

**Experience California's
Smaller, Boutique Wineries**

Each month, you or your giftee will receive two bottles of award-winning wines, plus an 8-page newsletter, *Uncorked*. $30.00 per month (includes shipping). **HOLIDAY GIFTS SHIPPED WITHIN 24 HOURS!** Visa / MasterCard / Am. Express

The California Wine Club

800/777-4443 Call 24 hours

Flatten your stomach with NordicTrack.

A NordicTrack® exerciser simulates cross-country skiing, the world's best aerobic workout. Its total-body motion burns more fat than ordinary exercisers that work only your legs — and burns up to 1,100 calories per hour. Plus, it raises your metabolism, so you can burn more calories even at rest. NordicTrack. It's the safe, enjoyable, efficient way to get rid of that spare tire for good.

30-day in-home trial

NordicTrack
A CML Company

**Call for a FREE
Video and Brochure**

1-800-328-5888 Ext. 200E3

or write: NordicTrack, Dept. 200E3
104 Peavey Road, Chaska, MN 55318
©1993 NordicTrack, Inc., A CML Company • All rights reserved

These little ads convey benefits in their headlines, use 800 numbers, show the products in action, and offer catalogs, brochures, or 24-hour information lines.

REMNANT SPACE AND PER INQUIRY

Guerrillas can buy left-over advertising space and save a bundle.

One minor league professional hockey team trying to break into a local sports market bought some remnant space through Media Networks (800-225-3457). They purchased a full-page black and white ad for 1/3 of full price and ran it for four consecutive months in regional issues of national magazines.

The first month it appeared in Sports Illustrated, *the second month in* Time, *the third in* Newsweek, *and the fourth in* US News and World Report. *The ad did wonders for the professional image of this relatively new team.*

Real guerrillas rarely pay full price for advertising. They realize that once the radio show is over, the show is broadcast, or the paper is printed, all the advertising opportunities in that segment or issue are gone forever. If a radio show has twenty minutes of advertising available but only sells fifteen, five minutes are gone, never to be sold again.

The alert guerrilla can buy this leftover space. The industry calls it remnant space, and sometimes it sells for as little as five cents on the dollar.

Here are some remnant strategies:

RADIO: If you buy a slate of ads with a radio station (which is smart, since single ads rarely work), insist on getting remnant space thrown in for free. For example, you could buy ten ads on a Saturday at the regular price, and ask for fifteen more ads to run, at the radio station's convenience, during the next three days. The ad might run at 3 in the morning or at noon, you never know. But the extra time is a bonus for you.

TELEVISION: Local stations, obscure cable broadcasters, and late night shows on network affiliates all have leftover space. It's not unusual to get a minute of air time for as little as $100. Again, you'll get a better deal if you buy a slate of time and ask for the remnant space as part of the bargain. Local network affiliates frequently have remnant space as well. While a nationwide spot on *Seinfeld* would bust your budget, you may be able to buy one of the local spots on the Omaha affiliate for a song.

NEWSPAPERS: The media with the most remnant space is usually the hardest to deal with. Most big city newspapers are hesitant to cut deals with anyone but their largest advertisers—but local papers are a different story. One technique we like is to run a full-page ad in the same spot every week. Then ask the paper to run dozens of tiny remnant space fillers throughout the

BASICS

REMNANT AND PER INQUIRY DEFINITIONS

PER INQUIRY: Ads that are run for no up-front cost. You pay the advertising outlet a fee for each phone call or letter that comes in response to the ad.

PER ORDER: Similar to per inquiry, but you pay the outlet for each order you receive as a result of the ad.

RUN OF STATION: Ads that have no guaranteed air time, but are instead given a time range—quite common, especially for remnant ads.

paper, referring readers to your ad on page 17. This makes your business seem like a big deal, but you only pay for one page of advertising.

MAGAZINES: Small, hobby-oriented magazines are great for remnant space because you get to deal with the owner. The strategy that works best for us is to present your ad, in ten different sizes, to the owner, and tell her that you'll pay 30% (or whatever) of the rate card rate whenever she runs the ad. You're offering a guaranteed cash flow to the magazine on a regular basis—money that they would not have made if the space wasn't filled.

National magazines offer a different opportunity. A magazine like *Time* runs dozens of different regional and demographic editions (that's how your local car dealer got an ad). These editions use inserts of 4, 8, or 16 pages that hold the local ads. If the local ad reps can only sell an odd number of pages, they're stuck with a leftover page. You can buy this page at the last minute for an extremely small amount of money ($300 for a full-page, black-and-white ad in *Time,* for example).

While the ad itself won't generate much new business for you (you only ran it once), the ad department will be happy to get you sample copies, and you can post a copy of your ad, with the "As seen in *Time* magazine" banner, in your window.

PER INQUIRY

When you're selling a product directly, or testing a new campaign, per inquiry ads are an even cheaper alternative to remnant space. In per inquiry ads, the publication becomes your partner. You pay nothing up front, but the publications gets a share of everything you sell as a result of the ad. Unfortunately, if your ad works, this turns out to cost you *more* than you would have paid up front. If it fails, neither side makes money, but you get a free test for your ad.

For example, a publisher ran a per inquiry ad for a book in a card deck (see *Inserts*). The ad usually costs $2,000. The publisher got the ad for free, but promised to pay the card deck company $15 for every book sold. To date, they've sold 400 books, meaning that they paid the card deck company $6,000 for a $2,000 ad. The good news is that they never would have run the ad if they had had to lay out the $2,000 for the test, so they learned something. Now they buy the ads using remnant space ($1,200 each) and keep the rest of the money for themselves.

Media Networks is a company that buys up remnant space from national magazines and then offers it at bargain prices to small businesses. Call them at (800) 225-3457.

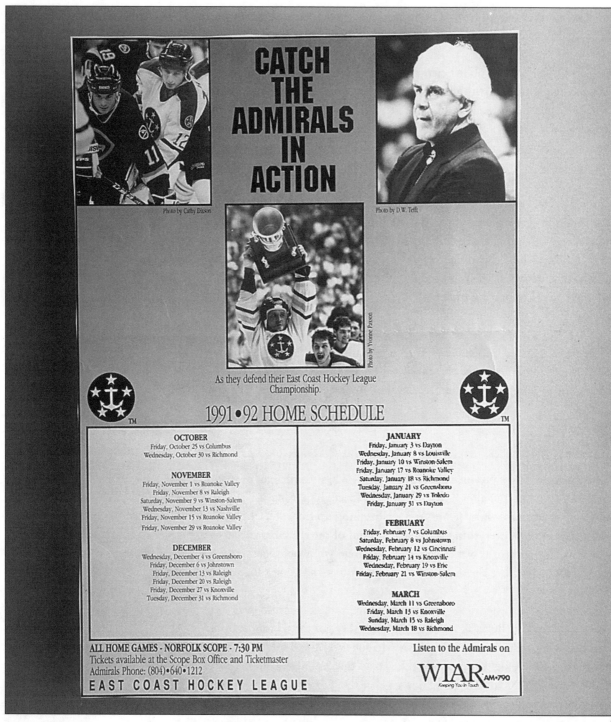

This remnant space ad was purchased by a local hockey team through Media Networks. The team paid a third of full price for it.

Don't expect many media outlets to jump at your offer of per inquiry advertising. Many have been burned in the past and are hesitant to test an unproven campaign (of course, if the campaign is proven, you're not interested in per inquiry anyway).

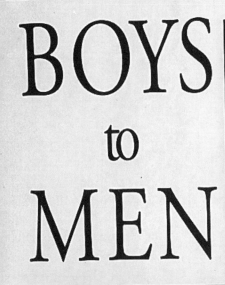

BOYS to MEN

"It's the people – older and younger students, teachers, staff, coaches. They all care about me. And you know, I care about them."

The forming of friendships, values and attitudes should take place in an atmosphere of care, inspiration and challenge. Iona Prep brings the individual into the family of Iona and offers each student the structure, goals and motivation to grow as a man and member of the community.

It is an exciting time in a young man's life and Iona Prep is alive with that excitement. We'd love for you to experience it. Call me, Brother William Stoldt, at 914 632-0714 or better yet drop by the school at Wilmot Road, New Rochelle.

The Catholic College Preparatory School of Westchester County. Founded in the tradition of Brother Edmund Rice and the Congregation of Christian Brothers.

WES 7

This regional ad ran in Time *magazine. Iona paid less than $1,000 for the ad, just a small fraction of the cost of nationwide exposure, but still gained the credibility of appearing in* Time.

REMNANT SPACE AND PER INQUIRY BRAINSTORMS

Use this space to brainstorm a two-step per inquiry campaign that will allow you to generate an initial sale via per inquiry, then follow-up with an additional sale to your new customers.

_____

_____

_____

_____

_____

_____

_____

_____

_____

_____

CLASSIFIED ADS

An economical alternative to display advertising.

 Every fall, a young entrepreneur in Wyoming buys carpet remnants by the truckload. He takes out an $8 classified ad in the University of Wyoming newspaper, offering carpets pre-cut to fit the campus-wide, ten-by-twelve foot dorm rooms. His average markup is 500%. In the spring, he buys the carpets back, for a buck each, and hauls them away, saving the University Housing Department a bundle and making a handsome profit for himself. He gets a fresh batch of prospects each semester.

• • • • • • • • • • • • • •

When you think of classified advertising, you probably think in terms of finding a job, looking for a car, selling a sofa, buying a boat, or locating a house or apartment. Think again. Classified advertising can also be used to support a business. And many a flourishing enterprise exists primarily on the pulling power of classified ads.

Generally, there are three places you can run classified ads: in magazines, in daily and weekly newspapers, and in classified-ad-only newspapers. Magazines are ideal if you are trying to sell country-wide. If your business is local in nature, you probably want to stay away from the national magazines and concentrate on the local papers and classified-ad-only publications. For example, if you run a carpet-cleaning service, it's probably a waste for you to place your classified in *Harper's Magazine*. You could hit a home run with an ad in the local Pennysaver, though.

Classified ads are extremely effective if you offer a specific product and service. Best of all, you have the opportunity in a classified to say, "Call or write for our FREE brochure."

More and more magazines are offering classified advertising. They know that the many new small businesses simply can't afford a display ad, and they know that classifieds work. Take a look at *Rolling Stone*, for example. You'll see that the same advertisers appear in the classifieds issue after issue.

It doesn't cost that much to run a classified ad—even in a major magazine. And most of the time you will be offered a frequency discount as well. This means that if your five-line classified ad costs you $20 to run once, it will cost only, say, $18 per insertion if you run it three times, and only $15 per insertion if you run it five times. The more frequently you run it, the lower your cost per insertion.

Just because classified ads are small and inexpensive doesn't mean they're ineffective. One guerrilla ran this ad:

Fast, efficient electrical work. Certified electricians with references. FREE estimates. Call 555-5656. All work fully guaranteed.

After it ran six times, he had to pull the ad because he couldn't handle all of the business it generated.

TIPS FOR WRITING A STRONG CLASSIFIED AD

➤ Keep your headline short, but make sure you *have* a headline and print it all in capital letters.

➤ Don't use abbreviations or esoteric terms unless you are sure people will understand them.

➤ Include a way to contact you.

➤ Test different categories. *USA Today* runs classified sections with headings like BUSINESS OPPORTUNITIES and DISTRIBUTORSHIPS OFFERED. While they seem similar, your ad might work far better in one category than the other.

➤ Test different days of the week in daily papers. Some days are far more effective than others.

➤ You may want to start with an ad that mimics one you've seen running for a while. If it has a history, that's because it works. However, for a real breakthrough, you'll probably want to create an ad that is dramatically different from your competitors'.

➤ You'll be tempted to keep your ad as short as possible to save money. Don't be so quick. Test short ads and long ones. Classifieds are so cheap that you should constantly test new ideas.

Agnes Franz of Agnes Franz Advertising publishes a monthly newsletter devoted solely to classified advertising. The newsletter is full of tips for the classified advertiser, including advice on ad layout, classified ad uses, where to advertise, and how to be more creative when designing a classified ad. In most issues, Agnes critiques actual classified ads—it's classified guerrilla gospel. Subscriptions are available for $29 a year or $50 for two years. Write to *Classified Communication* at P.O. Box 4242, Prescott, AZ 86302.

Classifieds offer guerrillas the charming benefits of low cost, flexibility, ready availability, free production, free copy consultation (albeit far from Pulitzer Prize quality), simplicity in alteration, ease in testing, and delightful productivity once you've crafted a winner.

There are more classifications in the classified section than ever, meaning more chances to hit bullseyes with inexpensive ads. Within the last several years, classified sections have started popping up with names like

Because 61% of Americans read magazines from the back to the front, your economical classified ad will have a decent shot at being read.

There are dozens of examples of successful papers that print nothing but classifieds.
Hemmings Motor News *is a multimillion-dollar business built around a monthly magazine that lists thousands of used cars and parts. Anyone reading* Hemmings *is a very motivated prospect—if you sell a product that is of interest to this market, you should be listed there.*

Realtors live and die by their classified advertising. Two realtors in the New York area have created distinctive approaches to building their business.

Sopher Real Estate in Manhattan places their logo in every ad they run in the New York Times, *making their presence very obvious.*

Lindsey Real Estate in Mt. Vernon, NY, uses the classifieds to sell their agency, not just houses. By stressing their staff and services, Lindsey is able to bring customers in even if they don't see the exact house they're looking for in the paper.

• • • • • • • • • • • • • • • •

"Employment Alternatives," "Air Ticket Awards," "Attorneys," "California Lottery," "Career Aids," "Carpools," "Computers," "CPAs"—and that's just down to the "C's." Does it make sense for a bookstore to run an ad for its computer books in the computer section? In fact, you should be testing as many sections as possible. There's no reason why you can't run the same ad in multiple sections in the same paper.

In only two lines, this limo ad conveys a benefit and a guarantee. If we needed a limo fast, we'd call them.

Note the detailed nature of the categories, the headlines, and the concise sales pitches.

Source: New York Magazine

YELLOW PAGES

The best way to reach the hottest prospects.

One local fast food restaurant recently started a catering service. Call them up, tell them how many people are coming to your party and when, and they'll have enough food to feed all of them ready when you come in. They placed an ad in the Yellow Pages under the "catering" heading and the phone hasn't stopped ringing.

Imagine a publication that went to every household in your market for free, and was used extensively—only by people who were serious about buying a product or service *every time* they used it. Would you be interested in advertising there?

Because of their high cost, the Yellow Pages are underused by many guerrillas. However, there are also thousands of businesses that have attributed their entire success to Yellow Pages advertising. Clever guerrillas can (and should) use this effective (but expensive) medium to their advantage.

Unlike other media, Yellow Pages ads are difficult to test (they only run once a year) and are plagued by countless rules enforced by the publisher of the directory. Your Yellow Pages sales rep is a fountain of knowledge, but he's also trying to sell you the biggest possible ad. Pump him for whatever info you can, but make your own decision about what you can afford.

TIPS FOR EFFECTIVE YELLOW PAGES ADS

➤ **Copy**
Include as much copy in a Yellow Pages advertisement as you can fit. Studies have shown that display ads with more information stimulate customer action. Russell Marketing Research conducted a study in which a set of prospective respondents were shown ads that were both heavy and light in terms of the amount of copy. The study revealed that the heavy copy ads drew more response by an average ratio of more than 2 to 1. It has been repeatedly shown that *more copy sells.* The more information you can convey to the prospective buyer the better.

➤ **Size**
Make your ad as large as possible within the constraints of your budget. In the same study cited above, respondents claimed that they would call the advertiser with the largest ad first by an overwhelming percentage. The larger the ad, the more information you can convey, and the more persuasive you can be. If prospects ignore your ad, it doesn't matter what you say.

BASICS

THE GOLDEN YELLOW PAGES

Yellow Pages advertising hits the very hottest of prospects. These people are taking the time to look up what you're offering, so you don't have to expend much energy getting their attention or selling the general benefits of your product or service. Careful: This advertising also places you side-by-side with your competition. Be focused, be precise, and be as large as you can afford.

➤ **Color**

If possible, include a second color in your ad—color attracts readers.

➤ **Reliability**

Convince the prospective buyer that you are reliable. Include information along the lines of the following: Years in business, experience, size of firm, licenses, certifications, degrees, awards. If you're the largest pizza parlor in town, say so.

➤ **Authorized Sales and Service**

State the brand names, trademarks, manufacturers, and dealers with whom you do business. Include any information about distribution and factory service depots.

➤ **Safety and Protection**

Mention any insurance, bonding, guarantees, association memberships, and specially trained employees.

➤ **Completeness of Line and Service**

Convince the prospective buyer that you are the best and most complete dealer for the product or service. Include type, scope, variety, cost, and quality of service or product. Don't forget to mention specialized services and features, availability, inventory, capacity, catalogs or brochures, financing, credit cards accepted, check cashing, pick-up and delivery, hours, and parking.

➤ **Illustrations**

Pictures and illustrations are interesting to look at and help attract the prospective buyers' eye. They can also help tell the story of your product or service. Consider inserting a picture of the owner, premises, or product. It's also a great idea to include you company name and logo in big type.

➤ **Location**

Let people know where they can find you—include nearest intersection, landmarks, shopping center, or even a map.

YELLOW PAGES ALTERNATIVES

With the break up of the Bell System, there are more Yellow Pages alternatives than ever. No one controls the words "Yellow Pages," so anyone can publish his own. In addition to large metro directories, there are business-to-business directories and industry and demographic specific directories as well.

It is difficult to measure the success of advertising in one directory versus another, but where you should advertise depends on the type of product or

One reason that the Yellow Pages are such a useful consumer tool is that they have very strict advertising guidelines. These guidelines ensure that there's a consistent look throughout the book, but they can also make it difficult for a guerrilla to get his ad to stand out. If your sales rep tries to dissuade you from a particular technique, find another ad in the same Yellow Pages that uses the same technique as proof that you're not violating standards.

service you sell. The business-to-business Yellow Pages is certainly more targeted than the consumer Yellow Pages. If you sell hydrolic filters, for example, it is unlikely that the average suburban housewife will have an interest in your product. You'll probably have more luck in the business-to-business book.

In general, more industrial products do better in the business-to-business directories. Remember though, businesses you are marketing to probably have both the business-to-business directory and the consumer directory in their offices. You need to have a presence in both. The question then becomes where do you spend the majority of your dollars. Place ads in both directories as a test and see which ad pulls better.

Our rule of thumb for choosing a directory: Look for your competitors. Businesses won't stay in a Yellow Pages unless it is generating new business for them. If your category in a given directory is almost empty, there's probably a good reason. But, if the section is filled with page after page of ads, can you afford to be left out?

GUIDELINES FOR YELLOW PAGE ADVERTISERS

➤ Always ask yourself: What's my unique selling proposition? How can I out-sell the competition, knowing that the Yellow Pages reader who sees my ad sees everyone's ad?

➤ Don't use fine-line artwork that won't reproduce well on the soft yellow newsprint.

➤ If you're afraid to ask questions of the Yellow Pages salesperson because you think it's an admission of ignorance, you're costing yourself the immeasurable ammunition this information represents.

➤ Do what you can to have a memorable phone number.

➤ If you have two strong selling points (e.g., "Open 24 Hours" and "Delivery Within One Hour"), consider two separate ads instead of one.

➤ Fight for your rights. Don't abandon a good piece of selling copy because the salesperson says, "I don't think they'll accept that." Give it a try.

➤ Unless you're in a city that has separate directories for consumer and commercial use, aim your copy at consumers if you service both types of buyers. In such circumstances, business clients are probably better recruited through direct mail or personal solicitation.

➤ If Yellow Pages regulations force dilution of your sales pitch or a complex explanation of a claim, you may be better off dropping it. This kind of copy, watered down by a lot of explanation, lacks punch and may kill off calls.

➤ If you're in a zoned area or one with tolls, either establish a local phone number that eliminates the toll or invite collect calls. Local suppliers are always favored by the consumer.

➤ Don't use dumb cartoons, puns, unclever slogans, or your children's pictures. People looking in the Yellow Pages are hot buyers looking for a professional source.

➤ Use strong borders—the blackest allowed. Lump type into smaller areas to give emphasis to those areas, and try to keep type away from the border. The reader's eye will go to your ad.

➤ Line illustrations usually reproduce better than photographs, but don't clown. Cartoons are for the comic strips, not the Yellow Pages.

➤ Don't be too sharp. The serious buyer resents smugness. Copy should be warm but businesslike.

➤ Don't rerun last year's ad just because you're at deadline and last year's ad is available.

➤ Don't be afraid of long copy. Research shows that long copy outpulls short copy in the Yellow Pages.

➤ Plan ahead. Analyze what works and what doesn't. Ask every new customer, "How did you hear about us?" Learn what the customer wants and gradually bend your copy approach to give a positive answer to those wants.

Source: How to Make Your Advertising Twice as Effective at Half the Cost *by Herschell Gordon Lewis.*

TESTING YOUR YELLOW PAGES AD

Typically, Yellow Pages ads are tested in one of two ways: metered ads and split run tests. The metered ad involves only one ad in a particular directory with one unique telephone number that is remote call forwarded (RCF) to the advertiser's existing office. Since the RCF number is not given out by directory assistance operators and is not included in any other print advertising, any call placed to this number is the direct result of a reference to the Yellow Pages. Each month, the telephone company provides a printout of the number of calls made to that number.

According to Mark O'Halloran of O'Halloran Advertising, Inc., over 80% of all Yellow Pages advertising is placed by local advertisers. He notes, however, that there is an increase of national, nontraditional advertising popping up in the Yellow Pages. Supermarkets, for example, do not typically advertise in the Yellow Pages, but they are beginning to do so. Some of the largest florists and pharmacies are now located within supermarkets and so those supermarkets are finding it profitable to advertise under the "pharmacy" or "florist" headings.

O'Halloran Advertising is one of the largest ad agencies specializing in Yellow Pages advertising. Give them a call at (800) 762-0054 if you need some help with your Yellow Pages campaign.

The ad for House of Honda has a good headline, positions the store well, shows customers how to get there with a map, and gives the phone numbers for all the individual departments. It is also the largest and best designed ad on the page.

Most directory publishers offer split-run testing opportunities for their advertisers. Within a given area, the Yellow Pages are printed so that every other copy contains one of two versions of your advertisement. The books are then distributed evenly throughout the area and you can track how many responses you get from each ad you ran.

Split-runs are most frequently used to test different ad sizes. For example, 50% of households and businesses within the directory distribution area receive version "A" with a small trademark ad, while the remaining 50% recieve version "B" with a 1/4 page display ad. You can put a distinct phone number in each ad (both unlisted elsewhere) and track the calls you receive to each number. Or you can code each ad and then ask for the code when prospects call citing your listing in the Yellow Pages.

Directories usually only offer a limited amount of space for split-runs, so ask your advertising account rep to keep you updated about split-runs going on in your area.

Remember to test only one aspect of your ad at a time. Test your headline, offer, and body copy. Then use the information you gather from the test to make the rest of your advertising more effective.

Source: O'Halloran Advertising, (203) 762-0054

YELLOW PAGES TERMS YOU SHOULD KNOW

ANCHOR LISTING—a tag line placed at the end of your Yellow Pages entry that references your display ad. For example, "See our display ad on page 335."

CERTIFIED MARKETING REPRESENTATIVE (CMR)—an advertising agent certified by the Yellow Pages Publishers Association to handle placement, design, and implementation of ads for local and national advertisers.

BOLD LISTING—a listing in the Yellow Pages printed in bold lettering.

HEADING—Classifications in the Yellow Pages under which different types of businesses are grouped.

IN-COLUMN AD—a Yellow Pages ad that appears alphabetically within the column, under the appropriate business classification.

UTILITY PUBLISHER—a company that publishes Yellow Pages directories for a telephone company, as opposed to an independent publisher that is unrelated to any particular telephone company.

RESOURCES FOR YELLOW PAGES ADVERTISERS

Yellow Pages Publishers Association (YPPA)

820 Kirts Blvd., Suite 100 • Troy, MI 48084 • (810) 244-6200

An association representing the Yellow Pages industry. The association represents industry-authorized sales representatives that assist advertisers in placing multiple-directory ads. They also publish the Yellow Pages Industry Fact Booklet.

Association of Directory Marketers

1187 Thorn Run Rd. Suite 202 • Moon Township, PA 15108
(412) 269-0663

Community Pride Association

P.O. Box 1479 • Redlands, CA 92373

This organization provides counseling to members on cost-effective strategies for advertising, particularly in the Yellow Pages.

Association of Directory Publishers

105 Summer Street • Wrentham, MA 02093 • (508) 883-3688

This association is made up of publishers of city, telephone, and special interest directories. With a membership of 200, the ADP maintains a library of telephone directory related materials and compiles mailing lists of directory publishers and advertising agencies that specialize in Yellow Pages advertising. The association also puts out a quarterly trade publication called Directory Journal.

YELLOW PAGES BRAINSTORMS

Use this page to prioritize the six elements you want to include in your next Yellow Pages ad (ranked from most prominent to least prominent).

_____

_____

_____

_____

_____

_____

_____

_____

_____

RADIO

Custom designed for guerrillas—low cost, high impact advertising on a local basis.

Guerrilla Marketer of the Year.

Brothers Barry and Eliot, owners of Jordan's Furniture, built their retail furniture empire on 22 years of radio advertising. In 1972, they launched their first "Barry and Eliot" campaign, featuring their own voices and personalities. Their on-air antics soon became famous and they have never abandoned radio advertising.

They are on at least twelve different radio stations in the Boston area at all times. Their selective media buying and savvy creative strategy have made them a mainstay on Boston radio stations. Most Bostonians can recite every one of Jordan's radio slogans and even the directions to their stores—from "Main Street to Moody Street" to "Right on Spitbrook, left on Daniel Webster."

Radio advertising is one of the most powerful guerrilla tools available. Radio stations are receptive to remnant and barter (see *Bartering*) deals, and they usually need what you have to offer. Play your cards right and you can receive three times the amount of radio exposure you pay for.

BENEFITS AND KEYS TO SUCCESSFUL RADIO ADVERTISING

➤ Radio is one of the best ways to reach a highly targeted market, but you have to make sure you are advertising on the right station. Do your research to pinpoint the stations in your market whose listeners most closely resemble your customer base.

➤ Radio works best in combination with other media. Use it to reinforce a direct mail or telemarketing campaign. It also works well in conjunction with 800 or 900 telephone numbers.

➤ Be creative. A humorous approach gets attention.

➤ Radio provides a great bang for the buck. Short commercials are great for building name recognition, and long commercials give you plenty of time to tell your story. Don't fill the time with dead space or boring copy. Sixty seconds is an eternity on radio.

➤ Repetition is even more important on radio than anywhere else. Because listeners tune in and out, do errands, drive through tunnels, and occasionally stop paying attention, you need to repeat yourself several times.

➤ Use the radio's "live" power. Have the station do a live remote from your place of business. The disc jockey drives a huge van to your parking lot and does his broadcast live. This is a particularly effective campaign if you are promoting a special event like a grand opening or a sale. Live remotes are a call to action: "Come right down and . . ." Remotes also get you far more ads for less money than a conventional radio campaign ever could. The station wants to draw attention to remote broadcasts (and to you). Remotes are great for advertisers, but they also allow the radion station to show off.

BASICS

BEST RADIO TIMES

Morning (6-9 A.M.) and evening (3-7 P.M.) drive times are going to cost the most. You can probably get times between 7 P.M. and 10 P.M. at a relatively good price, but you may not necessarily want it. That's during television prime time and radio listenership is down. Many stations have more listeners in the middle of the night than during TV prime time. Be sure to test to find the times that are most cost-effective for you.

➤ Radio is a powerful promotional medium. You can create a sense of urgency that just doesn't happen in print. Combine efforts with other businesses or organizations to create an attention-getting promotion. Hold a food drive at your place of business for a local charity. Advertise on the radio and use a live remote to push the drive. Run a contest asking for entries in your radio commercials. Institute a new toll-free customer service line and plug it on the radio.

➤ Radio is a particularly effective medium for car dealers. What better time to run an ad about Jeeps than during rush hour in a snow storm?

➤ Be a radio sponsor. How about the "WXYZ Weather Update brought to you by Acme Snow Removal?" Sponsor a public service announcement: "The Candlelight Pub and WXYZ remind you that friends don't let friends drink and drive." Sponsor the news or the sports, each of which run throughout the day on most radio stations

➤ Radio is the ultimate remnant space medium. Offer to pay the station for any unsold time during the day. Whenever the station has a couple of unsold minutes, they will run your ad for a small fee. You get low cost exposure and the station gets a little something for time that would have gone unsold.

➤ Radio stations are often open to bartering (see *Bartering*). If you own a restaurant, offer to provide free lunch for the deejays of your local radio station every day in exchange for two mentions a day on the air. There is a limousine company in our area that takes the morning deejay to work when he needs a lift in exchange for the deejay talking about the company on the air.

➤ If you create your own ads, don't forget to ask for a 15% agency commission. (See *Ad Agencies.*)

FIVE GUERRILLA HINTS FOR USING RADIO

➤ If you don't have the attention of the listener within five seconds, you've failed.

➤ Consider all the radio tools available: a voice alone or several voices, background music or foreground jingle, and sound effects in great abundance (see *Jingles* and *Music*).

➤ Mention your name at least five times within a 30-second spot. People won't remember it as well otherwise.

! *If you are going to pay the drive time rates, make sure the station is willing to "throw in" some added time during off hours. It doesn't take much wheeling and dealing to get price breaks from radio stations. In fact, discounted time is the norm, so work with your station to put together an ad schedule that works for both of you.*

! *Many guerrillas ignore public radio, believing that you can't advertise there. On the contrary, because of the lack of clutter, high loyalty, and excellent demographics, sponsoring a public radio program may be a great way to build business at your bookstore, pharmaceutical company, or restaurant. The cost of sponsorship can be quite reasonable, and you'll certainly win the loyalty of NPR's (National Public Radio) regular listeners.*

Most radio stations are happy to provide you with limited technical support in creating your ads. If you need a soundproof room for your announcer to record a few spots, just ask. For more involved production, it pays to hire a studio (the low prices will surprise you).

➤ Develop a radio persona so people know it's you regardless of the thrust of your radio message or the sound of the spot. Get yourself an identity. Someone should be able to identify your ad even if they miss the beginning or the end of the spot.

➤ Commit to only one or two stations. You need to repeat yourself to the same people, and you can only do that by focusing on a few stations.

HERSCHELL GORDON LEWIS'S 12 RULES FOR WRITING A RADIO SPOT

➤ Don't be funny at the expense of sincerity.

➤ If you become your own announcer, talk clearly and naturally—as though you're explaining something to your mother; pronounce the word "the" as "thuh" before a word starting with a consonant, "thee" before a word starting with a vowel, and pronounce "a" as "uh."

➤ Repeat the product name constantly.

➤ If the spot ends with a phone number, build up to it: "Have a pencil? Write down this number so you won't forget it: 555-6000. Did you get that? Just in case, here it is again: 555-6000." Then remind the listener that the phone number is in the Yellow (or White) Pages. (See the sidebar for an important note about the Yellow Pages.)

➤ Use a jingle as a memory jogger, but never use a jingle as the entire spot unless the commercial is ten seconds long. We all hate jingles, but the fact is, they work. (see *Jingles*).

➤ If your strategy emphasizes prices, try to mention only one item and one price. When listening to an ad, it's easy to confuse numerous facts and numbers.

Don't refer readers to the Yellow Pages unless you have the largest ad in the section—otherwise you're sending people to your competition. Instead, tell people they can find you in the White Pages. If you're going to make this referral often, pay some money and buy an ad in the white pages to make it even easier to find you.

➤ Use simple, straightforward sentences. Try the ad out on a ten-year-old. If he doesn't understand it, it's too complicated.

➤ When giving an address, help with a mnemonic device: "Three-oh-three Main Street—across from Blevins Hotel." Our Guerrilla Marketer of the Year emblazoned directions to their store across the mind of every radio listener in Boston.

➤ In the script, write out numbers so the announcer can't stumble. For example, don't write "1,001 reasons," but rather, "a thousand and one reasons;" don't write "9400 E. State St.," but "ninety-four-hundred East State Street."

➤ Read the commercial aloud several times to get rid of words that don't "sound": words with "s" and "l" often sound slurpy and slippery; "Louisiana legislature" is hard to pronounce (lots of l's plus a five-syllable word followed by a four syllable word); words such as "fastest" and "comfortable" are hard to pronounce, and words like "banal" and "elongated" are often mispronounced or misunderstood.

RADIO ADVERTISING TERMS YOU SHOULD KNOW

DAYPARTS—Radio stations break up the day into units called dayparts. Drive time, for example, is the daypart between 6 A.M. and 9 A.M.

AVERAGE QUARTER-HOUR AUDIENCE (AQH PERSONS)—The average number of people listening to a radio station for at least five minutes out of a particular quarter-hour segment of time.

DRIVE TIMES—The morning and afternoon radio dayparts during which times most people are driving to work (6 A.M. to 10 A.M., 3 P.M. to 7 P.M.). These are usually the most expensive times to advertise, but they will also bring you the largest audience.

FREQUENCY—The number of times one person is exposed to your commercial during the entire run of the campaign.

LIVE REMOTES—A promotion where the radio disc jockey comes to your place of business and does his broadcast live.

REACH—The number of people who actually hear your radio commercial.

SPOT—The industry name for a radio commercial. You don't run radio commercials, you run radio spots.

RADIO RESOURCES

Radio Success Stories
Published by The Interep Radio Store
100 Park Avenue • New York, NY 10017 • (212) 916-0524
Anecdotes of successful radio campaigns from across the country on the national, regional, and local level

The Interep Radio Store
100 Park Avenue • New York, NY 10017 • (212) 916-0524
Radio advertising brokers

Katz Radio Group
125 West 55th St. • New York, NY 10019 • (212) 424-6490
Radio advertising brokers

Should you do your own voiceover? While appearing as the voice in your radio ads saves you a little money and definitely ads personality to your ads, most guerrillas find that it's a mistake. Why? First, it may be less effective—an obnoxious or grating voice turns listeners off. Second, it's harder to keep to a regular schedule of ads if you've got to haul yourself down to the studio every time you need a new one. You've get better things to do.

An electronic repair shop specializing in VCR cleaning and repair bought a schedule of radio ads on a local rock radio station. By running on a consistent weekly basis (every Tuesday through Thursday) and sponsoring the station's morning newscasts, the shop attracted a loyal following and doubled its revenue.

! *American adults listen to the radio for an average of 2 hours and 58 minutes each day according to the Radio Advertising Bureau. Also, over 75% of all professional, managerial, clerical, and blue collar workers listen to the radio while they are at work.*

....

Radio Advertising Bureau
304 Park Ave. South • New York, NY 10010 • (800) 232-3131

Radio advertising trade association. Publish several publications including a free booklet called "Why Radio?" that you can request by calling their toll-free number.

Radio Co-op Directory
Published by the Radio Advertising Bureau
304 Park Ave. South • New York, NY 10010 • (800) 232-3131

A listing of over 6,000 manufacturers that offer co-op funds to retail radio advertisers

Radio Marketing Guide and Fact Book for Advertisers
Published by the Radio Advertising Bureau
304 Park Ave. South • New York, NY 10010 • (800) 232-3131

RADIO BRAINSTORMS

Use this page to list new ways your business can use radio. Include possibilities for remote broadcasts, product giveaways, and special program sponsorships.

_____

_____

_____

_____

_____

_____

_____

_____

_____

TELEVISION

High leverage, low cost advertising for the astute guerrilla.

!
TV commercials are sold by the second, so make every second count. If you can make a 15-second commercial just as effective as a 30-second commercial, you'll be able to run it twice as often for the same budget. Tighten, tighten, tighten.

Guerrillas know that television advertising has impact. More than any other medium, TV can generate an emotional reaction in viewers—and with the average household watching seven hours of television *every day*, you are guaranteed an audience.

Television can serve many purposes for your company. Use it to build store traffic, establish a brand name, or position yourself with consumers. But television is relatively expensive, so pick your shots carefully.

GUERRILLA INSIGHT: TV DOESN'T HAVE TO BE EXPENSIVE

A 30-second spot on the Super Bowl costs nearly a million dollars. Faced with these forbidding numbers, guerrillas have responded in two ways. Some, like Master Lock, have decided to take their entire TV budget and spend it on just one ad. The value of repetition is lost, but Master Lock's executives do get good seats at the Super Bowl.

Other smaller guerrillas have abandoned TV because they think that it is too expensive. But now television just may be worth reconsidering.

With the explosion of cable TV, there are too many stations chasing too few advertisers. You might find 30 channels broadcasting to one neighborhood. Each station runs about ten ads in a given half hour. That's 600 ads an hour—a huge opportunity for the guerrilla!

If you explore the opportunities on cable networks and local nonaffiliated stations, you'll find that you can buy a minute of TV advertising for as little as $100. Of course, you won't get nationwide coverage on *Seinfeld*, but so what? Test your ads, and soon you'll find yourself with the right balance of budget, reach, and frequency.

EIGHT QUALITIES OF A GOOD COMMERCIAL

1. Entertaining. A commercial that entertains is memorable.

2. Clear. The viewer understands the message immediately.

3. Visual. The viewer can *see* the message.

4. High quality. The quality of the commercial reflects the quality of the product. If your commercial is poor in quality and obviously cheap, people who see it will assume the product being sold is just as shoddy.

5. Truthful. A commercial full of obvious exaggerations will backfire on you.

6. Contains a call to action. Instruct the viewer to do something with the information you have just given him—ideally go to the store and buy your product.

7. Filled with content, not just special effects. Special effects get attention, but the content is what sells the product.

8. Uses actors or voiceovers that inspire confidence. Don't cast your kid as the star.

FOUR WAYS TO TEST A COMMERCIAL BEFORE YOU RUN IT

1. Watch it with the sound turned off. Can you still figure out who it is for and how to respond?

2. Show it to a roomful of 12-year-olds. Do they stop talking long enough to watch it? Then ask them what it was about.

3. Watch the commercial twenty times in a row. Is it so abrasive you become angry?

4. Watch just the first half or just the second half of the commercial. Do you still understand what's being sold?

EXPANDING YOUR PRODUCT'S DISTRIBUTION WITH TV ADVERTISING

Television advertising can be a great tool for a manufacturer trying to gain a distribution niche in a particular market.

Distribution is not easy to get because so many other companies are competing for the same shelf or floor space. Amazingly enough, many stores now charge for shelf space by the foot. Television advertising alone won't get you into Wal-Mart, but with local stores and small chains, it might be able to get you around the distribution barrier.

Write and produce a 30-second TV commercial for your product. Make it a good one, with music, an announcer with a voice that inspires confidence, and impressive visuals. Of greatest importance, make it a 25-second commercial, leaving the final five seconds to list the name(s) of the outlets where your product is stocked. In reality, this is a form of reverse co-op. Ordinarily, retailers advertise and then recoup some of the cost from the manufacturers of the products they feature in the ad. In this case, it is the manufacturer who is pay-

How about this for a unique approach to television? A Seattle department store produced a TV commercial advertising its exclusive line of candy. The spot was only one fourteenth of a second long! The New York Times *wrote a story about the commercial, and the department store will be in the Guinness Book of World Records with the shortest TV spot in history. Obviously, the ad wasn't seen, but the PR sure was.*

Television advertising is perhaps the single best way to persuade retailers to carry your product.

! *Make sure that you spend enough money to produce a high quality ad. A stranger should be able to watch it fifteen times without hating you.*

. . . .

A used car dealer in San Francisco became a household name by greeting his kids at the beginning of every television commercial he ran. The commercials were so memorable that they help establish his brand name, and so successful that the dealer ran the same format ad for many years.

. . . .

ing for and placing the advertising. In return the retailers featured in the ad give the manufacturer shelf space to sell his product.

Don't spend a fortune producing your spot. Although in 1993 the average TV spot cost $179,000 to produce, great TV commercials can be produced for well under $5,000. Still, to create a desire for your product and to impress the retailers who are your potential distribution outlets, it has to look sharp and professional.

Tell the retailer you'll televise the commercial in his area, aimed at his exact audience, and you'll even mention his name and location at the end of the spot. A quality commercial will persuade the viewer that your product is just what she needs and that the retailer mentioned by name is the best place to go to buy it.

Your offer to the retailer is simple: Stock my product and I'll mention your store. The vast majority of retailers, loving the thought of having their name mentioned on television and dazzled because you aren't asking for one penny for shared marketing costs, will make a beeline to your dotted line.

After all, they think that TV commercials are expensive to produce and run. They aren't guerrillas like you. Deep in their hearts, they've always wanted to be on TV, but knew they couldn't afford it.

Make this arrangement with as many retail outlets as you like, but show no more than five names at the end of each commercial. If you sign up fifty retailers (which isn't difficult with the glamour and pizazz of TV), you'll need ten five-second endings with five names on each. Run the spots alternately so that each retailer gets equal exposure.

If you'd like, ask for a mega-order and offer the retailer an exclusive for three to twelve months. Go after chains and franchises because they'll instantly see the worth and the fairness of your offer. Of course, they've probably discovered all the wonders of TV.

THE BIGGEST TV ADVERTISING MISTAKE: POOR QUALITY

With production costs plummeting and air time easier to buy, TV advertising is becoming a real possibility for most guerrillas. And therein lies the danger. Because it's so cheap, many small businesses (and even some larger ones) are tempted to create ads on their own.

One of the quickest, most effective ways to poorly position your company is to make a stupid, poorly written, badly produced commercial. While we've all gotten a laugh from pompous car salesmen or unctuous infomercial stars, the fact is that these ads generally don't work. And the damage they do in terms of positioning is incalculable. Here's our guerrilla advice: You wouldn't perform surgery on yourself—don't write, or direct, or edit your own TV ads.

ALTERNATIVE TO NETWORK ADVERTISING

There are a host of new targeted television networks that are worth exploring. The Turner Broadcasting Company is at the forefront of a movement called "place-based" marketing and it fits right into the guerrilla scheme. The Airport and Checkout channels are just two of the new media being introduced. The do just what the names suggest. The Airport Channel broadcasts news and travel features in airline terminals and the Checkout Channel broadcasts a loop of consumer features on television sets placed right by the checkout counters in grocery stores.

There are new television networks that are being developed to broadcast shows in school classrooms and Whittle's Special Reports is a series of shows broadcast to people in doctors' waiting rooms. Then there's Big Mo. The Big Mo Video Network is a group of huge Sony Jumbotron Screens that are transported around the country by the Dallas-based Motion Graphics. The screens are set up at events, festivals, and concerts.

You don't have to venture that far from the good old household television set to target your television advertising. Buy advertising time on specialty cable stations and you'll find yourself spending a lot less money to reach a smaller, albeit more motivated, audience for your product than if you bought a 30-second spot on the Super Bowl. For example, if you sell kitchen appliances, advertise on the Food Channel, not on CBS. Remember, when you pay to reach people who have no interest in your product, you're throwing money away.

Using new desktop video techniques, the cost of editing a commercial has come way down. But don't do it yourself. Companies like Otterson TV in New York City will edit your commercial for as little as $99 per hour. Check your yellow pages for a local editing facility or call Otterson at (212) 695-7417.

INFOMERCIALS

Visit your prospects in the comfort of their homes.

Advertising that pays for itself as it runs is a wonderful thing. When you run a successful direct response ad, either in a magazine or on television, two things happen. Some of the viewers watch it and buy your product right away. Others watch it, remember your brand name, but don't buy right away. If you can make the first group pay for the cost of running the commercial, then you make your impressions on the second group for *free*. And guerrillas love free advertising.

First popular in the 1950s, then barred by FCC regulations on length, infomercials are defined as long (at least ten minutes) commercials. With the relaxation of FCC rules and the explosion of cable, it is suddenly within the reach of most guerrillas to test an infomercial. Production and air costs for infomercials are relatively low compared with those for a conventional 30-second television spot, particularly if you take advantage of the local cable stations and small cable networks. GTE only spends about $59 per half hour to have their infomercial entitled "Get the Edge" run on a local cable station (albeit to a tiny audience).

Infomercials are on the rise. Over the past five years, the gross sales generated by infomercials have risen from $350 million to over $900 million. Here is just a sampling of the major corporate marketers who have used infomercials: American Airlines, Apple, Braun, Club Med, Ford Motor Company, Eastman Kodak, McDonald's, Visa, and Volvo. In every case, these companies are trying to flesh out a new advertising opportunity that will separate them from the competition.

Talk to your local cable station about running an infomercial on a per inquiry basis. Eleven percent of 709 television stations surveyed by the BJK & E Media group said they were willing to work with infomercial advertisers on

> **!** *According to William Thompson in* Inside Infomercials, *you can produce an infomercial for as little as three times the cost of producing a two-minute television spot. The real difference in cost between the two is not in production. It's in the air time you need to purchase in order to run the spot.*

BASICS

INFOMERCIALS: FOLLOW-UP IS THE KEY

If you are going to market your product or service through an infomercial, remember that your job doesn't end when the program airs. Infomercials often breed mistrust in customers, sometimes with good reason. In one survey conducted by Response TV *magazine, 30 percent of respondents who had purchased items through direct response TV (spots or infomercials) said they wouldn't do it again. The product they received did not meet their expectations or wasn't delivered fast enough or in good condition, or the service they received on the phone was not satisfactory. Follow up is the key to selling through an infomercial. You need to be honest and prompt in your response to the customer.*

just such a basis. While the commission charged is high—as much as 60% of the gross—the advantage of testing on a per inquiry basis is obvious: If the ad doesn't work, your air time costs are minimal.

Most communities also have a public access TV station which will give you an opportunity to create a test version of an infomercial at no cost. Cable networks are required to run local broadcasting, regardless of content. In many cases, they'll even offer you a studio and equipment that you can use to create your test spot.

Once you create a spot, you should test it. You can show it to a number of focus groups and get their reactions. Incorporate the feedback you get until you've got something worth putting into a real-life test on the air.

Guerrillas can take advantage of the infomercial to bring their salesperson directly into the customer's home. The marketplace has been oversaturated with 30-second sound bites and consumers are becoming more receptive to watching commercials that tell the product's whole story. By capturing the consumer's undivided attention for a half hour, infomercials allow the little guys to challenge the market's heavy hitters. The trick is to make the infomercial entertaining enough to arrest attention, but also informative enough to educate the viewer about the product's benefits.

Guerrillas also realize that an infomercial can be a platform from which they can launch retail success. A new product can benefit from exposure through an infomercial. A high response rate will make the product that much more attractive to retailers—there are some consumers who just won't buy a product by phone but will gladly do so at their local store. Braun Inc. produced an infomercial for their Oral-B Plaque Remover that doubled their retail sales. The success of the Abdominizer is a classic example of the way that infomercials can drive the retail market. When first introduced to the retail market, the Abdominizer failed miserably. The manufacturers launched an infomercial campaign and retail success followed soon thereafter.

GUIDELINES FOR CREATING A SUCCESSFUL INFOMERCIAL

➤ Strike a balance. Be entertaining, but don't skimp on information (and vice versa).

➤ Include a lot of testimonials. Use real people and celebrities, too.

➤ Show the product in use in as many ways and environments as possible.

Susan Powter is the ultimate infomercial guerrilla success story. Her "Stop the Insanity" infomercial catapulted her straight to the top of the multi-billion dollar wellness industry. Susan travels around the country giving workshops and seminars, publishes a quarterly audio newsletter, markets a line of fitness clothing for larger women, and sells both a book and a videotape based on the material she covers in her half-hour infomercial. She also gives seminars at the Susan Powter Wellness and Education Center in Dallas, TX. She can be reached through her toll-free number, (800) 637-3451.

➤ Celebrities can lend credibility to an infomercial. They are nice to have, but are not critical for success. Genuine testimonials are more important.

➤ Infomercials work best if you combine them with a toll-free telephone number. Your infomercial should stimulate immediate action on the part of the viewer. You can make that action easier if you offer them an 800 number they can call right then and there to order your product.

Make sure your product is well suited for an infomercial. Some are not. This list outlines the four most important elements.

ATTRIBUTES TO LOOK FOR WHEN CHOOSING AN INFOMERCIAL PRODUCT

➤ **Price**

If your product is too expensive, it won't sell, but if it's too cheap, it won't work either. For example, no one will buy a car directly from an infomercial, and while you may have wide appeal for your line of canned soups, it's unlikely that you'll make much profit from a 69¢ sale.

➤ **Wide Appeal**

If your product is too specialized, it will most likely bomb on television (you pay for everyone who watches the show, regardless of their interest level).

➤ **Explainability**

Good infomercial products don't require a personal trial before purchase. Before buying anything that is highly technical or specialized, people are going to want to be able to try it out. If your product is easily demonstrated, it's probably well suited for this format.

➤ **Visual Proof of Effectiveness**

A product that depends heavily on testimonials or one that can provide vivid before and after images is ideal. Watching and listening to a satisfied customer on television has a huge impact on a prospective buyer.

Exercise equipment, health and beauty products, and CDs and audiocassettes are all proven winners for infomercials. Kitchen appliances, cookware, jewelry, self-improvement products, and diet products have also been very successful.

LEAD GENERATION VERSUS RETAILING

It is crucial that you determine the purpose of your infomercial *before* you get started. An infomercial designed to generate leads is completely different, from beginning to end, than one trying to sell a product outright. The audience for these two types of infomercials is different as well. Even though you wouldn't want to try selling automobiles with infomercials (see notes on product selection on the previous page), a lead-generating infomercial is a great way to find *prospective customers* for your new line of cars—you can narrow down the huge audience of television viewers into just those who it pays for you to send an expensive brochure to. Infomercials that actually sell products directly are far harder to pull off than those that generate leads. They also tend to sell to a small, increasingly jaded audience.

Many of the most glamorous infomercial success stories revolve around slightly cheesy products that have attracted huge sales. Most of us, though, couldn't imagine buying a Popeil Pasta Maker or a spray that eliminates bald spots. As the industry evolves, we believe that the real impact will be made by infomercials that generate leads for aggressive guerrillas.

INFOMERCIAL PRODUCTION COMPANIES

As you search for a production company, keep in mind that different companies have different services and different fee schedules. Some companies buy into your project and reap the benefits that way, while others charge straight fees for the production of your infomercial. Find out what kind of company you are talking to before you begin negotiating.

American Telecast
16 Industrial Blvd. • Paoli, PA 19301 • (215) 251-9933

National Media
1700 Walnut St. • Philadelphia, PA 19103 • (215) 772-5000
Creators of one of the most successful infomercials, "Amazing Discoveries." Also produced infomercials for Bruce Jenner's Stair Climber Plus and Regalware's Royal Diamond Cookware.

Blue Marketing
20 Valley Stream Pky., Suite 220 • Malvern, PA 19355 • (215) 648-9370

Clark National Products
5234 S. Procyon Ave. • Las Vegas, NV 89118 • (800) 999-4009

Lieberman Productions
200 Green St. • San Francisco, CA 94111 • (415) 955-0855

Direct Hit Productions
3565 Piedmont Rd., Suite 300 • Atlanta, GA 30305 • (404) 233-0370
Producers of infomercials for Time-Life Books, Six Flags/Astroworld, Gale Hayman Cosmetics, and The Salvation Army.

According to Jordan Whitney, Inc, and as reported in Response TV *(April 1994), the top ten infomercials for the month of February 1994 were:*

• *Psychic Friends*

• *Jake Hip & Thigh Machine*

• *Gravity Edge*

• *Principal Secret III*

• *Making Love Work*

• *Cross Trainer*

• *Duralube II*

• *Fitness Tread*

• *Komputor Tutor*

• *Popeil Pasta Maker*

The industry is evolving fast. By the time you read this, a totally different roster of successes will be on this list. More than half of the companies on the Fortune 500 have already tested an infomercial.

The manufacturers of the Flowbee, the device you hook up to a vacuum cleaner to cut your own hair, struck it rich with an infomercial. Their use of testimonials was particularly effective. All the way through the infomercial, ordinary people demonstrated how easy it was to use the product by giving each other perfect haircuts on the air.

Transactional Media Incorporated
345 N. Maple Drive, Suite 205 • Beverly Hills, CA 90210
(310) 657-2225

Gunthy-Renker
41-550 Eclectic, Suite 200 • Palm Desert, CA 92260 • (619) 773-9022
Creators of the Anthony Robbins infomercial, a classic

Jim McNamara & Associates
5301 Calhoun Ave. • Van Nuys, CA 91401 • (818) 907-6212
Produced infomercials for Thighmaster, Playboy, Toastmaster, and many others

Script to Screen Productions
200 N. Tustin Ave., Suite 200 • Santa Ana, CA 92705 • (714) 558-3971

Arch Communications
3700 S. Las Vegas Blvd., Suite 1000 • Las Vegas, NV 89109
(702) 597-1829

Concepts Video Productions
170 Changebridge Rd., Suite B2 • Montville, NJ 07045 • (201) 808-5646

Television Marketing Group
8544 Sunset Blvd. • Los Angeles, CA 90069 • (310) 854-7554

Prescott/Levinson, Inc.
2727 Philmont Ave., Suite 110 • Huntington Valley, PA 19006
(215) 947-4100

E&M Advertising
60 Madison Ave. • New York, NY 10010 • (212) 481-3663

Brandt-Thompson Group
10810 72nd St., North, Suite 210 • Largo, FL 34647 • (813) 544-8118

INFOMERCIAL MEDIA BUYERS

Between the major networks, local cable stations, and satellite networks, there are many places to run your infomercial. Before launching your ad, it's probably a good idea to consult a company that specializes in buying media time specifically for infomercials. Remember that the media time accounts for 95% of your costs. Buy the right time in the right place! Also keep in mind that many media buyers pre-purchase chunks of time, thereby cornering the media market. As an individual buyer, you might not be able to get time because it's already gone. At the very least, it will cost you more to buy the time directly from the station than it will to go through a media buyer.

Here is a listing of some of the firms you can call. If you already deal with an ad agency, ask them if they are well versed in negotiating for infomercial television time. If they are, they are probably qualified to place your ad for you.

Barry Jacobs and Associates
5408 Nagle Ave. • Van Nuys, CA 91401 • (818) 780-1761

CSJ Advertising
506 The Woods • Cherry Hill, NJ 08003 • (609) 751-5542

Brandt Thompson Group, Inc./BTG, Inc.
10810 72nd St. N, Suite 210 • Largo, FL 34647 • (813) 544-8118

Cable Shows Unlimited
422 Route 206, Suite 192 • Somerville, NJ 08876 • (908) 725-7026

Infomercial Marketing Corp.
150 E. 52nd St., 23rd Fl. • New York, NY 10022 • (212) 486-0060

Mercury Media
1750 Ocean Park, Suite 204 • Santa Monica, CA 90405 • (310) 452-3999

Cannella Response TV
488 North Pine St. • Burlington, WI 53105 • (414) 763-4810

Williams Television Time
3130 Wilshire Blvd., 4th Floor • Santa Monica, CA 90403
(310) 828-8600

Meridian Media Management, Inc.
221 East Glenoaks Blvd., Suite 200 • Glendale, CA 91207
(818) 552-4000

INFOMERCIAL RESOURCES

National Infomercial Marketing Association
1201 New York Ave. N.W. , Suite 1000 • Washington, DC 20005
(202) 962-8342

Steve Dworman's Infomercial Marketing Report
11533 Thurston Circle, Suite 14 • Los Angeles, CA 90049
(310) 472-6360

Charitable organizations are slowly discovering the power of infomercials. In 1993, Direct Hit Productions worked with St. Jude's Hospital to produce a 30-minute TV special. Celebrity spokespeople John Goodman and Marlo Thomas hosted the show that featured three children from St. Jude's with life-threatening illnesses and their families. Viewers could respond to the show by making a pledge to St. Jude's. The show elicited tremendous emotional response from the audience.

❗ *Because the majority of the cost associated with using infomercials is in the TV time, you have to be smart about where you run your infomercial. Look for bits and pieces of available time on local networks and targeted cable stations. Realize that very few infomercials run on a nation-wide scale. When you see one on the local CBS station, the time was probably purchased as regional time on the local CBS affiliate. Take advantage of regional and remnant space advertising, and make sure you look into all the highly targeted possibilities on cable when purchasing air time for your infomercial.*

· · · · · · · · · · · · · · · · ·

Response TV
131 West 1st St. • Duluth, MN 55802
(800) 346-0085 (call to subscribe)

Response TV also produces a videotape called "Dynamics of DRTV." Response TV sells the video for $29.95 and you can order it by calling (800) 598-6008.

The Insiders' Infomercial Report
Published by Consulting-Joint Ventures-Management
10810 72nd Street, North Suite 210 • Largo, FL 34647 • (813) 544-8118

Jordan Whitney, Inc.
17300 17th St., Suite J-111 • Tustin, CA 92680 • (714) 832-0737

A direct response television consulting firm. Publishers of the Direct Response Television Monitoring Report *and the* Greensheet TV Merchandiser *newsletters. A monthly subscription to the* Monitoring Report *costs $250 per month. A weekly subscription includes over 3 hours of infomercials on videotape and costs $250 per week.*

Downpat Productions
11707 Cranford Way • Oakland, CA 94605 • (510) 569-8794

Specializes in producing original soundtracks for infomercials. Fee structure varies with product and production company.

Score Productions, Inc.
254 East 49th St. • New York, NY 10017 • (212) 751-2510

Operate Infoscore, a music service operation tailored for infomercial production. Score will absorb the costs of producing the music for your infomercial in exchange for the writing and publishing royalties associated with broadcasting it. Score also works on a traditional fee schedule. Call them for more information.

The Infomercial Producer Report
Published by Television Time, Inc.
178 Barsana Ave. • Austin, TX 78737 • (512) 288-6400

Report includes an index of infomercials, product categories, producers, and products

Catalyst Air Date Management Software
Developed and sold by Catalyst Computer Services
1711 South Corning St. • Los Angeles, CA 90035 • (800) 659-2267

IBM compatible software that manages placement and tracks profitability of direct response television infomercials

INFOMERCIAL BRAINSTORMS

Use this space to outline the content of a brief infomercial that you can produce on a shoestring and test on a local TV station.

_____

_____

_____

_____

_____

_____

_____

_____

_____

ADVERTISING

OUTDOOR ADS

Billboards and subway and bus advertising get great exposure, and they build image and credibility.

Billboards are a good tool to use if your business is seasonal. Use them right before your heavy season to remind people about you. One professional minor league ice hockey team in the south runs a billboard campaign for one month prior to the start of every hockey season. The billboards remind people that it's time to put away the surfboards and pull out the ice skates. Ticket sales increase the moment the billboards go up, and the team has been playing to 87% arena capacity for the last five years, an almost unheard of audience for minor league hockey.

Most advertisers worry about clutter. How will their ad stand out in a sea of commercials? Outdoor advertisers have a different problem—they're competing with trees, street signs, and beautiful sunsets.

The lack of clutter in outdoor advertising is one of its two biggest advantages. The other is boredom. People sitting in traffic or waiting for a bus have nothing to do. Their brains are hungry for information. The first billboard in sight burns itself into the prospect's mind. Home run!

Since childhood, we've all been conditioned to believe that only huge companies like Marlboro, Seagram's, and 7-Up can afford billboards. That's exactly the mentality the resourceful guerrilla is counting on. Billboards convey a sense of stability and give your message a larger-than-life appearance. A well-placed, well-designed billboard does wonders for your credibility and for your sales.

Several stores have built their entire business around billboards. Wall Drug, located in rural South Dakota, has billboards running for hundreds of miles in each direction. By the time the driver gets to Wall Drug, anyone who's curious, hungry, or just in need of one of their "free glasses of ice cold water" makes sure to stop. At last count, Wall Drug was doing several million dollars a year in sales.

A fledgling computer software company bought billboard space between the airport and the convention center in Chicago during the annual Consumer Electronics Show. Every buyer who attended the show saw the billboard. With one billboard, which probably cost about $5,000, Spinnaker made themselves the focus of the trade show and created a heavy-hitting impression.

You can do the same thing with the Super Bowl. Everybody knows a year in advance where and when the Super Bowl is going to occur. Buy a billboard on the major highway leading to the football stadium. Over 70,000 consumers, along with all the journalists attending the game, will see your message.

Billboards don't move. This means that your message is guaranteed to hit the same commuter every day at about the same time. As every guerrilla knows, repetition is the secret of advertising success, and billboards deliver repetition.

Properly used, your billboard can be a call to action, leading directly to sales. Ideally, the two most important words on your billboard are "next exit." For

92

example, a new store in the San Francisco Bay area that did not have enough money to advertise in more traditional media was able to afford a long-term contract for just one billboard. That billboard, fortunately, was able to contain the words "next exit." Success came rapidly and overwhelmingly. Of course, the store had to do everything else right to succeed, and it did. But the billboard takes most of the credit. If you can't use those two magic words, these three also work well: "two miles ahead."

You cannot do the entire marketing job with billboards alone. But of course, there are notable exceptions. A bedroom furniture store in San Jose not only had a hard-to-find location, but also suffered from a woeful lack of funds. However, the store did have the good fortune to be located near a billboard placed just before its freeway exit. So the store rented it, said, "Take a peek into The Bedroom—next exit," and eventually won over so many impulse drivers that the store was able to expand its marketing to include television and eventually became the leading store of its kind in the nation. It all started with one lonely, but very hard-working billboard.

Another furniture store, this one in Des Moines used a billboard to spice up its slowest month. During the summer doldrums, this store held a promotion and sung its praises on the radio, the store's usual medium. But it also added a downtown billboard, one in a very good location. Although the billboard was only rentable for one month, it helped make the promotion a success and the normally slow July into one of the store's most profitable months. Does the billboard get all the credit? Of course not. It's all part of the mix.

BILLBOARD PRICING

Billboards are sold in a way similar to TV shows—they're given a rating, based on the number of cars that will be exposed to the billboard in a one-month period. 3M, one of the largest billboard companies in the country, relies on the government to provide them with what they call their Daily Effective Circulation (a fancy term for the number of cars that pass by a billboard everyday).

Obviously, high-traffic billboards cost more than out of the way ones. In addition to traditional outdoor companies (which own thousands of billboards) there are smaller mom-and-pop operations. You also have the option of erecting and maintaining your own billboard. Look in the Yellow Pages under "Advertising-Outdoor." The listings will give you a good idea of the local versus national companies that broker the advertising in your area.

According to Robert Aaberg of Entrepreneur magazine, the "Golden Ratio" for any billboard or sign is 5:8—five units of height to eight units of width.

The price of billboards varies widely depending upon their location and whether you want to advertise on a superhighway or a local back road. Here's a rough comparison: It costs between $15,000 and $25,000 a month to advertise on a billboard by the Lincoln Tunnel in New York City. That's just about the top of the line. In Chicago, a highway billboard will cost between $2,500 and $6,000 a month.

ALTERNATIVES TO BILLBOARDS

There's more to outdoor advertising than large billboards. Cities offer all sorts of opportunities, including advertising on bus shelters, in subways, and on benches. Airports also offer indoor ads that work just like billboards. Some smaller communities even offer advertising on their parking meters. Don't forget about shopping mall displays, taxicab displays, and telephone kiosks.

Bus shelter ads are a relatively inexpensive way to make a lot of noise. New Yorkers are an egocentric group, and are quick to believe that anyone who is advertising in New York is advertising *everywhere*. Since most of the media is located in New York, an aggressive bus shelter campaign in Manhattan can translate into word of mouth and buzz nationwide.

The same theory works for airport advertising. The people stranded at the gate with nothing to do but stare at your ad are often the top business executives or high-income families that most guerrillas salivate over. While items like rental cars, hotels, and laptop computers are obvious products to feature in an airport, consider any product or service that appeals to the demographic that's paying all that money to fly. Local advertisers (restaurants especially) often do extremely well with this medium. The nation's largest provider of airport media is Ackerley Communications. You can reach them at (206) 624-2888.

Subway advertising can be an effective tool, especially if your business is near a subway stop. Kennedy Studios, a chain of framing shops in Boston, uses this medium extensively. They advertise the subway stop for each of their stores along with clever stories and copy. When Kennedy started advertising on the subway, they had far fewer stores than they have today—it's working.

Bus shelters, subway ads, and airport signs give you more than a split-second to convey your message. As with a billboard, you still have to get the prospects' attention with a catchy headline or killer graphic. But now that your audience isn't speeding by in a car, feel free to make your point with as much text as you need. Someone waiting for a bus has at least ten full minutes to read your ad.

A proven technique for use in the subway are Take One pads. Attach a pad of tear-off fliers to your ad that people can take with them. Use your ad to attract attention and your Take One flier to make an offer. Many of the firms that sell subway advertising will maintain your ad, checking the signs daily to be sure the Take One pads are full. The advantage of these pads is obvious—the person sees your ad on the subway, likes what you have to say, and takes a coupon. This call to action can translate directly into sales.

THE LARGEST OUTDOOR ADVERTISING COMPANIES

Ackerley Communications
3601 6th Ave. S. • Seattle, WA 98134 • (206) 624-2888
Handles most of the airport advertising in the United States

Gannett Outdoor Group
666 Third Ave., 4th Floor • New York, NY 10017 • (212) 297-6400

Naegele Outdoor Advertising
1700 W. 78th St. • Richfield, MN 55423 • (612) 869-1900

Penn Advertising
5953 Susquehanna Plaza Dr. • York, PA 17406 • (717) 252-1528

Patrick Media Group
338 N. Washington Ave. • Scranton, PA 18503 • (717) 347-7100

3M National Advertising
6850 S. Harlem Ave. • Argol, IL 60501 • (708) 496-6500

Whiteco Metrocom
1000 E. 80th Pl., Suite 700N • Merrillville, IN 46410 • (219) 769-6601

OUTDOOR ADVERTISING RESOURCES

Outdoor Advertising Association of America (OAAA)
12 E. 49th St. • 22nd Floor • New York, NY 10017 • (212) 688-3667

The OAAA provides marketing information services, creative services, and communication services, all of which can be of use to the guerrilla marketer.

The same retail tax firm that employs the 800-4REFUND telephone number once bought billboards during a slow first quarter. Instead of buying them for the typical thirty-day minimum period, they were able to negotiate for a two-week cycle at half the price. Since there were no buyers for the other two weeks of the cycle, their ads stayed up all month at half price. In fact, many of the ads ended up staying up for two months!

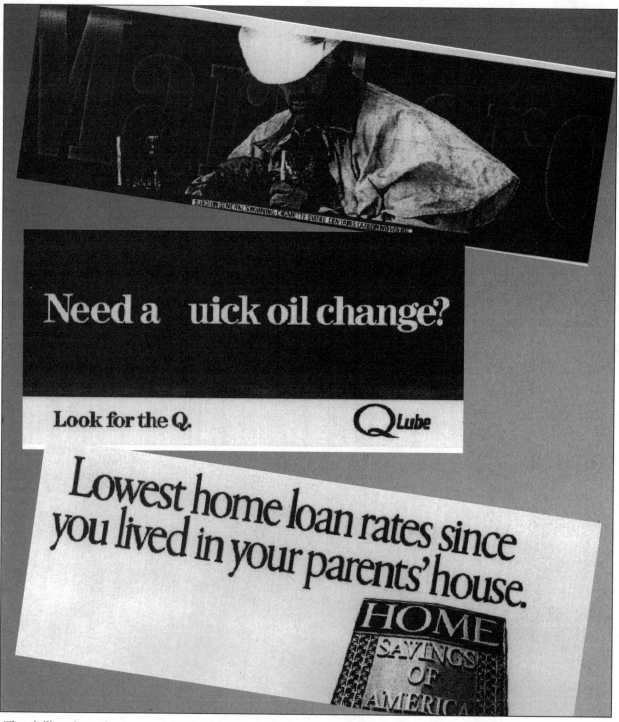

These billboards are short on words but long on impact. They are clear, clever, and immediately recognizable.

Billboard Basics
Published by the OAAA

The basics of outdoor advertising for easy reference. A small booklet containing the basics of the industry, from the definition of billboards and outdoor advertising to lists of outdoor advertising organizations and industry statistics.

Obie Awards
Available through the OAAA

This booklet, published annually by the OAAA, contains the billboards honored with an Obie Award for the best outdoor advertising.

American Council of Highway Advertisers
P.O. Box 809 • North Beach, MD 20714 • (301) 855-8886

Eight Sheet Outdoor Advertising Association
P.O. Box 13616 • Sacramento, CA 95853• (800) 874-3387

Association devoted to the use of 8-sheet posters for outdoor advertisers. 8-sheet signs are smaller than the more conventional 24-sheet billboards and typically measure 6 x 12 feet.

National Bench Advertising Association
(800) 999-2964

Promotes the use of advertising on benches

Shelter Advertising Association
1 Appletree Square, Suite 820 • Minneapolis, MN 55425 • (612) 854-2522

Information and promotional resource for bus shelter advertising

Traffic Audit Bureau for Media Measurement
114 E. 32nd St., Suite 102 • New York, NY 10016 • (212) 213-9640

Auditing association for the outdoor advertising industry that sets circulation and rate measurement standards and maintains visibility and circulation statistics. Also publishes several good resources including Planning for Out of Home Media *and* Standard Procedures for the Evaluation of Outdoor Advertising.

TIPS FOR NEGOTIATING A BILLBOARD CONTRACT

➤ Never take the published rate without negotiating for a lower price. You can often save 15% to 25% if you do.

➤ Negotiate to shorten the length of the billboard contract. They say twelve months. You may be able to get it for six (or even less).

➤ Buy at the end of the month. Billboard firms have quotas and often offer attractive discounts and incentives.

You can invent your own billboard spaces. One restaurant in New York placed a 30-foot iguana on the roof of their building. Another uses a spotlight to project the silhouette of a spider on the wall of the building.

If there's a building that might benefit from a paint job, perhaps the owner would let you add your own sign in exchange for painting his building. The Phoenix Hotel in San Francisco painted a huge mural on the side of a neighboring building, attracting lots of media attention and plenty of new business.

Of course, check with your zoning board before putting up a 30-foot iguana.

- ➤ Realize that the winter is off-season in most states, and you can save up to 50%. When public service billboards start to spring up, you've seen the buying signal—there's empty space and deals are being made.

- ➤ Remnant space is a problem with billboards. Tell the billboard company you're interested but quite patient.

- ➤ Ask for extra posters once you intend to buy. Once a billboard is being printed, the incremental costs for additional posters is small. You can place your own billboard on the side of your building.

- ➤ Consider bartering. Billboard firms may need what you sell.

- ➤ Look for billboard co-op funds from manufacturers with whom you deal. Some guerrillas cover 100% of the cost that way.

- ➤ If you sign up for a year, ask for a repaint or two during that period. You'll never get such freebies unless you ask.

TIPS FOR BILLBOARD DESIGN

- ➤ Don't use more than six words—more than six take too long to read.

- ➤ Keep the concept simple. Billboards are no place to discuss frequent buyer programs, graduated rebates, or computer operating systems.

- ➤ Give the person driving by one large graphic on which he can concentrate —one that will draw attention.

- ➤ Be sure the type is clear and easy to read.

- ➤ Be sure the words are large—a person driving by doesn't have time to read small type.

- ➤ Make sure the billboard is illuminated if it receives a lot of drive-by traffic at night.

When designing your billboard, use this handy template to decide if it will be effective. When the box below is held at arm's length, it looks approximately the same as a billboard when seen from the highway. If you can't read your copy on this template, your prospect won't be able to read it either.

NINE THINGS TO PUT ON A BILLBOARD (AND ONE NOT TO)

1. An easy-to-remember phone number.
2. Something that moves.
3. A smoke-generating machine.
4. A testimonial.
5. A vivid photograph.
6. A giant 3-D object, like a nose or rocket or whatever.
7. Your slogan.
8. A giant coupon.
9. A specific call to action ("Next Exit" is our favorite).

No one wants to see a photo of you or anyone in your family. Resist the temptation to make yourself famous.

OUTDOOR ADVERTISING TERMS YOU SHOULD KNOW

30-SHEET POSTERS—The standard size of billboard posters. They measure approximately $9\frac{1}{2}$ feet wide by $21\frac{1}{2}$ feet tall.

ANNUAL ADT—Annual Average Daily Traffic. This number represents the average number of vehicles passing a given billboard on a daily basis. It's used by the Traffic Audit Bureau to calculate Daily Effective Circulation.

BULLETINS—The largest of the billboards, it measures 14 feet high and 48 feet wide. It is often lighted and, unlike most billboards where the posters are mounted and then removed, the entire structure is periodically moved to a new location.

DAILY EFFECTIVE CIRCULATION—The Average number of people exposed to a particular billboard on a daily basis.

8-SHEET POSTERS—Smaller size posters for billboards. They measure 5 feet high by 11 feet wide and often appear in local areas and on smaller thoroughfares than 30-sheet posters.

GRP/SHOWING—The unit of sale for outdoor billboards, or the Gross Rating Points per Showing. For example, if you buy a billboard at #100 daily GRP per showing, the advertising package will provide you with enough billboards to reach 100% of the population in the area in which you are advertising in one day. A #50 daily GRP showing will reach 50% of the market's audience in one day.

LOAD FACTOR—A factor that takes into account how many people, on average, occupy each vehicle passing a particular billboard. It is used in calculating the daily effective circulation.

ONE-SHEET—Advertising panels in subway or train platforms. They usually measure 46 inches high by 30 inches wide.

RIDING THE SHOWING—A ride-through of the area in which you place your billboards. During a pre-buy ride-through, you examine the proposed locations for your boards. Be sure to check the presence of your competition in the area as well as the visibility of the boards you are going to advertise on. During a post-buy ride-through, you check the quality of the posters (no rips, tears, or color problems) and make sure the locations promised are where your posters actually appear.

OUTDOOR AD BRAINSTORMS

Billboards should be seven words or less. Use this space to create ten new
outdoor ad slogans for your company.

_____

_____

_____

_____

_____

_____

_____

_____

_____

_____

MIDAIR ADVERTISING

Blimps, balloons, and most anything that flies through the air can give you a lot of bang for the buck.

! *Not quite a billboard, not quite a blimp, side-of-bus advertising is an effective way to bring your message into a crowded urban area. You can advertise on the front, side, or back of the bus and reach thousands of pedestrians and drivers during the course of one day.*

Want to get noticed? Hire a blimp! It may cost you a lot, but the value for the money is unbeatable. There is no better way to break through the clutter. People have a mystical attraction for things in the sky and a blimp is your very own UFO. The Goodyear Blimp is an attraction, not just an advertisement. Goodyear gets billions of dollars worth of exposure from their blimp every year.

Blimps, hot air balloons, and skywriting are good ways to go if you want to build name brand recognition. You can't tell a story with a blimp, but you can sure make an impression. If you are a company trying to break into a market or an industry, fly a blimp over the crowd at the PGA Masters Golf Tournament—instant name recognition. Of course, you could always advertise on the Tournament's television broadcast instead, but for the same amount of money, you'll reach ten times more people with a blimp, and the blimp will have far more impact!

The single longest running promotion used by the 7-Up company is a hot air balloon in the shape of a 7-Up can that was created by Aerostar International. They take the balloon all over the country, setting it up at festivals and sporting events. If they sponsor a fun run or an outdoor carnival, the balloon is there. 7-Up has found that people will stop and get out of their cars just to take pictures of the inflated can. How many billboard advertisers can say that? The balloon attracts crowds, creates a postitive image for the 7-Up company, and positions the product as fun and lighthearted.

One of the most unusual guerrilla stories we've heard is the one about the writer who hired a plane to fly over the beaches in California promoting his unsold screenplay. He never sold the movie, but that's because it wasn't very good. He did, however, get lots of calls from agents who wanted to read it. Incidentally, if you own a bar in Daytona Beach, flying a plane with an advertising banner over the beach is a sure fire way to fill your bar!

Even smaller guerrillas can afford mid-air advertising. Dozens of companies offer hot air balloons and other helium-filled attention-grabbers that you can float over your store. They work just like a spotlight, but during the day.

There are also cold air inflatables that are even more affordable than the flying helium balloons. Those are the units that sit on the ground and have fans blowing air into them. They range in size from 6 to 60 feet tall. You can purchase one that's 6 feet tall in the shape of a can for under $500. The average size is 30 feet and they cost between $10,000 and $15,000.

Fly a tethered blimp outside your store or restaurant. They range in size from 12 to 40 feet and can be flown up to 150 feet above your store. Paint one with your logo or slogan and watch your store's recognition soar with it. The owner of a fireworks store in Alabama bought a custom helium blimp from Aerostar International. The blimp was the only part of their marketing plan that they changed from one year to the next. They kept the same Yellow Pages ad, the same outdoor billboard, and the same direct mail package. All they added was a helium blimp that cost them $895, and they saw a 15% increase in business!

Try looking into the new, high-tech features of blimps and airships to increase your exposure. There are night blimps that flash messages in neon, and new skywriting techniques that work just like dot matrix printers and make your message suddenly appear in the sky like magic. And then there's the new large screen television set perched on the Newsday building in New York's Times Square. No, it doesn't fly, but it achieves the same purpose—high impact recognition. Call Bright Lights Corporation at (201) 930-6426 if you're interested in advertising on it. It's not as expensive as you might think. It costs $40 to advertise on the TV for 60 seconds. You have to buy a minimum of 25 units per week, so for $1,000 you can buy one week of fame in New York's Times Square.

MIDAIR ADVERTISING COMPANIES

The first place you should look to find a company that handles mid-air advertising is the Yellow Pages. You'll find all the local companies that deal in skywriting, aerial billboards and banners, and blimps under "Advertising–Aerial" or "Balloons."

Airship International
7380 Sand Lake Rd., Suite 350 • Orlando, FL 32819 • (407) 351-0011

Boulder Blimp Company
2840 Wilderness Pl., Suite E • Boulder, CO 80301 • (303) 449-2190

Sky Promotions
RD2 Box 54 • Pittstown, NJ 08867 • (908) 996-2195
Specializes in hot air balloons, remote controlled blimps, and helium inflatables. They are also the East Coast distributor for Aerostar International, the makers of the Macy's Thanksgiving Day Parade balloons.

Aerostar International
P.O. Box 5057 • Sioux Falls, SD 57117 • (605) 331-3500
North America's largest and oldest manufacturer of hot air balloons. Makers of custom balloons, remote controlled blimps, helium and cold air inflatables.

An ad agent in Minneapolis organizes a megasale for sixteen car dealerships once a year. The dealerships fly blimps outside throughout the promotion and typically experience a 20% increase in store traffic.

A Baptist minister in Illinois recently instructed Aerostar International to construct a hot air balloon in the shape of Noah's Ark. The Ark has 28 different balloon animals in it and will be used all over the world to promote the minister's new series of books, memorabilia, and, hopefully, a new television show, all aimed at teaching children about the ark and other Bible stories.

! *Don't forget to test. Every one of your employees should ask each new customer how he heard about your business. Keep track of how many people the skywriting is bringing in—advertising without testing is a waste of money.*

. . . .

Air America Promotions
85 Glenmere Terrace • Mahwah, NJ 07430 • (800) 424-7871

Balloons, Etc.
5414-B Port Royal Rd. • Springfield, VA 22151 • (703) 425-1400

Virgin Lightships
5728 Major Blvd., Suite 314 • Orlando, FL 32819 • (407) 363-7777
Blimp company specializing in nighttime illumination.

MIDAIR ADVERTISING BRAINSTORMS

If you had a blimp, where would you fly it? Are there any outdoor attractions your customers frequent that are accessible by an airplane dragging a sign? List them here.

_____

_____

_____

_____

_____

_____

_____

_____

_____

CO-OP

A great source of advertising money for retailers. An opportunity for manufacturers to target local advertising and get price-off promotions run by suppliers.

If you're a retailer and are not receiving co-op funds from your suppliers, you're losing advertising exposure. Ever see those ads in the newspaper for computer stores? They scream brand names at you all the time, and why shouldn't they? Some store owners actually make money just by running those ads. The store advertises all of the brands it carries (Apple, Macintosh, IBM, Compaq, and so on) and then goes to each manufacturer and gets them to pay for some of the advertising. If the store owner is lucky, when he adds up the money paid by the manufacturers, he's collected more funds than he paid out to run the ad in the first place.

Be persistent and aggressive. Virtually all manufacturers have co-op programs and most are eager to provide retailers with advertising funds. Ask your sales representative about the procedures you need to follow in order to gain access to the funds. (Note: some unenlightened suppliers make redeeming co-op funds difficult. Ask *before* you run your ad, not after.)

If you're a manufacturer, don't overlook this opportunity. Co-op money isn't charity—it's often the very best way to enhance your presence in a local market, often at advantageous ad rates only available to the local retailer. Record companies don't want to buy ads in newspapers all over the country, but they're delighted to pay part of the bill for the record stores that do.

Whenever you see a television commercial that ends with the line "available at fine retailers like..." you know you've seen a co-op ad. All of the retailers mentioned have paid a fee or given shelf space to the manufacturer advertising the product in exchange for a mention in the ad. A good example is the co-op relationship between Sam's Club and Tide detergent. Procter & Gamble launched a television ad campaign for Tide in which they mentioned, "For low wholesale prices on Tide and most everything for your business, count on Sam's Club" at the end of the spot. Sam's also received a few other mentions in the ad. Procter & Gamble paid for the TV time and Sam's paid a fee to Proctor and Gamble for the mentions in the ad.

If you're a manufacturer, you'll need to create a co-op policy for your retailers. The two most important elements of the policy:
1. Be clear. If you have a simple, easy-to-use system, retailers will use it more often and get angry at you less.

2. Be fair and be legal. If you think you can cut a better deal with one account than another, you're sadly mistaken. The word will get out and you'll get caught. There's nothing wrong with creating a custom program, but you've got to offer it to anyone who qualifies.

This Yellow Pages advertisement was co-oped by Canon, Xerox, Okidata, Ricoh, and Fujitsu. Electronic Systems Plus gets a lot of its business from this ad, but they only pay a fraction of the cost of running it.

BENEFITS FOR A RETAILER

1. Low-cost or no-cost exposure
2. Prepaid, proven, professional sales materials
3. Shared advice on what works and what doesn't

BENEFITS FOR A MANUFACTURER

1. Focused local ads too cumbersome to set up from the home office
2. Leveraged ad spending
3. Increased in-store support from the retailer

If you're a manufacturer, explore the idea of paying for co-op with goods, not cash. Retailers are often willing to load up on a product (thus giving you enhanced shelf space) if the expanded size of their order buys them television advertising.

RESOURCES

The Co-op Source Directory
National Register Publishing Company
121 Chanlon Road • New Providence, NJ 07974 • (908) 464-6800

The Co-op Source Directory *lists every major cooperative advertising program available. The programs covered are divided into 52 product classifications and are indexed by manufacturer, trademark, and program description.*

CO-OP BRAINSTORMS

If you are a retailer, make a list of your ten largest suppliers, along with the co-op help you're getting from them. If you are a manufacturer, list your ten largest accounts, along with the funds you're giving them.

_____

_____

_____

_____

_____

_____

_____

_____

_____

_____

BARTERING

Trading can save big money for the shrewd guerrilla.

! *Chyron Inc. is a leading producer of television graphics equipment, expensive machines that place logos and type on-screen during TV shows. When first starting out, their goal was to establish themselves as the market leader, which meant getting a system installed at every network.*

They bartered their equipment to MTV, ESPN, and others in exchange for air time. They then turned around and sold the air time to a barter company for cash and office equipment. The barter company then traded the air time to other guerrillas, who paid in either products or services.

Everyone won. The networks got thousands of dollars in equipment for free. Chyron established itself and got enough cash to make a small profit. And the rest of the guerrillas got a great discount.

Even more sophisticated than buying remnant ad space is the practice of bartering for advertising. Because air time gets stale fast, advertising is one area of business where bartering is widely used. You will find that radio and television stations often need the products and services you have and are willing to trade them for advertising.

At the simplest level, if you own a restaurant, you may be able to trade meals for commercials on the local radio station. Our *Guerrilla Marketing Newsletter* gains quite a bit of circulation when Jay writes a column for a publication in exchange for the publication plugging the newsletter in a paragraph at the end of the column. They get a free column on marketing; we get free advertising for the newsletter. Readers get information that they might not normally get. As in most guerrilla marketing exchanges, everyone comes out a winner.

Rush Limbaugh got his start by offering a radio station a trade. They provided him with a studio where he could record his show, and he allowed them to broadcast his show at no cost.

Most barter, though, is far more sophisticated than these simple trades, but ideal for the guerrilla marketer with flexibility.

Many stations use middlemen who trade air time for your product, then trade your product for something else, and on and on. Amazingly enough, according to *Barter News*, in 1993 nearly 60% of all media was not purchased. Instead it was bartered for!

STRAIGHT TRADE

Straight trading works just like it sounds. Barter companies trade air time for goods, and no cash changes hands. Here's a simple example:

ZYX Widget company has $100,000 in unsold clock radios. They offer them to a barter company in exchange for air time.

The barter company's merchandising department estimates that the street value of the clocks is $20,000. They offer ZYX a certain value of air time or print space in exchange for the clocks (usually more than the value of the merchandise being traded)— in this case, an account worth $30,000 in advertising at selected magazines, radio stations, and TV stations across the country.

ZYX ends up with $30,000 in advertising and doesn't have to worry about an overflowing warehouse. The participating media outlets "sell" ad space to the barter company that would have gone empty. And the barter company is able to sell the clock radios to a flea market in Georgia for $25,000. Everyone profits.

CASH TRADE

Some items are not as easily disposed of as clock radios. In those cases, many barter companies engage in a cash trade. For example, XYZ approaches the barter company with 10,000 purple widgets. The barter company takes the widgets, and in return gives XYZ an amount of advertising credit equal to the widgets' wholesale value (let's say $60,000). They then use the $60,000 to match all of XYZ's media purchases from the outlets they represent. If XYZ chooses to buy a $20,000 ad in *Hot Rod News* for instance, the barter company puts up half the cost, requiring XYZ to pay just $10,000 for the ad.

XYZ wins because they only have to pay $10,000 for a $20,000 ad. The barter company wins because they bought that $20,000 ad from *Hot Rod News* as remnant space and only paid $5,000 for it. *Hot Rod News* wins because they sold space that might very well have gone unsold if the barter company had not bought it.

A cash trade is beneficial in cases where you are planning to spend the money anyway. By reducing your cash outlay, this sort of barter increases your profits and lets you move quickly.

BARTERING RESOURCES

While the mechanics of a barter deal can seem complicated, the organizations in the field work hard to make it as simple as possible. Contact these resources for more information.

BarterNews
P.O. Box 3024 • Mission Viejo, CA 92690 • (714) 831-0607

Trade publication on bartering. Full of resources and tips for companies looking to enter a barter arrangement. Ask for their special reports like No Need to Pay Cash for Broadcast Advertising *and others.*

International Reciprocal Trade Association
9513 Beach Mill Road • Great Falls, VA 22066 • (703) 759-1473

Send a stamped, self-addressed envelope to the Association and they'll send you a free publications list and several fact sheets on bartering.

Citicorp was stuck with an office building that was on their books for quite a lot of money. None of the offers for the building came close to covering their investment in it.

They contacted Tradewell and were able to trade the building for a cash payment plus a substantial radio advertising budget. They then used the advertising to promote their credit card, generating a significant savings on their media costs.

Before you enter into a barter agreement, talk to your accountant about any tax implications. Make sure whatever bartering you do positively affects your bottom line.

Tradewell

845 Third Ave. • New York, NY 10022 • (212) 888-8500

The nation's largest corporate barter firm. They trade just about anything that is produced by corporate America.

MINI-MEDIA

TOOLS, TECHNIQUES, AND TIPS IN THIS SECTION:

*MINI-MEDIA IDEAS
FOR GUERRILLAS*

*Whoever said it's the little
things that matter must have
had guerrillas in mind. The
impact that business cards,
banners, or newsletters have
on prospects is often overlooked
by traditional mass marketers.
Guerrillas know that these
tools can be crucial elements in
reaching a target market and
closing the sale.*

*In this section, you'll learn
to pay attention to the details
and take advantage of every
selling opportunity. You'll start
thinking about how to use
your order form to generate
additional sales, your business
card to position your product,
and gift certificates to induce
repeat buying.*

BUSINESS CARDS

Use a low-cost business card to separate yourself from the clutter.

To promote The Information Please Business Almanac and Desk Reference, *we created a business card that lists the toll-free 800 numbers for dozens of airlines on the back. It cost virtually nothing to add this useful information, and it made the card a valuable asset to anyone who travels.*

· · · · · · · · · · · · · · · · ·

Denise wanted to expand her accounting practice, so she bought a 2" x 3" ad in the small-town newspaper. She arranged in advance for the printer to leave the ad blank except for a line across the bottom inviting readers to file her business card for future reference. As the papers came off the press, she and her husband stuck the colorful photo business cards into the blank space with double-stick tape. Months later, she was still hearing from readers.

· · · · · · · · · · · · · · · · ·

One of the least expensive, highest-impact tools you can use to market yourself is your business card. Every business, from the largest conglomerate to the tiniest guerrilla, uses the same materials in creating a card. If you think of your business card as a chance to break through the clutter, you will distinguish yourself and your business.

At the very least, your card should include your name, company, address, phone, fax, and a positioning statement. This statement can be your slogan ("You Can't Buy a Better Hospital Crib") or a short description of what your company does ("Innovative Marketing Techniques for Shoe Stores"). You'd be amazed at how often someone will look at a business card with absolutely no recollection of who you are or what you do.

One large company, acting like a guerrilla, puts its executive's home phone numbers on their business cards. If you're trying to establish personal service (especially in an industry where speed counts) you can build trust by including these.

Never cut corners when producing your card. Use the best paper you can afford, and make sure it is professionally designed. Having a local printer design your card is shortsighted. In this era of desktop design, you can probably find a top-notch designer to do the work for just a few hundred dollars.

There are tremendous opportunities to dress your card up, to make it more useful or give it more impact. First thing to remember: Use the back of the card. It costs almost nothing and it is otherwise wasted space.

A joke and novelty shop near our office gives away a business card that has the following words emblazoned across the back: "ANOTHER FORM OF IDENTIFICATION." Lots of their customers carry it in their wallet, just waiting for a rental car clerk to ask for it. Wouldn't you rather have your card in a customer's wallet than in the trash?

The Infocard, shown later in this chapter, is an ingenious new print product that lets you create a business card–size brochure. You can include as many as eight panels of type, giving you plenty of room to include lots of useful information. Paul Schultze, the inventor of the Infocard, can be reached at (512) 795-9685.

SUGGESTIONS OF WHAT TO INCLUDE ON A BUSINESS CARD OR INFOCARD

➤ Describe your business with a tag line.

➤ Include your price list.

➤ Detail your services.

➤ Include a map of how to find your place of business.

➤ Give lists of toll-free 800 numbers or tourist information.

➤ Profile key employees.

➤ Tell the success story of someone who has used your product.

➤ Feature photographs of products, your office, or employees.

➤ Include quotes, jokes or aphorisms people might enjoy carrying around.

If Infocards seem excessive or inappropriate for you, you can still use the back of a regular business card to print handy information on postal rates, area codes, or some other piece of information that will keep your card on the top of the stack. A fold-over business card also works well and isn't that much more expensive.

If you have a retail business, consider turning your business card into a frequent customer discount card. A large record store in Manhattan gives a 10% discount to any customer who presents the manager's business card at the cash register.

Think of your card as a mini-billboard for your company. If you're a contractor, put them in the mailboxes of people in your neighborhood. Drop them into outbound mail, and hand them to everyone attending a meeting. If you've got something neat on the back, it's easy to say, "Here's a list of 800 numbers you'll need when you travel."

Try using your business card as an active selling tool. Print a double sided card and on one side print the phrase "Present this card for _____." Whenever you talk to a prospect, fill in the blank. For example, if you are a representative for a printing firm, you may come across a prospect who wishes she could print her brochures more efficiently. Fill out the back of your card "Present this card for a 10% discount on your next run of corporate brochures." This is a more personal offer tailored directly to the prospect's needs. Guerrillas love to get personal!

A guerrilla in Kansas uses her business card as a mini-billboard. Her typing service specializes in term papers for students at the University of Kansas. She puts all the relevant information on her card (turnaround, pricing, etc.), and posts 100 cards a week on bulletin boards around campus. The cost of 5,000 business cards a year is her entire marketing budget.

A real estate guerrilla in California hands an extra three dollars and a business card to the toll collector as he crosses the bridge from exclusive Marin County into San Francisco. "I'd like to pay for the car behind me as well. Please give the driver this." Nine out of ten times, the other driver calls, at least to say thank you. He's sold several expensive homes as a result, and at 6 % commission, he can afford to drive back and forth across the bridge all day, positioning himself in front of BMWs, Cadillacs, and Mercedes Benzes.

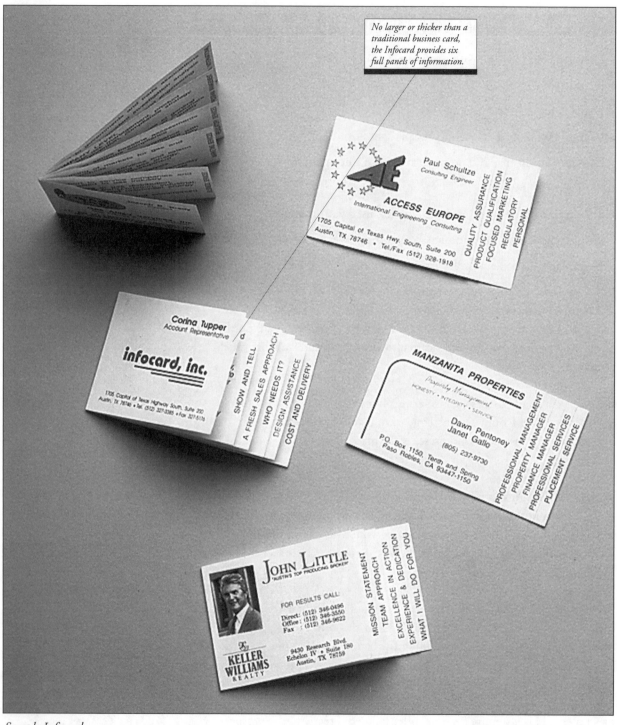

No larger or thicker than a traditional business card, the Infocard provides six full panels of information.

Sample Infocards

Source: Infocard • 1705 Capital of Texas Hwy. South, Suite 200 • Austin, TX 78746 • (512) 795-9685

Sample business cards. Note the interesting shapes, the fold-over card, the Rolodex card, and the way that the cards position the businesses they represent.

BROCHURES

Turn your brochure into an effective sales tool.

! *Many of the visual examples of guerrilla marketing that you see throughout this book were submitted by people who entered* How Magazine's *annual design contest.* How *magazine stands alone in its field. Geared mostly toward the graphic design world, it is full of tips, tricks, and shortcuts to help you master the art of computer imaging. It is an indispensable resource if you plan to design any of your own business cards, fliers, circulars, or other mini-media marketing tools on the computer.*

How also contains hints, ideas, and resources that will help you design marketing pieces that stand out from the crowd. You'll learn how to choose the right paper and the right design, work with printers, hire a designer, and more. Call (800) 333-1115 to subscribe.

When someone asks for more information on your company, what do you send them? Many companies use out-of-date, incomplete, unfocused brochures that scare away more customers than they attract. Others use over-priced, overproduced extravaganzas that just aren't effective enough to warrant their high cost.

Don't ask too much from your brochure and you won't be disappointed. Many businesses think of a brochure as an opportunity to close the sale without making a sales call. For most purchases, that's expecting too much. However, a brochure can do a great job of positioning your company and preparing the prospect to be sold.

Unlike an advertising insert, which you should spread far and wide, brochures should be distributed more selectively, to those who have requested more information or to carefully targeted prospects.

Most purchasing decisions cause people some anxiety; they're afraid of making a mistake, and reflexively hesitate before making a commitment. More prospects will be converted if you ask them to take a few tiny steps rather than one giant leap. Most people will be more receptive to your pitch if you say, "Take a small step and read my brochure. Now take another small step and talk to me on the phone. Then take one last step and buy something from me."

By adding these steps to the buying and the selling processes, your brochure gives the prospect the opportunity to learn more about you. Customers must come to know and trust you before they commit to buying something. A brochure breaks the ice.

ADVANTAGES TO USING A BROCHURE IN THE SELLING PROCESS

➤ Brochures work well when they amplify an introductory letter that initiates the relationship with a prospect.

BASICS

THE VALUE OF BROCHURES

Brochures offer the best opportunity to provide great detail about your product or service. People expect a lot of information from a brochure, so you should give it to them. This is not an invitation to be boring, but it is a hint that you can — and should—be very informative.

A self-mailing brochure sent out by Imagelab. This piece is two-color with a perforated business reply card, two die-cut Rolodex business cards, a free offer that calls for action, and clear, well-defined copy. Designed by Tieken Design and Creative Services.

Source: Tieken Design and Creative Services • 2800 North Central Ave, Suite 150 • Phoenix, AZ 85004 • (602) 230-0060

When you mail your company brochure, think about giving it that personal touch. Highlight points that you think will be particularly interesting to the prospect, write notes in the margins, or attach Post-its with additional comments. This gives the impression that you have put some time and thought into the prospect's needs.

➤ Brochures lend an aura of credibility to a company if they are professionally written, designed, and produced.

➤ Brochures remove the pressure from the sale, giving the prospect a chance to study what you have to say before you meet.

➤ Brochures enable you to answer important questions for your prospect before they are even asked. Use your brochure to give testimonials, illustrate benefits, and communicate verbally and visually.

Many guerrillas skimp on their brochure's design and production. Big mistake. This is your chance to position your company and establish a quality image. Your brochure should be at least as well dressed as you are. But you don't have to have a 32-page, four-color brochure (at $5 a piece) to compete with the big guys.

Two brochure types that have been successfully used by cost-conscious guerrillas are:
➤ Three-fold brochures printed on preprinted forms
➤ Low cost four-color fliers, folded into a booklet

One of the most cost-effective methods is to use preprinted brochure forms. These $8 \frac{1}{2}$" x 11" sheets are printed with borders and colors on both sides. Bring the paper to a local print shop or run it through your laser printer and you can customize the brochure with your own copy. Preprinted forms are also great for price lists or for other information that changes often. You can hire a designer to lay out your first one, then make the changes yourself as needed.

COMPANIES SPECIALIZING IN PREPRINTED BROCHURE FORMS

Until recently, preprinted papers were hard to find. If you wanted something fancier than colored paper, you had to print it yourself. Now, several mail order companies offer a wide variety of pre-folded, patterned papers at reasonable cost. On request, most offer a complete paper sampler for free with your first order. Start by ordering in small quantities. When you find a pattern or design that works for you. stick with it.

PaperDirect
205 Chubb Ave. • Lyndhurst, NJ 07071 • (800) 272-7377

Queblo Images
1000 Florida Ave. • Hagerstown, MD 21740 • (800) 523-9080

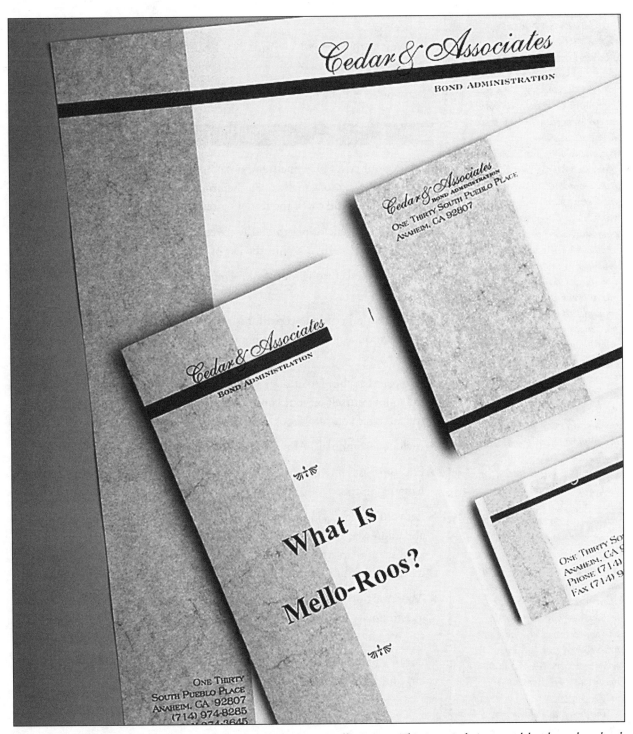

Cedar & Associates's entry into Paper Direct's "Show Us Your Stuff" Contest. This is a nicely integrated brochure, letterhead, and business card, all created with preprinted paper.

Source: Paper Direct • 205 Chubb Ave. • Lyndhurst, NJ 07071 • (800) 272-7377

Marcia Layton is one of hundreds of business plan writers all over the country. Yet her business is booming while others are struggling to keep their heads above water. Why? Because Marcia is a guerrilla, plain and simple. She follows her own advice and creates a marketing plan for herself every year. It's well thought out and, obviously, very effective.

She created a tri-fold brochure to promote her firm, Layton & Co., and she sends it out to break the ice with unqualified sales leads. She follows that up with a whole folder of information about herself and her firm, including sheets on her background, experience, and services, as well as some news clippings and writing samples. In all of her materials, she employs referrals and testimonials.

Her electronic classified ad on CompuServe only costs about $7.75 a week and allows her to reach a highly targeted group of prospects. Marcia also spends a lot of time online, networking with business owners and operators all over the country. She posts messages on bulletin boards, participates in electronic forums, and gives advice to other members. She has built many client relationships this way.

Publicity, one of the most effective yet cheapest forms of marketing, is Marcia's bread and butter. She has received

Paper Access
23 West 18th Street • New York, NY 10011 • (212) 463-7035

BeaverPrints
Main Street • Bellwood, PA 16617 • (800) 847-7237

BROCHURE TIPS

➤ Make your cover headline stand out. People should know who you are without having to actually open the brochure. Your headline should sell your product and catch the reader's attention.

➤ Include a graphic or photo on the cover that will draw the reader in. If possible, make it stand out with the use of color.

➤ Include visuals throughout the brochure. Show your product or service in use.

➤ Don't be afraid of long copy if it is needed. Give the prospect as much information as you can, describing clearly the benefits of your product or service.

➤ Use your brochure to create a relationship with your prospect. Tell a little bit about yourself or your company. Share your business credo and establish the fact that you care about what you do and about your customers.

➤ Include testimonials. Also list major clients or buyers.

➤ Put some useful reference material in your brochure that will make it worth hanging on to.

➤ Let your prospects know how to reach you. Include your telephone number and address at the very least. If you own a retail outlet, consider putting a local street map with your location starred in the brochure and include written directions. Always include your hours of operation.

➤ Ask for action. Include an order form, make an offer, or include a customer questionnaire in your brochure.

Color in a brochure adds to the professional quality. If you are going to use color, find a printer that specializes in color printing.

COLOR PRINTERS

In the past most color printers have been small, local operations. But in the last few years, a number of national firms have started to focus on short-run, high-quality, low-cost color printing. These companies will create several thousand brochures in full color, including color separations, for under $500. Call to request a price list and samples.

Clark Printing
63 Belmont Ave. • Garfield, NJ 07026 • (800) 574-2527

MultiPrint
5555 W. Howard St. • Skokie, IL 60077 • (800) 858-9999

American Color Printing
1731 Northwest 97th Ave. • Plantation, FL 33322 • (305) 473-4392

BROCHURE RESOURCES

Better Brochures, Catalogs and Mailing Pieces
by Jane Maas • Published by St. Martin's Press

This book is full of tips on every aspect of brochure production from concept through completion. Layout ideas and rules of thumb for production are covered. Also covers several types of brochures in detail, including those for the tourist industry and fundraising organizations. Catalogs and guidelines for other types of mailing pieces are covered in short chapters at the end of the book.

coverage in several trade publications, including CompuServe Magazine, MAC Home Journal, and Online Access.

Marcia even uses her fax cover letter to market her business. Besides the usual information (fax to and from), Marcia lists the services her firm offers, a sure reminder to customers and prospects that Layton & Co. can perform a wide variety of services.

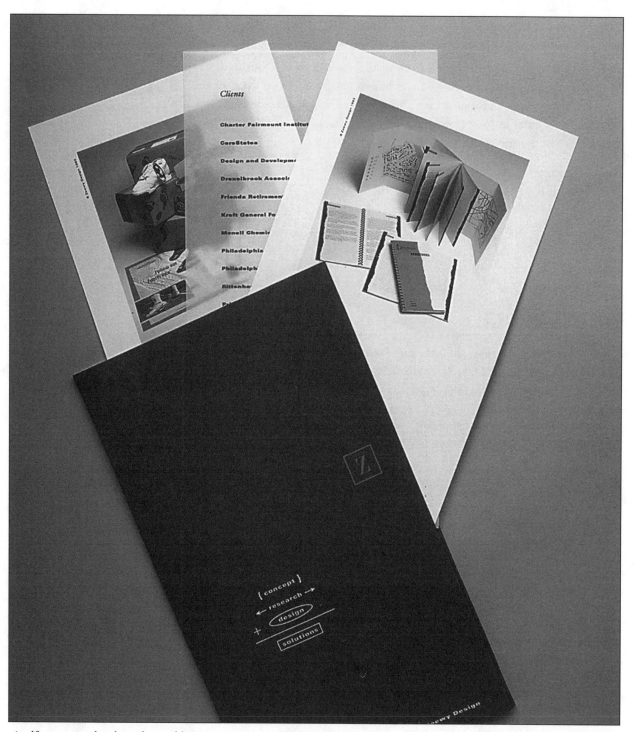

A self-promotion brochure designed by Zeewy Design. Inside the folder is a series of inserts, each of which has a photo and detailed description of Zeewy's work.

Source: Zeewy Design • 111 Forest Ave., Suite 2 • Narberth, PA 19072 • (610) 667-3459

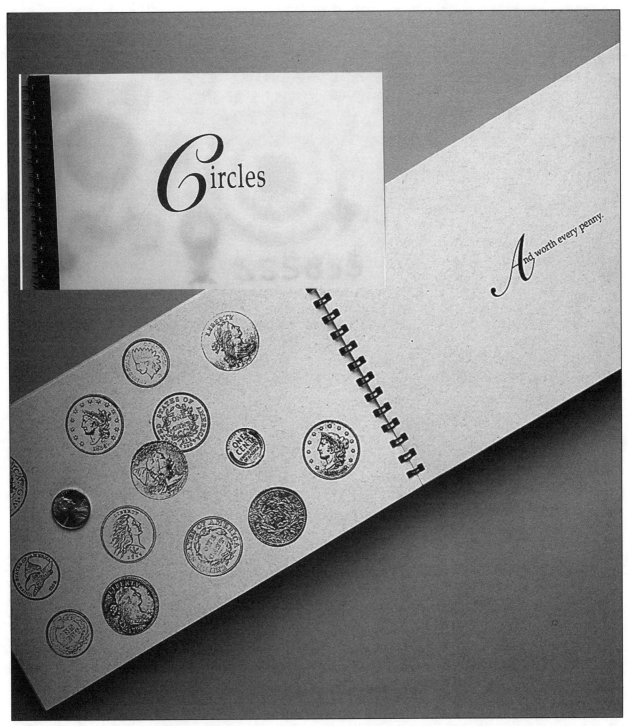

Self-promotion brochure designed by Full Circle Advertising and Design. Isn't the real penny great! Each page of the brochure has a clever graphic and a related selling statement about Full Circle.

Source: Full Circle Advertising and Design • 218 Parkwood Ave. • Kenmore, NY 14217 • (716) 875-7555

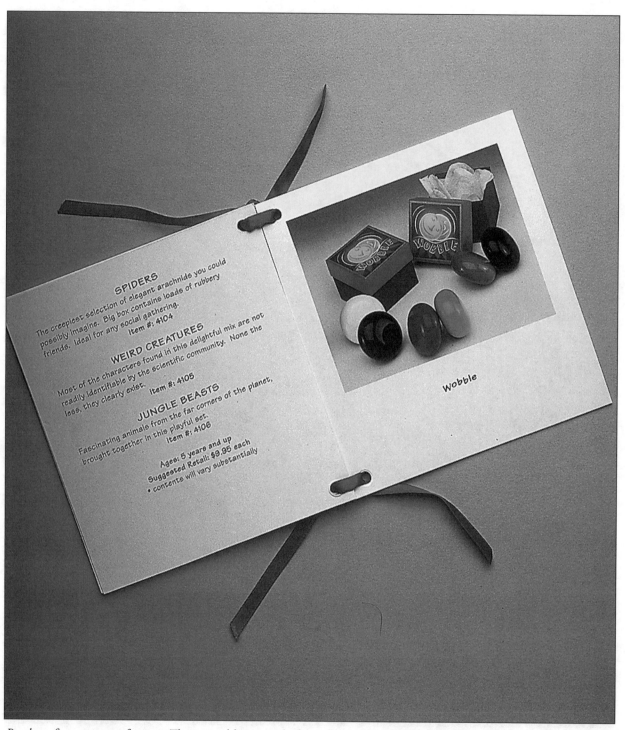

Brochure for a toy manufacturer. The text and layout is playful, and the pictures help to position the company as an upscale toy company. You won't find this stuff at Toys R Us.

BROCHURE BRAINSTORMS

Use this page to list the elements you should include in your next brochure. Think about possible headlines, testimonials, benefits, and offers you could use.

_____

_____

_____

_____

_____

_____

_____

_____

_____

VIDEO BROCHURES

A low-cost way of communicating one-on-one with your prospects.

Camp Arowhon in Algonquin Park, Canada, used to sell by word of mouth. They followed up every inquiry with a personal visit to the prospect's house. The closing rate for these visits was 10%. Unfortunately, this was time consuming and expensive. Two years ago, they replaced the in-home visits with a video brochure. The closing rate has dropped slightly, but the number of prospects has more than tripled. The camp is spending a lot less time and money to get twice as many paying customers.

. . . .

If anything can outdo a print brochure, it is an electronic one—a five- to nine-minute version of a printed brochure. Video brochures combine the impact of a TV commercial with the targeting power of a mailed print brochure.

The cost of duplicating short videos is about $2 each. With a print brochure, the cost per unit goes down the more you print (see *Brochures),* so, if you only need a small quantity, the cost per unit can be prohibitive. Unlike print brochures, no matter how many video brochures you make, the cost per unit remains the same. With video brochures, you can keep your per unit costs low and make duplicate tapes as needed.

The cost of producing videos is $100 to $10,000 per minute, but you should anticipate that it will cost at least $1,000 a minute to do a great job. You probably don't need more than four or five minutes, so the total cost isn't that out of line with a full-color print brochure.

A video brochure can often give more of an impression of worth and value than its printed equivalent. About 80% of Americans have access to a VCR, so you can reach the majority of your audience with a videotape. Prospects are likely to view it and, if interested, will probably view it again with one or more people. Remember, videotapes are still a novelty, unlike printed brochures. Most people don't instinctively throw them away.

Some large-scale guerrillas have successfully executed mass mailings of video brochures. Hart, Schaffner & Marx, the men's clothing king, replaced its Christmas catalog with a videotape. One car maker sent a video for a new model, introducing the local dealer's name at the beginning, including glitzy footage in the middle, and ending with the recipient's name superimposed across the video image—it was the first of a series of personalized video brochures created by this guerrilla. Very effective.

Prospects can learn of your video through magazines, direct mailings, trade shows, and other modes of communication. When they request a video from you, send it to them for free. Include a personal letter, just as you would with a printed brochure. Follow up within ten days with a phone call or letter. A request for the video should be construed as the first step in the purchasing process. Be sure to follow up—don't lose the momentum you've created.

VIDEO PRODUCTION COMPANIES

The following companies specialize in handling your video brochure from storyboard through fulfillment. When creating a video, make sure you spend enough time planning (pre-production) and you'll save lots of money in the actual production. Unless you're planning on spending more than $10,000, it probably pays to start by getting prices from local companies who don't have to factor travel into their budget.

Rank Video
555 Huehl Rd. • Northbrook, IL 60062 • (800) 800-7265

MediaLink
708 Third Ave., 21st Fl. • New York, NY 10017 • (212) 682-8300

Reality Film and Video
165 Passaic Ave • Fairfield, NJ 07004 • (201) 783-6754

Bryant Productions
5184 N. Blythe, Suite 103 • Fresno, CA 93722 • (800) 984-3367

Or look for a local production company in the Yellow Pages

VIDEO DUPLICATION SERVICES

Shop around before settling on a duplication house. Ask for references and check them carefully. Inquire about warehousing and fulfillment—it's often cheaper than doing it yourself.

Hauppauge Manufacturing Group
15 Gilpin Avenue • Hauppauge, NY 11788 • (516) 234-0200
video duplication, packaging, and fulfillment services

Sifford Video Services
121 Lyle Ln. • Nashville, TN 37210 • (800) 251-1009
videotape duplication

Technicolor
3233 E. Mission Oaks Blvd. • Camarillo, CA 93012 • (800) 732-4555
duplication, packaging, fulfillment

ABC Home Video Corp.
7045 Radford Ave. • North Hollywood, CA 91605 • (818) 982-6800

Hank Kashiwa, co-founder of Volant Ski Corporation, found that one of the most effective ways to introduce the market to his innovative stainless-steel ski was through a video brochure. In an eleven minute video, Volant educates both retailers and consumers about the new product.

If you call Advertising Age and mention this book, they'll send you a free video entitled Marketing with Video. It explains how to integrate video into a marketing campaign. Call (800) 613-3344.

Matrix Video Duplication Corp.
5429 McConnell Ave. • Los Angeles, CA 90066 • (310) 306-2600

Production Masters, Inc.
321 First Ave. • Pittsburgh, PA 15222 • (412) 281-8500

Duplication Factory
4275 Norex Dr. • Chaska, MN 55318 • (612) 448-9912
Specializes in creative videocassette packaging that increases the impact of the video

Or look in your local Yellow Pages

VIDEO BROCHURE BRAINSTORMS

Make a list of the ten big prospects you'd like to turn into customers. Talk to your salespeople and create a plan on how a video brochure can help capture their business.

BANNERS AND SIGNS

A great positioning tool that gets you noticed.

! *It is against federal law to create a banner or sign with a word spelled incorrectly. (Well, it's not against the law, but it should be.) Most common errors: You're, It's, and Stationary.*

Don't overlook the value of banners and signs in positioning your business and generating traffic. If you are located on a main freeway, as many as 50,000 people may drive by your door on the average day. An effective sign can make a huge difference.

Los Angeles is filled with businesses that have turned their buildings into huge signs. There are restaurants shaped like hot dogs and car washes shaped like whales—instantly communicating their position to the consumer.

SOME RULES OF THUMB FOR THE USE OF SIGNS

➤ Proofread exhaustively. Check and double check spelling. Mistakes happen often, and they are a turn-off to consumers.

➤ Make a sign you can commit to. Spend enough money to make a great sign, then leave it alone.

➤ Keep the message short. Drivers only have a few seconds to read your sign, so stick with ten words or less (six is even better).

➤ Use lights on signs, and flags on banners.

➤ Make sure the zoning regulations permit a sign or banner, then make the biggest, most obvious sign the regulations will allow.

➤ "Going Out of Business" is not a useful slogan for a guerrilla trying to build a business. Don't try to trick your customers.

A low-cost way to attract attention is to string multicolored flags (the kind used by car dealers). Or rent a searchlight. People love to come to a special event, even if the only thing special about it is that you've strung flags or rented a searchlight.

If you can get neighboring businesses to join in, you can create a special event in your business district. String a banner across your street, put tables out on the sidewalk, and create a bazaar. This is a great way to attract new prospects. If you think about it, it even works for dry cleaners (serve mini hotdogs as a refreshment, then offer discounted cleaning to anyone who spills mustard all over himself)!

A great technique for small businesses on busy thoroughfares: Erect a sign that lets you change the letters daily. If you're clever enough, your daily message to commuters can become a regular part of their day and you can actually have people looking forward to seeing your sign. That's a big first step to establishing a relationship and turning people into customers.

BANNER PRODUCERS

American Banner
9810-A E. 58 St. • Tulsa, OK 74146 • (918) 254-6151

Best Buy Banner
6750-C Central Ave. • Riverside, CA 92504 • (800) 624-1691

Davey Enterprises
44 Clinton St. • Newton, NJ 07860 • (201) 579-5889

Eastern Banner Supply
2582 Spring Lake Rd. • Mooresville, IN 46158 • (317) 831-6055

National Banner Company
11938 Harry Hines • Dallas, TX 75234 • (800) 527-0860

Royal Wholesale Banner
4660 Ironton • Denver, CO 80239 • (303) 371-1200

McCullough Manufacturing
27 Miller St. • Strasburg, PA 17579 • (800) 423-8204

SIGN COMPANIES

For local sign and banner companies in your area, check the Yellow Pages Business to Business Directory under "Signs and Banners."

Sign Co, Inc.
6047 Rte. 68 North • Kenton, OH 43326 • (419) 673-1261

Belsinger Sign Works, Inc.
1300 Bayard St. • Baltimore, MD 21230 • (800) 428-8848

A.R.K. Ramos
P.O. Box 26388 • Oklahoma City, OK 73126 • (405) 235-5505

ASI Sign Systems Inc.
3890 Northwest Highway, Suite 102, • Dallas, TX 75220 • (214) 352-9140

CAS
10909 Tuxford St. • Sun Valley, CA 91352 • (818) 768-7814

Cummings Signs
543 Expressway Park Dr. • Nashville, TN 37210 • (800) 489-4043

Three adjacent furniture stores compete for traffic in a Cleveland strip mall. The store on the south end put up a huge sign: CLEARANCE SALE: EVERYTHING MUST GO. The store on the north end put up an even bigger sign that read, GREAT SAVINGS, 50% OFF. The guerrilla in the middle hung up a small banner over his door that said only, MAIN ENTRANCE.

POSTERS

Economical, high-impact marketing tools.

! *Virtually every major town has at least one company that caters to graphic designers. They usually offer color copying, mounting, color rubdowns, and more.*

Check your Yellow Pages for a nearby firm. A good place to start is in the "Copying" section, or look in the Business to Business Directory under "Graphic Designers."

Posters pack a punch! Large, four-color posters that look more like art than advertising can be very effective guerrilla tools. Best of all, they aren't as expensive as you might think.

Once again, computers have come to the rescue. If you use traditional techniques to produce a four-color poster, color separation and printing are not cost effective for short print runs. These days, though, the whole process can be completely computerized. You can save hundreds of dollars if you only need a few dozen posters.

SHORT-RUN COMPUTERIZED POSTER COMPANIES

Using new computer technology, these companies can take an image or a computer file and inexpensively convert it into a very impressive, very large, color image.

Scangraphics
5300 Newport Drive • Rolling Meadows, IL 60008 • (708) 392-3980

Digicolor
1300 Dexter Ave. North, Suite 130 • Seattle, WA 98109 • (206) 284-2198

Digital Prism
820 American St. • San Carlos, CA 94070 • (415) 508-8800

Photo Lab, Inc.
1026 Redna Terrace • Cincinnati, OH 45215 • (800) 452-4420

If you are planning to produce a large quantity of posters, it pays to use a conventional printing house and have it print from a color separation. Once the separation is paid for, each poster can cost as little as a 25¢. Large quantities can further reduce the running cost.

Posters can be a useful tool depending upon how they are used. They are a great way to advertise a special event such as a grand opening or a holiday sale. Using a poster as a direct mail piece can be effective, especially if you send it to someone who puts it up on a wall where the rest of the world can see it (like a business office or retail store).

THINGS YOU CAN DO WITH A POSTER

➤ Posters make great in-store giveaway items. Customers, especially kids, love to get things for free.

➤ Hang them around the store. The Body Shop uses huge ones to create a sense of excitement. They frequently change the posters, keeping their decor interesting to the customer.

➤ When the circus comes to town, they hang posters all over the place. You can do the same thing to announce your special event.

➤ Capcom, a video game company, mailed a poster featuring their game graphics to the media on a monthly basis. If your poster is a piece of art, people will hold on to it and use it to decorate a room or an office. Your message becomes permanent.

➤ Use your poster as an freestanding insert by inserting it into your local newspaper or a regional magazine.

TWO THINGS NOT TO DO WITH A POSTER

➤ Don't mail posters to anyone unless you're willing to invest in a mailing tube. Folded posters don't get hung.

➤ It's not worth doing unless you execute it well.

FULL-COLOR PRINTERS

Every city has dozens of printers capable of printing posters (check your Yellow Pages). The printers below specialize in producing color images at low cost—with a standard pricing schedule, so you don't have to worry about getting the best deal.

MultiPrint
5555 W. Howard St. • Skokie, IL 60077 • (800) 858-9999

Service Web Offset Corporation
2500 S. Dearborn St • Chicago, IL 60616 • (800) 621-1567

Econocolor
7405 Industrial Rd. • Florence, KY 41042 • (800) 877-7405, ext. 245

National Posters
P.O. Box 1448 Chattanooga, TN 37406 • (800) 624-0408

Posters are a great way to advertise an event, especially if the event is one that occurs over time. For example, a hockey team in the East Coast Hockey League prints up posters at the beginning of every hockey season. The poster contains the team's home schedule for the season and some action photographs. The posters are distributed all over town. People love to hang them in store windows and inside their places of business (especially restaurants). They remind people when the team is playing and also become a collectors' item.

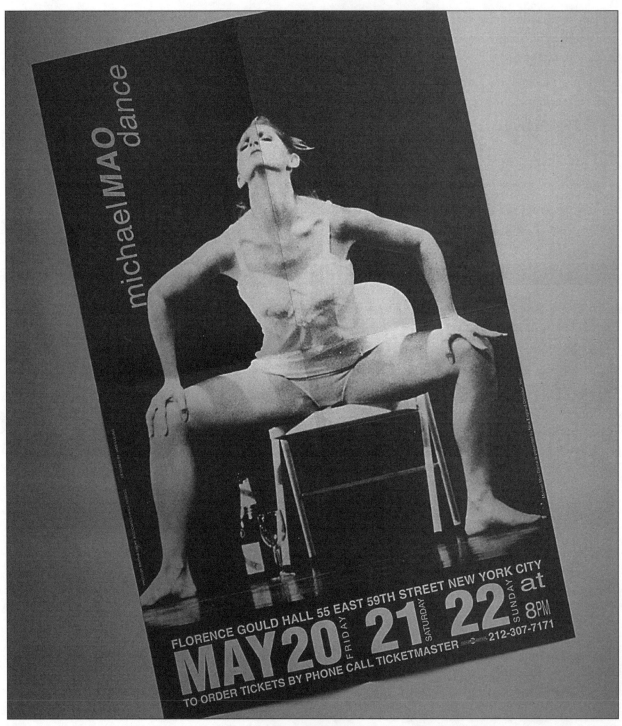

This poster promoting a performance by Michael Mao Dance also folds down into a self-mailer.

Source: James Leung Design Co. NY • 455 84th St. 1/F • Brooklyn, NY 11209

POSTER BRAINSTORMS

Use this space to draw a poster that you could use at a trade show, a media event, or in the streets of your town.

NEWSLETTERS

A great way to communicate with customers and prospects alike.

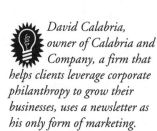

David Calabria, owner of Calabria and Company, a firm that helps clients leverage corporate philanthropy to grow their businesses, uses a newsletter as his only form of marketing.

He has never paid a dollar for advertising. Instead, he mails his newsletter to business trade journals and highly targeted prospects. It's brought him a tremendous amount of exposure in terms of publicity and direct inquiries from potential clients.

Since starting Profit and Philanthropy, *David has received so many requests for the publication that he is considering turning it into a subscription newsletter.*

The resourceful guerrilla looks for new, efficient ways to remind the consumer of his name and business constantly. One low-priced way to do this is with a newsletter.

If your business becomes a source of information as well as a source of products and services, you'll gain respect and increased loyalty from your customers.

A local fish market might use a newsletter to give customers recipes, tips on good values in fish, news about which fish are in season, etc. By positioning themselves as a company that really knows its fish, they gain credibility and help differentiate themselves from their competitors.

According to Howard Penn Hudson, the president of The Newsletter Clearinghouse, newsletters are effective because they are targeted. If you start a secretarial service, for example, you obviously want to reach business people. Through the local Chamber of Commerce, you can get a list of the presidents of area businesses. Go directly to the decision-makers who can make the purchase. Send them a newsletter full of anecdotal stories from companies that use your services, citing benefits and testimonials. Make it easy for recipients to contact you for more information. Try including a coupon or a special offer.

Don't be afraid to share your success. If your business provides a service, send out an announcement whenever you sign on a visible customer. Let everyone know which houses you're painting, which buildings you've rented or how many hamburgers you've served.

If your newsletter is interesting enough, you can gradually turn it into a catalog and sell your prospects while you entertain them.

BASICS

DO IT ECONOMICALLY

You probably don't want to spend a lot of money on your newsletter. One way to save money is to design a color masthead and gang run it—print up a quantity that will last you for several newsletters. Then, when it comes time to publish the newsletter, print the black and white copy on the already printed color masthead. You save time and money that way and end up with a professional looking piece for half the cost.

Another way you can save money is by eliminating the cost of an envelope. Design your newsletter as a self-mailer.

Don't forget about co-marketing. Find several businesses that complement each other (maybe a plumber, an electrician, and a painter) and combine their efforts into creating one newsletter that will help all three.

NEWSLETTER TIPS

➤ Fill your newsletter with interesting copy, including short facts and blurbs that people will find useful. If you fill your newsletter with long, boring copy, you will lose your audience fast.

➤ Proofread your newsletter carefully. It is a reflection of you and your company.

➤ Be informative. Cover a variety of topics. Don't bore them by going on too long about any one thing.

➤ Use your newsletter as a selling tool. Include your toll-free phone and fax numbers, perhaps on every page.

➤ Be succinct. Your newsletter does not have to be long to have impact. Most people look at a newsletter as something they can read quickly to get some useful information.

➤ Invest in a designer for advice on layout and graphics. Once you have a professional design that works, stick with it.

➤ Make your customers an important topic. People love to see their names in print.

➤ Your newsletter is a selling tool, but it has to educate the reader, too. Don't just fill it with advertising or you'll turn the reader off.

➤ Once you commit to a newsletter program, keep it coming regularly. Publish at least quarterly, but preferably bimonthly or even monthly.

➤ Have specific goals in mind when you create your newsletter. It should have a voice and a focus. If you are confused about what its purpose is, your audience will be, too.

RESOURCES FOR NEWSLETTER PUBLISHERS

Newsletter Publishers Association
1401 Wilson Blvd., Suite 207 • Arlington, VA 22209 • (703) 527-2333
trade association

Ivan Levison built a tremendously successful copywriting business by sending a monthly newsletter to all of his customers and prospects. The newsletter shares his tips on writing copy and gives case studies from successful mailings he's worked on.

Kimberly Stanséll, a Business Information Specialist, publishes a quarterly newsletter called Bootstrappin' Entrepreneur. *She charges a small fee for a yearly subscription and uses the newsletter as a forum for her business, Research Done Write!*
Bootstrappin' *has been named a top bargain by the* L.A. Bargain Book *two years in a row. It's full of tips, resources, and advice for small business owners. Call Research Done Write! at (310) 568-9861 to subscribe.*

Jessica's Biscuit, now the largest seller of cookbooks in America, started by sending a newsletter to its customers. The newsletter grew into a catalog, which is now distributed around the world. In-store sales are a fraction of those coming in by phone.

. . . .

Pages Filler Service

Berry Publishing
300 North State St. • Chicago, IL 60610 • (312) 222-9245

For about $16 a month, Pages will send you thirty pages of copyright-free editorial filler for your newsletter. Each issue contains articles and artwork having to do with a wide variety of subjects. One issue, for example, contained articles called, "Making the Phone an Effective Tool," "Be a Firesafe Apartment Neighbor," "Muted Tones Predicted for Home, Fashion," and "Coretta King Details the Progress, Goals of the Civil Rights Movement." Five pages of clip art and a page of short quotes and filler statements were included at the end of the issue. Pages is available either in camera-ready hard copy or on floppy disk for an additional fee.

ClipEdit

The Dartnell Corporation
4660 N. Ravenswood • Chicago, IL 60640 • (800) 621-5463

ClipEdit is a valuable tool for anyone who produces newsletters on the computer and needs filler articles. ClipEdit volumes sell for $79.95 each and contain 35 copyright-free articles on such topics as business, humor, health and fitness, sales and marketing, and more. Each volume is available on disk in DOS, Windows, or Macintosh format.

The Cartoon Bank

495 Warburton Ave • Hastings-on-Hudson, NY 10706 • (914) 478-5527

If you want to add a touch of humor to your newsletter, call The Cartoon Bank. Tell them what type of piece you're working on and the subject. They'll fax you a selection of suggested drawings and cartoons for you to choose from. Once you have selected, they will send you the camera-ready art you need to put the cartoon in your publication. What a great way to liven up your newsletter.

Cartoons by Johns

Box 1300 • Pebble Beach, CA 93953 • (408) 649-0303

Hudson's Subscription Newsletter Directory

Published by Howard Penn Hudson • Newsletter Clearinghouse
44 West Market St. • P.O Box 311 • Rhinebeck, NY 12572

The best source of information about subscription newsletters. You might want to look at some of the newsletters listed to get ideas on layout and content.

Oxbridge Directory of Newsletters

published by Oxbridge Communications, Inc.
150 Fifth Ave., Suite 302 • New York, NY 10011 • (212) 741-0231

The Oxbridge Directory lists over 20,000 titles, including, newsletters published by non-profit organizations and trade and professional associations.

Jane Wesman, a public relations executive in New York, puts out a newsletter called JW News & Views. *She includes publicity tips, industry news, and the latest public relations successes of Jane Wesman Public Relations. The newsletter gives Wesman a great deal of credibility and presents her as a public relations expert.*

. . . .

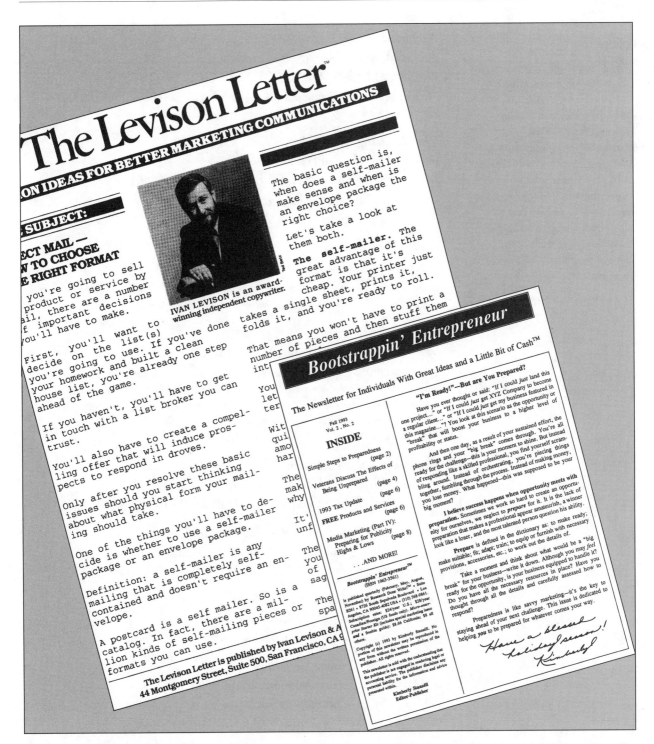

The Levison Letter™
ON IDEAS FOR BETTER MARKETING COMMUNICATIONS

SUBJECT:

**ECT MAIL —
W TO CHOOSE
E RIGHT FORMAT**

you're going to sell product or service by ail, there are a number f important decisions you'll have to make.

First, you'll want to decide on the list(s) you're going to use. If you've done your homework and built a clean house list, you're already one step ahead of the game.

If you haven't, you'll have to get in touch with a list broker you can trust.

You'll also have to create a compelling offer that will induce prospects to respond in droves.

Only after you resolve these basic issues should you start thinking about what physical form your mailing should take.

One of the things you'll have to decide is whether to use a self-mailer package or an envelope package.

Definition: a self-mailer is any mailing that is completely self-contained and doesn't require an envelope.

A postcard is a self mailer. So is a catalog. In fact, there are a million kinds of self-mailing pieces or formats you can use.

IVAN LEVISON is an award-winning independent copywriter.

The basic question is, when does a self-mailer make sense and when is an envelope package the right choice?

Let's take a look at them both.

The self-mailer. The great advantage of this format is that it's cheap. Your printer just takes a single sheet, prints it, folds it, and you're ready to roll.

That means you won't have to print a number of pieces and then stuff them int

You let ter

Wit qui amo har

The mak why

It' unf

The you of sag

The spa

*The Levison Letter is published by Ivan Levison &
44 Montgomery Street, Suite 500, San Francisco, CA*

Bootstrappin' Entrepreneur™

The Newsletter for Individuals With Great Ideas and a Little Bit of Cash™

Fall 1993
Vol. 2 , No. 2

INSIDE

Bootstrappin' Entrepreneur™
(ISSN 1063-3561)

is published quarterly (February, May, August, November) by Research Done Write™ • Suite B261 • 8726 South Sepulveda Boulevard • Los Angeles, CA 90045-4082 USA • (310) 568-9861. Subscription rates: $24/year U.S.; $28/year Canadian/Foreign (US funds only). Microfiche: prior Starter Kit (includes special marketing issue and a freebie guide); $8.66 California; $8 all others.

Kimberly Stansell
Editor-Publisher

"I'm Ready!"—But are You Prepared?

Have you ever thought or said: "If I could *just* land this one project..." or "If I could *just* get XYZ Company to become a regular client..." or "If I could *just* get my business featured in this magazine..."? You look at this scenario as the opportunity or "break" that will boost your business to a higher level of profitability or status.

And then one day, as a result of your sustained effort, the phone rings and your "big break" comes through. You're all ready for the challenge—this is your moment to shine. But instead of responding like a skilled professional, you find yourself scrambling around. Instead of orchestrating, you're piecing things together, fumbling through the process. Instead of making money, you lose money. What happened—this was supposed to be your big moment?

I believe success happens when opportunity meets with preparation. Sometimes we work so hard to create an opportunity for ourselves, we neglect to *prepare* for it. It is the lack of preparation that makes a professional appear amateurish, a winner look like a loser, and the most talented person question his ability.

Prepare is defined in the dictionary as: to make ready; make suitable; fit; adapt; train; to equip or furnish with necessary provisions, accessories, etc.; to work out the details of.

Take a moment and think about what would be a "big break" for your business—write it down. Although you may *feel* ready for the opportunity, is your business equipped to handle it? Do you have all the necessary resources in place? Have you thought through all the details and carefully assessed how to respond?

Preparedness is like savvy marketing—it's the key to staying ahead of your next challenge. This issue is dedicated to helping *you* to be prepared for whatever comes your way.

Have a blessed
holiday season!
Kimberly

The Levison Letter is a free promotional newsletter put out by copywriter Ivan Levison, and Bootstrappin' Entrepreneur is a subscription newsletter put out by business information specialist Kimberly Stansell.

The newsletter Chanel Dateline: Paris *contains offbeat articles about Chanel products, interviews with "celebrities" in the cosmetics field, and makeup tips and information. Customers continually bring the newsletter to makeup counters all over the country, requesting the products covered, and Chanel has had such an overwhelming response, they have decided to add a third issue to their yearly publication schedule.*

. . . .

Newsletter Design
published by The Newsletter Clearinghouse
P.O. Box 311 • Rhinebeck, NY 12572 • (914) 876-2561

Monthly newsletter that critiques existing newsletters. Full of great ideas and real examples of newsletter design.

The Newsletter on Newsletters
published by Howard Penn Hudson
P.O. Box 311 • Rhinebeck, NY 12572 • (914) 876-2561

One of the best resources for newsletter publishers. Published twice a month.

Before & After
published by Pagelab
331 J St., #150 • Sacramento, CA 95814 • (916) 443-4890

One of the best resources on desktop publishing design. This bimonthly newsletter is full of great ideas and step-by-step instructions that are easy to follow.

Newsletter Resources
6614 Pernod Ave. • St. Louis, MO 63139-2149 • (314) 647-6788

This company and its president, Elaine Floyd, is a one-stop resource for newsletter publishers. Elaine publishes a newsletter called Newsletter News & Resources *four times a year, maintains a bibliography of newsletter resources, and has written some of the best books and manuals about newsletter publishing you can find. Some of them are listed here. Contact her for the rest.*

Marketing with Newsletters
by Elaine Floyd • Published by EF Communications
6614 Pernod Ave. • St. Louis, MO 63139-2149 • (314) 647-6788

Quick & Easy Newsletters on a Shoestring Budget
by Elaine Floyd • Published by EF Communications
6614 Pernod Ave. • St. Louis, MO 63139-2149 • (314) 647-6788

Fundamentals of Successful Newsletters
by Thomas Bivens • Published by NTC Books
4255 W. Touhy Ave. • Chicago, IL 60646 • (800) 323-4900

The Newsletter Editor's Desk Book
by Marvin Arth, Helen Ashmore, and Elaine Floyd
Published by EF Communications
6614 Pernod Ave. • St. Louis, MO 63139-2149 • (314) 647-6788

Editing Your Newsletter
by Mark Beach • Published by Writer's Digest Books
1507 Dana Ave. • Cincinnati, OH 45207 • (513) 531-2222

Publishing Newsletters
by Howard Penn Hudson
P.O. Box 311 • Rhinebeck, NY 12572 • (914) 876-2561

Newsletter Sourcebook
by Mark Beach • Published by North Light Books
1507 Dana Ave. • Cincinnati, OH 45207 • (513) 531-2222

Newsletters from the Desktop
by Roger C. Parker • Published by Ventana Press
P.O. Box 2469 • Chapel Hill, NC 27515 • (919) 942-0220

This is a promotional newsletter put out by Camp Arowhon in Ontario. It keeps people interested and excited about the camp all year long, so it's easier to sign them up to come back to camp in the summer.

NEWSLETTER BRAINSTORMS

If your firm had a newsletter for existing customers, what exciting new developments would you cover?

_____

_____

_____

_____

_____

_____

_____

_____

TAKE-ONE BOX

Get your message directly into your prospect's hands by distributing your fliers, inserts, and coupons right on your premises or in your neighborhood.

American Express has built a huge portion of its cardmember acquisition program around take-one. By prominently posting the display at restaurants and colleges, they're carefully targeting their best prospects.

RETAILERS

If you own a retail store and don't have a take-one box on the counter, you're missing a lucrative opportunity. Guerrillas never stop selling once the customer is in the store; they use fliers, inserts, and coupons displayed in take-one boxes to help close the sale. So, for instance, if you have an electronics store, print a brochure or flier called "Basics for Buying a Stereo System."

Giving your customers something in writing that tells them about you and your product is a fundamental guerrilla tactic. Also use the brochure to include your qualifications, testimonials from previous customers, and other information that will persuade prospects to buy from you.

Visit every store in your neighborhood and arrange to put a coupon for your product on their counters. Offer to pay each store something (consider offering your product or service) for every resulting sale, or trade out the space by letting them put coupons on your counter. A local Chinese takeout restaurant has a box with take-one inserts from an auto lube and oil business, an automobile tire dealer, Carvel ice cream, and Sportime USA sitting on its counter. Rest assured that the restaurant has coupons on the counters of each of those outlets, too.

Pay attention to the details. Have a professional design your coupon or flier. If coupons aren't eye-catching, nobody will take them out of the box. Don't scrimp on the box itself. Something transparent is best. If people can't see what they are picking up, they'll probably ignore it.

For a more traditional approach to take-one inserts, go to the local supermarket. Everyone has seen the boxes mounted on supermarket walls by the door filled with fliers, circulars, and booklets advertising a variety of items. There are companies that specialize in distributing take-one space in supermarkets. You can contact one of them and have your insert put in every supermarket in the country. Chances are, though, you are more interested in regional or local coverage, and those same companies can sell you space by the region. Look them up in the Yellow Pages and call them about advertising only in your particular region.

Supermarket Communications in Norwalk, Connecticut, calls their supermarket take-one advertising their "Good Neighbor Direct Program." They offer national and regional distribution. Here is an example of cost: To place a standard 4" wide insert in the 449 stores representing the Baltimore/Washington,

DC/Virginia region costs about $2,000 per month. That cost does not include the cost of actually producing the insert so you need to figure that in.

NON-RETAILERS

Take-one boxes are primarily used by retailers to boost their sales, but a guerrilla manufacturer can also use the same technique to boost his sales by providing his retailers with take-one boxes.

For example, Apple faced a huge problem when it had to educate consumers about their new Newton computer. By describing the salient features of the machine in a simple take-one brochure, they made it easier for their retail distributors to disseminate the information.

So discuss with your reatailers the advisability of using take-one boxes and inserts that you would provide at no charge. You'll find that most of them are more than happy to give it a try.

THE NEXT GENERATION OF TAKE-ONE

The take-one concept has also gone high-tech. There are new take-one dispensers right on product shelves and in shopping carts, even inside the grocer's freezer. Even though the technology is more advanced, it's still not a very expensive advertising medium, especially if you are selling goods to outlets like supermarkets, pharmacies, or convenience stores. ActMedia in Norwalk, Connecticut, is one company that specializes in both in-store advertising and high-tech take-one. The following are the types of advertising they broker.

ADVERTISING BROKERED BY ACTMEDIA, INC.

➤ Instant coupon machines.

➤ Shopping cart advertising, including LCD displays.

➤ On-shelf advertising, including interactive audio and LCD units that give information as requested by the consumer and then dispense coupons.

➤ In-store demonstrations.

➤ Freezervision™ (signs inside your grocer's freezer).

➤ Point-of-purchase radio. You can have your radio commercial piped into supermarkets all over the country through ActMedia.

➤ Aisle signs.

Nexus (hair care products) relies exclusively on hairdressers for sales. Providing them with handsome take-one brochures enables Nexus to take their sales pitch directly to the consumer. This saves time for the hairdresser, while improving sales for Nexus.

Direct Mailers, Inc. is an independent Val-Pak dealer in New York's Westchester County. To separate themselves from the competition, they recently began brokering reciprocal take-one boxes. They started by printing an extra 1,000 or so inserts for their direct mail clients and distributed them in local stores. They color-coded the inserts so their clients could track which ones came back from the direct mail campaign and which ones were from the take-one boxes. The take-one boxes were so successful, they became another business for the company.

According to Direct Mailers' president, Neal Perlowitz, "In a tight economy, you will recover one town at a time, and local couponing is the way to grow your business."

Tops Appliances in the Northeast regularly uses in-store take-one to create incremental sales from customers once they're in the store. They have used coupons ("Save $100 today on any air conditioner") as well as special store maps to direct prospects to different departments.

....

TAKE-ONE DESIGN TIPS

➤ **Lead with Your Product or Service**
Your headline should be bold and to the point. The message should be clear and cause people to stop, look, and pick up the insert.

➤ **Make Your Masthead or Logo the Centerpiece.**
The insert should communicate the identity of your product and company. You have a split second to grab the customer's eye and a logo or masthead is an effective way of doing that.

➤ **Include a Valuable Offer**
The insert should have a coupon or special offer as the main point. Talk about a special sale, a promotional deadline, or a special feature that you offer. You must create a sense of urgency and the promise of benefit with your insert. There has to be a reason for someone to pick up your insert—now.

➤ **Use Color Intelligently**
The insert has to stand out, but clarity is more important than flashiness.

➤ **Use High-Quality, Coated Paper**
Give the customer something that will make her take you seriously.

➤ **Include an Easy Way for the Customer to Reply to Your Offer**
If your insert is a coupon, make it obvious and easy to redeem it.

Source: Supermarket Communications Systems

TAKE-ONE COMPANIES

Supermarket Communications Systems
148 East Ave. • Suite 2-I • Norwalk, CT 06851 • (203) 852-0888

ActMedia, Inc.
301 Merritt • P.O. Box 5102 • Norwalk, CT 06856 • (800) 543-1101

Many take-one companies are local. Check your Business to Business Yellow Pages for more suggestions.

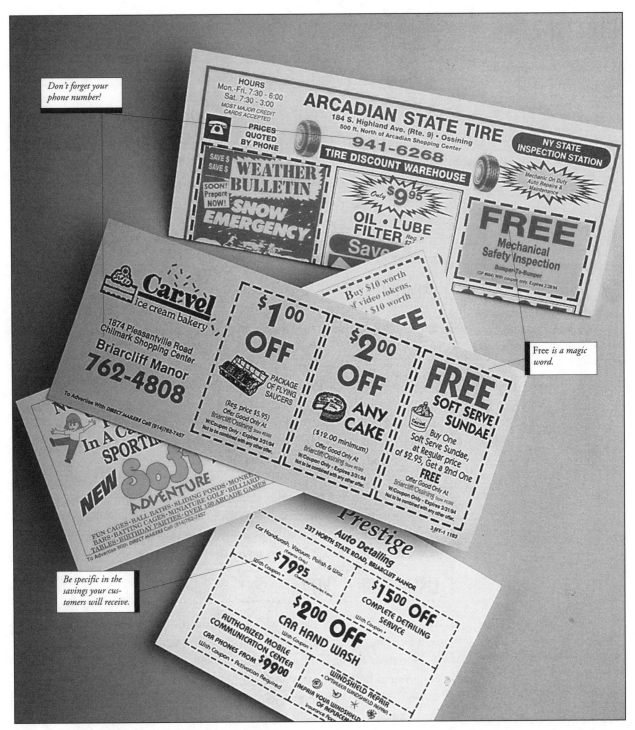

Don't forget your phone number!

Free is a magic word.

Be specific in the savings your customers will receive.

Three inserts found in a take-one box at a local Chinese restaurant and distributed by Direct Mailers, Inc., and one (Prestige Auto) found on the counter of the neighborhood florist.

CIRCULARS

A low-cost way to spread the word.

One of the largest SAT test prep companies hands out special #2 pencils and a circular to every student walking in to take the SAT. The circular includes a coupon, of which thousands are redeemed for their $600 course. Low cost, targeted, and savvy.

For the money, circulars are one of the most powerful of the guerrilla marketing weapons. They are pure power and pure economy. Why?

➤ They get instant action.

➤ They are astonishingly inexpensive (we're talking pennies).

➤ They let you use color in a sea of black and white.

➤ They are the essence of simplicity and flexibility.

Circulars can be distributed in a variety of locations: posted on community bulletin boards, handed out on street corners, given to sports and music fans as they leave the game or the concert, placed on car windshields, included in your mailings. You can even make deals with nearby non-competitive businesses to place your circular in their stores.

CREATING A CIRCULAR

You used to be able to save money by having a printer design your piece. But with the explosion of desktop publishing and cheap copy services, it makes more sense to spend more of your money on a first-rate designer and then photocopy whatever you need.

Don't skimp on copy. The difference between success and failure with a flier often comes down to how well it's written. Remember the primary importance of an attention-grabbing headline.

Include your offer, its expiration date, your address, fax and phone, and the major benefit or benefits that you provide. While the bulk of the sales you generate through circulars will come soon after distribution, you want to establish a brand image for sales down the road.

CIRCULATION IS CRITICAL

One local deli placed a stack of circulars in the lobby of our building. It contained their menu and phone number and advertised in large letters "FREE DELIVERY." We had never heard of the place. Now we order lunch from them almost daily.

Perhaps the biggest challenge with circulars is the effort it takes to get them well distributed. Consider hiring a high school student to distribute them door to door or at a busy street corner. Post them in your neighborhood on community bulletin boards and telephone poles (check your local posting regulations). Hand them out to people heading into the local movie theater or the baseball park. Make a donation to your local church and in return ask them to stick a pile of your circulars on the table at their next bake sale. Don't, however, hand them out in the middle of the mall or any other private establishment without first checking into the local laws about solicitation.

West Art Gallery circulars. The owner of the gallery plasters these all over the place—on car windshields, on bulletin boards, and on his own counters. The gallery has covered all the basics—good headline, an offer, and convenience.

Think before you act. Determine where your target market is likely to be. A Chinese restaurant places circulars under the windshield wipers of every car in the commuter parking lot—after all, every person parked there has a car, lives in the area, and will be reading the circular around dinner time. Great targeting.

Circulars are a great way to reach students. You can hire kids to hand them out on school buses or at after school athletic events or parties. Make it humorous and you'll be guaranteed to get a response.

Check your Yellow Pages under "Advertising Circulars" or "Distribution." Many cities have businesses that specialize in this service. Not as cheap as hiring a kid, but more reliable.

CIRCULAR BRAINSTORMS

Use this space to draw a circular. Keep it brief, and highlight the most important elements.

DOORHANGERS

A low-cost, highly personal way of communicating with prospects.

One businessman had a relatively complex product to sell – a video delivery and pickup service. So he started his selling process by having high school students hang doorhangers throughout his target area. The doorhangers briefly described the service, then asked readers to call the phone number printed on the colorful doorhanger (though they need not be in color) to receive more information.

An impressive 18% of the people who received doorhangers called for more information. Then they were visited by college students who closed the sales. There was no way our client could have signed up so many people if he used standard media.

Doorhangers were just the ticket in the residential neighborhoods he had targeted. He checked to see if it was legal to hang them. They were were legal as long as they were hung on doorknobs. Sticking them into mailboxes would have been illegal.

If you run a geographically based business and want to let your prospective customers know about you, one of the best tools you can use is a doorhanger. They are inexpensive to print and distribute and they reach your prospective customers directly. A doorhanger left at someone's house sends the message, "I was here personally, and I have something to say directly to YOU. As a customer, you are important to me."

The most effective doorhangers are the ones that look like oversize "Do Not Disturb" signs. Success with this type of advertising once again depends heavily on the headline. Your doorhanger must have an immediate impact on the recipient to produce results. A well-designed doorhanger is sure to be read by the person who pulls it off the doorknob. As soon as the person picks it up, the message is conveyed—now that's direct advertising!

The call to action should be primary: "You Could Eat a Hot Pizza Tonight Instead of Cooking" is a great headline. Imagine the person coming home from a long day at work to find a doorhanger with this headline and a coupon from the local pizzeria. The doorhanger certainly puts the bug in their ear.

Another tactic is to personalize your message. For example, if you run a diaper service, get the names and addresses of new parents (and their newborns) along your driver's route from the local hospital. Have the driver leave a personalized doorhanger at the home of the new baby.

It might say something like, "Welcome home, JACOB! If your mom or dad call us, we'll be delighted to give you a two-week supply of diapers *FREE.*" The personalized nature of the doorhanger, along with the irresistible offer, make it a cheap, effective way to generate new business.

TIPS FOR DOORHANGER DESIGN

➤ A short, punchy headline is most effective.

➤ Don't skimp on the production. They are already inexpensive, so don't cut corners. Print your doorhanger on a heavy paper or card stock and add a dash of color.

➤ Use testimonials. They are the most effective way to convince the prospect you are a reputable business.

➤ Describe your qualifications to provide the service. People need to know you are not just a fly-by-night operation.

➤ Make an offer—a discount, a coupon, a free estimate or a free brochure. Induce the prospect to give you a call.

Rarely does a marketing weapon do the entire selling job for a guerrilla. But they may get a guerrilla's foot in the door, and that can lead to a prospect's name on an order form.

The ubiquitous Chinese restaurant menus that are indiscriminately dumped in apartment building lobbies in most cities are the worst kind of marketing. The do not have a catchy headline or a special offer, and their approach is wasteful and annoying. We're sure many restaurants have actually lost customers by invading prospects' home territory. Whenever you try a new advertising medium, do some research to insure you're not going to offend people.

It's easy to test doorhangers. Just code each one (either with a color or a little number on the bottom of the coupon) and track the results. Rotate offers within different neighborhoods, but beware that this tactic can get tired. Experience has also shown though that doorhanger campaigns must be repeated several times before maximum results are realized. After all, a customer who does not order a pizza the first time he sees the offer may succumb the following week.

This doorhanger has a good headline, a call to action, and advertises a unique service for Big Shot Video.

DOORHANGER BRAINSTORMS

Use this space to outline a doorhanger that might be effective in your neighborhood.

GIFT CERTIFICATES

A low cost, revenue-producing marketing tool.

! *Don't be greedy. Too many retailers lose new customers by giving them a hard time when they try to cash their gift certificate. If a customer buys a $20 item with a $100 gift certificate, don't hesitate to give them their change in cash. Forcing a customer to shop for something he doesn't want does nothing but build animosity. Be generous—after all, the certificate is already paid for.*

Printing gift certificates is like printing money. Companies are never sorry when they do. Never? No, never. Don't make the mistake of thinking that they're solely the province of department stores. These days, juicy profits are being earned with gift certificates offered by movie theaters, massage therapists, computer stores, automobile dealers (for parts and service), bookstores, shoe stores, ski areas, airlines, and countless other types of businesses.

Hint: Gift certificates work especially well for businesses that have never offered them before. People are always on the lookout for new and unusual gift ideas. Gift certificates often fit the bill perfectly. Hardware stores, video stores, and coffee bars are perfect places to offer gift certificates.

Start your program by printing a sign or adding a line to your brochure, insert, or ad, that says, "Ask about our Gift Certificates." A quality paper stock is recommended for the certificate printing. Include your business name at the top, leaving space for the dollar amount, and allow room for the name of the recipient. A testimonial about the value of your gift certificates will enhance your program. Don't have a cutoff date. Like diamonds, gift certificates should be forever. Most people eventually use them and, despite the accounting hassle, telling a customer that the time has run out on their gift certificate is guaranteed to generate ill will.

As an alternative to the standard blank check gift certificate, try a more focused approach. Offer a certificate good for a car wash every week for a year, or a cup of espresso every morning, or a back rub, or whatever. By eliminating a cash value from the certificate, you can make it even more attractive to the gift giver.

Amost any business can benefit from a non-cash-value gift certificate. Here are some ideas to get you thinking about how your business could use one.

TEN GIFT CERTIFICATE IDEAS

➤ A free massage

➤ A bouquet of roses

➤ An evening of bowling

➤ A free dental exam (weird, sure, but don't you know someone who needs one?)

➤ A year of movies (rented or at the movie theater)

This is an elegant gift certificate designed by James Leung for a hair salon. The customer buys a set dollar amount of services. Each time the recipient of the gift comes in, it's marked off right on the certificate and the amount he spends is deducted.

Source: James Leung Design Co NY • 455 84th St. 1/F • Brooklyn, NY 11209

Tiffany's doesn't use gift certificates. Instead, they mint their own coins—hefty, solid metal disks that seem like they're worth even more than money.

Reusable metal gift certificates eliminate hassles, are easy to keep track of, and fun to buy and redeem.

➤ Dinner for two, with wine, at a pre-reserved romantic table

➤ Free housecleaning, from top to bottom

➤ Free tank of gas (thanks for lending me your car...)

➤ Free afternoon of babysitting

➤ Free month of E-mail connection with CompuServe

THE MOST IMPORTANT OPPORTUNITY

When you sell a gift certificate, the profit to your business isn't really generated from the first sale. A gift certificate is your opportunity to convert a first time customer into a repeat customer.

Instruct your staff that gift certificate redeemers should be given *special* attention. This is your opportunity to dazzle them and make them regulars.

Make sure you maintain a list of names and addresses of every customer who redeems a gift certificate in your store. Follow up those leads with a letter, a brochure, coupons, even a thank you note. You've found someone who's already been given a testimonial (from the person who gave them the certificate) and who has now sampled your goods and service. Do everything you can to keep her coming back as a paying customer.

GIFT CERTIFICATE BRAINSTORMS

Some of the most effective gift certificates aren't for cash—they're for a specific item or service. Make a list of ten things your business sells that might be appropriate as gifts.

_____

_____

_____

_____

_____

_____

_____

_____

_____

_____

ORDER FORMS

*Don't miss this
advertising opportunity.*

The King Arthur Flour Company, which is usually a guerrilla in all things, makes it virtually impossible to correctly compute the shipping charges they apply. Every item is charged at a different rate, and you need a calculator to compute how much you owe them. They've lost at least one regular customer because ordering is just too hard.

. . . .

If you have a product guarantee, state it on the order form in a prominent spot. If you guarantee swift delivery, put that on, too. Hard Manufacturing, the world's leading hospital crib company, puts this guarantee on every order form: "If we don't ship your order within two weeks, the freight is free. If we don't ship your order within four weeks, the cribs are free." With a guarantee like that, there's little doubt in the customer's mind that the order will get there on time.

. . . .

Guerrillas never overlook the little things. The seemingly small detail of the inclusion and the design of an order form is actually very important. If you sell by direct response or with a catalog, your order form may be the last hurdle between the customer and the order.

First, order forms should be as user-friendly as possible. They should include your guarantee, easy ordering directions, and even new or special product highlights or promotions.

INTRODUCE NEW PRODUCTS

When you introduce a new product, highlight it on the order form. Your regular customers might not realize that you've got something new, and they'll appreciate the chance to just check it off. If you want to offer a free trial, this is a great place to mention it.

You should also highlight special deals and promotions. When you print your order forms, consider writing the special deals along the side by hand. This personal touch will attract attention and personalize your presentation at the critical deciding moment.

ORDER FROM YOURSELF

As a test, sit down with your form and time how long it takes to fill out. Are there sections that are confusing? Are you asking the customer to do work that you could be doing (computing tax, figuring freight, etc.)? Make it user-friendly.

Shortsighted policies can cripple even the best conceived guerrilla marketing efforts. Hannah Andersson, usually a guerrilla, presents its wares in a beautiful, order-friendly catalog. But when the user confronts the order form, he sees shipping charges that can account for as much as 25% of the order total. By making it hard to do business, Hannah Andersson may be turning away some potential customers.

Offering different ordering and payment methods makes it easier for people to do business with you. For repeat customers, offer automatic debiting, credit card payment or subscription rates, even if they are not normally associated with your business. For example, you'd be surprised at how many people find paying bills, especially small ones, a big hassle. Many mortgage banks have discovered this, and greatly increase profitability and cash flow by offering to

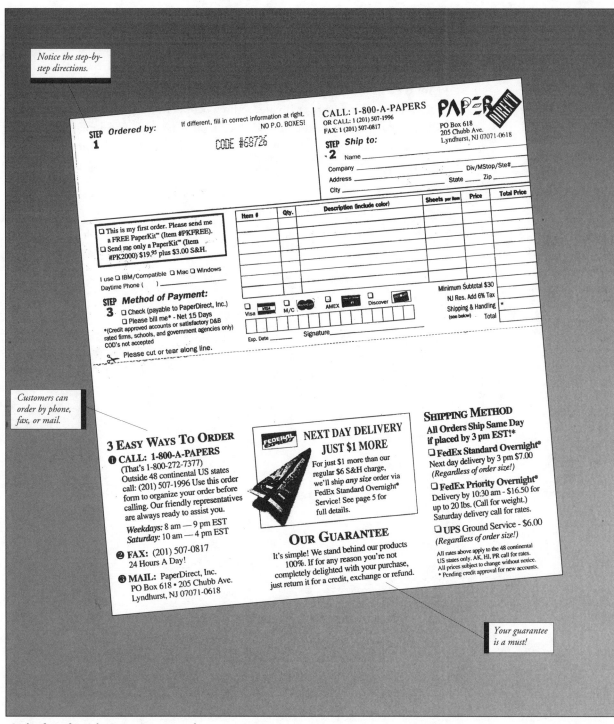

Notice the step-by-step directions.

Customers can order by phone, fax, or mail.

Your guarantee is a must!

Order form from the Paper Direct catalog.

Source: Paper Direct • P.O. Box 618 • Lyndhurst, NJ 07071 • (800) 272-7377

deduct payments directly from a bank account. If you run a local newspaper, try allowing your customers to pay by credit card rather than always requiring a check.

You'd be surprised by how many people will fill out your form, but you never see it because it never gets mailed. Allow people to fax you their orders, or if you want them to use the mail, include a business reply envelope in your catalog. You should always do anything you can to make the order process easy and flexible.

ORDER FORM BRAINSTORMS

Take out one of your company's order forms. Make a list of the most prominent elements and rank the form on ease of use, promotional value, and clarity.

_____

_____

_____

_____

_____

_____

_____

_____

_____

_____

STATIONERY

Make your letterhead work for you.

Designing stationery seems like a simple enough task. We've all seen letterheads from thousands of companies. How hard can it be to get it right?

Fortunately for guerrillas, most of their competitors don't use one-tenth of the potential of their letterhead. A guerrilla has a real opportunity to create an alternative that delivers the impact needed to make more sales.

Remember that your stationery acts as your stand-in when you don't make a personal appearance. It should be as well dressed as you would be for an important meeting. Use the most expensive paper you can afford, and stay away from colors. Use white or buff.

Letterhead should feature your name, address, phone number, fax number, and E-mail address. But it should also include your one-sentence positioning statement ("The Nation's #1 Manufacturer of Hospital Cribs"). A positioning statement does two things for you: First, it helps ensure that the reader of the letter understands the position of your company. Second, it reminds the busy reader exactly who you are.

In addition to a positioning statement, many guerrillas have turned their letterhead into mini-brochures. List the full range of services you offer. For example, if your mail-receiving business also does typing, put it on your letterhead.

MORE THAN JUST YOUR LETTERHEAD

Also, give some thought to what you put in the envelope along with your stationery. Many businesses have found that inserting a business card or a Rolodex card is a low-cost way to get their name and number into the hands of prospects. Think about inserting something into every piece of mail that leaves your office, not just direct mail letters. One business includes a business card with every check they mail out when they pay the bills. A car wash inserts a coupon good for $2 off every wash, while the people at M&M/Mars frequently drop a coupon good for a free pound of M&Ms in every letter they send to a consumer (see *Inserts*).

Quality is everything. The care you put into the stationery you send out reflects the care you put into your business. Don Slavin, founder of International Testing Services, Inc. found out the hard way. After advertising his fledgling software company in a trade journal five years ago, he was asked to quote a job for a Fortune 500 company.

He printed some homemade stationery and company literature and sent it off to the prospect. After receiving the information, the prospect was no longer interested. As Don notes, "I was treated somewhat rudely. She [the prospect] wasn't even interested in the quality of my product! The fact that my literature was shoddy had caused her to be more concerned about my company than the product. Needless to say, I immediately had new stationery, business cards, and brochures printed."

Don Slavin's company eventually sold more than 15,000 copies of job-training software.

Hard Manufacturing uses their letterhead and memo pad paper to position their product and their company.

TARGETED MEDIA

TARGETED MEDIA FOR GUERRILLAS
Concentrate on the word "targeted." With direct mail, catalogs, and the like you can speak directly to each of your customers, one customer at a time.

In this section, you'll discover the most important elements of a targeted media campaign and how to make the best use of them. You will learn about how to find the best prospects for your product or service before you start communicating with them, and then you'll learn how to reach them over and over and over again.

Guerrillas get a higher rate of response to their targeted media and in the long run generate a more loyal following than the traditional marketer who simply tries to stuff his message into as many mailboxes as possible. Quality is certainly better than quantity when it comes to targeted media.

CUSTOMER MAILING LISTS

The most important element contributing to the success of your direct mail campaign.

Customer lists are the gold mine of an established business. Keeping an existing customer (and increasing your business with him) is far, far easier than finding a new customer. Yet very few businesses spend enough time selling to their existing customer base. Start your customer mailing list on the day you open and never stop collecting names.

SEVEN WAYS TO GENERATE MAILING LISTS

➤ Whenever you deal with someone who calls your business, take her phone number right at the start. If you offer to send the person a brochure or free coupon, you've got her address, too.

➤ When a customer leaves something (shoes for repair, or dry cleaning) or special orders something (like books) make sure you get her address and phone number.

➤ Run frequent sweepstakes (see *Contests and Sweepstakes*) that require customers to fill out a form with their address and phone number. The owners of a new hockey team in Norfolk, VA, went to every business-to-business trade show they could find when they first moved into the area. At each show, they placed a fishbowl on their table and invited people to toss their business cards in the bowl for a free chance at winning a hockey jersey. The contest generated traffic at the table and also provided the owners of the team with an immediate list of names and addresses of people to whom they sent ticket and advertising sales materials. Several people who entered that contest eventually became some of the team's most loyal fans and corporate sponsors.

➤ Install a prominent SUGGESTIONS box. This is good business anyway, but it also gives you a way to collect addresses. Not only should you place the names of people who enter suggestions on your mailing list, but you should respond personally to each suggestion. Send a handwritten note to the person thanking him for his input—a great first step in trying to build your business one customer at a time.

➤ Create a free newsletter or catalog and offer it to anyone who gives you their address and phone.

➤ Insert an offer with your product that requires customers to write in to redeem. For example, Mister Coffee prints an offer on the inside of their coffee filter packages for one of their water purifiers. Not only are they reaching hot prospects for another one of their products, but they are also collecting names and addresses for their database. Customers must fill out and mail in a form to take advantage of the water purifier offer.

Calyx and Corolla is a florist specializing in nationwide delivery of fresh orchids. If you order a bouquet for a friend's birthday or anniversary, they carefully note the date in their computer.

Eleven months later, you'll get a call from Calyx, reminding you of the occasion and asking if you'd like to send another bouquet. It costs them very little, and most customers are delighted with the reminder.

➤ All products sold in this country come with an automatic implied warranty. Smart marketers insert a warranty card. Even though there is little legal basis for the card (the warranty stands whether you mail it in or not) it is also a great tool to find out more about your customers. The warranty card collects names and addresses, as well as other valuable marketing information.

➤ Offer a new customer starter kit that includes coupons, a catalog, etc.

➤ Put a fishbowl on your counter and invite your customers to throw their business cards in to win something from your store. For example, if you own a shoe store, tell people to drop their names and addresses in the bowl and after they buy five pairs of shoes, you'll give them the sixth for free.

MAILING LIST USES

➤ Send a coupon good for 10% off any purchase. Highlight different areas of your store, and be sure to attach an expiration date to get people to visit you *now.*

➤ Send greeting cards on holidays, birthdays, etc.

➤ Send keychains, pocket knives, pocket flashlights, little plastic pumpkins—send something—once a month. (See *Premiums and Ad Specialties.*)

➤ Clip articles and send them to customers who might be interested.

➤ Send a thank you note after any particularly big purchase. It furthers your relationship with a customer at a critical moment.

➤ Start a company newsletter. You can feature a variety of topics, including: car care tips, high school sports news, neighborhood news (everyone likes to read about himself), new product news (especially good for hobbies, etc.) and even press clippings and achievements (include photos).

➤ Send magazine subscriptions—great for dentists, barbers, even floor waxing and chimney cleaning companies. They have a high perceived value and remind your customer of you regularly.

THE SECRET SALE

A powerful tool to bring existing customers into your store is called the Secret Sale. Dittler Brothers of Atlanta [(404) 355-3423] is one company that specializes in creating this customer-grabbing tool.

Lowes, a home improvement retail store chain based in North Carolina, recently started a newsletter called Select Connection. *The newsletter provides stories and information on all types of do-it-yourself projects. By mailing the newsletter to everyone on its customer mailing list likely to be involved in these types of projects, Lowes positions itself as the expert in the field, and once customers read about their project in the newsletter, they will be that much more likely to buy their supplies at Lowes.*

One car salesman collects the name and address of every person who comes in to look at a car. The next day, he sends them a personalized thank you note just for dropping by, citing the car they looked at, its features, and its price. We know of at least one buyer who returned to the dealership citing the kind note he received in the mail as the reason for his second visit.

The Secret Sale is a postcard that offers your customer a discount of 10% to 60% on everything they buy on one visit. The hook is that the amount of the discount is hidden beneath a rub-off seal similar to those used for lottery tickets. The customer isn't permitted to rub off the seal until he's in the store and at the cash register, ready to make a purchase. For most shoppers, the suspense is irresistible. The chance that a coupon is worth 60% off any purchase at a favorite shoe store is usually enough incentive to bring a customer rushing in.

Because you only send Secret Sale cards to your existing customers, your costs are quite low. Of course, the number of people with a 60% discount is also quite small, so most of your customers will only earn a 10% discount.

CUSTOMER MAILING LIST BRAINSTORMS

Use this space to make a list of what you're using your customer mailing list for. If the list isn't long, brainstorm ten additional ways you can use it.

DIRECT MAIL POSTCARDS

An economical, innovative way to engage in direct mail.

 Glen Oaks Hospital and Medical Center in Glendale Heights, IL, was looking for a way to encourage more women to have mammograms. They printed up 30,000 direct mail postcards at a cost of 31¢ per piece (including design, printing, list, and postage). After the mailing, the radiology department recorded a 300% increase in the number of mammograms performed over the previous year during the same time period.

. . . .

! *TIP: Don't feel like you have to print up postcards from scratch. How about sending a scenic shot of the Caribbean islands to announce your new travel service?*

. . . .

If you're about to do a direct mailing, you might try it with a postcard. You can save money and increase your response rate at the same time. Make it a color postcard and you'll get the best of both worlds: Color increases readership by 41% and raises a buyer's inclination to buy by 26%. The cost? Lower than you think.

Direct mail is expensive. At a cost of nearly $1 a letter (by the time you include postage, envelope, insert, stuffing, and handling) and a response rate of one or two percent, you can see that you need a hefty profit per order to make it worth your while.

Direct postcards are cheaper. You save a dime per piece in postage, you don't have an insert or an envelope, and you don't have to stuff. Figure you can get a postcard mailing out the door for less than 40¢ each. Ask your local postmaster before printing your postcards how much it will cost to send them. There are certain size limits you should be aware of also.

Because people don't have to open the postcard, the chance that they will at least glance at the message is much greater. Postcards are lousy at closing a sale, but are very good at making announcements or getting attention.

When you design your postcard, remember that you get only one chance to make an impression, so make sure your headline is dynamic; use colored paper or two-color printing (black and red ink, for example). If you can, test a full-color postcard with a photo of your product on it. Because your first impression is so important, pay special attention to the colors you test. They may double your sales. They already have for some guerrillas.

The maximum size for a 19¢ postcard is 4.25 inches by 6 inches. Don't be afraid to turn your postcard sideways and design it so it's 6 inches wide by 4.25 inches tall.

FIVE WAYS TO USE A DIRECT MAIL POSTCARD CAMPAIGN

➤ Announce a private sale to your best customers.

➤ Announce the grand opening of a new store to your best customers.

➤ Offer a secret sale discount or a special contest ("bring this card with you and you'll be entered in our drawing...").

➤ Share a good review. This is great for restaurants or theaters.

➤ Announce a promotion or a new hire—super for hairdressers.

COMPANIES SPECIALIZING IN DIRECT MAIL POSTCARDS

Adcolor
141 Industrial St. • San Francisco, CA 94124 • (415) 575-3611

Adcolor is a company that specializes in printing four-color postcards. You'll pay about $600 to print 2,500 four-color postcards (4" x 6"). That comes to about 50¢ each including postage and a label.

American Color Printing
1731 Northwest 97th Ave. • Plantation, FL 33322 • (302) 473-4392

Color Magic Corp.
381 Brook Ave. • Passaic, NJ 07055 • (800) 832-3107

Pat Rickey, a self-proclaimed guerrilla and owner of Downpat Productions, relies heavily on direct mail postcards to gain new clients for his music production studio. Every two months he sends out 700 postcards to commercial, infomercial, and media producers, telling them about the work he has done most recently. On average, he generates a 1% response rate. It costs him a couple hundred dollars to send out the postcards, and he lands at least one job out of each mailing.

As a direct result of his bimonthly mailing, he was recently signed on to produce the music on Zsa Zsa Gabor's new television show about cooking.

One printer we know sent out postcards she bought in Las Vegas. She hand-addressed them and used the slogan "Don't Gamble on Your Printing Needs" while offering a discount on her services. The mailing turned in a 10% response rate, very high for a direct mail campaign.

Series of direct mail postcards sent out by Stewart Monderer Design. They sent out a postcard every two weeks and co-oped some of the cost by allowing the printer to place a credit line on the piece.

Source: Stewart Monderer Design • 10 Thatcher St., Suite 112 • Boston, MA 02113

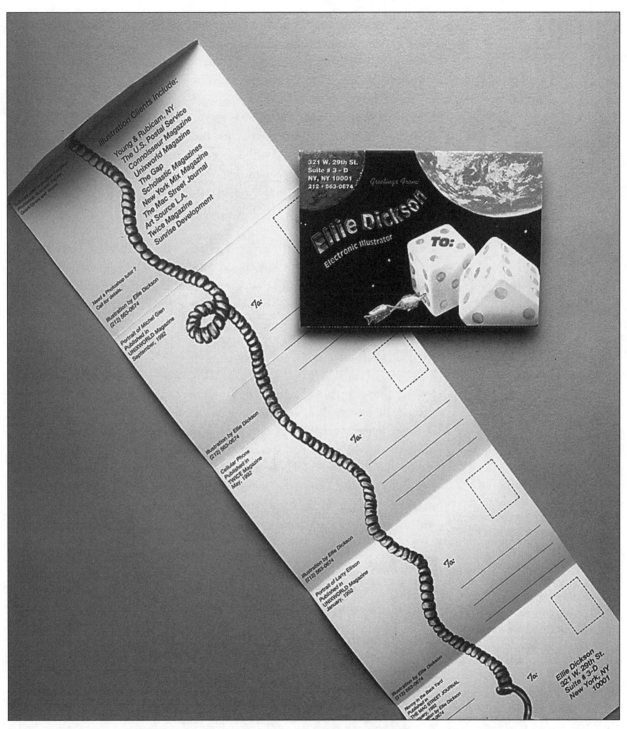

Not one postcard but many! This self-promo piece mailed out by Ellie Dickson (an electronic illustrator) was actually perforated so that each card could be detached and used by the recipient. On the back of each card is one of Ellie's illustrations.

Source: Ellie Dickson • 321 W. 29th St., Suite 3-D • New York, NY 10001 • (212) 563-0674

INSERTS

Highly targeted, low cost advertising that lets guerrillas combine forces to reach viable prospects.

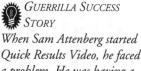

GUERRILLA SUCCESS STORY

When Sam Attenberg started Quick Results Video, he faced a problem. He was having a hard time getting information about his new line of computer-instruction videotapes to the people most likely to buy them.

Traditional marketing would have you run ads in all the computer magazines, and place the videotapes in computer stores. The problem is that a very small percentage of the readers of these magazines actually need help with any particular program. Sam would waste money reaching people he didn't need to reach.

Instead, he pursued a guerrilla approach. Reasoning that training users was also in the interest of the software companies, he approached them with the following offer: He'd make the video and pay all expenses, and the software company would agree to place a flier for

Inserts take advantage of someone else's money. They offer a flexible, timely, and inexpensive means of reaching a highly targeted market. Find a marketer who's already reaching a market you're interested in, insert your message along with theirs, and you both win.

Inserts can have a very low distribution cost, but guerrillas know that they must carefully manage the impact of any insert program by making sure it only goes to hot prospects. As with any direct mail campaign, the quality of prospects is much more important than the quantity. It doesn't do you any good to mail an insert to 100,000 people who have no use for or interest in your business. So do your research first.

Unlike brochures, inserts are never requested by the prospect, so you've got to overcome the clutter hurdle. Your insert must have impact—offer a benefit that is so irresistible it can't be passed over. Use inserts to generate leads, to follow up with existing customers, to initiate or close a sale, or in support of a promotional campaign.

RIDE-ALONGS

Several different types of advertising fall under the category of inserts. Package inserts are also called ride-alongs. These are the direct mail pieces included in packages already being mailed to customers or prospects. Include them in your own mailings or contact a company that provides a related product and arrange to include your insert in any of their mailings. One guerrilla landscaper we know arranged to place a coupon for his services in every statement sent out by the local gardening supply store. The landscaper reached his target market and generated new business. The gardening supply

---

BASICS

Insert Definitions

RIDE-ALONGS: Inserts or advertisements you place inside another marketer's mail.

CARD DECKS: Stacks of ride-alongs that share the cost of the mailing. Usually in the form of 3 x 5 cards.

SPLIT TEST: Testing one element within the same mailing. If you send out a mailing of 1,000 pieces, you can split test by sending out 500 with one headline and 500 with another. Make sure only one element is different in each half of the mailing, and that the two halves get mailed at the same time. This ensures the accuracy of the test.

FSI: Free Standing Insert—those coupon-filled circulars that are stuffed into your Sunday paper.

store also won because the landscaper's clients always needed to buy more gardening supplies and equipment.

FREE-STANDING INSERTS

Free-Standing Inserts (FSIs), are the tag-along inserts that come in your daily newspaper. Most of the time they are produced by large companies aiming to blanket a huge market with coupons or word of a special sale. The advertiser pays to produce the insert and simply pays the newspaper to stuff it in the publication—not very targeted.

These types of campaigns can cost millions of dollars, and they reach all sorts of people, including those who have absolutely no interest in the advertiser's offering. But, as a guerrilla, you can take advantage of this same method and the technology behind it. Your neighborhood paper probably isn't used to using FSI's. Offer to print a high-quality, colorful insert they can stuff in their paper. If you have an ad salesman who's also a guerrilla, he'll understand the importance of targeting a market—you might be able to have your insert included in newspapers going only to certain zip codes.

Try testing your FSI by printing several different ones. Stuff them in regional editions of the publication and then track the response. This is a great approach for contractors, chiropractors, retailers, or anyone else targeting a specific neighborhood.

MAILBOX INSERTS

Every region of the country has a company that brokers direct mail inserts. Just look them up in the Yellow Pages. These brokers are in the business of collecting a number of local advertisers that want to share in the costs of sending an envelope filled with offers and coupons to every person in the neighborhood. "Val-Pak" and "Mailbox Values" are prime examples of brand names used by brokers. They put together shared mailings by contacting a number of retailers in the same geographic area. You can contact a broker or you can do it yourself. Get together with several businesses in your neighborhood and send out a packet of inserts or coupons to all of your mailing lists. You'll receive all of the same benefits, but your mailing will be even more targeted.

the video in the box.the software came in. Now, 100% of all new users would see a flier for the video, and they could order it by phone instead of traveling all the way to a computer store.

One product converted 4% of all software purchases into video purchases—an astonishingly high figure. The line of ten tapes generated more than a million dollars in sales.

Almost anything can be promoted through inserts. Nabisco recently ventured into inserts by putting a trial size package of their new product, chocolate graham crackers, in a polybag along with the local daily newspaper delivered throughout one New York suburb.

John Wiley and Sons is a book publisher that sends out their own card deck. Because they are selling a specialized product (business and marketing books) to a highly targeted market and are willing to send out free trial copies, a card deck is a great marketing tool for them. As evidenced by their frequent use of card decks, it must be working.

• • • • • • • • • • • • • • • •

The publishers of the Information Please Business Almanac *use card decks to reach small businesses. One deck, mailed to marketing executives, generated more than 800 responses— nearly a 1% response rate.*

• • • • • • • • • • • • • • • •

CARD DECKS

Card decks are magic for some guerrillas. These stacks of index cards are mailed to targeted audiences (usually small businesses). Each deck contains 50 to 200 cards, each a tiny advertisement, usually with a business reply card on the back. The recipient flips through the deck, stopping at anything that catches his eye.

Because the decks are inexpensively produced, the cost of inclusion is low. It is possible to reach as many as 100,000 businesses for as little as $2,500—less than 3 cents apiece. Decks are highly targeted. Venture Communications, for example, brokers card decks such as The Business and Management Books card deck, the Biochemistry and Molecular Biology card deck, and the Teacher's card deck.

TIPS FOR CARD DECK SUCCESS

➤ A card deck's ability to target a niche is its greatest strength. Do your research and pick the deck that is right for you.

➤ As with most types of advertising, the headline is the kicker. It has to be bold and meaningful. The person flipping through the deck has to be compelled to stop and read your card. The word "FREE" usually gives people a reason to stop and look.

➤ Show a picture of your product. People rarely buy anything without seeing it. If possible, show the product in use.

➤ The insert must call for action on the part of the prospect. Ask her to mail back the card to order (most cards double as business reply cards that the prospect can mail back free of charge), or to take advantage of a free offer. Give an 800 number, or at least ask the prospect to fill out a questionnaire. If you don't ask for anything, you won't get anything. You get one chance with a card deck. If the prospect is not compelled to act on the spot, chances are your card will end up in the trash.

➤ Guerrillas rarely pay full price for card decks. Be sure to ask about remnant space or try to negotiate the price.

➤ Look for card decks with repeat advertisers. If an advertiser buys space in a deck more than once, the ad is probably working for her.

➤ Offer a free sample of your product, or at least a free gift for ordering. It's the norm for card deck advertising, and it's a great motivator.

Note the use of the word FREE, the built-in survey, the easy response mechanism, and the product photo.

Source: Various card decks

CARD DECK PUBLISHERS AND BROKERS

Some of the companies listed here publish their own card decks, while others broker decks and help you find the one that's right for your product.

Venture Communications
60 Madison Ave. • 3rd Floor • New York, NY 10010 • (212) 684-4800

Simon Direct
F-4 Brier Hill Court • East Brunswick, NJ 08816 • (908) 651-7222

Trump Card Marketing
222 Cedar Lane • Teaneck, NJ 07666 • (201) 836-8000

Card Deck Printers
Rose Printing Co. • Box 5078 • Tallahassee, FL 32314 • (904) 576-4151

Scoville Press, Inc
575 Madison Ave. • New York, NY 10022 • (212) 605-0109

Solar Press
38 South Finley Ave. • Basking Ridge, NJ 07920 • (201) 236-7060

Lifestyle Change Communications, Inc.
5885 Glenridge Drive, Suite 150 • Atlanta, GA 30328 • (404) 252-0554

Lifestyle Change Communications specializes in "synchographics," or reaching the right market at the right time. They maintain databases of new brides, new parents, home buyers, and other groups that are at major crossroads in their lives and are primed to make major purchases. They also broker ride-alongs and insert programs designed to reach these specialized markets.

Leon Henry, Inc.
455 Central Ave. • Scarsdale, NY 10583 • (914) 723-3176

Leon Henry is a card deck pioneer. His firm acts as a broker, placing ads with the appropriate decks and earning a commission from the publisher. His service is invaluable—we don't recommend advertising in a card deck without consulting him.

MAILBOX INSERT COMPANIES

Lifestyle Change Communications, Inc.
5885 Glenridge Drive, Suite 150 • Atlanta, GA 30328 • (404) 252-0554

ADVO
239 West Service Rd. • Hartford, CT 06120 • (203) 520-3200

When Canon wanted to reach office supply buyers, they placed a ride-along in the bills mailed out by Staples, a large office supply retailer. For minimal cost, Canon was virtually guaranteed to reach the decision-makers in companies all over the country. Staples won because they deferred some of the cost of mailing out their bills, and Canon gave Staples customers a discount.

Val-Pak Advertising of Englewood, CO

6456 S. Quebec St. • Bldg. 5, Suite 550 • Englewood, CO 80111

To locate the Val-Pak broker in your area, look in the business White Pages under V.

TEN RULES FOR THE MOST EFFECTIVE INSERT AD PLACEMENT

➤ **Choose the Right Distribution Program**

Look for demographics that are geared to your product or service and try to insure that the merchandise your package insert accompanies will heighten the response to your offer.

➤ **Test at Least Ten Programs at a Time**

Out of every ten programs tested you will have an average of three losers. Experiment with new inserts to get an accurate measure of success.

➤ **Go with the Maximum Size**

Different programs have different physical limitations. Go with the maximum size allowed by each program to prevent your insert from being lost in the shuffle.

➤ **Test with Copy that You Know Works**

Do not write new copy, create new graphics, or introduce a new offer when you first test your insert. Test what you already know works in direct mail or space advertising. If your program fails, you'll know it was the program and not your copy or offer that was at fault.

➤ **Be Patient When Evaluating a Program**

Inserts that accompany retail merchandise may take six months before they are fully distributed. Calculate a final cost-per-order you can be comfortable with, and as long as you come in under that number, you can consider your insert program a success.

➤ **Try to Transform Marginal Performers into New Profit Makers**

By reducing printing costs, changing layout, or changing stock, color, or copy, you might be able to manipulate the cost of participation in a program. Creative renegotiation can turn a marginal program into a real success.

➤ **Always Key Every Insert Package**

Using a five- or six-digit code, mark every insert you send out with a key that will allow you to identify what package it was part of. It's better to pay the extra money to stop the press and change keys than it is to be unsure of your results.

➤ **Include an Appropriate Number of Inserts**

Unless you have at least 10,000 inserts in each program you test, your returns may not be statistically reliable. On the other hand, if the number

Direct Micro is a company that sells computer modems. Who better to sell fast modem upgrades to than the subscribers to online services like CompuServe? So, Direct Micro slips an advertising insert in with every one of the 1,000,000 copies of CompuServe *magazine that* CompuServe *sends out each month.*

. . . .

HINT: Never mail out anything without including an advertising insert for one of your products. Whenever you ship out a product, include an insert that invites the customer to order from you again. Put inserts in your invoices, catalogs, statements, and newsletters. Take advantage of every opportunity to put an offer to buy in front of your customers.

. . . .

of inserts you put in one program is too high, it will force you to wait too long a time until all of your inserts have been distributed and you can evaluate the results. One way around this is to break up a large number of inserts into several keys and evaluate them as you go along.

➤ **Choose a Dependable Broker**

Many inserts miss the program they were intended for because of foul-ups in production or shipping. Your broker must make sure your materials are printed accurately, shipped to where they're supposed to go, received by the appropriate people, and inserted in the right program.

➤ **Always Re-test Favorable Returns**

If you don't, a competitor may jump in and preempt you from profiting from your success. On the other hand, you should maintain sizable reserves of pre-keyed inserts so that you may take advantage of a new program or a competitor's failure to re-test promptly.

Source: Leon Henry, President of Leon Henry, Inc. (914) 723-3176

! *CAREFUL: Most people aren't as honest as you are.*
■ *There are numerous scam artists using card decks to increase the inventory of their flea markets and used book-stores. When you first start testing card decks, be sure to check for multiple responses from the same names or addresses—you can save yourself a lot of time and trouble by eliminating troublemakers early.*

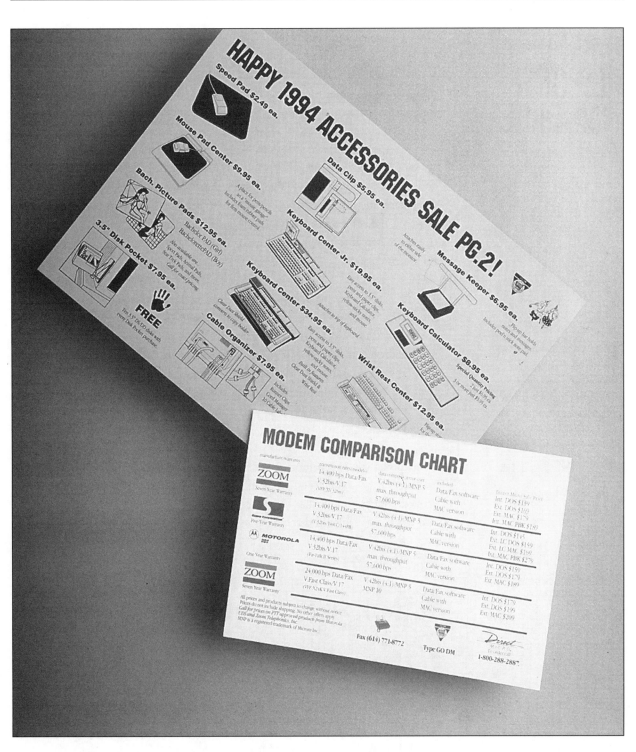

The inserts that Direct Micro puts into every CompuServe *magazine (see page 183)*

DIRECT RESPONSE MAIL ORDER

The key to mail order success is repeat buying.

! *DIRECT RESPONSE IS NOT DIRECT MAIL.*

Direct response gives the prospect an opportunity to respond to your ad in a magazine or on television.

Direct mail is a letter that goes to a targeted prospect, specifically asking for an order.

The first is passive. The second is active.

Direct response mail order is a useful tool for some guerrillas. To begin with, the startup costs are low. Countless mail order businesses have been started at the kitchen table for under $1,000. More important, mail order gives you the opportunity to establish strong, direct links with individual consumers— something that's much more difficult if you have to deal with a retailer.

Direct response is far less targeted than other direct mail techniques. You pick a medium—a magazine, a TV show, a radio program—and then run your ad and hope for the best. Inevitably, you'll reach a large number of people with no interest in your product. But when you reach the right audience with the right ad, the results can be extremely profitable. Several successful ads have run for thirty, forty, or fifty years, consistently generating predictable profits for their creators.

The reason for the low start-up cost is testing. Guerrillas know that for a small cost they can conduct a comprehensive testing program that will predict, with a high degree of certainty, whether or not a product will be profitable. A retail store can't do the same thing? Retail store owners have to cover their eyes and take the plunge right into the marketplace, hoping that their investment in rent, fixtures, cash register, and staff pays off. The direct mail marketer can build the business at her own pace and with comparatively little overhead.

Don't invest too much money without first testing your product, your price, and most importantly, your advertising. Once a product has been tested and proved a success, guerrillas can increase their sales exponentially just by launching a full-blown direct response advertising campaign.

The one disadvantage for mail order guerrillas is the lack of word of mouth.

BASICS

THE MAIL ORDER GUERRILLA

The traditional mass marketer, the opposite of a guerrilla, can be successful in mail order, focusing on reaching as many prospects as possible with one product at a time. The guerrilla, though, takes this traditionally impersonal form of sales and turns it into a relational selling process that builds a network of loyal customers who purchase a whole line of goods over a long period of time. She sells more goods to fewer customers than the traditional mass marketer, but by doing so constructs a much stronger and more profitable market base that will support her business far into the future.

Most guerrillas thrive on the recommendations of their customers, but if you sell exclusively through the mail, it's difficult to cultivate the relationship necessary to generate valuable word-of-mouth advertising. Fortunately, there are ways to overcome the barrier between the mail order seller and buyer, and the guerrilla makes use of these opportunities to build personal relationships with customers.

The key to starting the mail order relationship, though, is advertising. Some techniques for classified advertising are covered in our chapter, *Classifieds*. The rest follow:

GUIDELINES FOR EFFECTIVE DIRECT RESPONSE CLASSIFIED ADVERTISING

➤ Get the reader's attention. The headline is especially important. In his book *Mail Order: Starting Up, Making It Pay* (published by Chilton Book Company), J. Frank Brumbaugh suggests using one of the following grabbers in your headline:

The Secret Of...

Revealed...

New Discovery...

What You Should Know About...

Free! Secrets...

Is Prosperity Worth $5.75...?

Mistakes that Cost...

273 Ways to...

➤ Make sure your ad is placed under the appropriate classification. Possible categories include "Business Opportunities," "Books, Periodicals," "Mail Order Opportunities," "Of Interest to Women." These categories will vary widely depending on the publication.

➤ Keep it short and simple. Make every word in your classified ad count, especially since every word costs you money.

➤ Ask for action and make it easy for the customer to respond. The reader should be compelled to do something—ideally, to place an order. Provide a toll-free phone number.

➤ Have a promotional time limit on your mail order offer. These types of offers push prospects to act. For example, advertise that "for the next month, you can buy my book for the special price of $9.95." We recommend that time limits be tested, though, as some customers are turned off by deadlines. Test to see if it works for you.

➤ Feature a money-back guarantee. Without one, don't expect many people to take a chance on your product.

➤ Make a trial offer. Allow the prospect to try your product for free and to pay for it only if he is satisfied.

➤ Keep your copy as simple and straightforward as possible. The mail order customer wants the straight facts about the product she is buying sight unseen. She will be skeptical of flashy, hard-sell advertising.

GUIDELINES FOR DIRECT RESPONSE DISPLAY ADS

➤ Consider using both classified and display advertising, even in the same publication. Most mail order businesses confine their advertising to the classified section. You definitely want to be there because that's where people look first for mail order goods. You might, however, be able to gain an edge by exploring the potential of a well-designed display ad.

➤ In a display ad, include as many customer testimonials as you can. This is your best opportunity to use word-of-mouth marketing. Your satisfied customers don't have many forums in which to recommend your product, so do it for them.

➤ Use pictures when you can, but make sure they are relevant. The best pictures show the product in use.

➤ Negotiate for good positioning of your ad. Ideally, you want your ad to appear on the outside of a right-hand page that is situated toward the front of the magazine.

If you need to hire an ad agency to manage your marketing effort, consider hiring one that specializes in direct response. In our experience, traditional ad agencies, without the unforgiving numbers of direct response to keep them on the straight and narrow, are frequently more interested in creativity than results. Direct response agencies understand that without response, there are no clients.

Note that most agencies have a stiff minimum fee, preferring to work with larger firms. Here are several, but there are hundreds of firms working in this field. Check with the American Association of Advertising Agencies at (212) 682-2500 for a complete listing.

AGENCIES SPECIALIZING IN DIRECT RESPONSE MARKETING

To find an agency to help you market your mail order business, start by calling the American Association of Advertising Agencies at (212) 682-2500, or looking in the Adweek Agency Directory *which lists firms by location and specialty. The Yellow Pages can also be helpful, or you might start by calling the agency on the list below that is closest to you.*

Barry Blau & Partners
Greenfield Commons • 1960 Bronson Road • Fairfield, CT 06430
(203) 254-6341

Dimac Direct
757 Third Avenue • New York, NY 10017 • (212) 355-2530

Ogilvy & Mather Direct
309 West 49th St. • New York, NY 10019 • (212) 237-6000

Wunderman Cato Johnson
675 6th Ave. • New York, NY 10010 • (212) 941-3000

Bronner Slosberg Humphrey
695 Atlantic Ave. • Boston, MA 02111 • (617) 737-2020

Gillespie
191 Clarksville Rd. • Lawrenceville, NJ 08648 • (609) 799-6000

Targetcom (Chicago)
401 East Illinois • Suite 333 • Chicago, IL 60611 • (312) 822-1100

YOUR PRODUCT CAN MAKE OR BREAK YOU

Not surprisingly, you must also select the right product, or the rest of your efforts will go to waste. Mail order products where the sale to the consumer begins and ends with just one transaction must have a high margin of profit in order to pay for the advertising used to promote them. Lands' End doesn't have to make a huge profit on every pair of pants you buy because they know you'll buy a number of items from them over your lifetime.

Books and booklets make great mail order products. A self-published booklet on real estate sales might cost you 50¢ to print and could be sold for $10, $20, or even $30. One guerrilla had some success selling a $500 special report in a loose-leaf binder—which cost a total of $10 to produce. Guerrillas know that they don't always have to make a huge profit on the product they advertise, especially if the purpose of the mail order is to generate a prospect list or a loyal customer following. An accountant, for example, can sell his self-published book entitled *How to Save Money on Your Taxes* with a mail order ad in the classified section of *Money* magazine. He may sell the book for $4.95, only $1 more than he paid to have it produced. So, what's the point? This accountant knows that for every customer who orders his book, he has a name to add to his prospect list. Chances are, too, that if the customer likes the book, he'll be receptive to the idea of using the accountant's services at tax time.

You'll frequently see this technique used in card decks. The guerrilla will sell a product for very little—or even for free—just to establish a relationship with the customer.

TIPS TO SELECTING THE RIGHT PRODUCT

➤ Repeat-buy products are traditionally more profitable in the long run than one-shot fad items. Products like uniforms, clothing, or office supplies may not bring you a profit the first time the customer buys, but the key here is the repeat buyer. These products will pay off heartily on the second, third, and fourth buys. If you sell a product that people are only going to buy once, the business is dead two months after you run your last ad. One-shot successes also draw direct competition faster than you can say "bankrupt."

➤ Successful mail order businesses are based on extensive research and trial and error, but mail order is not the place to be fickle. Advertise again and again, in the same place and in the same format. You may find that of the thirty products in your inventory, only one seems to draw in a direct response ad. Once you have found a product and an ad that work together, stick with them.

➤ Do some research. Write down the names of all the publications that carry a number of mail order ads regularly. Use the Standard Rate and Data Service to compile your list. Obtain review copies and advertising rate cards from a wide variety of publications. Browse through the display pages and the classifieds. Familiarize yourself with the types of ads and the companies that you come across most often. Write away for their free offers. Eventually, you will have a good idea of the types of products that have been most successful. How will you know? You'll see them advertised again and again and again!

➤ Choose a product with high markup potential. Items with a low profit margin rarely pay in the mail order business. A good rule of thumb: A product must sell for at least three times its cost to make a decent profit in ad-driven mail order.

➤ Narrow your choice of products and test a few before committing all of your resources to just one. Run a few well-placed test ads and monitor the response. Select the product that shows the most potential. You may even find that more than one of the products you've chosen can be marketed together.

➤ Your product should fit into the logistics of the mail order business. It should be inexpensive to mail, nonbreakable, and require no special packaging or handling.

➤ Select a product through which you can expand your business down the road. Mail order often leads to catalogs. If your first product is successful, try adding another to your line. Continue to advertise the original product in the classifieds, but also offer your free catalog to anyone who orders. The catalog then becomes the basis for a continued relationship with the customer and for repeat buys.

➤ Overseas markets are a good place to look for products. Try scouting trade journals from England. Adapt the product to fit the American market and test it. Imported items are often unique and specialized, and have been proven winners in the mail order market.

SUGGESTED PRODUCT CATEGORIES FOR MAIL ORDER

➤ **Food and Drink**
Stick with specialty items that can't be readily obtained in the retail market. For example, salmon is the specialty of the Seattle area and people all over the country order it from vendors in Washington because it isn't available where they live.

➤ **Books**
Self-published books are often sold through mail order. How-to and self-help books are particularly profitable mail order items. Reselling books published by others doesn't offer enough margin for most businesses.

➤ **Correspondence Courses**
Mail order was made for the correspondence course. What better way to sell education by mail than through the mail!

➤ **Clothing**
Specialty clothing is a big seller through mail order. One company sells shoes to women with large feet and another sells custom-made mens' suits imported from Hong Kong.

➤ **Sporting Goods**

Golf balls, specialized performance-related products, and camping equipment are all proven successes. Stick with a product people will need to buy more than once, or one that is not readily available at the local sporting goods store.

➤ **Gardening Supplies**

Bulbs, tools, and gardening books are proven winners.

➤ **Hobbyist Information and Supplies**

The best businesses are irresistible to a small niche. If you sell the best hand-tied flies in the world, fishermen will beat a path to your door. Find a niche, become indispensable, and reap the profits for a long time.

PRICING

Test your pricing. When doing so, however, set aside your assumptions. You may find that a higher price works better than a lower one. Make sure you do your math.

Unlike a retail environment, mail order makes it easy to test pricing. Run two ads and see which pulls better. Keep adjusting your offer (maybe free shipping makes a difference) until you find the ideal combination.

FULFILLMENT

Once you have your product and your advertising campaign, you'll need to decide how to deliver your product to the customer. You can do it yourself, or you can have a fulfillment house do it for you. If you like, your fulfillment house will set up an around-the-clock toll-free number that will be answered by operators who will take orders over the phone, charge them to the customer's credit card, send out the product, and send you a check. When looking for a fulfillment house, make sure you find out exactly what services they provide before hiring them. Some provide all of the services mentioned above, while others simply take orders and let you handle mailing out the product. Know what you need before you start looking for a service.

While fulfillment houses remove many hassles, they add to your costs and remove a level of control. By all means, interview a number of firms, and if you choose to hire one, watch them very carefully. After all, you've worked hard to acquire a customer, and one error in fulfillment can lose them forever.

! *DON'T GET*
■ *BURNED.*

It's easy to be seduced by a fulfillment house, but be vigilant. Here are a few ways you can get hurt:

- *The phone isn't answered promptly or in a way that makes you happy. Test the service regularly.*

- *Orders aren't shipped promptly.*

- *Credit cards aren't processed correctly.*

- *Orders and returns are not clearly accounted for.*

Constantly monitor your fulfillment house and all parties will be happier.

If you choose to use an outside firm to fulfill your product orders, add a personal touch to the packaging. Always include a thank you letter, your catalog, and news of any special promotions or sales that you may be having. The package should be used as an advertising vehicle to encourage repeat buying.

FULFILLMENT HOUSES

The companies below all take orders and provide product fulfillment. Try looking in the Yellow Pages if you want a firm near you, or call one of the companies below.

Tylie Jones & Associates
3519 West Pacific Ave • Burbank, CA 91505 • (800) 922-0662

Promotional Distribution Services Worldwide
82 South Street • Hopkinton, MA 01748 • (508) 435-0001

American Fulfillment Packaging Corporation
440 New Haven Ave. • Milford, CT 06460 • (203) 877-8969

ICT Response
800 Town Center Drive • Langhorne, PA 19047 • (215) 757-0200

American Industries
300 McCann St. • Nashville, TN 37210 • (615) 242-0931

SimTel Communications
31220 LaBaya Dr., Suite 254 • Westlake Village, CA 91362
(818) 706-1921

Motivational Fulfillment & Packaging Services
5959 Triumph St. • Commerce, CA 90040 • (213) 723-0997

USA 800, Inc.
6616 Raytown Rd. • Kansas City, MO 64133 • (800) 821-7539

BACK END BUSINESS

All of the business you get after the initial sale is called back end business. For most companies, the profit made from back end business is far greater than that made from the front end.

The cost of acquiring a mail order customer is very high. The cost of selling additional products can be quite low if you've chosen your product line well. Once someone buys from you, make sure you do everything you can to turn

Ted Nicholas, in his book The Golden Mailbox, *suggests not using a P.O. box in your direct mail advertising. Post office boxes are impersonal. Give prospects a real address to which they can mail their order. Street addresses are traceable and lead the customer to believe that you are on the up-and-up, and have nothing to hide.*

them into repeat buyers. Mail order pros refer to this as the back end. There are many businesses, like book clubs, that make 100% of their profit from the back end.

Track your customers by which products they buy, how often they buy, and how much money they spend. Follow up their purchases with more mailings. Reward them for buying by sending them exclusive offers, coupons, and a copy of your catalog. Personalize the relationship by sending reminders when it's time to reorder.

MAIL ORDER RESOURCES

Mail Order...Starting Up, Making It Pay
by J. Frank Brumbaugh • Published by Chilton Book Company

Getting into the Mail Order Business
by Julian L. Simon • Published by McGraw-Hill, Inc.

MAIL ORDER BRAINSTORMS

Do you offer goods or services that appeal to a targeted audience? Describe the most specific mailing list you can imagine ("Left-handed horseback riding instructors," for example) then see if you can rent it from a broker.

_____

_____

_____

_____

_____

_____

_____

_____

_____

_____

DIRECT MAIL

A one-to-one, inexpensive means of pinpointing and reaching prospects.

Direct mail is a perfect guerrilla tool. It is targeted, easy to test, and low cost. It allows you to contact prospects directly, make your pitch, and invite them to become customers. Big budgets have no advantage inside the mailbox.

Unlike direct mail giants like Lillian Vernon or L.L. Bean, your goal isn't to stuff a catalog into every mailbox in America. Instead, by focusing your energy and dollars on a very small, highly targeted population, you can translate postage into big dollars.

Direct mail allows David to compete with Goliath. It's the great equalizer. Big non-guerrillas don't have the patience to attract one customer at a time. While they're worrying about market segments and media plans, you can focus on Tess Deutsch, who lives in suburban Illinois.

The entire key to direct mail success revolves around testing. You must constantly test both the successes and the failures. Send out two different offers and monitor which offer gets the most response. Try different pricing scales, or different order forms. Direct mail is the best way to study your market.

THE ADVANTAGES OF DIRECT MAIL OVER OTHER ADVERTISING MEDIA

➤ You can measure results more accurately.

➤ You can be as expansive or concise as you wish.

➤ You can zero in on almost any target audience.

➤ You can personalize your marketing.

➤ You have unlimited opportunities for testing.

➤ You can develop repeat sales to proven customers.

➤ You can compete with, and even beat, the giants.

There are three key elements to consider when using direct mail: the list, the offer, and the package. Of the three, the list is by far the most important. Choosing the right list is the critical difference between success and failure in direct mail.

LIST MANIA!

Most people don't realize just how scientific and targeted the list business has become. For a cost of less than ten cents a name, you can buy mailing labels for members of an unbelievable number of groups.

List rentals are a major source of income for many publications and direct mailers. By offering their lists to other marketers, (at a cost ranging from $50 to $100 per thousand) list managers are able to generate substantial income. As the market clamors for more specialized lists, the managers respond. Here are some examples:

➤ Women in Manhattan with a license to carry a gun

➤ Doctors who have purchased medical stat kits by mail

➤ Subscribers to *Design News* who live in downtown Chicago

➤ Librarians at junior colleges

➤ Islamic families living in Wyoming with more than two children

Don't forget to start with your own customer list (see *Customer Mailing Lists*). It is the most effective list you can use because your best sales prospects are your existing customers. Then use rented lists to expand your market.

FOCUS LIKE A LASER

Non-guerrillas are preoccupied with volume. They buy names by the millions, and don't use the specialized lists that are ideal for the guerrilla who knows that mailing to 100 people who have an interest in her product is much more effective than mailing to 1,000 unqualified leads.

Your first step is to browse the SRDS (Standard Rate and Data Service—see the resource list at the end of this chapter) direct mail catalog. This massive book contains more than 10,000 different mailing lists. These lists allow you to carefully select exactly which group of people you'll be marketing to.

If you can define the precise market you're selling to (and you ought to be able to do that in your sleep) then you can find a mailing list that's ideal. There are subscribers to magazines, members of clubs, purchasers of similar products, demographic groups, and more.

While SRDS is an excellent idea source, they don't rent lists. You should probably rent your list through a broker. List brokers are paid by the list managers, so there's no charge to you. Like travel agents, their advice and experience is usually worth the investment.

In addition to these commercially available lists, guerrillas often barter their own customer lists for less well-known but often more effective lists. A carpenter could trade his customer list with a plumber, or a travel agent might

like a family member and remembered his name.

Joe's best innovation was his monthly card campaign. If you had ever bought a car from Joe Gerard, every single month for the rest of your life you received a greeting card from him. Joe used these opportunities to remind you that he cared about you and, not incidentally, to remind you that he was the person you should buy your next car from.

Sound silly? It worked. On any given day during the peak of his career, Joe would sell as many as 10 cars. Most car salesmen don't do that in two weeks. More than half of all of his sales were to people he'd already sold at least one car to—a pretty easy sale to make after you've done all that preparation. Many others were referrals.

This low-tech, low-cost marketing technique demonstrates that enthusiasm and a little creativity alone can make a successful guerrilla.

One company we know mailed Christmas cards in May, just ahead of a postal rate increase. Each card showed Benjamin Franklin, our first postmaster, and the quote, "A penny saved is a penny earned." The result: national PR and a high response.

buy a list of soon-to-be-married couples from a caterer. Even if there are only 50 names on a mailing list, it can turn into a significant asset.

When you rent a list, you're usually granted only one use. However, if the person you mail to responds to you, you own that name. As you rent and use lists, keep careful records of which lists perform better than others and be certain to segregate the people who respond from those who don't.

Lists get stale very quickly—as many as 20% of the people on a list move every year, so make sure your list is as up-to-date as possible. Once you find a list that works for you, you should periodically contact the list manager for the latest additions to the list—this new flow of names is virtually guaranteed to do as well as the last batch.

Too many guerrillas focus on the creative aspect of the package without worrying about the list. The list is king.

MAILING LIST BROKERS

Abelow Response
181 S. Franklin Ave. • Valley Stream, NY 11581 • (516) 791-7900

American Business Lists
5711 South 86th Circle • Omaha, NE 68127 • (402) 331-7169

AZ Marketing Services
31 River Rd. • Cos Cob, CT 06807 • (203) 629-8088

Direct Media
200 Pemberwick Rd. • Greenwich, CT 06830 • (203) 532-1000

The Kaplan Agency
1200 High Ridge Rd. • Stamford, CT 06905 • (203) 968-8800

Kleid Company
530 Fifth Ave., 17th Floor • New York, NY 10036 • (212) 819-3400

Leon Henry
455 Central Ave. • Scarsdale, NY 10583 • (914) 723-3176
brokers card deck lists

Mal Dunn & Associates
Hardscrabble Rd. • Croton Falls, NY 10519 • (914) 277-5558

When planning a direct mail campaign, remember to follow the commonly known 60-30-10 rule. Sixty percent of direct mail success lies in using the right mailing list; thirty percent depends on your making the right offer; ten percent depends upon your creative package.

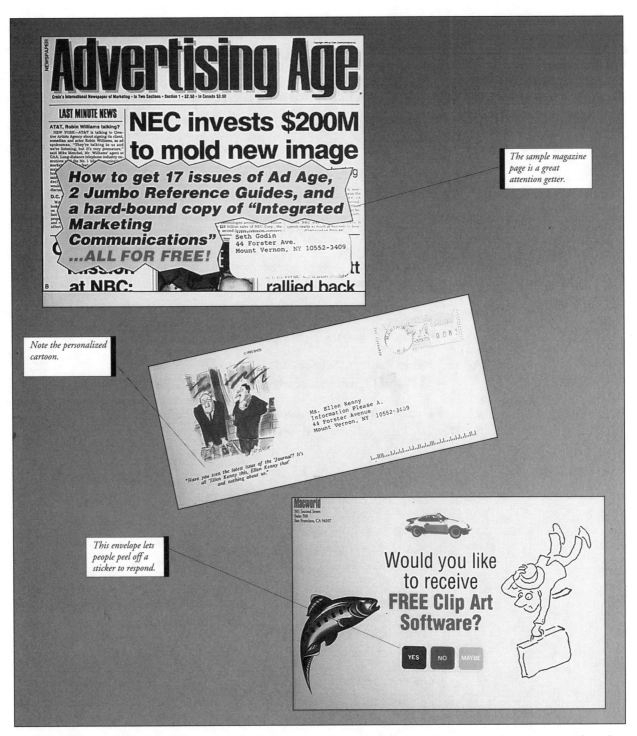

Three great direct mail envelopes. One way to tell if a campaign is a success it to see how long it's been running. These three campaigns have been running for years.

Mease and Associates created a direct mail campaign for Beechcraft, a manufacturer of business jets. They sent a small crate containing a real apple and a plastic apple to a group of CEOs. They invited the CEOs to compare apples to apples, or in this case, business jets to business jets. CEOs who responded by allowing a Beechcraft representative to make a presentation to them received an entire crate of apples. The campaign generated a response rate of 6.35%—quite a feat considering how hard it is to reach top execs.

Media Horizons
94 East Ave. • Norwalk, CT 06851 • (203) 857-0770

Millard Group
10 Vose Farm Rd. • Peterborough, NH 03458 • (603) 924-9262

Names and Addresses
4096 Commercial Ave. • Northbrook, IL 60062 • (708) 272-7933

Qualified Lists Corp.
135 Bedford Rd. • Armonk, NY 10504 • (914) 273-6606

MAILING LIST COMPANIES

In addition to brokering other people's lists (like the brokers listed above), these companies compile and sell their own unique mailing lists.

American List Counsel
88 Orchard Road, CN-5219 • Princeton, NJ 08540 • (800) 526-3973

Rubin Response Services, Inc.
1111 Plaza Drive • Schaumburg, IL 60173 • (708) 619-9800

Database America Companies
100 Paragon Drive • Montvale, NJ 07645 • (201) 476-2300

Pentron Lists
1100 Superior Ave. • Cleveland, OH 44114 • (216) 696-7000
Specializes in lists of subscibers to business, industrial, and technical publications

Quality Lists
Dept. EN-144-Wholesale List Selection
P.O. Box 6060 • Miller Place, NY 11764 • (516) 744-7289

MAILING LIST RESOURCES

Standard Rate and Data Service
3004 Glenview Rd. • Wilmette, IL 60091 • (708) 256-6067

Directory of Mailing List Companies
Published by Todd Publications
18 N. Greenbush Rd. • West Nyack, NY 10994 • (914) 358-6213
This book lists names, addresses, and telephone numbers of hundreds of mailing list brokers.

1993 Lifestyle Zip Code Analyst

Published by the Standard Rate and Data Service (SRDS)

1,669 pages of market analysis organized by zip code and covering the top 25 metro markets and counties with populations of 150,000 or more. Markets are profiled by lifestyles, demographics, and economics. Direct mail lists targeted to each lifestyle profile are also included.

The Direct Marketing Market Place

Published by the Standard Rate and Data Service

5201 Old Orchard Rd. • Skokie, IL 60077 • (708) 256-6067

A Standard Rate and Data Service reference book

Direct Mail List Rates and Data

Published by the Standard Rate and Data Service

5201 Old Orchard Rd. • Skokie, IL 60077 • (708) 256-6067

Contains descriptions of over 12,000 mailing lists available to rent

THE OFFER

Every direct mail piece invites the recipient to take action, even if it's only to call for a free estimate or a free sample. The goal is to offer the prospect something so irresistible he or she will immediately order it.

For expensive items or services, offering a free estimate or sample is nearly always more effective than trying to sell a product in the letter. You can overcome fear and answer questions better in person, so getting an appointment is probably in your best interests.

People often test the creative, but don't spent a lot of time on the offer. While you test the color of the paper, the size of the package, and the use of a photo versus a drawing, test the offer you are making. This is seemingly the simplest part of the three elements in a direct mail package, but if your offer isn't effective you're guaranteed to fail.

SPECIAL OFFER ALTERNATIVES

➤ Offer a 30-day free trial

➤ Advertise a free gift with purchase

➤ Allow installment payments

➤ Sell your product for a *higher* than retail price

Janet Hughes and Associates, marketing consultants, wages a very effective direct mail campaign. Every month they mail out a piece to prospects and existing customers that highlights a different aspect of the services Janet Hughes provides. On one mailer, the prospect is asked to fill out and fax back a brief questionnaire. They have been running the campaign for over two years and receive an average of 25 calls per quarter in response. Eleven or twelve of those inquiries usually turn into paying clients for the firm.

Direct mail piece sent out by Tops Appliance Stores. The mailer stresses customer service, special buyers' club card, the word "FREE," and a guarantee.

- ➤ Sell your product for a *lower* than retail price
- ➤ Offer to send your product by COD
- ➤ Give people the choice of being billed later
- ➤ Offer people a free gift for allowing you to set up a demonstration

THE CREATIVE ELEMENT

The most celebrated part of direct mail selling is creating the package. This begins with the stamps and appearance of the mailing package you use and includes the paper, copy, layout, and design of the piece itself. While your list and your offer are far more important than the creative, this is the part you can haggle over forever. Here are some ideas that will help you create better materials.

SUGGESTED ENVELOPE TEASERS

If you are doing a large-scale direct mailing to a broad audience, you may want to use an envelope teaser to grab attention. After all, if your envelope isn't opened, it doesn't matter how wonderful your creative or your offer are. Here are a few examples:
- ➤ "Free gift enclosed"
- ➤ "Money-saving offer inside"
- ➤ "Wealth-building secrets for the nineties"
- ➤ "Private information for your eyes only"
- ➤ "Did you know that you can double your profits?"
- ➤ "What every business like yours needs to know"
- ➤ "How to add new profits for only six cents a day!"
- ➤ "See inside for exciting details about _____"
- ➤ "Read what's in store for you—this week only!"

There are a host of different techniques that you can use to make your envelope jump out at your prospect. Brightly colored envelopes grab attention. White is always the safest for business-related mail. Red and blue are time-honored favorites, but yellow, orange, and pink are on the rise. Oversized addressing stimulates the unconscious pleasure that people get from seeing their name in print. The bigger, the better. Take a look:

There is an advantage to keeping your mailings small. Guerrillas have had great success with smaller, more tarketed mailings that get a higher response rate.

If you can reach 50 super-targeted prospects with a personal letter and convert 2% into customers, you just gained a new customer for less than $20!

Guerrillas do direct mail with real stamps (as opposed to a bulk mail indicia), hand-addressed envelopes, and personalized letters.

John Polstein
123 Main Street
Davis, CA 12345

**John Polstein
123 Main Street
Davis, CA 12345**

A white business-size (#10) envelope with no return address is intriguing and gets opened.

Depending on the scale of your mailing, you can take advantage of the personal touch. Use real stamps instead of a postage meter. Hand address the envelope. Do a custom mail merge that says something special about each customer in the opening paragraph. Insert a handwritten Post-it.

HOW TO GET A 22% RESPONSE RATE

Our favorite campaign of all time involved a target market of 1,000 people to whom a company was trying to sell an expensive product. In order for the project to succeed, the company needed to receive at least a 10% response rate on the mailing.

They started by using Federal Express to deliver the letter. While using Fedex in small quantities can be expensive, they're happy to negotiate a special rate for anyone willing to mail 1,000 letters on one day. In this case, they charged about $6 per letter.

Inside, the recipient found a laser-printed letter mail-merged to include their name, address, and firm. Their name and the name of the firm were mentioned several times in the letter. There was a handwritten Post-it as well. Every package was followed up with a personal phone call.

Nearly 100% of the respondents opened the letter. More than 50% took the salesman's follow-up call. And an incredible 22% of the respondents (220 people) ordered the product and sent in a check for $1,000. As you can see, the cost of the mailing was tiny compared to the amount of revenue it generated.

If you sell a product or service that is *very* attractive to a small group of people, consider testing a similar campaign.

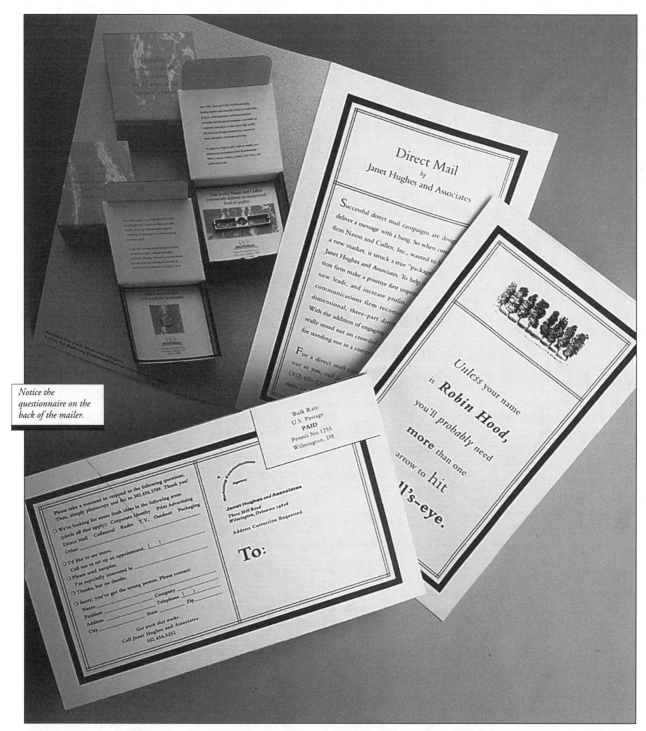

Notice the questionnaire on the back of the mailer.

Samples of the monthly mailing sent out by Janet Hughes and Associates (see page 201). The firm receives eleven or twelve new clients from the mailing every quarter.

Source: Janet Hughes and Associates • Three Mill Rd. • Wilmington, DE 19806 • (302) 656-5252

A car dealership consultant sent a brand new Hot Wheels car with his mailing to grab the attention of the sales manager. Profits from one customer covered the cost of the entire mailing.

ENVELOPE RESOURCES

The Yellow Pages is a good place to start when you are looking for a company that specializes in printing direct mail envelopes. If you need some design advice or direct mail campaign development, try calling one of the companies below.

Tension Envelope Corporation
819 East 19th Street • Kansas City, MO 64108 • (816) 471-3800

Tension envelope specializes in designing and producing envelopes for direct mail campaigns. Call them for a free envelope idea kit and a free fifteen-minute envelope analysis.

Dimac Direct
#1 Corporate Woods Dr. • Bridgeton, MO 63044 • (314) 344-8000

Transo Envelope Co.
P.O. Box 3006 • Glendale, CA 91221 • (818) 240-8383

EIGHT RULES OF THUMB FOR DIRECT MAIL MARKETING

➤ The most important element is the right list.

➤ Make it easy for the recipient to take action.

➤ Letters almost always outpull mailing packages with no letters.

➤ The best buyers are those who have bought by mail before, a rapidly growing number.

➤ Do anything to get your envelope opened. Unopened mail is another word for trash.

➤ Keeping good records is paramount.

➤ Testimonials improve response rate.

➤ Remember that nothing is as simple as it seems.

! MAIL VERSUS THE PHONE

When a customer calls your toll free number to order, it costs you just under a dollar and gets you an order on the spot. If the prospect has questions, you can answer them. If they need other products, you can sell them now.

When a prospect returns a postcard, it can take up to two weeks, it frequently contains innacurate information (or is missing critical data) and it leaves no opportunity for add-on products.

What's your reason for not having a toll free number?

TEN EASY WAYS TO IMPROVE YOUR BUSINESS REPLY CARD (BRC)

Including a business reply card in your mailing is a good way to encourage response. Sometimes people won't respond to a direct mail piece because it's too much work for them either to call you on the phone or stuff something into an envelope, address and mail it. It's easy if all they have to do to respond is check off a box on your reply card and stick it in the mail. Be careful though, because if you make it too easy, you may get a lot of people responding who are not very serious about buying your product. You'll have to spend a lot of time weeding them out as you follow up on your mailing. If you want to set up a business reply account, call your local post office.

➤ **State the Offer Clearly**

Once people are ready to order, they want you to cut to the chase. Don't disappoint them. Let them know what's for sale by getting to the point.

➤ **Avoid Writing Like a Lawyer**

A lot of BRC card copy often sounds stilted and legalistic. Try to make your copy sound like it was written by an accessible human being.

➤ **Write with Energy and Personality**

When you are writing selling copy, keep the benefits in the reader's face.

➤ **Stress that the Offer Is Risk-Free**

Restate your guarantee on the BRC.

➤ **Include Checkboxes**

If there are ordering options, checkboxes are a must. If there are no options, put a pre-checked box in front of the "YES."

➤ **Remember to Punch Up the 800 number.**

You hope that readers will call rather than send a coupon (you shorten the sales cycle and strike while the iron is hot). That's why you must say, "To order now, call 800-123-1234" right on the coupon.

➤ **Don't Put Important Information on the Reverse Side**

The back of your BRC can have a supportive message, but don't put the key elements of the offer there. Make certain that everything important goes on the front.

➤ **Use Visuals to Spur Action and Guide the Reader**

A well-placed red arrow can point to key copy (and higher return rates).

➤ **Attach a Stub**

BRCs often get better results when there's a stub perfed along the edge of the card. What should go back there? How about a copy of the money-back guarantee that the buyer can retain for her records?

➤ **Give Your Business Reply Card an Appropriate Title.**

Instead of calling your BRC an "order form" or "order card," try "action card," or "preferred customer upgrade card."

Reprinted with permission from The Levison Letter: Action Ideas For Better Marketing Communications. *Published by Ivan Levison & Associates • 14 Los Cerros Dr. • Greenbrae, CA 94904 • (415) 461-0672*

TWELVE HEADLINES YOU MIGHT USE TO PROMOTE A LIGHT BULB

As with most types of advertising, the headline has to grab 'em. Here are some example headlines you could use if you were selling light bulbs. They can be adapted to almost any type of product and give you an idea of how to sell the features of your product in the headline.

➤ News. "New Light Bulbs Last 30% Longer."

➤ Featured Benefit. "Save up to 30% on lighting costs."

➤ Boastful. "Tests show ABC Bulbs last longest."

➤ Command. "Try the light bulb preferred by Fortune 500 firms."

➤ Emotional. "Will your lights work when your family needs them most?"

➤ Trick. "Thomas Edison wouldn't believe it."

➤ Curiosity. "How often do you change?"

➤ Slogan. "ABC Bulbs put you in a good light."

➤ Offer. "Try ABC light bulbs free for 30 days."

➤ Information. "Most people spend more money than they need to to light their homes."

➤ Testimonial. "How I cut my lighting costs by 30%."

➤ Prediction. "Five years from now, all light bulbs will be made like ABC bulbs."

Source: The Golden Mailbox *by Ted Nicholas*

One personalized mailing included a piece that looked like a full-page newspaper ad with a Post-it stuck on it. Handwritten on the Post-it was "Daniel, try it. This works!—N."

WHAT TO INCLUDE IN YOUR DIRECT MAIL LETTER

➤ Describe the problem your prospects face.

➤ Tell why that problem won't go away. Add that it may become more bothersome.

➤ Tell the benefit your product or service provides that solves or eases this problem.

➤ Describe how easy and affordable your solution is.

➤ Back up that statement with testimonials from current customers.

➤ Now that your prospects see and believe your benefit, start pushing the deal. Tell them how much previous customers have gladly paid for this product or service, and then tell how much lower the price is in your current offering—if they act now.

➤ Sweeten the deal. Offer an additional free bonus product if the prospects order soon.

➤ Give prospects your personal promise that the product or service will provide the benefits you're describing in the letter.

➤ Add your money-back, no questions asked guarantee for additional reassurance.

➤ Stress that action must be taken now. Tell prospects that there is a time limit on this exceptional offer.

➤ Tell what prospects will lose if they pass up purchasing your product or service.

➤ As a postscript to your letter, you can repeat the benefit or the offer, or sweeten the deal even more. Often it's best at that point just to encourage action. Tell prospects to send no money now but to make sure their name and address are correct on the mailing label. Ask the prospect to peel the label off, place it on the order coupon, and mail it in the enclosed business reply envelope.

FIVE PRACTICAL TIPS FOR GETTING THE MOST FROM YOUR POSTSCRIPT

➤ Don't be afraid of writing a long P.S. If you're communicating important news or information and you can keep the reader with you, don't worry about length. The postscript is the part of your letter that is most likely to get read, so use it.

➤ Make sure the tone is personal. The P.S. is the place to add some color and personality. Don't use this valuable space to communicate dry, factual information. Loosen up and write with a little energy.

➤ Use underlinings or a second color. To make your postscript jump out, use boldface, italics, or even a typeface that simulates handwriting. Make it pop.

➤ Avoid a P.P.S. Moderation is the key to everything, and postscripts are no exception. A P.P.S. cheapens the letter and screams "junk mail."

Source: The Golden Mailbox *by Ted Nicholas*

Slap a dollar on the next personal letter you send out. It only costs a dollar and it makes quite an impression. We use spray glue (rubber cement in a can) to apply a thin film of glue along the top of the bill. This removes easily from the letter and the bill is still usable.

Be sure to use only brand new dollars. And make a point of mentioning the dollar in the body of the letter. (We sent one to a government agency by mistake and received a letter— with the bill—pointing out that they couldn't accept it. Of course, it costs more *than a dollar to return it to us!)*

💡 *The Vantec Can*
Vantec in Milwaukee, WI, sells a unique service to the direct mail marketer. They will print up an eye-catching four color label, wrap it around a small can (either 4.5" or 6" in height), stick your mailer inside and deliver it by third class mail to your prospect or customer list. Vantec will also send a four-color detached address card so the label will not have to be affixed directly to the can.

This is a great attention-getting mailer, especially because you can put something inside the can. Include a sample of your product or a premium giveaway item. Vantec sends out their samples with a flyer and a piece of candy inside.

Using a supplier like Vantec makes sense if you are mailing to more than a couple thousand addresses. The minimum order is 10,000 at a unit price of just over a dollar per each 4" can. If you are doing a smaller mailing, you can do this yourself by printing a four color label and manually affixing it to a coffee can.

Contact Vantec at (800) 475-0660.

TED NICHOLAS'S COPY MISTAKE CHECKLIST

➤ **Not Doing Enough Research**

Have I looked at the competition carefully enough? Have I looked at the needs that my customers or clients really have and determined that the product meets *their* needs?

➤ **Not Beginning the Sales Letter or Ad with the Biggest Benefit the Product Offers the Prospect**

Writers sometimes try to lead with an argument for why the prospect needs the product or service being offered. Meet needs that your prospects know they have. Don't try to "create" needs by trying to convince prospects they have needs they aren't aware of. Another problem is beginning the ad or letter with a "me" message. No one cares about your company. People will read your material only when you tell how you can meet their needs.

➤ **Not Ending the Ad or Letter by Requesting Specific Action**

You want your prospect to make an order or inquiry. You need to specifically ask for what you want, and give your prospect instructions on how to fulfill your request. Don't be modest. If your prospects have read the ad or letter to the end, they must be interested. Tell them what to do about it.

➤ **Taking Too Long to Introduce the Product or Service**

Let people know within the first eight or ten lines what you are selling. You don't have to detail the offer at that time, but you'll lose people if you don't tell them quickly what it is you have to offer.

DIRECT MAIL PUBLICATIONS AND RESOURCES

Direct Marketing Association (DMA)
11 W. 42nd Street • New York, NY 10036-8096 • (212) 768-7277

Members of the DMA can call the association to obtain examples of effective types of direct mail pieces. The DMA also publishes the annual Statistical Fact Book. *It provides extremely useful statistical information for direct marketers.*

DM News
19 W. 21st Street • New York, NY 10010 • (212) 741-2095

Direct Marketing Magazine
Hoke Communications • 224 Seventh Avenue • Garden City, NY 11530 • (516) 746-6700

Direct **Magazine**
911 Hope Street • P.O. Box 4949 • Stamford, CT 06907 • (203) 358-9900

Advertising Age
Crain Communications • 740 Rush Street North • Chicago, IL 60611
(312) 649-5200

The Golden Mailbox
by Ted Nicholas • Published by Enterprise Dearborn

Mail Order Know-How
by Cecil C. Hoge, Sr. • Published by Ten Speed Press

Mailing List Strategies
by Rose Harper • Published by McGraw-Hill

Mail Order Magic
by Herman Holtz • Published by McGraw-Hill

Direct Mail Copy That Sells
by Herschell Gordon Lewis • Published by Prentice Hall

Revolution in the Mailbox
by Mal Warwich • Published by Strathmore Press

Do-It-Yourself Direct Marketing
by Mark S. Bacon • Published by John Wiley & Sons

Mark S. Bacon breaks direct mail down into all of its elements and takes you through a step-by-step description of each. Dozens of successful direct mail pieces are used to show the secrets of direct mail success for the small business owner.

BYPASSING THE POSTAL SERVICE

Alternate delivery companies deliver products in polybags that are hung from the customer's doorknob. Catalog makers, magazine publishers, and newspaper companies are all jumping on the alternate delivery bandwagon. Through alternate delivery, publications can offer ride-along opportunities for their advertisers while reducing their mailing costs. Numerous advertising partnerships are fostered through alternate delivery, as there is virtually no limit to the number of items that can be placed in the same polybag.

Rates for alternate delivery depend on the size of the insert or product sample and the number of households reached. For example,. sending a one half ounce piece in a ride-along (5 $\frac{1}{2}$" by 8 $\frac{1}{2}$") with Alternate Postal Delivery will cost about $100 per thousand delivered, with a minimum delivery of 50,000.

Family Circle *magazine ran a special promotional section on the cold and flu season targeted to cold weather regions. They offered advertisers in the special section the opportunity to include samples of their products with the 25,000 issues of the magazine that were delivered by alternate methods. The advertisers had another chance (in addition to their ad in the magazine) to reach a very targeted segment of the market and the whole package was delivered in its own separate polybag.*

Who said you need to use an envelope? The postal service will deliver mylar pouches, Chinese food takeout containers, wooden crates, transparent portfolios, canoe paddles, or hubcaps. The goal is to get the prospect to pay attention. While we don't recommend it, we know one marketer who sent a live chicken to a prospect by courier. He saved the chicken from the butcher, but wreaked havoc and lost the sale.

Alternate delivery reduces postage costs on large mailings, but unlike tradiitional second and third class mail, alternate delivery can guarantee delivery dates and cut down on undelivered mail. It's a low-cost way to put samples, coupons, or promotional items in the hands of prospective customers. Crayola delivered their new washable crayons to mothers, and Minute Rice used alternate delivery to put their recipe books directly in the consumers' hands.

Ride-along advertising opportunities with major magazines and catalogs that use alternate delivery are also on the rise. Hershey's chocolate and Pantene hair products are among dozens of advertisers that have included product literature and samples as ride-alongs with *McCall's* magazine.

ALTERNATE DELIVERY COMPANIES

Publishers Express
1850 Parkway Pl., Suite 920 • Marietta, GA 30067 • (404) 429-4500

Alternate Postal Delivery
1 Ionia SW, Suite 300 • Grand Rapids, MI 49503 • (800) 438-9430

GUERRILLAS ALWAYS TEST

No one knows why one direct mail letter works better than another. But, unlike most things in this world, it's easy to tell. Either your direct mail letter works, or it doesn't.

We know that long letters do better than short ones, that letters received on Tuesday do the best, and that adding a P.S. always increases response. None of these facts necessarily makes sense, and the only way they were discovered was by testing them.

When sending direct mail, a guerrilla always tests. Every mailing should contain at least one test—larger mailings should contain more. Yet many smaller direct mail marketers don't test as often as they should. While it seems obvious, this example points out how important testing can be: If you mail 100,000 letters with a 2% response rate, you will receive 2,000 orders. If you can increase the rate to 2.1%, you'll get 100 more orders. If your profit per order is $100, that's $10,000.

Test your copy, the size of the envelope, the type of stamp, the color of the ink, the type style you use, the photos—everything. There are only three rules you need to follow when testing:

➤ Run tests on a random distribution of the same list. Don't test one mailing in Denver and the other in Reno.

➤ Test only one thing at a time. If you change copy and color at once, you'll never know which made the difference.

➤ Test on at least 200 names at a time. You probably don't need to test on more than 400 names—statistically, it's overkill.

To keep track of your tests, put a little 3 digit code on the bottom of your coupon. In fact, make sure the code is on something the recipient will have in her hand when she calls your 800 number to order. Instruct your operators to ask for the code. It will make it easy for you to figure out which calls came from where.

Testing works on more than direct mail. Some cable TV stations will let you test two ads during the same time slot (dividing by neighborhood) and many newspapers and magazines offer different editions for comparison. Most of these are geographically based, so the test isn't 100% pure, but it's better than nothing.

If you're not testing, you're leaving money on the table.

ELEVEN ELEMENTS OF A DIRECT MAIL CAMPAIGN YOU CAN TEST

Maximize your testing opportunities. In each mailing you do, run as many tests as your audience and your logistics allow. Remember, you can't test a mailing to different audiences. As long as you have at least 250 people in a group that is demographically similar to your control group, then you can run a test. Don't make the mistake of testing one offer to a wealthy zip code and another offer to a poor one—your results will be skewed by the different income levels.

Here are several elements you can test:
➤ Color vs. black and white printing

➤ Motivators

➤ Price of your product

➤ Length of letter

➤ First class vs. third class

> **!** *It's important that you learn a lot about postal rates before you design your direct mail piece. You don't want to design something that is too expensive to mail. Also, look into bulk mail rates and second class mail to see if you qualify for either discounted rate.*
>
> *The United States Postal Service has all the information you need regarding postal rates, zip codes, size requirements, insurance and registration of mail, and more. Call them at (800) 222-1811.*

Direct mail Christmas card mailed out by Framer's Workshop and designed by 226 Design.

Source: 226 Design • 1440 East Missouri Ave., Suite 110 • Phoenix, AZ 85014 • (602) 230-0226

➤ Your mailing lists

➤ Envelope color and treatment

➤ Means of ordering

➤ Number of enclosures in your envelope

➤ Postage paid vs. buyer pays return postage vs. toll-free number

➤ One-step vs. two-step conversion (Do you ask people to buy from you immediately, or do you ask them to call you to receive a brochure, or to set up a meeting, and then ask them to buy from you?).

Source: How to Make Your Advertising Twice as Effective at Half the Cost *by Herschell Gordon Lewis*

DIRECT MAIL TERMS YOU SHOULD KNOW

ALTERNATE DELIVERY—a delivery method that bypasses the postal system. Alternate delivery companies will deliver your advertising piece directly to the prospect, usually in a polybag hung on the doorknob.

BOUNCE BACK COUPON—a coupon included in a direct mail piece that is redeemed when the customer mails it back to you.

BUSINESS REPLY CARD (BRC)—a form of direct mail response. A BRC is a card enclosed in a direct mail package (letter, card deck, insert, etc.) that the recipient can fill out and send back to the advertiser, responding in some way to the offer being made. Typically, BRCs have a postage paid address so all the customer has to do is fill it out and drop it in a mailbox.

CO-OP MAILING—several advertisers mail their direct mail inserts together in one envelope. Val-Pak and Carol Wright are examples of co-op mailings.

ONE-STEP—a mailing that asks the prospect to buy the product. The goal is to have people respond by buying the product, as opposed to a two-step offer that generates leads. People respond to a two-step mailing by either writing or calling for more information about the product.

RIDE-ALONG—a direct mail advertising piece that is inserted into a package that someone else is already mailing out. For example, the product samples that arrive with your favorite magazine are ride-alongs.

SELF-MAILERS—a direct mail piece that, when folded, forms its own envelope. They are usually stapled closed and cost less money to produce than a typical direct mail piece with a separate envelope.

STATEMENT STUFFERS— advertisements or direct mail offers included with bills and statements sent out to either existing customers or another company's customers.

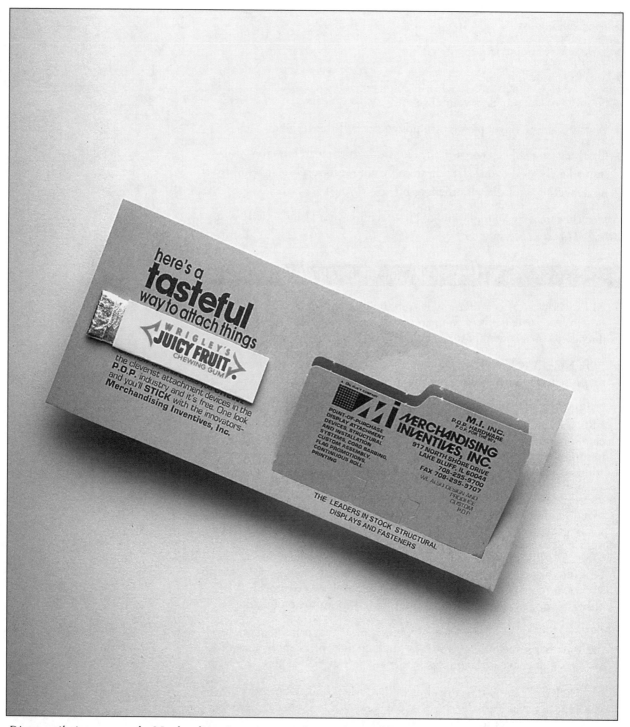

Direct mail piece sent out by Merchandising Incentives, an advertising specialty company. Notice the die-cut business card that recipients can cut out and put in their Rolodex.

The Vantec Can (see story page 210). This unique direct mail piece can be a real attention getter.

Source: Vantec, (800) 475-0660

CATALOGS

Great for positioning your business and grabbing the attention of real prospects.

J. Peterman is a guerrilla who can write. Peterman found a manufacturer who produced a long canvas coat straight out of Butch Cassidy and the Sundance Kid. *Starting from scratch, he wrote a tiny ad for* The New Yorker *and from there created a small catalog with pithy, funny descriptions of his offerings. Within a few years, the J. Peterman catalog turned into a multimillion dollar venture, all based on the writing style of one man. He doesn't even use photographs. Call (800) 231-7341 to receive a copy of the catalog.*

Catalogs are a guerrilla tactic par excellence. They allow you to reach far more prospects, help position your company and your products, and make life easier for your customers.

Your catalog doesn't have to look like the J. Crew catalog to be effective. If the product or service you offer appeals to a select group of motivated people, even the simplest catalog can be incredibly effective. But it does help if your customer service and follow-through is as good as J. Crew's. As a catalog marketer, you have to build your customer base one customer at a time, using your catalog as your primary salesperson. Don't put out a catalog unless you are prepared to back it up with outstanding service and attentiveness to your customers' needs.

THREE RULES FOR CATALOG MARKETERS

➤ **Start small.**
Try a simple one- or two-page flier first, judge the response, then move on from there.

➤ **Target your mailings.**
The largest cost, by far, in catalogs is the cost of wasted mailings. Sending a catalog to someone who isn't interested is like throwing money away. Start by sending the catalog to your existing customer list. Then expand by using carefully selected and researched mailing lists (see *Customer Mailing Lists* and *Direct Mail*).

➤ **Test, test, test.**
Keep altering your lists, your catalog, your pricing—everything—until you have the mix that works for you.

Guerrilla catalog sellers take advantage of the mail order relationship to deal with each prospect on an individual basis—something Macy's can't do. Because you are able to deal with each customer one-on-one, your business can start small and grow.

Take advantage of every selling opportunity when producing your catalog. Obviously, the focus is on the products you are selling, their descriptions, and their prices, but there are countless other ways to sell your product and your company. Emphasize that your catalog is an extension of you. You are bringing your retail store to the customer. Take advantage of it.

Use all of the catalog's elements to make an impression on your customer and to sell your product. Make sure your catalog has a voice—there should be real people behind it, for example. The descriptions might read like personal recommendations. Give the customer a visual frame of reference so he can characterize your company. This lends credibility to your company, something the customer needs before he buys from you sight unseen.

Welcome the customer just as you would if he walked into your retail store. Include a letter telling the customer how valuable he is. Sign the letter for a more personal touch.

Use your order form to its fullest potential to sell your product. Besides making the form easy to read, use, and understand, fill it with product descriptions and special offers. Select a "product of the month" from your catalog and preprint the product number and price on the order form. Then all the customer has to do to order the item is check the box next to it.

Include testimonials throughout the catalog. Written letters of recommendation from customers who have already purchased your products will boost credibility. If prospects see that others have benefited, they will want to order, too. Besides, if they order, they become part of your club.

Make it easy to order. Include ordering instructions and options in several places in the catalog, not just on the order form. Allow customers to order by phone, mail, or even by fax. Give them a toll-free number to use. Some catalog companies have an operator standing by 24 hours a day. If you can't do that, at least have a fax machine operational all the time so people can fax in their orders. Also, make sure you accept credit cards. For customers' convenience, that's a must.

Remember that according to a recent survey, 36% of people shop by mail because it is convenient. Make it even more convenient to shop in your catalog and you'll gain the edge over your competition fast.

At MacConnection, the largest mail order company selling Macintosh software, a computer displays for the operator a repeat customer's name, address, computer set-up, and past order history—before the phone is even answered. Having that information allows the operator to treat the customer more quickly and personally. This attention to speed and personal service makes them even more successful at filling their niche.

Guarantee satisfaction—no ifs, ands, or buts. While there is no way to guar-

According to a recent survey, 36% of people questioned say that convenience is what they like most about shopping by catalog; 19% say it's the increased variety of products available; 17% like the low prices; 6% go for the high quality offered; and 22% list "other" or say nothing.

Catalogs are not always used as direct mail pieces. Some retail stores use them solely as in-store giveaways. Walk into any supermarket or discount store and there's a stack of them by the door. Hammacher Schlemmer and The Sharper Image both use them in their stores. Customers pick them up on their way in and read them while walking through the store.

antee the customers will get exactly what they expect, the next best thing is to promise that you will take the merchandise back if the customer is not completely satisfied.

Order a shirt from Lands' End, drag it through the mud, light the sleeve on fire, and then send it back, and they'll replace it with a brand new one—no questions asked, guaranteed. And the policy pays off for Lands' End over the long haul.

The copy in your catalog has to be consistent and reflect the character of the products being sold. Your catalog can be snobbish, loud, educational, or folksy in nature, but regardless, its copy must be clear, concise, and contain all the basic information. Here is a set of suggestions to help you fill a catalog with copy that sells.

CATALOG COPY SUGGESTIONS

➤ Keep your copy straightforward and concise. You want to give the reader as much information as possible in as clear a manner as possible.

➤ Motivate the prospect to buy. Get them excited about your product. Your catalog is your salesperson so give it your best pitch.

➤ Make sure the photograph or illustration matches the copy.

➤ Compliment the reader with your copy: "Only you are worthy..."

➤ Make your copy timely in nature. If your catalog is scheduled to come out during the Christmas season, for example, make a lot of references to Old Saint Nick.

➤ Make the copy on your order form simple and easy to understand, but detailed enough that the customer won't have any problems following directions.

➤ Write in the active tense!

➤ Highlight the key selling points of each item and repeat them at least twice.

➤ Make your headlines sing out. They have to make the browser stop and look.

➤ The copy should convey the identity not only of the product, but of your company as well. All of the elements in your catalog need to come together to form an image to which the customer can relate.

GUIDELINES FOR CATALOG MARKETING

➤ Set specific objectives on what the catalog should do for your business.

➤ Define your audience so that you know who will receive your catalog; that helps in creating and producing it.

➤ Pre-plan all the elements of your catalog business before going into production: Products, prices, fulfillment, and more.

➤ If possible, organize your offerings into clearly defined groups so that the catalog is not a hodgepodge.

➤ Make a rough outline of the contents of your catalog, including everything you wish to have in it—the order form, promotional inserts, products, etc.

➤ Determine the exact format you want: size, typeface, color or not, paper, binding.

➤ Make a layout that is organized, logical, and pleasing to the eye of your target audience.

➤ Plan, write, and perfect the copy. Then set up a timetable and stick to it.

COMPETING WITH THE BIG GUYS IN THE CATALOG TRENCHES

Define your audience. Pick a niche and ignore everyone else. That's your secret weapon.

Niche marketing is the key to success for the guerrilla catalog marketer. Outposition the big guys by selling a specialty product to a highly targeted audience. The big guys often overlook the smaller specialty markets, leaving them wide open for the smaller guys to dominate.

Guerrillas do what it takes to transform the impersonal mail order method into an opportunity to create a personal relationship with customers. They start with toll-free telephone salespeople who are pleasant, friendly, and knowledgeable about the company and the product.

CATALOG PRINTERS

Companies that specialize in catalogs and similar tools.

Alden Press
2000 Author Avenue • Elk Grove Village, IL 60007-6071 • (708) 640-6000

Jackson's Orchard and Nursery in Bowling Green, KY, is built on a guerrilla foundation. Bill and Shirley Jackson have taken the down-home approach all the way to the bank. Hospitality has turned their nursery and orchard into a tourist attraction, bringing in as many as 100,000 visitors each weekend. Their mail order catalog is an extension of the down-home image, filled with quant illustrations and homestyle recipes. Call the Jacksons at (502) 781-5303.

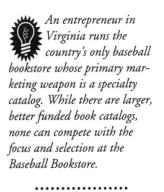

An entrepreneur in Virginia runs the country's only baseball bookstore whose primary marketing weapon is a specialty catalog. While there are larger, better funded book catalogs, none can compete with the focus and selection at the Baseball Bookstore.

!

"We're going to see the catalog industry and the department-store industry look very much alike in the future....The fact is that people will be dealing with a retail store that is delivered to their homes...the processes that I can now do at home, bring into my home, the marketplace. Instead of going to it, it will come to me"
– Lester Wunderman, direct marketing expert and founder of Wunderman Cato Johnson, a direct marketing agency.

....

American Spirit Graphics Corp.
104 Park Rd. • West Hartford, CT 06119 • (203) 236-4247

B & W Press
401 E. Main St. • Georgetown, MA 01833 • (508) 774-2200

Catalog King
One Entin Rd. • Clifton, NJ 07014 • (800) 223-5751
Specializes in catalog production and quotes all prices including photography .

Noll Printing Co. Inc.
100 Noll Plaza • Huntington, IN 46750 • (219) 356-2020

Perryscope/Perry Printing Co.
P.O. Box 97 • Waterloo, WI 53594 • (414) 478-3551

Scoville Press, Inc.
575 Madison Ave. • New York, NY 10022 • (212) 605-0109

Triangle/Expercolor
3737 Chase Avenue • Skoki, IL 60076 • (312) 465-3400

Vermont Graphics, Inc.
18 Granger Street • Bellows Falls, VT 05101 • (802) 463-9515

PIGGYBACKING

Another way to take advantage of marketing through catalogs is to put your product in someone else's catalog. First make sure that the catalog you choose has the right image and message for your product and company. You probably wouldn't want to try selling your gourmet, secret-recipe chocolate torte through a health food catalog.

There are a number of companies that specialize in finding the right catalog for your product. Try to find a company that will work with you on a commission basis—you only pay them for the orders you actually receive.

CATALOG PRODUCT BROKERS

Catalog Solutions
521 Riverside Ave. • Westport, CT 06880 • (203) 454-1919

Direct to Catalogs Inc.
6600 Coffman Farms Rd. • Keedysville, MD 21756 • (301) 432-4410

CATALOG PRODUCT FULFILLMENT

The following is a list of fulfillment houses that provide catalog product fulfillment. They will take orders, process credit cards and billings, and send out your product.

Comar Acquisition, Inc.
25060 Avenue Tibbitts • Valencia, CA 91355 • (805) 294-2700

Fosdick Fulfillment Services
500 South Broad Street • Meriden, CT 06450 • (800) 759-5558

Fusion Industries
17311 Fusion Way • Country Club Hills, IL 60478 • (708) 799-1997

National Fulfillment Incorporated
507 Maple Leaf Drive • Nashville, TN 37210 • (615) 391-0047

CATALOG RESOURCES

How to Create Successful Catalogs
by Maxwell Sroge

A comprehensive volume covering the step-by-step methods for creating an effective mail order catalog. Author Maxwell Sroge, a well-regarded expert in the field of catalog production, takes the reader through every step involved from concept through final production. He includes checklists of ideas the reader should keep in mind when producing each part of the catalog. The different types of catalogs are discussed along with the role of each element in a catalog, and the organization and format options for catalogs. Art, photography, copy, page layout, pre-press production, color, and paper type are examples of the topics that Sroge covers in great detail.

101 Tips for More Profitable Catalogs
by Maxwell Sroge

A selection of the most successful proven techniques for catalog marketers from The Catalog Marketer *newsletter. This is a how-to for the catalog marketer. Topics covered include: seven ideas for successful catalog marketing; the twelve most important features of successful catalogs; seven tested ways to put more oomph into your catalog; How to write powerful captions; ten ways to improve your order form.*

How to Write Powerful Catalog Copy
by Herschell Gordon Lewis

Lewis details many of the do's and don'ts of writing responsive catalog copy. Through challenging hands-on practice exercises and a plethora of real-life examples, Lewis shows you how to get the most out of your catalog. His method revolves around tightening and strengthening copy with gripping headlines and meaningful and accurate product descriptions.

King Arthur Flour is a small, regional flour manufacturer, producing unbleached and whole grain flours that appeal to the home baker. To combat difficulties in getting distribution at major supermarkets, the guerrillas at King Arthur started a catalog (which, by the way, they advertise on the side of their flour bags). It has now grown to more than 40 pages, and offers everything from caraway seeds to $400 mixers. The success of the catalog has allowed them to "brand" the flour, and has even helped in-store sales.

223

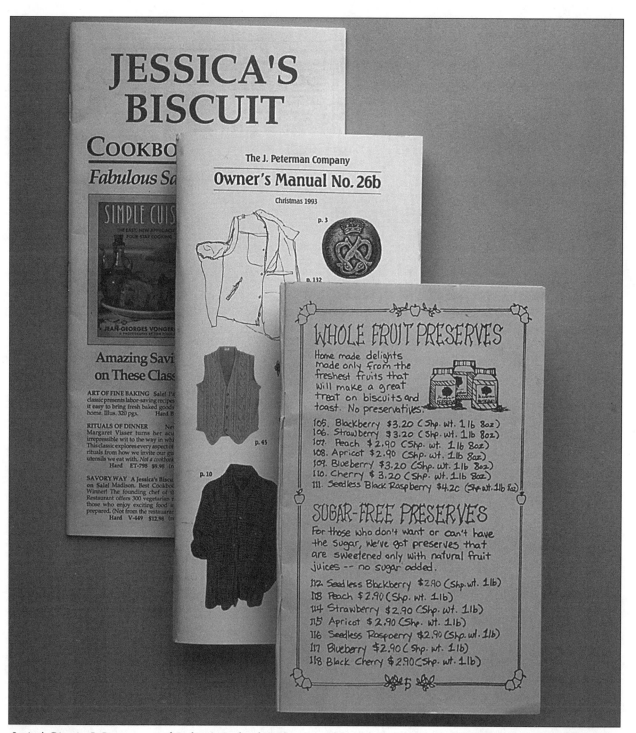

Jessica's Biscuit, J. Peterman, and Jackson's Orchard catalogs (see sidebars throughout chapter). Despite their obvious differences, each catalog has a distinct personality and vision.

The Coyote Cocina catalog is full of guerrilla techniques. There are great product photos, an after-hours fax order number printed at the bottom of every other page, and the telephone number is (800) 866-HOWL. This is great positioning, too.

DATABASE MARKETING

Relational selling will take you into the future.

Companies that sell by mail order or catalog are in a great position to engage in database marketing. If you sell computer products through a catalog, keep track of everyone who buys a color printer. Chances are these same people are interested in buying software that lets them paint things on the screen in color. You know they just bought a color monitor, but your competitors don't. Beat them to the punch and send the customer a coupon for the software you know they want. That customer is yours—do everything you can to keep it that way.

Database marketing is the perfect weapon for any guerrilla, big or small. It gives you a way to dominate your competition by using your knowledge of your customers to deliver unique products and services. In the dark ages (twenty years ago), the most a guerrilla could get out of his customer list, even if he personally knew every customer on that list, was some repeat business (see *Customer Lists*). Now, with the power of computers, you can divide and recombine your customer list in a thousand ways depending upon your knowledge of every single customer. Today, that customer list can help you create new niches that you can expand and deliver new products to.

So take a new look at your customer base, thinking of every customer as an individual, not as a mass market statistic. Database marketers make the extra effort to learn about their customers' individual interests, needs, and desires. They create relationships based on what they've learned and market to those same individuals over and over again.

For example, if you had a list of every customer who bought fax paper last month, you could contact them again this month to arrange for a refill order. If you know what your customers want even before they do, you can provide it for them before your competitors can.

Technology has opened the doors to database marketing for small businesses of all kinds. It's the great equalizer and it can, in fact, help you not only compete with the big guys, but surpass them in the marketplace. Ironically, it's the technology that allows you to reach your customers on a very personal level. Your mailing list is maintained on a computer database—yes? If it's not, it should be. Take great pains to keep that database of customers and prospects current. Every time you learn something about a customer, put it in your database. If you knew which 250 of your customers were most likely to buy extra-large Christmas trees, you could send them a letter two weeks before your shipment arrived, thereby guaranteeing that they would find the tree they want—and that they'll buy it from you.

Each time a guerrilla sells something to a new customer, she realizes the value that customer could have to her business over the long haul. She doesn't just sell the product and call it quits. She records what the customer purchased, when and why she purchased it, and when she may need to make a repeat or related purchase. The guerrilla keeps that information in her computer database and sends out a friendly reminder or a coupon when she gets a special shipment of an appropriate product, or when the computer tells her it's time for the customer to buy again.

Pizza Hut maintains a list of customers according to the type of pizza they order and then sends out tailored coupons and promotional materials. Buyers of Meatlovers pizza receive coupons for Meatlovers pizza, and so on.

As a guerrilla, you already realize the need to build your market one customer at a time. Database marketing takes this thinking one step further. Once you've established a relationship with a customer, it is far cheaper and easier to sell more to that customer than it is to find a new customer.

The guerrilla establishes a special relationship with his customer base. This means that he knows what the customer is buying, what he needs, and what he wants. It also means that he's set up communication with the customer, and is able to listen to what the customer is saying.

Milkmen were great database marketers. They had a relationship with each customer, and new exactly when they needed milk. Most expanded into butter, juice, and eggs—they increased the sales to each customer, since it was cheaper and easier than adding new ones. They made it very easy for people to keep their pantries stocked, and as a result, once they captured a customer, they profited from a steady income stream. The birth of the supermarket doomed the milkman, but the concept works.

Most people aren't very loyal about where they buy gasoline or get their oil changed. A gas station in Austin, Texas, uses database marketing to improve the chances that they get as much business from each loyal customer as they can. A computer keeps track of when you had your last oil change and sends out a discount coupon two weeks before you're due for your next one. This simple reminder and discount has increased their profitable oil change business by 60%.

Take this to the next step. If you paint houses, you've got first hand knowledge of how many of your customers need their windows cleaned, their floors scraped, their gutters cleaned, and their roofs fixed. Since you've done such a good job painting their houses, you've already built their trust. Making the additional sale is a benefit to both you and the customer—you've saved him from having to search out another contractor.

Fifty years ago, the corner grocery store owner made his living by knowing each of his customers on a first name basis. He knew what they bought and when they needed certain items. He socialized with them and built a rapport that turned most of his customers into "regulars." That kind of relational

United Artists recently ventured into database marketing. They have begun giving out membership cards, and each time a customer goes to a movie, the card is swiped through a scanner that records the customer, the movie he is going to see, the time, and the day of the week. The information is then stored in their database and they use it to mail special promotions for new movies to the patrons they know have an interest in that type of movie. If, like United Artists, you are marketing a low-cost, low-price item like a movie ticket, this tactic is a sure-fire way to increase sales and stimulate repeat buyers.

marketing was abandoned with the arrival of huge department stores, franchises, and conglomerates. Guerrillas now use relational selling to gain an edge on these Goliaths. Whether or not they own a computer, this tool is the key to selling success and to establishing yourself as a player in the marketplace.

Let's say you own a local drug and convenience store. Make sure to get the name and address of every parent who comes in to buy infant products; chances are good that he or she has an infant in the household. If you play your cards right, you should get that same customer spending $10,000 in your store over the next twenty years by mailing him fliers, promotional literature, and coupons for everything a kid needs while growing up.

Imagine the waste involved in sending back-to-school sale announcements to every house in a neighborhood when you could target your existing customers—and only those with kids.

Here's another example. A large record store routinely signs up customers for its Music Lovers Club. The customer gets a card entitling him to discounts and special sales. The store puts the customer's name and address into a database and then records every CD the cardholder buys. For example, if you buy a copy of *Harvest Moon,* by Neil Young, that information is recorded in the database. When the singer comes out with a new CD, the store mails a postcard announcing its arrival and offering a discount. A more highly targeted mailing doesn't exist.

At Staples office supply stores, customers are signed up for a membership card that gives a hidden discount on many items. They've gone halfway—they know who their customers are and what they buy. The last step of the equation—offering customers products and services customized for them—is on its way.

THE POWER OF YOUR DATABASE

Once you've created a database of your hundreds, thousands, or tens of thousands of customers, all sorts of good things happen.

➤ Take a look at the demographics of your audience. What do they have in common? Do they live in the same neighborhoods, drive the same model cars, read the same magazines? Understanding their hobbies and habits helps you figure out how to advertise to people just like them and increase your customer base.

If you own a large grocery store you can be like your corner grocery store ancestors and start building relationships with your customers. Print membership cards for your frequent and "most loyal" customers and keep a database of members. Record their purchases. Then approach a manufacturer like Procter & Gamble and offer them a list of all your customers who buy their competitor's brand of paper towels. Use co-op money to target these customers on behalf of P&G. For example, you could send an offer for a free roll of paper towels. It brings customers into your store, and it creates goodwill because your customers get a free offer through their contact with you.

➤ Watch their habits. Study your data, looking for patterns that you can capitalize on. Do certain people buy certain products? If you discover that the teenagers in your database are renting action movies on Sundays, find out why. If your bookstore sells more romances to single women in February, you can probably do something with that information.

➤ Figure out what they want. Are your customers leaving your store wanting more? If you discovered, for example, that 10% of your customers are buying 90% of the diet food sold in your supermarket, perhaps you should survey this niche and discover what other products they might buy.

➤ Identify your best customers. Nearly every business has a small, loyal niche of customers that account for a bulk of their profits (the folks who always fly first class to Asia are a core market for Northwest Airline). Identify these all-stars, pamper them, and keep them forever.

➤ Organize your customers into categories. The more you know about your customers, the more likely you'll be able to satisfy them—getting their business instead of losing it to a competitor.

DATABASE MARKETING TOOLS

At the simplest level, all you need to perform database miracles is a well-organized stack of 3" x 5" index cards. However, most businesses have more customers and more products than this technique will support, and computer hardware and software has become so inexpensive that even the smallest business can afford to ramp up with one.

The next level of complexity involves using a computer database to track your customers. Filemaker Pro, made by Claris, works on both Macintosh and Windows platforms. It's easy to use, very powerful, and capable of creating tables, forms, and personalized letters.

If you're a retailer, you'll need something far more powerful than a flat file database. Your current point of sale (POS) system probably supports a computerized information-capturing utility. Talk to your vendor about the available options.

The goal in database marketing is to discover what your customer wants and needs and to make it easy for the customer to get the job done. While computers make this job easier, they can also cloud the concept behind it. If you can do it with index cards, that's fine. Don't let the complexity and cost of a computer system stop you from getting started.

DATABASE MARKETING SPECIALISTS

D.A. Lewis
P.O. Box 815 • Doylestown, PA 18901 • (215) 340-6860
database marketing firm

Rosenfield & Associates
7676 Hazard Center Drive, 5th Floor • San Diego, CA 92108
(619) 497-2568
database marketing expert, consultant to Cowles, publishers of Direct *magazine*

MarketPulse
Four Cambridge Center • Cambridge, MA 02142 • (617) 868-6220
database marketing firm

Raab Associates
19 Price's Lane • Rose Valley, PA 19063 • (215) 565-8188
consultant specializing in selection and evaluation of marketing database systems

DiMark
2050 Cabot Blvd. West • Langhorne, PA 19047 • (800) 543-2212

Acxiom Corp.
301 Industrial Blvd. • Conway, AR 72032 • (800) 922-9466

Washburn Direct Marketing
1123 S. Church St. • Charlotte, NC 28203 • (704) 334-5371

DATABASE MARKETING COMPUTER SOFTWARE COMPANIES

Customer Insight Company
6855 South Havana • Englewood, CO 80112 • (708) 932-2680
experts in database software and systems

Group 1 Software
4200 Parliament Place • Lanham, MD 20706 • (800) 368-5806

May & Speh
1501 Opus Place • Downers Grove, IL 60515 • (708) 964-1501

Mercantile Software Systems
255 Old Brunswick Rd. • Piscataway, NJ 08854 • (908) 981-1290

Metromail Corporation
360 East 22nd St. • Lombard, IL 60148 • (708) 932-3074

TRW Target Marketing Services
701 TRW Pkwy. • Allen, TX 75002 • (214) 390-5160

DATABASE MARKETING RESOURCES

Direct **Magazine**
911 Hope Street • Box 4949 • Stanford, CT 06907 • (203) 358-9900

The Cowles Report on Database Marketing
470 Park Ave. South, 7th floor North • New York, NY 10016
(212) 683-3986
for subscriptions, call (800) 775-3777

The One-to-One Future
by Don Peppers and Martha Rogers, Ph.D. • Published by Doubleday
This is a brilliant book. After purchasing all the books in the Guerrilla Marketing series, this should be the next one you buy.

Database Marketing
by Edward L. Nash • Published by McGraw-Hill, Inc.

PROMOTION

GUERRILLA MARKETER
OF THE YEAR
Promotion can bring it all
together for the astute guerrilla. Once the foundation is in
place, promotion can be the
element that puts you over the
top and ahead of the competition.

An effective promotion can
put you in the prospect's mind
and keep you there. Our
Guerrilla Marketer of the
Year, Jordan's Furniture in
Boston, is a great example.
They built a Disney-like ride
called MOM that they opened
to the public on Mother's Day
in 1992. The ride has generated a lot of publicity and people come from all over just to
ride MOM. Of course, while
they are there, they just have to
look at the furniture Jordan's
sells, too!

A contest, unique package,
or innovative trade show promotion can help you break
through the clutter and reach
your prospects directly.

CONTESTS & SWEEPSTAKES

Build traffic and customer loyalty.

💡 GUERRILLA MARKETER OF THE YEAR.
In 1983, Jordan's Furniture ran a contest during which they gave away a $40,000 house. All that customers had to do to register was go to the store and lie on a waterbed for 60 seconds.

• • • • • • • • • • • • • • • •

People love to play games. Last year, more than half of all Americans bought a lottery ticket. And Ed McMahon and the Publisher's Clearing House sweepstakes generate several million new magazine subscriptions a year.

For very little investment you can create a sweepstakes that will focus attention on your business, build traffic in your store, encourage people to try your product, and generate word of mouth.

Sweepstakes are a great guerrilla weapon. But you'll need to be careful—mistakes can cost you money, time, and even a brush with the law.

There are critical differences between contests, sweepstakes, and lotteries (see the definitions below). The most important thing to keep in mind is that private lotteries (sometimes referred to as raffles) are illegal in all fifty states, and if you run one, you'll probably get shut down. The defining element of all three is that there's a prize. If you don't give away a prize worth more than a few bucks, you've got nothing to worry about.

If there's a prize, the next issue is what lawyers call consideration. Does it cost money to play? This can be tricky. Most states consider a purchase in your store to be consideration. That means that collecting store receipts as entries is illegal. In some states, just buying a stamp to mail in an entry can be called consideration. So be careful.

The final issue is chance. Lotteries are obviously games of chance—no one ever won Lotto because he was a genius. Games of skill (like golf tournaments, spelling bees, and Jeopardy!) are generally considered to be an entirely different category, called, not surprisingly, games of skill.

BASICS

IMPORTANT CONTEST DEFINITIONS

LOTTERIES: Games of chance that involve an entry fee. They're illegal.

SWEEPSTAKES: These are games of chance that make it clear that there is no purchase required. These are the most common promotions.

CONTESTS: These are games of skill that involve an entry fee. They're legal in many states, but often tricky to administer.

ELEMENTS OF A SUCCESSFUL SWEEPSTAKES

➤ Require people to enter your store to enter the sweepstakes. While you can't require a purchase, you can require people to walk all the way to the back of your store to enter the sweepstakes. If you're a manufacturer, feel free to ask consumers to answer a bunch of questions that can only be found by reading your ads or studying your box.

➤ Make the prize fantastic. Cash isn't usually a good prize unless the amount is stupendous. So consider travel, sporting events, services (free car washes for a year), or other publicity-generating prizes. A prize awarded over time is usually cheaper for you and just as enticing to the winner.

Even better, make the prize an event. One radio station gives the winner the opportunity to host a station-sponsored concert in his high school. The concert generates news and every single student in the school becomes grateful to the station.

➤ Make sure people think they've got a chance. By adding a skill component to a contest (answer these three questions) you can encourage people who think they never win anything to enter.

➤ Require names, addresess, and phone numbers to enter. People are usually very forthcoming with data if you ask for it in a sweepstakes entry. Put all the names on your mailing list for future reference.

➤ Make it cheat-proof. If people can cheat, they will. Count on it.

➤ Publicize the winner. Invite the local paper to take photos. Send out press releases with quotes from the grateful winner.

FIVE SWEEPSTAKES THAT CAN BUILD TRAFFIC AND GENERATE A MAILING LIST

➤ **Testimonials**
Ask your customers to submit, in 25 words or less, why they like shopping at your store. Post all your favorites (use them in your ads, too), then have a drawing and randomly choose one entry to win a gift certificate at your store.

➤ **Cross Promotion**
Find five merchants who make complementary products (like a caterer, a band, and a banquet hall; or maybe a bakery, a deli, and a florist) and offer a prize package to the customers of all three businesses. You'll get the names of their customers, they'll get yours, and you'll end up generating a substantial mailing list of people definitely interested in your product.

A pub borrowed twenty-five crabs from a pet store and publicized a crab race. Crabs raced on a table in the pub. Nearly 400 people showed up. The winner was Crab-o'-War — and the pub owner.

• • • • • • • • • • • • • • • •

A store owner calls consistent attention to his windows by placing "a mystery initial" in the front window each week. If your last initial matches it, you get substantial discounts.

The No Name bar in New York gives free drinks to anyone who's name matches the name of the day. Of course, the lucky winners probably have their friends along as well, so the bar ends up way ahead.

• • • • • • • • • • • • • • • •

One detergent company ran a promotion where they advertised that a certain number of product containers on retail shelves had diamonds in them. The person who bought a container with a diamond got to keep the diamond. Sales of the detergent skyrocketed as people bought up bottles just to see if there was a diamond inside. Be careful, as this type of promotion falls under the contest, lottery, and sweepstakes laws. A safer way to do this would be to put a coupon in each package of your product. Have people fill out the coupon with a 25-word essay on why they like your product and send it in to enter a contest to win a diamond. Tell people they can enter as many times as they want, but only with an original coupon—no facsimiles accepted.

➤ **Instant Win**

This is similar to those scratch-and-win tickets you find at McDonald's. Every time a customer visits your store, she grabs a number from a big bowl. If the number matches the one on the wall, she wins on the spot. Builds repeat traffic.

➤ **Jelly Beans in the Window**

If you're in a heavy foot-traffic area and want to entice people to walk in, put a big jar of jelly beans in the window and a sign that invites people to guess how many jelly beans are in the jar. The person who comes closest to the right number wins a gift certificate to your store. To enter, people have to walk in and fill out the form.

➤ **Everybody Wins**

This works great for health clubs and other try-before-you-buy establishments. Create a small entry box and offer 90 days free (a $100 value!) to a lucky winner. Ask local merchants to place the box on their counters. The twist is, every single entry actually wins. (Though you don't have to tell anyone that) People love to win, and you'll find a much higher acceptance rate than if you promoted the fact that everyone wins.

SWEEPSTAKES RESOURCES

Look in the Yellow Pages under "Contests" to find a company near you that manages and creates contest and sweepstakes promotions. Below are some of the largest companies you can call.

The Wessel Company

370 Lexington Ave. • New York, NY 10017 • (212) 490-1570

The Wessel Company is a full service printer that specializes in producing scratch-off games, coupons, and pop-up game pieces.

Dittler Brothers

1375 Seaboard Industrial Boulevard • Atlanta, GA 30318 • (404) 355-3423

Promotions company specializing in developing sweepstakes programs including scratch-off games and mystery discounts.

American Games, Inc.

504 34th Ave. • Council Bluffs, IA 51501 • (712) 366-9553

Specializes in manufacturing pull-tab game pieces and lottery tickets.

Ventura Associates

1211 Avenue of the Americas • New York, NY 10036 • (212) 302-8277

ETHICAL GUIDELINES FOR SWEEPSTAKES AND CONTESTS

Here is a partial list of guidelines suggested by the Direct Marketing Association. It is probably a good idea to check with a lawyer to make sure you are not violating any laws with your contest. No matter what, the following should be set forth clearly in the rules of your sweepstakes or contest.

➤ No purchase of the advertised product or service is required in order to win a prize.

➤ The procedure for entering the sweepstakes or contest.

➤ If applicable, disclosure that a facsimile of the entry blank or other alternate means (such as a 3" x 5" card) may be used to enter the sweepstakes.

➤ The termination date for eligibility in the sweepstakes. The termination date should specify whether it is the date of mailing or receipt of entry deadline.

➤ The number, retail value (of non-cash prizes), and complete description of all prizes offered, and whether cash may be awarded instead of merchandise. If a cash prize is to be awarded by installment payments, that fact should be clearly disclosed, along with the nature and timing of the payments.

➤ The approximate odds of winning a prize or a statement that such odds depend on number of entrants.

➤ The method by which winners will be selected.

➤ The geographic area covered by the sweepstakes and those areas in which the offer is void.

➤ All eligibility requirements, if any.

➤ Approximate dates when winners will be selected and notified.

➤ Publicity rights regarding the use of winner's name.

➤ Taxes are the responsibility of the winner.

➤ Provision of a mailing address to allow consumers to receive a list of winners of prizes over $25.00 in value.

Also, no sweepstakes promotion or any of its parts should state or imply that a recipient has won a prize when this is not the case. Winners should be selected in a manner that ensures fair application of the laws of chance.

Keep in mind that these are only guidelines, suggestions to get you started. A sweepstakes can by complicated, so you'll probably want to run it by your lawyer before going forward.

FREQUENT BUYER PROGRAMS

Get more sales from each customer.

Have you ever flown a particular airline in order to earn their frequent flier miles? Guerrillas can use that same technique to build long-term product loyalty.

With competition as stiff as it is, anything you can do to keep a customer from trying an alternative helps you maintain your market share. A successful frequent buyer program can encourage people to stay with you without costing you a lot of money.

Another benefit of a frequent buyer program is that it helps you identify your most important customers. If 20% of your customers account for 80% (or even 50%) of your business, you want to watch those customers very closely. By introducing a frequent buyer program, your best customers are immediately singled out by your staff for special treatment.

Be careful not to make the requirements for rewards too stringent. If it's too hard to participate, or if the prizes aren't worth the hassle, you'll alienate your customers. An entire frequent flier service business, Air-Miles, folded because it was just too much work for customers to participate. In order to collect frequent flier miles, you had to take all the receipts from your trips, staple them to an application form in a certain way, and mail them in a special envelope. You also had to fly a prohibitive number of paid miles before you were eligible for anything, so their customers quickly abandoned the participating carriers.

By contrast, USAir's frequent flier program is particularly user-friendly. The sign-up procedure is easy, and by simply presenting your ID number at the departure gate, the mileage gets credited to your account. Quarterly statements explain current offers and reward requirements and tell you how many miles you have earned.

You don't have to lose money on your frequent buyer program. National Car Rental actually charges customers a $50 annual fee. The rationale is that the benefits of membership (which include fast check-in, free upgrades, and no hassles) are so great that the frequent business renter will pay for them. Entry fees or annual fees can also weed out nonproductive members.

You don't always have to offer your own product as the frequent buyer's reward. In fact, while the cost of using your own product may seem low, doing so may have the effect of devaluing it in your customers' eyes. Instead, consider offering a related product or service to customers who buy from you.

Eukanuba dog food offers a free forty-pound bag of food after you've purchased ten bags. For most dog owners, this translates into a free bag every year. Eukanuba ensures that dog food buyers (who don't even eat the stuff) won't switch if there is a promotion on another brand—once you've got eight checks on your card, you have a big incentive to shovel your way through those last two bags!

Hotels and airlines often combine efforts this way. It's called "partnering," and it's one of the hottest guerrilla techniques going. Marriott Hotels offer frequent flier miles on any of a number of airlines to their guests. The hotel and the airline both benefit.

A concert promoter offers a special telephone access line for his frequent customers. They can buy tickets and get into the auditorium quicker and easier than everyone else. This VIP treatment costs nothing, keeps loyal customers, and encourages others to sign up for the same service.

You can also use a frequent buyer program to differentiate your pricing. By offering frequent customers an exclusive discount, you can reward those who buy from you regularly. Staples, Inc. does this with office supplies, and A&P has just begun doing it with groceries.

THINGS TO CONSIDER WHEN SETTING UP A PROGRAM

➤ What is your objective? Are you trying to reach people who are already customers or are you setting up a continuity program to attract new business and attract your competition's clients to your company?

➤ What are the logistics? Decide exactly what it is that will earn your customers the prizes or the points. Will they need to have a card stamped every time they buy, or mail in a coupon to redeem their prize? Keep it as simple as possible.

➤ What is the reward? The prize or reward has to be perceived by your customers as sufficiently valuable to induce action. At the same time, the rewards can't be so lavish as to make the program a loser. The estimated increase in sales must offset the costs to make it a success.

➤ How long will the program last? You have to give customers enough time to benefit from the program.

➤ How will you handle the fulfillment of the prizes? Make sure you can accommodate all of the people who join the program. If you require proofs of purchase to redeem the gift, consider hiring a fulfillment house to process the orders and mail out the rewards. If customers have to wait too long, the program will backfire, creating more dissatisfied customers than loyal repeat-buyers.

Why not cross-promote your frequent buyer's club? Arrange with the local gas station, parking garage, or restaurant to give a discount to your best customers. Your partner benefits from the new business, and you benefit in two ways: your customers are pleased to get the discount, and those who haven't yet joined the club might hear about it at dinner.

The New York Times is using this technique with great results. Subscribers get a 25% discount at more than 1,000 participating restaurants around the country.

Allen Sports stimulates frequent purchases by handing out Allen Sports Dollars. With every $10 worth of merchandise you buy, the salesperson gives you a gift certificate good for $1 off your next purchase. You can accumulate the certificates as long as you like, and redeem them whenever you are ready. The more you buy, the more certificates you get.

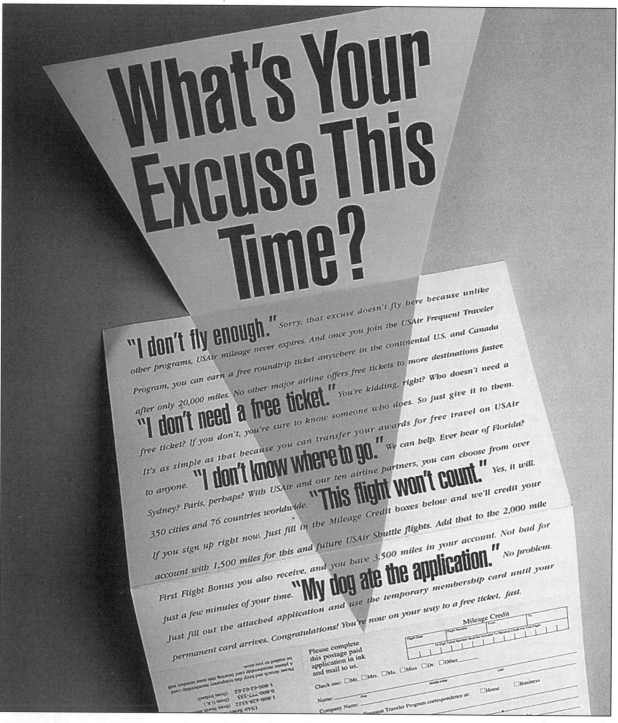

This is a promotional mailer and application form for USAir's frequent flier program. It's easy to join, easy to rack up the miles, and easy to use your prize.

Allen Sports Dollars (see page 239). For every $10 you spend in the store, you get a coupon good for $1 off any other purchase. You can accumulate unlimited Allen Sports Dollars and spend them at any time. Be careful: Your mechanism to fulfill these bonuses could last for a long time. Customers may take you up on your offer years later.

MUSIC

In your store and in your advertising.

Music can benefit your business in two ways.

First, music is an excellent motivator. Studies performed by Muzak and others have shown that shoppers will buy more when surrounded by the appropriate music. One Muzak study showed that in one major department store, 17% more shoppers purchased goods when music was played.

Before you smirk and announce, "Not in my store," understand that Muzak isn't just elevator music. They package a variety of mixes, each designed to work best in a particular environment. Walk into any mall and you're likely to hear Muzak-packaged music playing in the teenage clothing boutique as well as the corner jewelry store.

For information on retail music, call Muzak at (800) 331-3340 and ask for the name of your local affiliate. While it may seem cheaper to just play the radio, we think you'll be impressed by the statistics that Muzak can show you.

Of course, you don't have to hire Muzak or another service to comply with copyright laws. ASCAP and BMI will license your store to play any mix of music you choose. With a license, you can use the radio (not our favorite solution) or let your staff choose from a stack of CDs.

MUSIC AND YOUR IMAGE

Just as important as music in your store, your advertising has far more impact when you use the right music. (See *Jingles*.) Some radio and TV mavens claim that music increases a commercial's effectiveness by as much as 30%.

Try this experiment. Watch a drama or a commercial on TV with the sound turned off. You'll see that it looks flat and lifeless. Now watch again, focusing on the background music. You'll see how it is intentionally used to toy with your emotions.

Because music has such a direct connection to our subconscious, concentrate on the music you choose to use in your advertising. Jimi Hendrix might be ideal for a used jeans store, but consider how it positions your new French restaurant.

There are a number of low-cost ways to include music in your ads. One of the easiest is to use "needle-drop" clips. These are collections of music, available on CD, that you can use at no additional charge in your advertising. Every

A used CD store in Manhattan lost our business because the heavy metal music blasting out of their speakers at 100 dB was so offensive we couldn't stay in the store for more than a few minutes.

Think twice about the message you send with the music you play. Just because you like it doesn't mean that your customers do.

recording studio has a set of these, or you can buy your own.

In addition to using music in your ads and in your store, there's a second, even more powerful way to use music. It gives a guerrilla credibility.

The cost of hiring Mick Jagger, Willie Nelson, or Whitney Houston (assuming you could) to promote your store would be astronomical (not very guerrilla-like). The cost of licensing their music is far more reasonable. When a consumer hears familiar music, he subconsciously associates his feelings about it (positive, warm all over, romantic, excited—whatever) with your business. It gives you credibility and it gives you an emotional connection with your customers. Fruit of the Loom uses music from Crosby, Stills and Nash to sell underwear. They use it because the emotional connection baby boomers feel toward that era rubs off on their product.

Licensing music to use in your advertising is a tricky business—you need to license the composition (the song itself) as well as the performance. If you decide to include the *Hawaii Five-0* theme in your bikini store ads, or *Rhapsody in Blue* in your taco store ads (which worked great for Buffalo's #1 taco chain) be sure to get all the permissions first.

The easiest way to deal with permission to use music in your ads is to let your ad agency worry about it. If you don't have an agency, call either BMI or ASCAP (the two main music performing rights licensing organizations) for the performance permission, and EMI Music Publishing or Harry Fox Agency for permission to use the composition.

If you want to play music in your store or restaurant, you may need a license from BMI or ASCAP. They license performances of millions of copyrighted compositions.

LICENSING AGENCIES

ASCAP (The American Society of Composers, Authors and Publishers)
1 Lincoln Plaza • New York, NY 10023 • (212) 682-7227

BMI (Broadcast Music, Inc.)
320 W. 57th St. • New York, NY 10019 • (212) 586-2000

Harry Fox Agency
205 E. 42nd St. • New York, NY 10017 • (212) 370-5330

The Nature Company has effectively used music to create a unique atmosphere in their stores. Every time you walk into a Nature Company store, you know it just from what you hear. There's always the sound of a babbling brook or soothing, New Age music.

The music they use is so appealing, they have decided to offer the CDs for sale to their customers. The CDs are on display near the register. On top of the display is a sign that says "Now Playing." When people enter the store and hear music they like, they will very often go over to the display and buy whatever is playing or one of the other CDs offered for sale.

EMI Music Publishing
810 E. 7th Ave. • New York, NY 10019 • (212) 830-2000

MUSIC LIBRARIES

The companies listed below (and all music libraries) will help you find music to use in your commercials. Some of them will even help you compose your own. Look in the Yellow Pages to find a library near you or call one of these. They are some of the largest in the country.

Aircraft Music Library
162 Columbus Ave. • Boston, MA 02116 • (800) 343-2514

Airforce Broadcast Services, Inc.
216 Carlton St., Main floor • Toronto, Canada M5A 2L1 • (416) 961-2541

Associated Production Music
6255 Sunset Blvd., Suite 820 • Hollywood, CA 90028 • (800) 543-4276

Capitol Production Music
6922 Hollywood Blvd., Suite 718 • Hollywood, CA 90028
(800) 421-4163

Davenport Productions
P.O. Box 25636 • Charlotte, NC 28229 • (800) 951-6666

De Wolfe Music Library
25 W. 45th St. • New York, NY 10036 • (212) 382-0220

Firstcom
13747 Montfort Drive • Suite 220 • Dallas, TX 75240 • (800) 858-8880

HLC Killer Music/Killer Tracks
6534 Sunset Blvd. • Hollywood, CA 90028 • (800) 877-0078

JAM Creative Productions
5454 Parkdale Dr. • Dallas, TX 75227 • (214) 388-5454

James & Aster Music, Inc.
115 East 23rd St. • New York, NY 10010 • (212) 982-0300

Lavsky Music
16 East 42nd St., 8th floor • New York, NY 10017 • (212) 697-9800

Manhattan Production Music
355 W. 52nd St., 6th floor • New York, NY 10019 • (212) 333-5766

MusicMatch, Inc.
P.O. Box 120021 • Nashville, TN 37212 • (615) 259-9155

OmniMusic
6255 Sunset Blvd., Suite 803 • Hollywood, CA 90028 • (800) 828-6664

The Production Garden
15335 San Pedro, Suite A • San Antonio, TX 78232 • (800) 247-5317

Ross-Gaffney, Inc.
21 West 46th St. • New York, NY 10036 • (212) 719-2744

Shelton Leigh Palmer & Co.
19 West 36th St., 11th floor • New York, NY 10018 • (212) 714-1710

Silvertree, Inc.
2831 Camino del Rio South, Suite 212 • San Diego, CA 92108
(619) 296-1601

Sopersound Music Library
P.O. Box 498 • Palo Alto, CA 94301 • (800) 227-9980

Sound Ideas
105 West Beaver Creek Rd., Suite 4 • Richmond Hill, Ontario,
Canada L4B 1C6 • (800) 387-3030

Sound of Birmingham Productions
3625 5th Ave. South • Birmingham, AL 35222 • (205) 595-8497

Thomas J. Valentino, Inc.
500 Executive Blvd. • Elmsford, NY 10523 • (800) 223-6278

TM Century, Inc.
2002 Academy • Dallas, TX 75234 • (800) 937-2100

Toby Arnold & Associates
3234 Commander Dr. • Carrollton, TX 75006 • (214) 661-8201

TRF Production Music Libraries
747 Chestnut Ridge Rd, Suite 301 • Chestnut Ridge, NY 10977
(800) 899-6874

JINGLES AND SLOGANS

A message that plays over and over and over and over...

Fill in the blank: *Winston tastes good, _____.*

If you're over 30, odds are you knew that the next four words were *Like a cigarette should.* Here's the amazing fact: That jingle has not been broadcast in this country in more than 25 years! The power of jingles is awe-inspiring.

A memorable jingle that positions your company can pay dividends for generations. Millions of people still remember the end of the couplet *Plop, Plop, Fizz, Fizz...* You can create your own phenomenon, if you plan properly and follow a few simple steps.

IS A JINGLE RIGHT FOR YOU?

Before spending the time and money to create a jingle, use this checklist to determine if you'll get your money's worth:

➤ Do you advertise intensely on radio or TV?

➤ Is your product too serious for a jingle?

➤ Is your product an impulse purchase?

➤ Are you willing to offend some people?

Jingles have room for just one message. You need to take a long, hard look at your positioning statement and find the one benefit of your business that you want to stress. If your business can't live with that sort of pigeonholing, you'll need to reconsider using a jingle. In the case of Winston, the taste of the cigarette was the position—not the price, the size, the glamour, or the nicotine level.

Your existing customers may like your jingle at first, but sooner or later you'll start hearing complaints. By their very nature, jingles are a bit obnoxious. They creep under our skin and begin to drive us crazy. Is this a weapon you're willing to use? It's up to you.

SLOGANS VS. JINGLES

The main difference is the use of music — slogans don't have any. They're usually far less invasive than jingles, but less effective as well. We like them because they force you to decide on your positioning statement and stick with it. Wisk used the "ring around the collar" slogan as an excellent way to position their product as totally different from their competition. Even the United States of America has a slogan ("In God We Trust") though it periodically comes under fire.

CREATING YOUR SLOGAN OR JINGLE

Because they're so short and so catchy, creating a great slogan or jingle is not easy for an amateur. The best jingles are written by a small cadre of jingle writers based in New York. These folks are very good, very quick, and not inexpensive. To find a list of jingle writers, look in the Yellow Pages under "Music" and start calling the companies listed under "Original Music" or "Composers" or a similar category.

Slogans are a little easier. We recommend you try to come up with 100 alternatives at a company get together, then start narrowing down your list.

PACKAGING

The window to the soul of your product.

There are a lot of things you can do with your packaging. Packaging should make the product visually appealing, but there are also opportunities to use the package in other ways. Try using special packages, like high-volume packages ("Special one gallon economy size"), or use the package to ride-along a premium item or promotional piece (Buy Acme shaving cream and get a razor, free).

It's fashionable to be cynical about packaging. After the explosion of the packaged goods industry in the sixties and seventies, many consumers got turned off. Packages overpromised and became extravagant. They drove up the prices of the products without offering any added benefits.

But don't dismiss it so quickly. Entire businesses have been built around packaging. L'eggs is our favorite example. Here's an ordinary pair of pantyhose, brilliantly marketed in a low-cost, self-service package that revolutionized the way women buy pantyhose. Without the package (and the name/pun tie-in) there would be no product.

Other products that have been built around their packaging include L'Air du Temps perfume, Paul Newman's salad dressing (who ever thought to put the face of a movie star on a bottle of salad dressing?), and Tic Tacs.

Take a look at these five fabulous packages:
> Perrier

> Softsoap

> Pez

> Capri juice bags

> Kentucky Fried Chicken's bucket

These well-known products owe much of their success to their superior packaging. The product's identity is in the package.

But you can be a guerrilla without inventing the world's best package. First thing to do is make sure you create a package that doesn't hurt you. If your package makes life difficult for the retailer, it will fail before it even gets a chance. Make sure every package passes this checklist:

PRACTICAL PACKAGE CONSIDERATIONS

> Your package should be easy for the retailer to handle and display on his store shelves. If you make it difficult for the retailer, he won't want to be bothered and he'll replace your product with someone else's. Ask yourself whether or not your package is too tall to fit on the shelves, too flimsy to stand up to being handled, or too awkward to be arranged on the store shelf. If it is, redesign it.

> Make sure your package is sturdy enough to stand up to the handling

248

process. One glass company packages its products in a flimsy cardboard container. Almost 15% of the goods are already broken when they reach the retailer, and another 5% break while on the store shelves. That leads to profit loss and generates badwill with the customer who tried to buy the product, but broke it in the process.

➤ Don't be afraid to make your packaging more expensive than your product—perfume or other fantasy products sell because the package *is* the product. When Infocom started selling computer games, they packaged a 60¢ floppy disk in a $3 box. It made it easier for them to charge $40 for their product, and the markup quickly translated into a very profitable strategy.

➤ If you are selling by mail, take into consideration the cost of mailing the product with the packaging. If the packaging increases the postage necessary by too much, change the packaging.

➤ You can't forget about the law when designing your package. There are strict regulations about package design, the product claims that are put on packages, and even the sizes of some packages. Do your homework, or you might get stuck with a warehouse full of goods you can't sell.

POSITIONING

Your package should communicate your positioning distinctively. Experiment with shapes, textures, colors, and materials to find a niche. Most baking soda comes in an orange box because that's what Arm & Hammer, the market dominator uses. If a guerrilla introduced a new baking soda, the color of the box would be a critical decision.

Look at products like flour or breakfast cereal or antiperspirant. Every product in each category is packaged similarly. Break the rules a little bit and you might be able to grab significant market share. G.E. did it with their air conditioners. They reduced the size of their package by taking out some of the packing material. Then they stuck handles on the sides of the box, thereby transforming it from a product the deliveryman would bring to your house, to something you could buy and carry out of the store yourself.

Sometimes the package is the product. For example, take the Colgate toothpaste pump or the Capri Sun juice bags. When these products came on the market, they were hailed as revolutionary. Why? The juice was still basically sugar water and the toothpaste was still the same stuff Colgate had been sell-

When Manco Inc. of Westlake, OH, decided to go after the big guys, the first thing they looked to was their packaging. Makers of duct tape, Manco decided to play on the fact that people often refer to duct tape as "duck tape." They redesigned all of their product packaging and displays to feature a big yellow cartoon duck. Customer recognition grew, as did shelf space allocated by the retail market for Manco's tape.

They also built on the campaign by sending 32,000 greeting cards four times a year to buyers and retail store managers. Manco also produces a company newsletter and sends it to all of their retailers. When it comes time to buy duct tape, the retailers remember Manco, helping the small company increase its market share to 40%, up from almost zero in 1979.

Source: BusinessWeek.

The company that makes Chubs baby wipes gets our award for the most innovative use of packaging. They turned their package into a product all its own. Once all of the wipes are gone, the package becomes a colorful, stackable container that they market as a Lego-like toy kids can play with. Containers come in four different colors and have interlocking pegs that make them easy to stack. Parents can also use them as stackable storage containers, and they can even be refilled with Chubs wipes.

ing for generations. The packages made all the difference. They were so radically different that both were able to enter the market as virtually new products. The package created the product.

TIPS FOR SOUND PACKAGE DESIGN

➤ The words, design, colors, and materials all have to work together to inspire confidence. If the package is low quality, the customer will assume that the product is, too.

➤ The customer should be able to obtain enough information about what is inside to make an educated buying decision. The copy must outline the product's description and key selling points.

➤ Do you need a window? Many products, especially kids' toys, profit greatly from showing the consumer exactly what's inside.

➤ If you are considering using point-of-purchase displays, be sure that your package fits the standard sizes offered by the industry. This will save big money in the long run.

➤ The package must fit into the overall identity of your company. Your logo should be prominently displayed and your company theme or slogan boldly stated.

➤ The best packages say "pick me up." Once the consumer has your product in his hand, the battle for the sale is more than half over.

➤ How much should your package weigh? People have expectations, and you should take these into account. Bicycle helmets should feel light as a feather when hefted, while expensive software products are expected to be bulky and heavy.

➤ Test. Test the production line. Test shipping. Test retailer acceptance. Test consumer opinion.

25 QUESTIONS TO ASK ABOUT YOUR PACKAGE IF IT SITS ON A SHELF

➤ Does it stand out on the shelf?

➤ Is it competitive in shape?

➤ Is it competitive in size?

➤ Is it competitive in labeling?

➤ Is it competitive in overall appearance?

➤ Does it have eye appeal?

➤ Does it have taste appeal?

➤ It the name on the package easy to read?

➤ Is the name in the same typeface used in the advertising?

➤ Is the visual symbol from the advertising on the package?

➤ Is the theme line on the package?

➤ Does your package design reflect the quality and price of your product?

➤ Are the proper colors used to depict the type of your product?

➤ Does your package serve as a mini-billboard in the store?

➤ Is your package easy to handle?

➤ Does your package tell your story in words or pictures or both?

➤ Are the package colors apt to appeal to the type of prospect you seek?

➤ Does your package have the instructions or recipes to make it easy for your customers to use what's inside the package?

➤ Does your package encourage and suggest new uses for your product?

➤ Does your package stack well?

➤ Is your package designed so that retailers will gladly recommend it?

➤ Does your package have a distinct personality?

➤ Is the label as good as the best ad you have ever written?

➤ Is your package placed in a dominant, eye-level position?

➤ Are you prepared to needle, bug, demand, and motivate your salespeople, distributors, and retailers to prominently feature your package? If you aren't, the other 24 questions approach irrelevancy.

PACKAGE DESIGN SPECIALISTS

If you decide to hire a company to help you design or produce your packaging, make sure you hire a firm that specializes in what you need. You may want a firm that specializes in any number of packaging areas, including brand and corporate identity, environmental design, or exhibit design.

Look in the Yellow Pages under "Package Design and Development" to find a local company, or call one of the firms on our partial listing of package design specialists throughout the country.

The wave of warehouse superstores (Costco, Price Club, Sam's) is built on packaging. Bulk packaging is in! At the same time, (ironically enough) small sizes are in. The single-serving soup cans and juice boxes on the market are good examples of popular small packages.

Find out what your consumer wants, and make it.

Adams/Flock & Associates
521 Fifth Ave. • New York, NY 10175 • (212) 986-0692

Monnens-Addis Design
5800 Shellmound #250 • Emeryville, CA 94608 • (510) 652-1331

Bailey Spiker, Inc.
805 E. Germantown Pike • Norristown, PA 19401 • (215) 275-4353

Waliner Harbauer Bruce
500 N. Michigan Ave. • Chicago, IL 60611 • (312) 787-7039

Design North, Inc.
8007 Douglas Ave. • Racine, WI 53402 • (414) 639-2080

Fitch Richardson Smith
139 Lewis Wharf • Boston, MA 02110 • (617) 367-1491

Sean Michael Edwards Design
28 W. 25th St. • New York, NY 10010 • (212) 924-5700

Obata Design, Inc.
1610 Menard St. • St. Louis, MO 63104 • (314) 241-1710

The Design Company
165 Page St. • San Francisco, CA 94102 • (415) 989-0800

Addison Design Consultants
79 5th Ave., 6th floor • New York, NY 10003 • (212) 532-6166

Libby Perszyk Kathman
19 Garfield Pl., 5th floor • Cincinnati, OH 45202 • (513) 241-6401

King-Casey, Inc
199 Elm St. • New Canaan, CT 06840 • (203) 966-3581

PACKAGE RESOURCES

Package Design Council
481 Carlysle Drive • Herndon, VA 22070 • (703) 318-7225
trade association

Packaging Magazine
Cahners Plaza • 1350 E. Touhy Ave. • P.O. Box 5080 • Des Plaines, IL 60018
(708) 635-8800

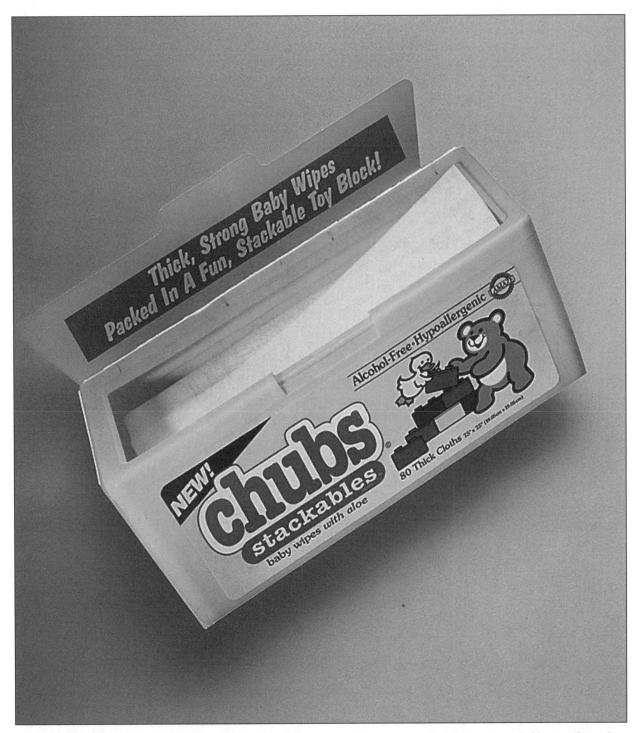

Package for Chubs baby wipes (see page 250). Once all of the wipes are used, the package becomes a stackable toy. The package can also be refilled with Chubs wipes.

Packaging Marketplace
Gale Research Inc.
835 Penobscot Bldg. • Detroit, MI 48226 • (313) 961-2242
listing of packaging manufacturers

Boxboard Containers
MacLean Hunter Publishing Company
29 N. Wacker Drive • Chicago, IL 60606 • (312) 726-2802
trade journal

Food and Drug Packaging
210 S. 5th St., Suite 202 • St. Charles, IL 60174 • (708) 377-0100
trade magazine

Shelf Presence
740 Shady Grove Ln. • Buffalo Grove, IL 60089 • (708) 215-8910
packaging monthly newsletter

Talk about a unique packaging idea! This maker of graphics software packaged a new product called Painter in a paint can.

This is an annual report for a packaging firm called Shorewood Packaging Corporation. Who better to show off their packaging talents than a packaging firm!

PACKAGING BRAINSTORMS

Take a look at your competitors' packaging. How does it position itself
(and you)? Make a list of the attributes of your packaging versus that of
the competition.

_____

_____

_____

_____

_____

_____

_____

_____

_____

_____

POINT-OF-PURCHASE

A high-impact way to close the sale.

Hanes made L'eggs a household name with brilliant point-of-purchase advertising. Mention the brand name and most people picture those display bins stacked with plastic egg-shaped packages (a great packaging example too!).

Many guerrillas forget that the most important moment for any marketer is when the cash register finally rings. Having a store full of prospects may look good, but it doesn't increase your profits. Getting the customer in the store is not enough. You have to close the sale.

Guerrillas use point-of-purchase displays such as signs, product displays, countertop dispensers, and shelf decorations to motivate sales. Such advertising serves two purposes. It's a reminder to customers that your product exists and that they need or want it. Second, point-of-purchase advertising can persuade a customer to buy one product over another. The way a product is displayed or merchandised can affect the buying decision.

Most point-of-purchase advertising is paid for by manufacturers. They send displays to the retailer with the product, hoping the retailer will use them in the store. Chances are, the retailer carries several brands of the same product and it makes no difference to them which one they sell. Whichever sells the best will receive more shelf space, resulting in larger orders for the manufacturer. Point-of-purchase displays give the manufacturer a means of reaching the consumer directly at the most crucial time in the buying process.

Retailers also benefit from point-of-purchase advertising. Studies have shown that retailers who use point-of-purchase advertising generate more sales from the customers that visit their stores. In one study conducted by the Point-of-Purchase Advertising Institute, 56% of convenience store managers said that point-of-purchase materials are extremely effective in increasing sales; 48% of supermarket managers agreed.

Point-of-purchase advertising can be extravagant and expensive, but it doesn't have to be. Guerrilla POP signs direct people to the things they came in to buy, but they also steer customers toward other products they hadn't planned

BASICS

POP USES

BRAND ADVERTISING: Create brand awareness over other products.

SUPPORT OF PROMOTIONAL EVENTS: Use signs and freestanding product holders to announce upcoming promotions. Push giveaways, sweepstakes, and new product announcements.

CROSS MERCHANDISING: The manufacturer can tie into the retailers' products—"Buy a bag of Acme brand potato chips and get a free bottle of soda."

ANNOUNCEMENTS: Announce special packs, new products, freestanding inserts in newspapers, or coupon campaigns.

on buying. POP enlarges the size of transactions, stresses your selection, and wins new customers as well as new profits.

Think about what attracts you to certain products. Which bag of chips are you more likely to pick up when you go to the corner convenience store—the one displayed on the neon-lighted rack at the end of the aisle or the one stuffed in with all the other brands on the plain white metal shelf?

WHAT ERNEST GALLO AND JAY LEVINSON HAVE IN COMMON

The largest winery in the world is E&J Gallo, even though the United States is certainly not the largest producer of wines. So how did Gallo get so big? Quality? Price? Selection? Wrong, wrong, and wrong.

Ernest, the marketing genius behind the winery, saw that liquor stores were not putting up the signs he gave them. So he made it part of his salesmen's job to place and actually put up Gallo wine signs at the point-of-purchase. While salesmen were there, they also found time to put the wine bottles at eye level in a place where they would obtain maximum visibility.

Many stores will accept your offer of POP, but end up tossing it out. You've got to do what Ernest did and take the action for the POP to be visible in all stores and at all times. If your salespeople can't do it, your distributors can. If they can't, you must. Point-of-purchase signs are a powerful marketing weapon, but not if they're gathering dust in the backroom.

Many industry experts will tell you that this is naive advice. They'll point out that retailers won't let just any guerrilla walk in off the street and dictate displays. While it's true that giants like WalMart and Sears are a little complicated to deal with, most POPs don't get placed primarily because of lack of effort.

Jay Levinson does not run a large or even a small winery. But he did write a book called *The Most Important $1.00 Book Ever Written*. He offered it, along with a stock wire rack that held twenty-four books, to booksellers *if* they would put the rack next to the cash register. Jay knew that without a POP at the front of the store, his book was doomed.

Many retailers refused. Some wanted the book but wouldn't agree to put the rack next to the register. Jay said thanks, but no thanks, and moved on to the next bookseller. Eventually, the racks were in fifteen stores. The power of

Everyone who's been through high school remembers Cliffs Notes. How did these little yellow books become (and stay) so popular? A big part of their success lies in the use of POP.

Every single bookstore in America is visited by a Cliffs Notes rep at least once a month. In addition to doing a quick inventory of what needs to be ordered, the rep makes sure that the custom-made Cliffs display is still there, and still being used exclusively for Cliffs products. By keeping competitors out of their racks, and by making it easy for panicked high school students to find the notes they need, Cliffs is maximizing its sales and ensuring that bookstores are seeing a steady profit.

* * *

One of our favorite types of POP is a live demonstration. Everything from cooking dumplings in the aisle of the supermarket to using a Cuisinart at Macy's qualifies as a live demo. These demos, while not cheap, provide an atmosphere of excitement and festivity that translates into sales. If you're a manufacturer, send someone on the road to try it out. Retailers, encourage your suppliers to set these salesmakers up.

* * *

POP was demonstrated when within one month all 15 stores had sold all the books and reordered. With persistence, this could become the core element of regional marketing success.

DISPOSABLE VS. PERMANENT

When creating your POP, decide how long it must last. In many industries self-shipping, disposable displays are the norm. These corregated cardboard containers (sometimes called dumps) can be quickly assembled and then discarded when depleted. While easy to place, these displays don't ensure you long-term presence in the store.

Far more expensive are permanent displays. These are used by cosmetics companies at their counters in department stores, by the folks who make golf clubs for pro shops, even by toothbrush manufacturers. If your product is going to stay in the store for a long time, you should investigate this alternative.

In addition to displays, you should also investigate alternatives such as posters, shelf talkers (little signs that hang below your item), and cutaways. Cutaways display how your product works. They include telephones made out of clear plastic, skis cut in half, or any other means of revealing the guts of your product. One of our favorites is the hard hat display used by Krazy Glue that refers back to their memorable TV commercial in which a construction worker glues himself by the hard hat to a steel girder hanging in midair. The display is a vivid way to educate people about the effectiveness of the product.

In most cases, if you can demonstrate that you'll increase profits for the retailer, she'll be willing to listen to your pitch and to include your permanent POP in her store.

RETAILER-DRIVEN POP

Savvy guerrilla retailers will realize that POP can increase sales per customer, which translates directly into bottom line. Does your store have a map making it easy to find items? Have you shopped the competition to discover the innovative ways they promote their product?

Appoint a trusted employee to act as vice president of POP. Her job is constantly to improve the way you're talking with the customer at the point-of-purchase—increasing the information you're presenting and the excitement you create.

POINT-OF-PURCHASE RESOURCES

POPAI (point-of-purchase Advertising Institute)
66 North Van Brunt Street • Englewood, NJ 07631 • (201) 894-8899
Offers members and the public a wide range of information, including buyer's guides, samples, and more.

P-O-P Times
7400 Skokie Blvd. • Skokie, IL 60077 • (708) 675-7400

***Retail Store Image* magazine**
6151 Powers Ferry Rd., NW, Suite 200 • Atlanta, GA 30339
(404) 955-2500

POINT-OF-PURCHASE DISPLAY COMPANIES

The companies listed below offer POP materials to clients nationwide. For local providers, check your Yellow Pages.

Academy Display
750 Pasquinelli Drive, Suite 204 • Westmont, IL 60559 • (708) 655-3010

Graphic Communications, Inc.
922 Washington Ave. • Golden, CO 80401 • (303) 277-9444

Display One
N83 W13330 Leon Rd. • Menomonee Falls, WI 53051 • (800) 678-5880
POP display company and also publishers of the Merchandising Insights *newsletter. Call them for a free copy.*

AG Industries, Inc.
1 American Road • Cleveland, OH 44144 • (800) 388-1244

Marketing Displays International
38271 West Twelve Mile Road • Farmington Hills, MI 48331
(313) 553-1900

Display Technologies
30-56 Whitestone Expwy. • Whitestone, NY 11354 • (718) 321-3100

Phoenix Display & Packaging Corp.
1300 Metropolitan Avenue • W. Deptford, NJ 08066 • (609) 853-7000

Indoor Media Group has developed a new point-of-purchase advertising medium called In-Floor. The company produces floor tiles with advertising messages that can replace ordinary floor tiles at the point-of-purchase. It's high impact and low cost, at only 96¢ per 1,000 impressions. Call Indoor Media Group at (214) 871-2277.

Thirty years ago, an innovative pen manufacturer wanted to show how much easier it was to write with his new pen. He created a small display that held 100 pens, as well as a small pad. This "try before you buy" pad begged the customer to reach out and touch the pens— and translated into big sales.

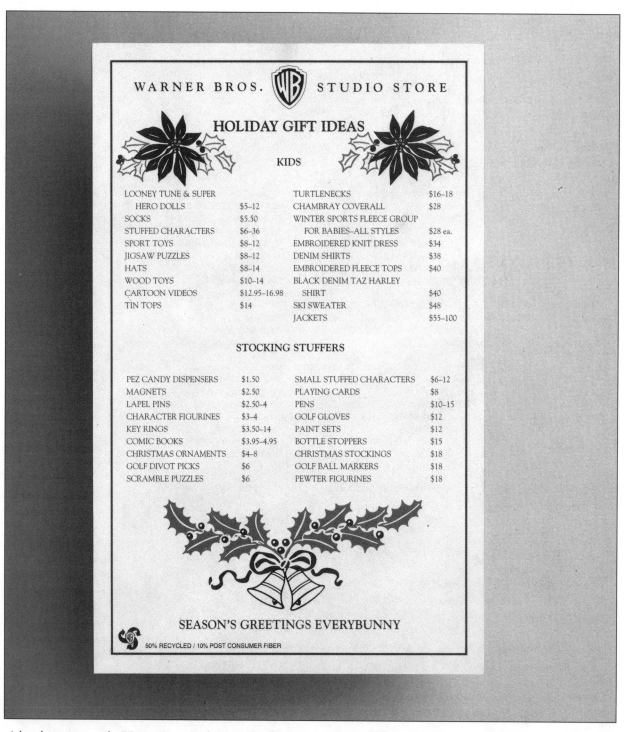

A handout given at the Warner Bros. Studio Store during the holidays. The handout is filled with great ideas for gifts sold at the store, broken down by price range.

INNOVATIVE POINT-OF-PURCHASE

Genesis Creative Group, Inc.

640 Three Mile Rd. N.W. • Grand Rapids, MI 49504 • (616) 784-3803

Alvimar Manufacturing Co.

51-02 21st Street • Long Island City, NY 11101 • (718) 937-0404

Both of these companies specialize in point-of-purchase inflatables. Large, freestanding inflatables can be used to promote products and smaller point-of-purchase inflatables can sit on countertops where products are sold.

Telestar Interactive Corporation

11541 Goldcoast Drive • Cincinnati, OH 45249 • (513) 469-9800

Telestar Interactive provides innovative microchip speech products, called Microtalk, for the point-of-purchase advertising industry.

Kinetics, LTD.

2805 Prospect • Colorado Springs, CO 80907 • (719) 636-3379

Kinetics, Ltd. sells a product called "The Grabbers." A grabber is a series of motion frames that are completely self-contained and battery operated. For just pennies a day, holographic decals on precision spinning gears use ambient light to turn a sign into a piece that looks like a theater marquee.

Catalina Marketing Network

11300 9th St. • St. Petersburg, FL 33716 • (800) 955-9770

Catalina Marketing Network is at the forefront of electronic point-of-purchase marketing. They can bring Checkout Coupon into your store. Checkout Coupon is a method of giving customers coupons based on what they buy. At the grocery store, for example, if a customer buys dog food, the register will print a coupon for dog food on the back of the register tape—very targeted and very effective.

! *The color of your point-of-purchase display is important. In a recent study, Joseph Bellizzi and Robert Hite placed television sets in front of red and blue displays. The sets placed in front of the blue displays generated 50% more in sales than those placed in front of the red ones..*

! *According to* Progressive Grocer *magazine, the position of your product on the shelf is crucial. A move from the top to the bottom shelf can reduce sales by up to 80%.*

PREMIUMS & SPECIALTY GIFTS

A miniature billboard on your prospect's desk.

GUERRILLA MARKETER OF THE YEAR
Jordan's likes to give something away to customers who buy furniture. At one point, they gave away a teddy bear with every mattress they sold.

If you could create a daily reminder of your business, the benefits you offer, and the quality you deliver, and place that reminder in front of your very best prospects, that would be a pretty good way to spend your money. In fact, an entire industry has grown out of this concept, and there are countless guerrilla uses for premiums and ad specialties.

Marketers divide giveaways into two categories: Premiums and Ad Specialties. Ad specialties are usually quite inexpensive and are designed to build goodwill and display your logo. Premiums can be quite valuable and are offered to increase the perceived value of a product. But these rules don't always hold true—the premium at the bottom of a box of Cheerios is worth just a few pennies, while the golf umbrellas given away at the Masters are worth nearly $100 each.

For the purposes of this chapter, we won't distinguish between the two categories—we'll just call them premiums. But when dealing with suppliers, you'll probably want to call an ad specialty and ad specialty.

Premiums generate goodwill, remind prospects about your business, and can even add perceived value to your product. They're fun, too.

Cracker Jacks built their business on premiums. When you're seven years old, the prospect of a 3¢ prize at the bottom of the box can be even more enticing than the popcorn you need to eat to get there. *Sports Illustrated* sells hundreds of thousands of subscriptions by selling the premium instead—usually a sports highlight videotape. In both cases, the premium is an additional benefit to purchase. Of course, every time you watch the tape, you're reminded of how much you enjoy the magazine—a nice benefit for *SI.*

While graft is frowned upon in this country, you can still bring along a gift when you call on a prospective client. One sports marketer brings along hockey pucks imprinted with the company's logo when they call on potential

BASICS

PREMIUMS VS. AD SPECIALTIES

PREMIUMS: Giveaway items that generate goodwill and are given to customers along with your product when they purchase from you. They add perceived value to your product. The toy you find at the bottom of a cereal box is a premium.

AD SPECIALTIES: Giveaway items that help you build a relationship with a prospective client or customer. The perceived value isn't nearly as important as whether or not it will be used. The goal is to drill your name into the mind of the consumer. The T-shirt imprinted with your company logo that you give to prospective clients when you meet with them is an ad specialty.

advertising clients. They spend about 50¢ on each puck, but the perceived value of the gift is a lot higher. The puck is a great icebreaker too.

SET GOALS FOR YOUR PREMIUMS

As you can imagine, a category as varied as premiums can satisfy a number of goals for your company. Before spending a penny, be sure you've clearly defined exactly what you expect from your premium. Some choices:

➤ **Make an impact on carefully selected prospects who might otherwise not notice your company.**

Do a quick analysis to determine how much a new order might be worth, and how much you'll need to spend to get the attention of prospects. A company selling multi-million-dollar consulting contracts can spend a little bit more than a housepainter on an icebreaking premium. You need to compare the cost of the premium with the cost of an alternative—direct mail or an ad campaign, for example.

➤ **Generate brand awareness among a large group of people.**

At public events, people notice what other people are wearing. If everyone on the beach has your logo on their hat, it makes an impression. Be careful though—brand awareness and real sales are two different things, and a guerrilla is careful not to confuse them. While it may boost your ego to see everyone wearing your picture, test the premium to be sure it works.

➤ **Increase the perceived value of the product you sell without dramatically increasing your cost of goods.**

Just like the kid attracted by the Cracker Jacks, many of us are swayed by the prize inside. If you can offer a bonus with purchase, it helps to focus attention on your product. Cosmetic companies do this all the time, offering a makeup case or free perfume with a significant purchase. You can also investigate using travel as a premium for an expensive sale ("Buy this couch and get a trip to France...").

➤ **Generate store traffic.**

For many retailers, attracting a crowd is a surefire way to generate sales. Giving concert tickets or T-shirts to the first 100 people is a cheap way to have a long line standing outside your store. Be sure you have adequate security—riots are bad for business.

➤ **Position your company.**

Establishing your company's image in the consumer's mind is difficult and expensive. The right premium can often do this for you in a hurry. A dentist trying to establish himself as a children's specialist can give away toys with his name on them—immediately establishing himself as someone interested in kids.

An investment bank was trying to sell its services to the 100 largest companies in America. They were having no luck reaching the chief financial officer at each company until they used a premium.

Once a week, over the course of a month, they sent each CFO an autographed baseball—using signed baseballs they had purchased for about $100 each. After the third ball was delivered, a note said that the fourth ball (which would fill the final spot in the display case they sent) would be hand delivered by their sales rep. Not willing to miss out on a Ted Williams autographed ball, 80% of the CFOs set up an appointment. According to the investment bank, the promotion led to $50,000,000 in new business for the bank.

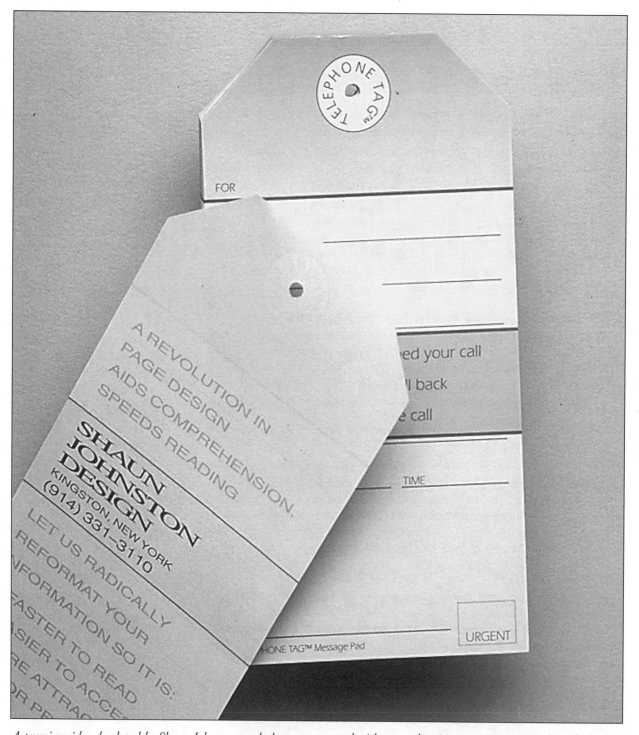

A premium idea developed by Shaun Johnston: a telephone message pad with your advertising message imprinted on the back of every sheet. It will always be by the phone and keep your name in the prospect's eye.

Source: Shaun Johnston Design • 276 Fair St. • Kingston, NY 12401 • (914) 331-3110

➤ **Put your name and phone number in front of the prospect at order time.**
An ambulance company is almost totally reliant on last-minute calls. But if
the consumer doesn't have the number, the sales may go to someone else.
By giving away emergency phone directories, listing police, fire, ambulance,
and hospital numbers, the ambulance company can be assured that their
number is exactly where it needs to be.

BUY IN BULK

Be prepared to order premiums in large quantities. Price breaks can be enormous. For example, a hardcover book might sell for $20 in the store, but if
you're going to buy 1,000 or more, you can easily get the book for under half
that (in some cases you may only spend $1 or so). The largest part of the cost
for many of the cheaper items is the cost to imprint your logo. Once the
imprint is made, the cost per item decreases the more you order.

DISTRIBUTION

You can either distribute your premium item yourself, or you can have somebody else do it for you. Find a means of distribution that will enhance the
image of the item and of your company. Athletic events are a great outlet for
premium items. Contact the local sports team (professional or collegiate) and
find out about premium night giveaway sponsorships. Maybe you can sponsor their cap night, and send thousands of fans home with your message on a
team cap. The team will probably give you some additional advertising with
your promotion. They'll want to advertise the giveaway and you will always
get a mention as the sponsor of the event.

At a trade show or public event you'll need to balance the waste involved in
giving premiums to people who will never purchase your product against the
ill will generated by turning down someone who asks for one. For this reason,
if you're giving a premium away in public, be prepared to give one to everyone who attends the event.

KEEP YOUR NAME AS THE FOCUS

One photography studio sponsors a team photo night with the local college's
basketball team. They give away 5,000 team photos with their logo imprinted
on them. Not only do fans keep the photos for years, but the quality of the
photo reinforces the work the photographer does. This investment in promotion pays dividends for years to come.

! *CAREFUL: Always make
sure the ad specialty you
use doesn't produce more
problems for you than it's
worth. One minor league ice
hockey team gave away seat
cushions to fans attending a
game. When the home team
made some errors, the enraged
fans showered the ice with seat
cushions. The incident delayed
the game, was a hazard to the
players and turned off the
advertisers who paid to have
their logos on the cushions. It's
safe to say that the promotion
backfired.*

*Domino's Pizza has
used refrigerator mag-
nets for years to pro-
mote their home-delivery pizza
business. The magnets keep
Domino's name and telephone
number in the eye of the consumer. When there's nothing
in the refrigerator, you can
always look on the refrigerator,
make a phone call, and
presto—dinner!*

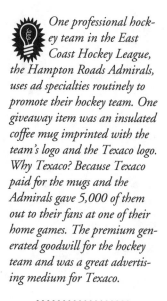

One professional hockey team in the East Coast Hockey League, the Hampton Roads Admirals, uses ad specialties routinely to promote their hockey team. One giveaway item was an insulated coffee mug imprinted with the team's logo and the Texaco logo. Why Texaco? Because Texaco paid for the mugs and the Admirals gave 5,000 of them out to their fans at one of their home games. The premium generated goodwill for the hockey team and was a great advertising medium for Texaco.

Try this for a great homemade premium. Invest in a luggage tag machine and every time you collect a business card from a customer or prospect, turn it into a luggage tag with your logo on the back. Enclose the tag in a follow-up letter. It's personalized and useful. Most importantly, it's a tangible reminder to the client that you are there and are ready to do business.

There are many items you can buy for under $1 to put your logo and name on. Refrigerator magnets, pens, pencils, and bumper stickers are some of the most popular. People also love to get T-shirts and hats for free. They make great giveaways, and when worn they serve as walking billboards for your business. Of course, there are expensive premiums as well, and these make great sense when dealing with a small, targeted audience of qualified prospects. Remember, the cost of the premium is irrelevant. What matters is the cost of the premium *per dollar generated in sales*. A premium that costs a nickel and generates no sales is worthless.

SUGGESTED GUIDELINES FOR A SUCCESSFUL SPECIALTY PROMOTION

➤ Select a premium that the recipient needs, wants, or desires. The item has to trigger a positive response or it is useless. People love to get something for nothing, but if they don't have a use for it, the item will end up in the trash once the novelty has worn off.

➤ Carefully plan your method of distribution. A premium item can be distributed before or after the sale depending upon its purpose.

➤ Choose an advertising theme that complements the product or service you offer. If you're an accountant, try handing out calculator business cards to your clients. It's a nice touch, especially at tax time.

➤ Put your phone number on the item if you can. Remember, your ultimate goal is to turn your goodwill gesture into sales, and a phone number (and an offer of some sort if you can) makes that even easier.

➤ Make sure the quality of your premium is at least as good as the quality of your product. A broken corkscrew with your name on it is quite a damper on your reputation.

➤ A clever guerrilla technique: Find a fellow guerrilla looking to publicize his product and cross-promote. He can generate awareness by having you distribute his item, and you can save money on the premium by buying from him at cost.

SELF-LIQUIDATING PREMIUMS

A guerrilla's favorite premium is a self-liquidating premium. These are items that you offer to your customers at a small charge, and they end up costing you nothing while substantially building your sales.

You've probably seen these premiums on the backs of cereal boxes (FREE plus

Here's a sampling of some of the hottest premiums on the market right now. The most popular are clothing items and pens.

Source: Promotional Products Association International

Magazine subscriptions are a great premium. They are extremely inexpensive (a subscription to Vanity Fair is only $12 a year), they last a full year, and they have a high perceived quality. The same is true for reference books that prospects use regularly, like dictionaries or directories.

$4 postage and handling) or addressed to frequent purchasers (Ten proofs of purchase plus $10).

The secret of a self-liquidating premium is finding a product with a very high perceived value and a very low actual cost. Many manufacturers are happy to work with you—premiums increase their production runs and generate publicity.

Here's how a self-liquidating premium might work:
➤ Buy 10,000 Frisbees, imprinted with your brand name, from Wham-O for 95¢ each (they regularly sell for $9 each.)

➤ Run a college promotion. "Send us a used six-pack, along with $3 for postage and handling, and we'll send you a Blitzed Beer Frisbee worth $9."

➤ Your fulfillment house charges you $2.05 to open the envelope, destroy the six pack, cash the check, and mail the Frisbee. You break even but have generated significant sales.

USING PREMIUMS AS A POSITIONING TOOL

If your product is hard to differentiate, creating a position in the marketplace can be difficult. For example, all beers taste approximately the same. One beer doesn't taste more "fun" or "yuppie" or "sports" than another. Yet breweries need to establish this position to grab market share.

One tactic is to use a premium. Offering free mud wrestling tickets with every six-pack, for example, will clearly identify which audience you're after.

The possibilities are limitless. A breakfast cereal can use a diet book, a cosmetics company can offer costume jewelry, and a particularly aggressive aftershave could offer condoms!

PREMIUM AND AD SPECIALTY RESOURCES

Association of Incentive Marketing
1600 Rt. 22 • Union, NJ 07083 • (908) 687-3090
trade association

The Specialty Advertising Association
3125 Skyway Circle N. • Irving, TX 75038 • (214) 252-0404
trade association

Dunkin' Donuts promotional calender sold during the holidays in their stores. Every month, Dunkin' Donuts included coupons good for that month only. It was a good way to spur sales throughout the year, and the calendars made a nice holiday gift.

The Aurora Casket Co. sent out its company literature accompanied by an imprinted coffee mug and a package of coffee. The premise was that the recipient would "take a coffee break on us" while reviewing the materials. The cup, imprinted with Aurora's phone number, made a useful, high-impact premium giveaway. It didn't end up in the trash, and it made the prospect stop and think about what Aurora had to offer.

• • • • • • • • • • • • • • • •

Advertising Age
(312) 649-5200

Business & Incentive Strategies
(212) 869-1300

Incentive
(714) 379-2200

Potentials in Marketing
(612) 333-0471

Promo Magazine
(800) 345-8112

Sales & Marketing Management
(212) 592-6300

The Complete Manager's Guide to Promotional Merchandise
by Louis Tharp • published by Dow Jones-Irwin

PREMIUM AND AD SPECIALTY COMPANIES

This a partial listing of some national premium brokers and manufacturers. For a premium company in your area, check the Yellow Pages or the Business to Business Directory.

American Premium Corp.
125 Walnut Street • Watertown, MA 02172 • (617) 923-1111

Brown & Bigelow
P.O. Box 64539 • St. Paul, MN 55164 • (800) 628-1749

Betras Plastics
Highway 221 North @ I-85 • Spartanburg, SC 29303 • (803) 599-0855

Chocolate By Design, Inc.
700-4 Union Pkwy. • Ronkonkoma, NY 11779 • (516) 737-0082

Competitive Edge Ad Specialty Manufacturing Co.
2711 Grand Avenue • Des Moines, IA 50312 • (800) 458-3343

Gift Creations
10310 Norris Ave. • Arleta, CA 91331 • (818) 896-7466

National Premium & Merchandising
2330 Commerce Drive • P.O. Box 247 • New Berlin, WI 53151
(414) 782-1510

New York Advertising Giveaways
309 Pittsfield Rd. • Lenox, MA 01240 • (800) 628-5037

Specialty Products Company
3198-F Airport Loop Drive • Costa Mesa, CA 92626 • (714) 549-1955

Spectrum Source Corporation
1212 Avenue of the Americas, #2201 • New York, NY 10036
(212) 840-5544

Van Schaack Premium Corp.
4600 S. Ulster St., Suite 650 • Denver, CO 80237 • (303) 779-6000

CALENDARS

One premium item you may want to consider is a calendar. There are many companies that will take your logo and company graphics and print them on calendars in a variety of different formats. Try mailing out pocket calendars with your imprint on them. They make nice gifts and people will use them all year long. Wall and desk calendars can give you even more for your dollar. You can say a lot more and you'll be seen by everyone who walks into the office where your calendar is hanging.

CALENDAR RESOURCES

Calendar Marketing Association
621 East Park Ave. • Libertyville, IL 60048 • (708) 816-8660
The Calendar Marketing Association prints a newsletter called Calendar News *that is full of ideas and contacts for calendar marketers.*

Calendar Promotions, Inc.
1010 S. 9th Ave. • Washington IA 52353 • (800) 421-5254
specialty calendar publishers

Sirivantana Interprint
(800) 995-8976
An international printing company specializing in calendars.

New York Advertising Giveaways
309 Pittsfield Rd. • Lenox, MA 01240 • (800) 628-5037
Sellers of Falco premium calendars.

TRADE SHOWS

One of the best ways to reach the hottest prospects.

According to the Trade Show Bureau, 34% of visitors to trade shows are top or middle managers. Chances are the prospects you speak to at trade shows are the decision-makers. 21% are sales/marketing professionals. 20% are in engineering or research. 12% are production or operation supervisors.

• • • • • • • • • • • • • • •

One publishing company gives its sales reps custom made engraved nametags to wear while manning the trade show booth. These tags look much better than the standard plastic variety and they create a classier atmosphere in the booth.

• • • • • • • • • • • • • • •

A trade show is the best place to reach the greatest number of real prospects all in the same place at the same time. If you handle it right, you can obtain enough contacts to generate a year's worth of orders by attending just one trade show. But that's not the real reason to go. Trade shows are perfect for establishing long-term relationships that will pay off for years to come. Even in this age of faxes and e-mail, the personal contacts that come out of a trade show can last for years.

Unlike almost all other settings, the sole purpose of a trade show is to sell. The attendees expect you to offer them products—the newer and more exciting, the better. This atmosphere of buyer curiosity and seller enthusiasm is perfect for the motivated guerrilla.

TIPS TO TRADE SHOW SUCCESS

➤ Select the Right Trade Show

Chances are there are hundreds of regional shows and national shows you can attend. In some industries, there are one or more relevant trade shows *each week*. Obviously, you can't go to all of them. You have to take into consideration factors like who is attending, how much it costs, how much lost time in the office it will cost you to attend, the quality of the show, and who the other exhibitors are before deciding whether or not attending is worth your while.

➤ Remember: Your Job Begins Way Before the Show Starts

There's lots to do before the show. Send invitations to all of your prospects to pick up a free product at your booth when they attend the show. Send people a show schedule and a map of the exhibit hall so they can find you easily. Send out an entry form for a contest that people can enter by visiting your booth at the show. Put out a press release telling about the show and your plans to exhibit. If you are a local business planning to attend a national show, this can be particularly effective. Work with show management—there are often special seminars, parties, and mailing lists available to exhibitors.

➤ Go to the Show with a Definite Goal in Mind

Know whether you plan to penetrate your existing market or expand into a new market. Know if you're going for sales or for leads. Without a goal, a show can be overwhelming. You can spread your efforts too thin and end up with nothing.

➤ Concentrate on the Design of Your Display

Make sure it blends with your marketing identity and your current marketing theme. If you can, include a hands-on demonstration or something that people can handle. Studies show that people love to touch things. At the very least, have something you can give away, ideally a sample of your product. Because most people don't like to walk into a booth where they might feel trapped, be sure your booth has an open feel. It's possible to spend a million dollars on a booth, but certainly not required. When you visit a trade show, find a booth you like and ask who designed it.

➤ **Make Sure You Have the Right People Staffing Your Booth**

Experts say profitability of a show is determined primarily by the quality of your people and how they work the booth. They must be personable and knowledgeable about your company and your product. They must also be empowered to make the sale and deal directly with customers. When someone is ready to buy, you don't want your employee having to say, "Well, I can't really place that order for you. Let me take your name and number and I'll have a salesperson call you in a few days." The customer will take her business elsewhere.

➤ **Wow 'em!**

Rent a limo and offer it to your biggest buyers to use at their convenience during the days of the show. Former video game giant Activision booked the Beach Boys to play at a Las Vegas trade show—and invited only their suppliers and customers to attend.

The annual *Playboy* party at the Consumer Electronics Show (one of the world's largest trade shows) is a magnet for major advertisers, and makes it easier for *Playboy* to make contact with key executives.

➤ **Run a Contest**

Try giving away a large-screen television set. In order to enter the contest, people must visit your booth and pick up a button, half of which is imprinted with your logo and a promotional message. The other half has a number on it. Hire someone to walk around the show and write down the numbers of all the buttons they see being worn. The winner is selected from those numbers. Sunsoft used this technique to sell their Batman video game at a show. Over 8,000 people were seen at the show wearing a button promoting the Sunsoft product. Sunsoft probably spent $3,000 for the television set and $1,000 for the buttons, but the impact of the promotion was priceless—even if only ten people saw each button, they made 80,000 positive impressions with key buyers.

FOCUS ON THE CRITICAL 20%

At every trade show, you'll find that 20% of the visitors account for 80% of your sales. It is critical that you *qualify your leads*. Immediately on meeting someone in your booth, introduce yourself and start asking questions. Find out what they do, what they want, how much they plan to spend.

A visitor will stop at about twenty booths per trade show. The average stop lasts about fifteen minutes, so keep your demonstrations to less than ten minutes to allow for conversation.

Informix software wanted to make a big splash when they introduced their first consumer software product, so they arranged to give away a tote bag (worth about $3) to each person who visited their booth. They intentionally kept the giveaway section of the booth small, and made people who wanted the tote bag watch a one-minute demo of their software. Because the line moved so slowly, there were thirty people outside the booth immediately, and by midday the line was more than 300 people long.

The buzz at the show was that Informix had the hottest new product, when in fact all they had was the longest line for a free tote bag.

A guerrilla in the consumer electronics business wanted to attract only qualified buyers to his booth at a major trade show. Instead of creating a friendly, open booth, his booth was sealed on four sides, and admission was limited to invited guests. Once word got out that there was a secret demonstration going on, buyers and the press flocked to the booth, begging for admission.

Unqualified visitors should be treated kindly, given a brochure and invited to look around (after all, you never know when an unqualified visitor will get a new job). Qualified prospects, on the other hand, should be immediately given the first class treatment. Invite them to meet executives. Ask them to sit down (a welcome relief at most trade shows). If possible, set up an appointment for them to return and speak when the environment isn't as crazy.

Before you get to the show, create a special box for the business cards of qualified prospects. Every night, enter these cards into your laptop computer or business diary. On the morning you return from the show, output all the names to mailing labels and send every person you met at the show a personal mail-merged letter along with another brochure. You'll be amazed at how few people bother to follow up at all.

Don't forget about your business cards as well (see *Business Cards*). Bring twice as many as you think you need and give them to everyone you meet.

DON'T FORGET THE MEDIA

Trade shows are vitally important to the media. This is the easiest way for them to cover the trends that affect an industry.

An alert guerrilla makes sure that the press room is well stocked with his press releases, is certain to attend relevant press conferences, gets a list of press attendees for follow-up, and keeps an eagle eye out for any press that may wander by.

ASK FOR ADVICE

Go to a trade show as a visitor before investing money to run your own booth. Visit other booths, (preferably not direct competitors) tell them you'll be exhibiting at the next show and ask them what works. You can also call your trade association and ask for their insight. *The Encyclopedia of Associations* lists the name and address of virtually every trade association in the country. You can probably find a copy at your local library.

TRADE SHOW RESOURCES

Your local Chamber of Commerce is one of the best sources of information about trade shows. Call them to find out when certain shows that come into your area normally take place and who runs them. Below is a listing of additional resources you should consult if you are thinking about venturing out on the trade show circuit. Also look in the Yellow Pages under "Display Designers" to find a local firm that can help you put your display together.

Tradeshow & Convention Guide
published by Amusement Business
P.O. Box 24970 • Nashville, TN 37202 • (615) 321-4250
published annually by Amusement Business, can be ordered for $85 by calling or writing.

Trade Shows Worldwide
published by Gale Research
835 Penobscot Bldg. • Detroit, MI 48226 • (800) 877-4253

Tradeshow Week Data Book
published by R.R. Bowker
121 Chanlon Rd. • New Providence, NJ 07974 • (800) 521-8110

Directory of Fairs, Festivals & Expositions
published by Amusement Business
Box 24970 • Nasvhille, TN 37202 • (615) 321-4251

PUBLICITY

Publicity is free advertising, plain and simple.

The guerrilla already knows that word of mouth is the most powerful marketing weapon. One of the best ways of generating word of mouth is through publicity. The "unbiased" nature of stories in the press generates interest from consumers who you could never reach with advertising.

Understand that the press needs your stories as much as you need to see them in print. Every day there are newspapers to fill, broadcasts to film, and radio shows to produce. Without stories like yours, the newspapers would carry nothing but articles about wars in foreign countries.

There are a number of great books about publicity and public relations (see the end of the chapter for some recommendations), but there are a few guerrilla techniques that you can use to break through the clutter.

PUBLICITY GUIDELINES

> **Don't Send Material to Everyone**

A press release sent to *Time* magazine is almost certain to be a waste of time. Instead, pick five or ten publications/media outlets that you'd really like to see your story appear in. Focus on them like a laser beam. Find out which editors have created stories similar to yours, and go straight to them. Don't forget, for most business, a local story is better than a national one.

> **Break the Rules**

If you're not a PR professional, don't worry so much about appearing to be one. If you want to send a dozen bagels from your new bagel bakery, go ahead. Some editors may frown, but at least you got their attention.

> **Be Persistent**

Just because your story didn't get picked up this week, don't give up. You can probably come up with one newsworthy event every month. So every month send a press release to your target list of five or ten. Sooner or later, it'll work.

One great way to generate publicity is to give an award in your field. Gale Research gives out an annual award honoring the Libraries and Librarians of the year. As sponsors of the award, Gale is mentioned in all media coverage of the award. The winning library is also featured in The Library Journal, *so Gale receives several mentions there, too. Can you think of a better way to reach your target market? Gale Research generates a lot of goodwill and puts themselves in the position of being the authority in the research field.*

PUBLICITY BASICS

Reprint any publicity stories about you or your company and use them in your mailings, as signs, in brochures, in press kits, as framed display pieces, and as sales aids for your sales representatives. Yesterday's newspaper is dead and gone; yesterday's PR story can—and should—live forever.

➤ **Buy Some PR**

The smaller the paper, the better the odds. Most advertiser-supported small papers and radio stations will be happy to publicize your event if you're a regular advertiser. Remember: ask the ad guy, not the editor, or your chances of being covered by the editor will be ruined forever.

HOW TO GET COVERED BY THE PRESS

The business owner who sends out several hundred press releases and then sits back and waits is probably not going to get a lot of return on his effort. Public relations takes a lot more ingenuity than that.

Your press release is a good place to start, but make sure you've done your homework. Make a list of all the publications you think might be interested in your product and research them. Find out what kinds of stories they tend to cover the most, and who the key editors and writers are. Call the editorial offices and find out who should receive your materials and if there are any special requirements. Personalize your cover letter and show off your knowledge of the publication. Mention an article you've read or an issue you found particularly interesting. Make suggestions of where your story might be run in the next issue.

Most important, your press release must be newsworthy. Why are you sending it? What's so interesting about your product, service, or store, and why now? Your story has to be compelling. Make sure you've written your story clearly and with a minimum of hype. Remember, editors read thousands of press releases, and they're not going to bother with yours if it is clumsy or difficult to read.

Your public relations job does not end with the press release. Follow up with a phone call. Ask the editor if she needs any more information to write the story. If you reach a dead end, don't despair. It frequently takes more than one effort to get the coverage you want. Send out releases on a regular basis and continue to follow them up. Your persistence will pay off with a headline, or at least with a valuable blurb that you can use to build credibility with your customers and prospects alike.

Want publicity? Try publishing a book. The architectural firm of Swanke Hayden Connell was involved in the restoration of the Statue of Liberty. The project was quite a feather in the firm's cap and so, to let people know what they had done, they wrote a book about it. Restoring the Statue of Liberty *by Richard Seth Hayden and Thierry W. Despont was published in 1986 by McGraw-Hill.*

This was a press release sent out with a new book written by Seth Godin. The book fit inside the fold-up package and the release was printed inside. The eye-catching package captured media attention and resulted in a lot of interviews for the author.

PUBLICITY RESOURCES

There are hundreds of resources out there to help you get your publicity campaign off the ground. Listed below are some newsletters, magazines, associations, and books that you can use. We've also included a list of resources that can help you locate an outside PR firm if you need one. The Yellow Pages is a good place to start looking for a local firm. You can expand your search from there.

Radio-TV Interview Report

135 E. Plumstead Ave. • Landsdowne, PA 19050 • (215) 259-1070

Bimonthly magazine listing project pitches and profiles and mailed to over 5,000 radio and TV talk show and TV news programming executives nationwide.

Public Relations Quarterly

P.O. Box 311 • Rhinebeck, NY 12572 • (914) 876-2081

Communications Briefing

700 Black Horse Pike, Suite 110 • Blackwood, NJ 08012 • (609) 232-6380

monthly newsletter

Jack O'Dwyer's PR Newsletter

271 Madison Ave. • New York, NY 10016 • (212) 679-2471

weekly newsletter

PR Reporter

P.O. Box 600 • Exeter, NH 03833 • (603) 778-0514

Weekly newsletter. The publishers of the PR Reporter also put out three supplements entitled Tips & Tactics *(how-to PR techniques),* Purview *(a list of books and other resources), and* Managing the Human Climate *(an analysis of specific events with an eye on public relations).*

PR Newswire (PRN)

1515 Broadway • New York, NY 10036 • (800) 832-5522

daily news service

Audio TV Features

149 Madison Ave., No. 804 • New York, NY 10016 • (212) 889-1342

daily radio feed

North American Precis Syndicate

1901 Ave. of the Stars, Suite 202 • Los Angeles, CA 90067
(818) 761-8400

Monthly distributor of multimedia script and slide packages to radio and tv

---

McKenzie Communications is a publicity success story of the first magnitude. One client, the law firm of Morrison & Foerster, had a senior executive who was a former associate general counsel to the U.S. Trade Representative. The executive wrote a summary of the North American Free Trade Agreement. Gordon Wright of McKenzie Communications contacted USA Today *with the news that a synopsis of the NAFTA had been written and that the law firm would give anyone who asked a free copy. The resulting publicity brought in over 14,000 inquiries to the law firm, many of which have turned into solid business leads.*

Robert Half is a very well-known employment agency. They established their fame by sending out at least one press release every month, year in and year out. They conduct surveys of chief executives and summarize the results in press releases. They do an analysis of the life of the average paper clip in an office and do a press release. Like clockwork, editors can expect a useful business blurb from Robert Half. Inevitably, Half is quoted as a leading expert in the field.

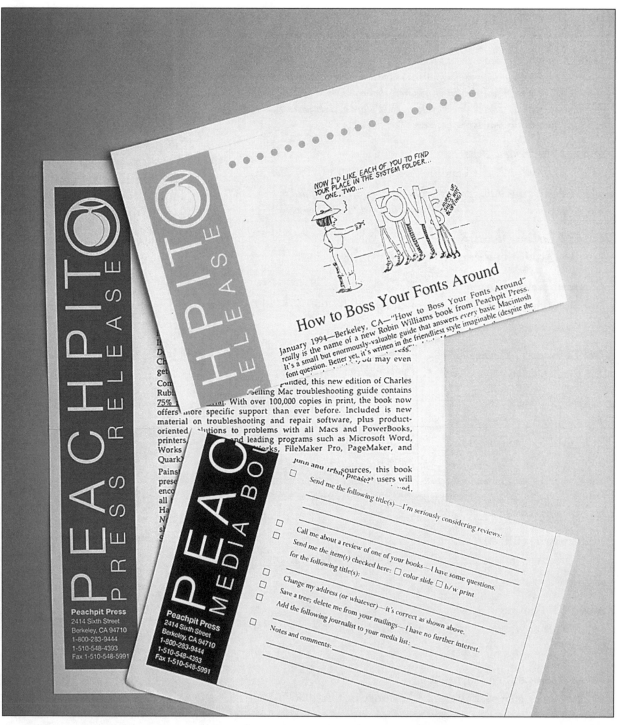

Peachpit Press sends this press release in the form of a newsletter to the media on a regular basis. It generates a lot of publicity for the books they publish and keeps the media apprised of new ventures in which Peachpit is involved.

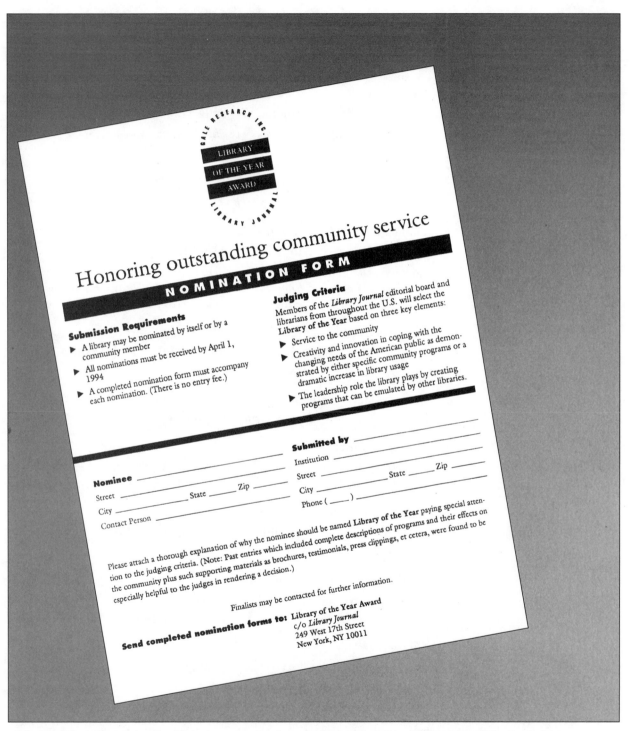

GALE RESEARCH INC.
LIBRARY
OF THE YEAR
AWARD
LIBRARY JOURNAL

Honoring outstanding community service

NOMINATION FORM

Submission Requirements

▶ A library may be nominated by itself or by a community member

▶ All nominations must be received by April 1, 1994

▶ A completed nomination form must accompany each nomination. (There is no entry fee.)

Judging Criteria

Members of the *Library Journal* editorial board and librarians from throughout the U.S. will select the **Library of the Year** based on three key elements:

▶ Service to the community

▶ Creativity and innovation in coping with the changing needs of the American public as demonstrated by either specific community programs or a dramatic increase in library usage

▶ The leadership role the library plays by creating programs that can be emulated by other libraries.

Submitted by _____

Institution _____

Nominee _____   Street _____ State _____ Zip _____

Street _____ State _____ Zip _____   City _____

City _____   Phone (____) _____

Contact Person _____

Please attach a thorough explanation of why the nominee should be named **Library of the Year** paying special attention to the judging criteria. (Note: Past entries which included complete descriptions of programs and their effects on the community plus such supporting materials as brochures, testimonials, press clippings, et cetera, were found to be especially helpful to the judges in rendering a decision.)

Finalists may be contacted for further information.

Send completed nomination forms to: Library of the Year Award
c/o *Library Journal*
249 West 17th Street
New York, NY 10011

Gale Research generates a lot of publicity by sponsoring the annual award honoring the libraries and librarians of the year.

Source: Gale Research

Medialink is a video public relations firm specializing in the production of video news releases and video public relations tours by satellite. For $8,000 Medialink can set up simultaneous interviews from the same location via satellite with a dozen or more media outlets. They can also provide special event videoconferences, public service announcements, and electronic press kits. If you need big-time publicity, this is a great deal. Call Medialink at (212) 682-8300.

Derus Media
500 N. Dearborn, No. 516 • Chicago, IL 60601 • (312) 644-4360
Monthly distributor of multimedia script and slide packages to radio and TV.

News USA
4601 Eisenhower • Alexandria, VA 22304 • (800) 868-6872
Distributor of monthly media releases and editorial feature camera-ready art.

Metro Publicity Services
33 W. 34th St. • New York, NY 10001 • (212) 947-5100
Service does monthly mailings to 7,000 newspapers.

Public Relations Society of America
33 Irving Place • New York, NY 10003 • (212) 995-2230
Publishers of the Public Relations Journal. *The PRSA is also a great resource for books, periodicals, videotapes, and audiotapes on marketing and publicity. They also put out the* Bibliography for Public Relations Professionals, *a comprehensive listing of books.*

International Association of Business Communicators
1 Hallidie Plaza, Suite 600 • San Francisco, CA 94102 • (415) 433-3400

Writing Effective News Releases
by Catherine V. McIntyre • published by Piccadilly Books
P.O. Box 25203 • Colorado Springs, CO 80936

Getting Publicity
by Tana Fletcher and Julia Rockler • published by Self-Counsel Press
1481 Charlotte Rd. • North Vancouver, British Columbia, Canada V7J 1H1

How to Get Publicity
by William Parkhurst • published by Random House, Inc.
201 E. 50th St., 31st floor • New York, NY 10022

Lesly's Public Relations Handbook
by Philip Lesly • published by Prentice-Hall, Inc.
15 Columbus Circle, 15th floor • New York, NY 10023

On the Air
by Al Parinello • published by Career Press, Inc.
180 5th Ave. • Hawthorne, NJ 07507
Covers the basics of getting yourself on a radio or TV talk show.

The Publicity Manual
by Kate Kelly • published by Visibility Enterprises
11 Rockwood Dr. • Larchmont, NY 10538

PUBLICITY DIRECTORIES

Most of the directories listed below should be available at your local library. You can also order them directly through their publishers.

Bacon's Publicity Checker
Bacon's Radio/TV Directory
Bacon's Publishing Company
332 South Michigan Avenue • Chicago, IL 60604 • (800) 621-0561

The Internal Publications Directory
Gebbie Press Inc.
Box 1000 • New Paltz, NY 12561 • (914) 255-7560

Working Press of the Nation
National Research Bureau
310 South Michigan, Suite 1150 • Chicago, IL • (312) 663-5580
Listing of companies that produce in-house publications. A unique way to target publicity.

Broadcasting Cable Yearbook
Broadcasting Publications, Inc.
1705 DeSales St., N.W. • Washington, DC 20036
Directory of broadcast media

All-In-One Directory
Gebbie Press, Inc.
Box 1000 • New Paltz, NY 12561 • (914) 255-7560
Lists publicity outlets in newspapers, magazine, radio, and television.

GETTING TV COVERAGE WITHOUT PAYING FOR IT

Anytime that you can take your ads or your product and make them TV-friendly, you'll increase the chances of getting more exposure than you've paid for. Sometimes you can even get free coverage if the media decides to cover you as a news item.

For instance, Nutri-System launched a nationwide campaign during which they received at least ten times the amount of advertising they paid for. They gave radio personalities all over the country free membership in the Nutri-System program. In exchange, the personalities went on the air and talked about how much weight they had lost on their diet plan. You cannot buy such testimonials at any price. Nutri-System also bought some air time on these stations, which turned them into paying advertisers and made the stations even more receptive to continuing these endorsements.

Nutri-System signed up celebrities like Tommy Lasorda and Kathy Lee Gifford to endorse the diet plan in TV ads. Each spokesperson actually used the diet plan to lose weight. Nutri-System boosted their credibility by showing before and after photos of the celebrities.

Many groundbreaking advertisers have managed to have their commercials covered on the evening news. If your commercial is controversial, consider sending it to news directors. If it gets picked up, you could see your ad—free—on newscasts around the country.

Another good tactic is to give your product away as a prize on a televised game show. Game-Show Placements, Ltd., specializes in getting exposure for your products on these shows. Call them in Hollywood, CA, at (213) 874-7818 to find out if they can make your product a star.

TELEPHONE

TELEPHONE FOR GUERRILLAS

The telephone is the ideal guerrilla tool. Careful, though – it can be abused all too easily. A true guerrilla knows the real value of the telephone: one-to-one communication.

The telephone is the best way to reach your prospects directly and in a way that makes them feel like you are bringing something of value into their lives. In this section, you'll learn the secrets to making the telephone a more effective selling tool. From toll-free numbers to selling on hold, you'll see how the telephone can make the buying experience more pleasant and efficient for your customers, and more profitable for you.

TELEPHONE SELLING

One-on-one communication with your prospect.

The telephone is a great tool for the guerrilla. Unlike mass marketing media, the telephone is a one-on-one tool. It *requires* you to treat the prospect as an individual, and guarantees that you'll get instant feedback.

Used properly, telephone selling is fast, efficient, and effective. It allows you reach a small but targeted market and make a substantial impact. There are potholes, but once you've identified the right strategy, telephone selling can be a powerhouse.

THE GOLDEN RULE OF TELPHONE SELLING

Never call someone without a referral. If you can't tell the caller the name of a mutual friend, acquaintance, or organization, don't bother calling. Phone selling is powerful, but it is also a dangerous weapon. Remember, when you're using a phone, you are essentially barging your way into your prospect's home or office.

Properly used, the telephone is a great way to break through the clutter and have a one-on-one communication with a prospect—the goal of every guerrilla. Improperly used, it will build up resentment and animosity and lose customers for life.

All of us have been pestered during dinner by a telemarketer who uses a script, is getting paid by the call, and has absolutely no idea what he or she is selling. The next time one calls you, try this trick. Say to her, "I'm very interested in what you're calling about. Can you tell me about it in your own words?" Ten to one the telemarketer will revert to the script within five seconds.

There's a substantial difference between phone selling as used by a guerrilla and the shotgun tactics that inevitably lead to resentment. The guerrilla uses the phone to reach a carefully targeted individual. You must know something special about the prospect to justify using the phone.

The best way to use the phone is to call people who are already your customers. "Hi, just wanted to remind you that your gutters need to be cleaned again this year." You have a relationship with these clients, and they'll probably welcome your call.

The second best way is to mention the name of an organization, company, or individual in the first sentence of your pitch.

On the previous page, we talked about acquiring referrals. Another way to get your foot in the telemarketing door is to work with a partner organization. For example, a company in New York sells Oriental rugs. They work with local churches and synagogues and give half the profit to the sponsoring charity.

Using their partnering organization's membership lists to promote their rug sale, the company is able to convince hundreds of members to attend the auction they run. The phone call goes something like this:

"Hello."
"Hi, I'm calling on behalf of the Methodist Church in New Rochelle. Did I catch you at a bad time?"
<NOTE: In one sentence we've identified our referral and asked for permission to have a conversation. There are two possible responses:>

"Yes. It's a bad time."
<If the person doesn't want to talk, don't force them. Give them a chance to get back to you or to give you a time when you can get back to them, then move on.>

Or:

"I've got just a minute. What can I do for you?"
<In this case, you've got the door opened just an inch. Don't take too much advantage of it. Lay out your proposal quickly and then give the prospect a chance to respond.>

"I'm with Acme Rug. We're running an Oriental rug auction for the church. Last year we donated more than $15,000. Do you think you and your family might be willing to attend this year?"

"Sure, we're regular members of the church. What's up?"
<This prospect is motivated by your referral. You can be more subtle here, build up more of a relationship.>
"My name's Bob. I'm an auctioneer at Acme Rug. As I'm sure you know, the church does a lot of charitable work each year, and now the church is in need of a new roof. We gave $15,000 to the church last year, and we're working to do it again this year..."

Note that we're not selling anything over the phone. There are just too many

L.L. Bean should give lessons on proper telephone selling techniques. They have phone operators manning the lines 24 hours a day, 7 days a week. That's not what sets them apart though. Every call is answered by a live person, not a machine, and customers are rarely, if ever, put on hold. The phone salespeople are knowledgeable, friendly, and very personable. When you get off the phone, you feel like you've been to the L.L. Bean store and have been waited on like royalty. Best of all, you never had to leave the house. One operator spent forty minutes on the phone with one customer, waiting for her to measure her son's foot size and discussing the pros and cons of all the different product choices. Now that's telephone selling!

barriers involved in getting someone to commit to a cash purchase on the telephone. Instead, work to sell a meeting, or even just to send a brochure or pamphlet.

Remember, trust is the guerrilla's secret weapon, and you must take your time to build it carefully. Telemarketing can be the first step to building trust, but it rarely works as an effective way to close the sale.

CHECKLIST FOR PLANNING THE CALL

1. Set Your Objective

What are you trying to do in this call? Sell a new product? Answer a question? Make an appointment? Qualify a prospect? Set your goal. You have to have a target before you can hit it. Don't expect that you'll sell many products by phone. Far better to use the phone to qualify prospects, to arrange a meeting, or to obtain information for a customized proposal.

2. Plan Your Introduction

Your first impression is your best, so make sure it counts. Steps to a successful introduction include:

➤ Your name

➤ Your company's name

➤ Personalize your introduction to the customer. Be positive and friendly, but react according to your customer's style. If he or she wants to chat a little at first, follow that lead.

➤ Make sure you're talking to the decision-maker. Does this person have the authority to purchase your product or service?

➤ Express a willingness to help, if the situation calls for it. Example: Your customer may need help with a problem. By offering to help, you position yourself as a team player.

➤ Develop an interest-creating remark. This remark ought to answer the question: Why should I listen to you? Example: "I'm calling to discuss the three techniques we used to increase Jones Heating's sales by 31% last year." or "I'm calling to discuss the article about you in last week's *Boston Globe*."

3. Manage Screeners

When you call a business, you'll probably run into a receptionist or secretary before reaching the person you want. They may be hesitant about letting you talk to the person in charge. Remember, they handle hundreds of business representatives every day. Here are several hints that can help you deal with a screening assistant or secretary:

➤ Ask for their help. You're offering a potential benefit to this company. Ask him to help you identify the person you need to talk to. Besides, it's very difficult for him to say no when someone is asking for their help. Example: "Could you help me? I'm new to this account, and I'm not sure who is in charge of purchasing maintenance supplies. Who would that be?"

➤ Be direct. You have many customers, and wasting their time is as bad as wasting yours. No one is fooled when you try to be cute by not indicating why you are calling.

➤ Use third-party references. A familiar name gives credibility to a stranger.

➤ Follow up on letters you send in advance. Sometimes a person will pay attention to a piece of mail and be much more receptive to a follow-up call. A letter can break the ice and also help you get past the screeners. "I'm calling to follow up on a letter I sent Mr. Jones last week."

➤ If you're returning a call, say so.

➤ Call after office hours. If the screener is particularly difficult to deal with, call before or after normal hours or during lunch when the odds are greater that the decision-maker will answer her own phone.

4. Develop Probing Questions

If you're working without a script, you may find yourself stymied after a minute or two of conversation. Many people get defensive on the telephone, and without the right questions, you may have to end the conversation prematurely. Ask lots of questions—people like talking about themselves, and interesting questions are a great way to keep a conversation going.

5. Distinguish Benefits from Features

All too often, a salesperson pays more attention to the features than the benefits. However, the customer buys because of the *benefits.*

Every benefit ultimately does one of three things for your customer:

➤ It increases sales.

➤ It decreases costs. (Costs don't have to be actual cash. Getting killed or losing a valuable employee or wasting time are costs as well).

➤ It increases profits.

In one successful phone campaign, a guerrilla enclosed a box of Cracker Jacks along with an introductory letter. A week later, he called to follow up. "I'm calling about the letter with the Cracker Jacks" was all he needed to get through to more than half the prospects he had targeted with his letter.

6. Ask for the Order

As a guerrilla, you're probably not going to try to sell your product by phone. But you are selling something—a brochure, a meeting, or an in-store visit. Don't be shy. Ask for the order. Try to close with the alternate choice, "Would Monday at 3 P.M. be a good time for a meeting, or is Tuesday morning better?" You'll find hundreds of other closes in Zig Ziglar's classic, *Secrets of Closing the Sale.*

Source: Powerful Telephone Skills, *published by Career Press*

A TOOL THAT EVERY TELEMARKETER MUST OWN

Don't consider a serious telemarketing effort without investing in a tape recorder that will allow you to keep a record of your calls. (This is legal—what's not permitted is recording a conversation where both parties aren't aware of the recorder, but if you know it's there, then you're fine.).

The tape recorder will dramatically improve the quality of your telemarketing. You and your staff can dissect which approaches work—and eliminate the ones that don't.

EFFECTIVE TELEPHONE TECHNIQUES

➤ Smile (it comes through in your voice)

➤ Speak clearly and concisely

➤ Be enthusiastic

➤ Lower your voice pitch

➤ Be positive

➤ Be prepared for objections

➤ Talk directly into the mouthpiece

➤ Consider your customer's personality

➤ Speak in terms of benefits

➤ Discuss rather than tell

➤ Always thank the listener for his time

➤ Follow up if necessary

INEFFECTIVE TELEPHONE TECHNIQUES

➤ Frowning

➤ Muttering

➤ Sounding tired

➤ Speaking in a monotone

➤ Being negative

➤ Being overconfident

➤ Holding the phone under your chin

➤ Rambling

➤ Making accusatory remarks

➤ Arguing

➤ Hanging up abruptly

➤ Forgetting to thank the listener

➤ Trying to talk and do something else at the same time.

Source: Powerful Telephone Skills, *published by Career Press*

TELEMARKETING RESOURCES

Powerful Telephone Skills
published by Career Press • (800) 227-3371
A great tool for guerrillas who rely on the telephone as a lifeline to their customers.

Secrets of Closing the Sale
by Zig Ziglar • Published by Berkley Books
The best book ever written on selling. The tapes are invaluable.

Successful Telemarketing
by Bob Stone & John Wyman • Published by NTC Business Books
Outlines case histories of firms that have successfully employed telemarketing to build their businesses (for example, the GE Answer Center and the AT&T Sales Center)

Successful Telephone Selling in the 90's
by Martin D. Shafiroff & Robert L. Shook • Published by Harper Collins

900 NUMBERS

Offer something of value and watch prospects pay to call.

Fifteen years ago, the phone company created a technology that would allow companies to earn money by generating calls to their offices. 900 numbers cost a fixed fee from anywhere in the country and generate income of 10% to 50% of the cost of the call.

Because 900 numbers have been used heavily for porn lines and ripping off unsuspecting callers, many individuals are suspicious of this technique. Many companies have altered their phones to lock out this exchange.

That doesn't mean you should abandon 900 numbers, though. Here are two scenarios in which you could make use of them:

➤ You offer a piece of short, highly valuable verbal information that is very timely. For example, giving sports scores, financial results, or weather information is a perfect use for a 900 number. People will gladly pay for this information again and again, and if you promote yourself correctly, you can establish a profitable, stand-alone business.

➤ You want to collect the names and phone numbers of prospects without exposing yourself to a lot of risk. You can run a 900 number that offers some sort of reward—either a prize (see *Sweepstakes and Contests* for legal issues) or a gift, or a fun or valuable audio snippet (last year, you could call the Pope on a 900 number).

Then you can use public relations and advertising to promote your number. Once you've established a relationship with the caller, these names and numbers give you an opportunity for repeat buyers.

CAUTION: There are significant financial and marketing risks associated with setting up a 900 number. You're responsible for the bills if your callers don't pay, so be sure to test extensively and be prepared for chargebacks.

FACTS ABOUT 900 NUMBERS

➤ Calls to a 900 number will be fewer than to a free 800 number, but the callers will be more motivated.

➤ A 900 line can help build a qualified base of prospects if you offer something other than your main service or product.

➤ 900 numbers require no investment in equipment. Don't be afraid to run one for a short time as an experiment.

➤ When supplying prospects with data, offer to fax it to callers who use your

Kimberly-Clark offered parents a 900 number that played a personalized lullaby. They gained revenues from the more than 100,000 calls they received, as well as a chance to mail coupons or materials to the callers as a follow up.

900 number. Those needing your data instantly will gladly pay the $5 toll for the call.

➤ Think twice before offering incentives for a 900 call. The call costs money (legally defined as "consideration"). You don't want to end up accidentally running a lottery and wind up in the slammer.

➤ Your 900 number can be used as a self-liquidating sample center. For example, if you sell perfume, try setting up a 900 number that people can call to get a free sample of your perfume. If the cost of the call covers the cost of producing and mailing the sample, you break even.

➤ Memberships and subscriptions can easily be sold through a 900 number. Prospects get convenience and instant gratification.

➤ Using a 900 number is a proven way for fundraisers to obtain money from small contributors.

SERVICE BUREAUS

If you are going to establish a 900 number, hire a service bureau to set up the number and handle the incoming calls. Hire a company that is well-versed in interactive telephone marketing. One of the hardest things to overcome is the history of fraudulent use of 900 numbers, so you need to hire a reputable firm that will enhance your campaign, not drag it into the muck. It may be more economical to use a service bureau that also provides product fulfillment.

West Telemarketing Corporation
9223 Bedford Ave. • Omaha, NE 68134 • (800) 841-9000

Interactive Telemedia Services Corporation
14651 Ventura Blvd. • Sherman Oaks, CA 91403 • (800) 441-4486

Network Telephone Services, Inc.
6233 Variel Ave. • Woodland Hills, CA 91367 • (800) 727-6874

Scherers Communications Inc.
575 Scherers Court • Worthington, OH 43085 • (800) 356-6161

Simtel Communications
31220 LaBaya Dr., Suite 254 • Westlake Village, CA 91362
(818) 706-1921

B.U.M Equipment ran a 900 campaign that involved the use of several great guerrilla tools. They set up a 900 number that customers could call to play the B.U.M. trivia game and receive a $10 gift certificate. They supported the campaign with an outdoor billboard that proclaimed "It Pays to Be a B.U.M." B.U.M. has gone from a start-up company to a genuine competitor in the activewear market over the last four years.

900 TELEPHONE RESOURCES

Infotext **magazine**
201 E. Sandpointe Ave., Suite 600 • Santa Ana, CA 92707
(714) 513-8400

900 Advertising Club
P.O. Box 5048 • Newport Beach, CA 92662 • (714) 721-9280
Among other services, the Club runs the Last Minute Media Hotline. Call (900) 446-2446 and listen to the recording that gives you low-cost advertising options

The "900" Source Reference Guide
Edited by Michael Landers • Published by Robins Press • (800) 238-7130

900 Know-How
By Robert Maston • Available from Robins Press • (800) 238-7130

VoiceNews
Edited by Bill Creitz • Stoneridge Technical Services
(800) 238-7130
monthy publication on voice processing technology and its applications

Robins Press
2675 Henry Hudson Pkwy., #6J • Riverdale, N.Y. 10463 • (800) 238-7130
Publishers of a wide variety of voice/fax processing publications. Call them for their free catalog.

900 NUMBER BRAINSTORMS

What information does your company possess that people might be willing to pay for?

_____

_____

_____

_____

_____

_____

_____

_____

_____

TOLL-FREE NUMBERS

Make your company accessible and your product easy to order.

Try using an 800 number when you introduce a new product. Have consumers use it to order free samples. Not only do you get exposure for the product, but you also generate a mailing list of qualified prospects. Ciba-Geigy corporation did it with a pain reliever they developed. They advertised the new product and the 800 number on a freestanding insert that went into the Sunday daily newspapers.

When people called the 800 number, Ciba-Geigy recorded their names and addresses in a database. They sent out a free sample of the pain reliever and then used the mailing list to market to those people again.

Guerrillas make it even easier for customers to call them by offering an 800 number. According to AT&T, prospects are seven times as likely to phone if the call is toll-free. When 800 numbers were first introduced, they made mail order possible. Today they have become so ubiquitous that running a business almost requires one.

You don't need to be a huge company to benefit from toll-free service. If your business attracts customers from more than one area code, an 800 number must be seriously considered. Companies are now starting to install toll-free fax machines, further encouraging their customers to contact them.

Acquiring a toll-free number is easy and surprisingly inexpensive. AT&T offers a service called Readyline, Sprint calls its service Fonline 800, and MCI has Preferred 800 service. Any of the three can give your business the 800 advantage for a base charge of about twenty dollars a month, plus about twenty cents a minute or less. The number can be programmed to ring to any phone in the U.S.—you don't need a special line—as your business grows, your 800 number can move with you.

COOL NUMBERS

Unless you can get a custom number that is a complete key word or phrase, like 1-800-SOFTWARE or 1-800-FLOWERS, stay away from clever combinations like 1-800-777-1234. People think they will remember them and then forget. Better to have a number they *have* to write down, like ours: 1-800-247-9145.

Be careful though. While using a clever mnemonic like 800-FLOWERS can make your business, make sure you use a word that people know how to spell easily. One company that makes water purifiers advertises their phone number as "1-800-BRITA44." It's easy for people to get that wrong by spelling Brita with two T's. Oh, by the way, 1-800-GUERRILLA would be a bad idea, too. Nobody knows how to spell "guerrilla."

One accounting firm in Houston, Texas, set up an 800 number that people could call to get information about taxes. The number is 800-4REFUND. Since introducing the number, the firm has tripled in size. Then there is Hooked on Phonics, a company that sells educational materials to teach kids how to read. Hooked on Phonics built their business on the 800 number: (800) ABCDEFG. Their toll-free number is so important to their business that before they even opened their doors, they found out who already had the number that spelled "ABCDEFG" and paid him $10,000 for the right to use it.

How about 1-800-MATTRES "and leave off the last S for Savings." This mattress delivery company built itself solely on a clever telephone number and good customer service. An 800 number often implies quick, convenient service and fast delivery of product. Dial-A-Mattress takes it to an extreme. They promise same day delivery, a 30-day exchange policy, removal of your old bed, and they have a delivery acceptance policy. If, once they have delivered and set up the bed, you decide you don't like it, they'll disassemble it and take it away no questions asked—and they won't charge you a thing! Is there any better way to buy a mattress?

SERVICE BUREAUS

The use of an 800 number on a radio or television commercial invites direct and immediate response from the viewer or listener. If that is the case, you'll need to be ready to field the calls whenever the spot airs. Consider using an 800 service bureau specializing in direct response calls. Research the company you choose to insure that they have enough workstations to handle the volume.

When advertising an 800 number, make sure that you let customers know when they can call. Unqualified 800 numbers imply 24-hour, 7-day a week service.

800 SERVICE BUREAUS

Before looking for a service bureau, decide what services you want them to provide. Are you looking for a service that will fulfill your product orders or just take them and turn them over to you? Below are some of the largest bureaus, most of which provide product fulfillment. You can start your search by calling them, or look in the Yellow Pages for a service bureau near you. (See also the list of fullfillment houses in the Mail Order *chapter.)*

Matrix Marketing
2121 N. 117th Ave. • Omaha, NE 68164 • (402) 498-4000

West Telemarketing
9910 Maple St. • Omaha, NE 68134 • (402) 571-7700

Call Phone Music Express at (800) 746-6368 and you can listen to a 90-second snippet of music from an album over the phone before you decide to buy it. Once you've decided, you can buy the album with your credit card or have it charged directly to your phone bill.

• • • • • • • • • • • • • • • • •

Health Valley Foods, an Irwindale, CA, health food manufacturer, broke into the market by setting up an 800 number that consumers could call to get advice on healthy living and eating. The names of those who called were put on a mailing list to receive special promotions on Health Valley foods. Eventually, Health Valley generated customer loyalty and a large customer base. From here, they were able to move from the small health food store market into the big supermarket chains, where they are growing by leaps and bounds.

• • • • • • • • • • • • • • • • •

Over 11 billion calls are made to toll-free telephone numbers each year.

Advanced Telemarketing Corp.
8001 Bent Branch Dr. • Irving, TX 75063 • (214) 830-1800

American Transtech
8000 Baymeadows Way • Jacksonville, FL 32256 • (904) 636-1000

Neodata
100 Crescent Ct., Suite 650 • Dallas, TX 75201 • (214) 871-5588

Precision Response Corp.
1505 NW 167th St. • Miami, FL 33169 • (305) 681-1188

The Product Line
2370 S. Trenton Way • Denver, CO 80231 • (303) 671-8000

Sitel
5601 N. 103rd St. • Omaha, NE 68134 • (402) 498-6810

Teletech
15355 Morrison St. • Sherman Oaks, CA 91403 • (818) 501-5595

TOLL-FREE TELEPHONE RESOURCES

Infotext **magazine**
201 E. Sandpointe Ave, Suite 600 • Santa Ana, CA 92707
(714) 513-8400

This is the ultimate guide to using your phone for incoming or outgoing business. Well worth the cost of a subscription.

Enterprise Communications Magazine
201 East Sandpointe Ave., Suite 600 • Santa Ana, CA 92707
(800) 346-0085

TOLL-FREE NUMBER BRAINSTORMS

If you could have any 800 number available, what would it spell? Write down a dozen selections, then call the phone company and see if any of them are available.

_____

_____

_____

_____

_____

_____

_____

_____

_____

SELLING ON HOLD

Using the time you must put customers on hold to your advantage.

Federal Express prides itself on fast and reliable service, so when you call them, you are not often put on hold. Sometimes, though, like in the middle of a snowstorm when they are being inundated with calls, Fedex has to put you on hold. But, before they do, they tell you that due to unusual circumstances, you are going to be put on hold, and it may take a few minutes for your call to be answered. People are much more agreeable to holding when they have been forewarned.

Don't you hate being put on hold? It shows disrespect for the customer and it is a waste of time. But as we all know, it can't always be avoided. How can a guerrilla keep holding customers from hanging up, or even better, make them happy?

Studies have shown that music on hold will increase the amount of time that people will wait. Choosing a type of music that is appropriate for all customers is tough—radio stations can be unpredictable, and no one wants to hear a screaming car ad while they wait. Worst of all are those tinny digital loop recordings of Beethoven.

Microsoft Corporation receives tens of thousands of tech support phone calls every day, most of which are on hold at one point or another. They have solved the music on hold problem by hiring their own disc jockey who plays music and gives "traffic updates" to appraise customers of how long the wait is on each line. Microsoft reports that people are willing to wait nearly twice as long if they know where they stand.

A cheaper alternative is hiring a company like Muzak or AEI to provide tapes. They offer a wide variety of tapes, not just elevator music. If you are going to play music, it is a good idea to interrupt with a voice every now and then that tells customers that their call is important to you and you will be right with them. The music is a good distraction, but it won't keep people from thinking you have forgotten about them. You need to break up their time on hold with a variety of things that will keep their attention. The last thing you want is for them to hang up.

An aggressive guerrilla won't stop with music. Why not provide information also? You can create a five minute endless tape that gives listeners news about your new products, or about specials. One guerrilla we know puts a secret discount on hold. ("Tell the operator that today's on-hold discount is 4% with any order over $100. It's our way of saying thanks for waiting.") If you hear it and mention it to the operator, you get the discount. The customer feels great about the two or three minutes spent on hold.

A comedy club in New Orleans uses a tape of some of its best comedians when it puts people on hold. There have been instances of people *asking to be put back on hold!*

NEW TECHNOLOGY

Inexpensive desktop computers can now be used to create sophisticated voice mail systems. For just a few thousand dollars, you can create a system that allows customers to interact with your computer while they're on hold. For example, you could give them a choice of five different products that they might want to hear more about. You could offer answers to the most frequently asked questions—a hotel in Greenwich, Connecticut, put the travel directions to the hotel in this system. It guarantees that the directions are accurate, and saves the harried operators from the chore.

STATISTICS

As a guerrilla, you should know exactly how long the average wait time to get through to you on the phone is. You should know what percentage of callers hang up (taking their business with them) and how much it would cost to hire enough people to deal with the overflow. We're constantly amazed at businesses that *always* put people on hold. That's a dumb way to manage your customers—after all, you need to deal with people sooner or later, and if there's always a hold queue, you postpone satisfying your customers to save a few bucks. This won't pay off in the long run.

One way of dealing with the overflow is to empower all of your employees to answer the phones when it gets busy. Spinnaker Software, once one of the leading providers of educational computer games, had a small army of Harvard M.B.A.s answering technical questions during the week after Christmas. Not only did it help satisfy the customers, it allowed top management to get a better understanding of what customers liked and didn't like.

ON-HOLD RESOURCES

Muzac
400 North 34 St., Suite 200 • Seattle, WA 98103 • (800) 331-3340

AEI
900 East Pine • Seattle, WA 98122 • (206) 329-1400

NON-MEDIA

NON-MEDIA IDEAS FOR GUERRILLAS
Often, what sets a successful guerrilla apart is the relationship that she has built with her customers. In this section, you'll learn all about building relationships—how to earn your customers' trust, how to amaze them with your service, and how to make them feel like you care about them in a way that your competitors do not.

Community involvement, speed and service, and customer research all generate more loyal customers, and repeat buyers—one of the keys to guerrilla success.

PRICING

Guerrillas don't price at the bottom of the market.

Three years ago, we loaded 2,500 copies of one of our books into a truck and drove to Washington, DC for a huge outdoor demonstration. We felt like this was the perfect place to sell the rest of our stock of this book, which was designed especially for the activists who would be attending the demonstration.

We bought a booth on the Mall, set up a banner and some balloons, and stood outside in the 34-degree weather. Approximately 50,000 people walked past our booth, and we sold exactly one copy of the book for $6.

"The price is too high," I was told by my shivering compatriots. After more than an hour of resisting them, I decided to prove a point about pricing. I lowered the price to $1.

During the next hour, as it warmed up to 39 degrees, another 100,000 people (no exaggeration) walked past our booth. And I sold two more books. We went home and had soup.

Here's the point: Your price is rarely the problem. Worry instead about benefits, positioning, and service.

Whenever business slows, the temptation is to lower your prices. When people don't buy, the reason they give is often that the price is too high. Your friends, associates and employees will all tell you that you must lower the price.

This doesn't make sense, and there are a lot of reasons why.

First, extensive market research has shown that people often don't care that much about price. For instance, when ranking why they switched dry cleaners, customers gave the following reasons (ranked by the importance they attached to each):

➤ Service

➤ Location

➤ Quality of workmanship

➤ Price

The same has been proven true in banking, food, even automobile sales. Take a look at the best-selling brands in any industry, from cigarettes to cars to jeans, and you'll see that *the lowest-priced item is rarely the best-selling item.*

When a customer tells you that your price is too high, what he's really saying is, that you don't give enough value for what you're charging. Time and time again, aggressive businesses have shown that people will pay for quality and service.

Here's a simple test. Below we've listed two items from each category. One is the cheapest. Which do you buy?

Yugo	Honda
Nike	Thom McAnn
Campbell's Soup	generic
Sony	Gerrard

In each case, from lowly cans of soup to expensive cars, the market leader is always the brand that delivers quality, service, and convenience at a reasonable, rather than the lowest, cost.

There's an old saying: "There's always someone willing to make something a little shoddier, a little cheaper, and charge a penny less."

As you consider your position in the market, realize that you can always out-deliver your competitors in service and convenience, and there's always someone out there who can beat you on price. You need to find your niche and defend it.

To put it another way—if all you have to compete with is price, how can you make a living? If your competitor is always willing to beat you by a dollar, the two of you will eventually find yourselves bankrupt. Your goal is not to sell something cheaper than everyone else, it is to deliver more value than your competitors. And value is created by understanding your customers' needs, not by selling on the cheap.

VALUE VS. COST-BASED PRICING

Many guerrillas are hung up on the idea that the price of an item has to have something to do with how much it costs to make. We are frequently asked for advice by businesses that have been determining their pricing by figuring out their out of pocket costs and adjusting upward. This method is *guaranteed not to work*. Here's why:

The customer couldn't care less what it costs you to make something. A person starving in the desert will gladly pay a million dollars for a glass of water that cost you nothing. A screaming teenager will pay $40 to see a concert (the marginal profit on the ticket is $38) and people continue to support DeBeers, even though the price of diamonds is kept artificially high through hoarding—do you really think it costs a million dollars to get a diamond out of the ground?

Consumers are faced with a decision every time they contemplate buying something: "Is the money I'll need to give up to get this item worth less to me than the item itself?" As long as the value of your product is greater than its price, you will be able to sell it.

The next time you price an item, do the pricing without figuring in how much it cost you to manufacture. Try to determine what a customer would be willing to pay—both with and without advertising—and *then* look at the cost. Guerrillas understand that offering consumers a good deal, consistently giving them more than they pay for, is the way to build customer loyalty. But don't give away the store by pricing low because your costs are low. Instead, price based on value.

Yale University charges more than $20,000 for a year at their fine institution. Just down the street, Bridgeport Community College offers a year of schooling for about $2,000. Of course, despite the fact that Yale is 1,000% more expensive, the waiting list at Yale is far longer than it is at BCC. Why? Because people buy the product that satisfies their needs, not the product that's the cheapest.

PRICING AT MULTIPLE LEVELS

What should you do when various segments of your customer base aren't willing to pay the same price for an item? Price it near the top of the range and you'll lose those customers who are price sensitive. Price it too low and you give away money you could have collected from less sensitive consumers.

Don't be afraid to segment your pricing. Many builders' supply stores are using computers to offer as many as six different prices on every item. When a customer sets up an account, the management assigns a discount rate to the customer based on his estimated annual sales. Large contractors (those most likely to buy a lot of stuff) get huge discounts, while individuals without accounts pay the standard price. By offering multiple prices, the store is able to sell products to each market at the prices it demands.

Note that manufacturers and wholesalers are often prohibited by law from segmenting prices. Check with your lawyer first. Retailers, on the other hand, can always take advantage of segmented pricing policies.

Concert promoters do this all the time. They sell the good seats for one price, while seats just a few rows back go for much less money. Consumers don't mind, because they're able to pick the pricing level that best satisfies their needs.

Obviously, you've got to be careful here. Nothing alienates a customer quicker than the discovery that she payed double the person sitting next to her. The airlines have to deal with this problem all the time. The solution: Be sure your pricing is fair and consistent in its application. Offer the higher-priced consumer the opportunity to become a high-discount consumer (by booking in advance, or by having a certain annual sales level). This will almost always assuage any concerns your customers have.

SIMPLIFY YOUR PRICING

One technique that's been successful for guerrillas is pricing simplification. In industries where there is a maze of complicated and often conflicting prices, many consumers choose to do nothing. For example, hiring a public relations firm is a scary act for most companies. The costs can vary widely, as can the product that's actually delivered. Realize, though, that while price segmentation (discussed above) may seem complex to you, the customer sees only her own price and it's all very simple from her perspective.

Alexis Parks, the founder of Media Syndicate, addressed this need by offering one-price PR. For $499, she writes a press release and sends it to her regular list of 400 press contacts. By standardizing the process, she has made her service much more palatable to small businesses on a budget.

Carpet shampooing companies use a similar approach. Rather than worry about calculating the exact square footage of a house, they offer homeowners one price to clean every carpet in their house. By shifting to value-based pricing and offering the consumer simplicity, they've made it easy to do business with them.

Prix Fixe, a restaurant in Manhattan, has only two prices on the entire menu. Unlike other fine restaurants where the costs can spiral out of control, Prix Fixe offers complete menus at a single price. A simple concept, but certainly attractive to diners on a budget. While the price for dinner at Prix Fixe isn't necessarily lower than that at any other fine restaurant, the peace of mind that comes from knowing the price in advance is worth quite a bit to some customers.

NAME

Your name should reflect your image and your positioning.

Naming a product or company is a difficult decision. Unlike most of the challenges you'll face, this one is in a field in which virtually everyone claims expertise. The first thing to remember when naming something is not to rely too heavily on others' advice. Names created by committee are usually losers.

Start by sitting down and making a list of what you want your name to stand for in the mind of the consumer. Haagen Dazs is supposed to make you think of cold fjørds and rich, creamy milk. It doesn't matter that there's no such person as Haagen, or no such place as Dazs—the name serves its purpose.

You must decide what you want your name to imply. It is usually the first thing your prospects learn about you. Here is a partial list of things that your name can tell your prospects about you. Check off all those that apply:

Quick	Reliable
The best	Inexpensive
Convenient	Guaranteed
Highest quality	Recommended
Experienced	Honest
Fun	Dangerous
Outrageous	Unique

Once you've got your list of attributes, try it out on peers and focus groups. For example, if you're starting a dry cleaner, ask them if the attributes you've chosen—fast, reliable and inexpensive—would meet their needs. Adjust your list and try again.

Now that you've got a list, you've got to make a decision. Do you want a

Fanciful names often have plebian origins. Some fanciful names that have become hits:

Reebok is an Australian animal.

1-2-3 was invented by a computer-illiterate copywriter at an ad agency, searching for a phrase that means easy.

Nike is the Greek goddess of victory.

The Gap was originally called The Generation Gap.

BASICS

DON'T FORGET ABOUT THE LAW

Your name can cause a Jurassic Park-size problem if you don't first conduct a legal name search. The last thing you want is to hit it big, then be forced to change your name because a tiny company has the same name and wants $100 million from you for the rights to it.

name that is generic, descriptive, or fanciful? Any lawyer will tell you that a fanciful name is the best sort of trademark. It's the easiest to protect from encroachment by competitors, and eventually it makes the strongest name. A fanciful name is one where no picture comes to mind. No one knows what a Nike or a Xerox or a Lotus looks like.

The problem with fanciful names is that it takes an awful lot of time and money to persuade the consumer that they stand for something. The name itself doesn't begin by positioning the product or the company. So for most guerrillas, a fanciful name is too expensive to develope into an asset.

The second alternative, which is more difficult to protect, is a descriptive name. These names help position your company or product, and they telegraph information about what you do. Some examples:
    Speedy Muffler

    Ultimate Auto Body

    College Pro Painters

Descriptive names are the guerrilla's favorites. They communicate enough about your product to help the sale, but they're unique and stick in the customer's mind and help stop the competition.

Lastly, you can use a generic name. These names are virtually unprotectable, but they have the ability to immediately telegraph what your business does. Some generic names include:
    International Business Machines

    U.S. Steel

    Park Avenue Cleaners

    FontHaus

    General Foods

    Mister Donut

As you can see, sometimes a generic name takes off and works, but in general, it's an uphill battle—you've positioned your company, but your company has no identity.

EXAMPLES OF GOOD NAMES

➤ **Fearless Computing**

indicates the positioning of the firm—they will alleviate the fear you feel when you face the prospect of using your computer.

➤ **Faith Popcorn**

A memorable name that reminds you that she doesn't take things too seriously.

➤ **National Public Radio**

A simple name that immediately connotes weight, seriousness, and the fact that everyone is involved.

➤ **Beverly Hills Brownies**

Instantly connotes richness and elegance.

➤ **Staples**

A simple word that brings together a ubiquitous office supply with another word for "essentials". Once learned, the user never forgets what it stands for.

➤ **Federal Express**

The word "Federal" is great in this instance. It helped them get off the ground when competing with the Postal Service.

➤ **Head and Shoulders**

The name lets you see the benefit of the product—no dandruff on your shoulders.

➤ **Apple Computer**

Simple, friendly, basic, easy to remember.

➤ **Tic Tacs**

Easy to remember and pronounce but not necessarily reminiscent of the tic, tac, toe game. Without the toe, connotes clean and crisp.

PRODUCT OR COMPANY NAMES TO AVOID

➤ **A name that starts with INTERNATIONAL**

It's not unique, it usually doesn't mean anything, and it's confusing. So many companies use the word International to begin their name, it often gets ignored. For example, when you think of International Business Machines, you rarely focus on the International part. Your competitors also do business internationally, so make sure that part of your name separates you from them.

> ➤ **Anything with a pun or joke**

You want your business to have a name that attracts potential customers not one that elicits a long groan and a snide remark. Remember, you have to live with your name for a long time. Hairdressers are notorious for bad names. Consider these examples:

Shear Madness

Mane Attraction

Hair Today, Gone Tomorrow

➤ **Names that are technology sensitive**

No one wants to buy a car from Consolidated Buggywhips. If you name your business after the technology that you sell, you are wedded to it. For example, if you call your business "Fax-Modems, Inc.," you may be positioning yourself as a dealer of an obsolete technology several years down the line. Don't get yourself trapped like that.

➤ **Most names that include the name of a person**

Wilson, Wilson and Dundas

Davis Consulting Group

Stew Leonard's

These names are fanciful, just like Lotus or Reebok. Unlike a truly fanciful name, though, these businesses are harder to grow (Everyone wants to work with the guy whose name is on the door), hard to sell once the founder leaves, and especially vulnerable to scandal. If a scandal involving the owner occurs, it reflects poorly on the business that bears his name. They have one advantage: If the business is very personal, the names tell the customer exactly who stands behind it.

RULES FOR CHOOSING A BUSINESS NAME

➤ Your name should have a positive ring. Avoid anything negative. Your name should make people enthusiastic and optimistic about working with you.

➤ Avoid difficult names. If people have trouble pronouncing and spelling it, they won't remember it.

➤ Make your name unique. You don't want people confusing you with a business that already exists, especially if it is one with a poor reputation.

➤ Don't use a name that will limit you down the road. Acme Sleep Shop will limit you to selling sleep products. Acme Interiors is more open to expansion.

People get very emotional about naming a company or a product. Be careful to limit your naming team—wait until you've narrowed your choices down to two or three before allowing others to vote or comment. One company we know spent more than 250 man-hours (at $50 an hour) arguing about the name for a product line.

Magazines are great at names. With only a nanosecond to position themselves, they spend a lot of effort choosing a name that will do the job quickly and well. Here are some favorites:

• Time

• Success

• American Demographics

• Wired

• MacWeek

• Vogue

• Sassy

Then there are the magazines that have managed to succeed despite their confusing names, thus rewarding their owners with powerful, fanciful names:

• Forbes

• Vanity Fair

• The Utne Reader

➤ Use a descriptive name, such as Jiffy Lube. Note that this name also conveys a benefit.

➤ Don't get caught up in trends or fads. While it may be very profitable in the short run, you can't ride a fad for the long haul and guerrillas are more focused on the long haul.

➤ Your name should reflect your identity: dignity, largeness, local identification, quality, whatever.

➤ Pick a name that looks and sounds attractive: On the phone, on the radio, and on your letterhead.

➤ If you plan to advertise in the Yellow Pages, consider a name that starts with "A." Your name will always come at the beginning.

International Association Of Fire
Chiefs Foundation
1329 18th St NW ------------- 833-8323

INTERNATIONAL ASSOCIATION OF FIRE FIGHTERS—
1750 NY Av NW ------------- **737-8484**
Local 36 2120 Bladensburg Rd NE --- 635-8500

International Association Of Fish
And Wildlife Agencies
444 N Cap St ------------- 624-7890

International Association Of Jewish
Lawyers & Jurists 1828 L St NW 775-0991

International Association Of Law
Enforcement Planners
7200 Wis Av Beth MD ------- 857-8485

International Association Of
Machinist & Aerospace Workers
grand lodge
9000 Machinist Pl Suitland --- 301 967-4500

International Association Of
Machinist & Aerospace Workers
Headquarters --- See Mary Land
Suburban Listing

International & Association Of
Machinists & Aerospace
Workers --- See Automotive Mechanics
Lodge No 1486

International Association Of
NVOCC's 1220 L St NW ------- 682-9474

International Association Of Official
Human Rights Agencies
444 N Cap St ------------- 624-5410

International Association Of
Professional Bureaucrats
Wash DC ------------- 347-2490

International Association Of
Refrigerated Warehouses
7315 Wis Av Beth ------- 301 652-5674

International Association Of Truck
Parts 2233 Wis Av NW ------- 544-3090

International Association Of Visual
Artists 52 O St NW ------------- 232-6456

INTERNATIONAL AUTO CARE
Monday Thru Friday 8 - 8
3426 18th St NE ------------- **832-0800**

International Auto Center
8656 Richmond Hwy Alex --- 703 780-7850

International Autopen Co
1349 Shepard Dr Sterling --- 703 450-6620

International Aviation Supply Co
8201 NH Av Hyatts ------- 301 439-5599

International Banana Association
1627 K St NW ------------- 223-1183

International Bank
4601 N Fairfx Dr Arl ------- 703 875-3700

International Barber Shop
1505 U St NW ------------- 387-9281

International Beverage Industry
Exhibition And Congress --- Call
Interbev Ltd ------------- 463-6794

International Bioaccess System
Corp 1611 North Kent St Arl VA
CA Tel No--415 323-2138

International Bridge Tunnel &
Turnpike Assn 2120 L St NW --- 659-4620

International Business Group
1419 27th St NW ------------- 785-4000

International Business Link
1221 Pa Av SE ------------- 543-2525

International Business Machines
Corp --- See IBM Corp

International Business Network
Corporation
8212-C Old Courthse Rd ---- 703 506-4734

International Business Services
8219 Leesburg Pk Vienna --- 703 903-9800

International Business Venture Corp
1606 7th St NW ------------- 588-9245

International Campaign For Tibet
1518 K St NW ------------- 628-4123

International Cancer Alliance for
Research and Education
4853 Cordell Av Beth ---- 301 654-7933

International Cargo Management
Specialist 1455 Pa Av NW ------- 783-2358

International Cargo And Ship
Chartering Consultants Inc
1828 L St NW ------------- 296-4911

International Carpet & Rugs Inc
8150 Leesburg Pk Vienna --- 703 356-2550
1800 Rockvl Pike Rockvl ---- 301 881-5555

International Cartridge Recycling
Association 1101 Conn Av NW --- 857-1100

International Cartridge Recycling
Association 1101 Conn Av NW --- 857-1154

INTERNATIONAL CATHOLIC MIGRATION COMMISSION
1319 F St NW ------------- **393-2904**

International Center 731 8th St SE 547-3800

International Center For Information
Technologies Washngtn DC ---- 337-2688

INTERNATIONAL CENTER FOR LANGUAGE STUDIES INC
727 Fifteen St NW ------------- **639-8800**

International Center For Research
On Women 1717 Mass Av NW --- 797-0007

International Center For Settlement
Of Investment Disputes
1818 H St NW ------------- 477-1234

International Chemical Workers
Union 1126 16th St NW ------- 659-3747

International Christian Embassy
Jerusalem 1331 H St NW ------- 638-5830

International Church Relief Fund
Wash DC ------------- 244-8713

International City Management
Association 777 N Cap St NE ---- 289-4262

International Cleaners
3420 Conn Av NW ------------- 966-2966

International Club Of Washington
1800 K St NW ------------- 862-1400

International Coal Report
4545 Conn Av NW ------------- 362-5164

International Commission On English
In The Liturgy 1275 K St NW --- 347-0800

International Commission On
Medical Neutrality
1224 M St NW ------------- 783-1303

International Commission On
Radiation Units And Measurements
Inc 7910 Woodmont Av Beth - 301 657-2652

International Committee For The
Prevention Of Alcoholism

International Consultants Of
America ------------- 619 222-1178

International Consulting Firm
1825 I St NW ------------- 429-2036

International Contract Furnishings
Inc 300 D St SW ------------- 554-7941

International Contractors Inc
6718 3rd St NW ------------- 882-2120

International Contractors Inc fax tn
6718 3rd St NW ------------- 882-2120

International Cooperative Publishing
House 13801 Old Columbia Pke
Fairland Md ------------- 301 384-2627

International Cooperative Publishing
House Of Washington Inc
13801 Old Columbia Pke
Fairland Md ------------- 301 384-2627

International Coordination Center
1511 K St NW ------------- 393-3953

International Corporate Domiciles
11800 Sunrise Valley Dr
Reston ------------- 703 620-4880

International Corporate Yellow
Book 1301 Pa Av NW ------------- 347-7757

International Cotton Advisory
Committee 1901 Pa Av NW ----- 463-6660

International Council For Bird
Preservation 1250 24th St NW --- 778-9563

International Council For Dispute
Resolution 1835 K St NW ------- 775-9172

International Council Of Cruise
Lines 1211 Conn Av NW ------- 296-8463

International Council Of Employers
815 15th St NW ------------- 737-5062

International Council Of Museums
1225 I St NW ------------- 289-1818

International Council On Education
For Teaching
2009 N 14th St Arl VA ----- 703 525-5253

International Council On Monuments
And Sites US Committee Of
1785 Mass Av NW ------------- 673-4093

International Counsel For Bird
Protection 666 Pa Av SE ------- 547-9009

International Counseling Center
3000 Conn Av NW ------------- 483-0700

International Cover Model Search
2627 Conn Av NW ------------- 232-2800

International Cover Model Search-
Fax 2627 Conn Av NW ------- 387-8891

International Crating & Container
Corp 45-50 Court Sq Long Island City NY
From DC MD & VA Telephones
Toll Free Dial "1" & Then - 800 221-9583
Washington DC Office 2025 I St NW - 861-0640

International Cruise Line Inc
7315 Wis Av ------------- 301 907-7305

International Cuisine 1825 I St NW 775-6941

International Cultural Foundation
1015 18th St NW ------------- 293-7440

International Dairy Foods
Association 888 16th St NW --- 296-4250

International Data Control Systems
Corp 310 Swann Av Alex ---- 703 548-8177

International Defense Technology
Inc 21 Dupont Circle Nw ------- 833-4578

Internat'
Corpo
Internat'
3045
Internat
1629
Internat
Schoo
Internat
6031
Internat
Monit
Internat
1618
Internat
Devel
Internat
1458
Internat
1133
Internat
4201
Internat
Surve
Assoc
Interna
Garm
Interna
Oppo
Interna
Limit
3211
Interna
Inc 14
Interna
1730
Interna
, 533!
Interna
790!
Interna
451!
Interna
Interna
249!
Interna
Wa!
Interna
182!
Interna
717!
Interna
780!
Interna
5 T
Interna
Insti!
100!
Interna
601!

INTEI VID

Interna
181!
Interna
65!

Here is a sample page from the Business White Pages. It's very difficult to separate yourself from the competition when your name begins with "International."

MANUFACTURERS' AGENTS

Getting your product into the store is half the battle.

There are thousands of bookstores in the United States. Most large publishers have a sales force that calls on them directly to sell each and every title published. But a small publisher could never afford such a luxury. Companies like Publishers Group West handle the sales and distribution for a large group of smaller firms. They currently represent more than forty publishers and 3,000 titles. One of the bestselling books of 1991, 50 Simple Things You Can Do to Save the Earth, *was distributed by Publishers Group West.*

Manufacturers' agents are great resources if you need to expand your sales force without directly hiring more employees. They work on commission and enable you to get your products out into the marketplace quickly and with little effort. Instead of having a sales rep in Missouri, for example, you could hire a manufacturers' agent with ten employees that cover the state. Each employee only works part time on your product, and you pay on a straight commission. There are other types of firms called distribution firms that also perform warehousing and distribution functions. Sometimes these firms also sell for you, but not always.

There are several thousand manufacturers' sales agents throughout the country. Each has a sales force of one or more professionals that specialize in selling particular types of products to buyers in specific regional (or industrial) locales. These firms handle everything from canning and processing equipment to advertising products and services to medical and surgical supplies. Here is a list of some of the advantages of hiring an outside distribution firm to supplement your sales force or to introduce your product into a new market or location.

ADVANTAGES TO HIRING A MANUFACTURERS' AGENT

➤ Hiring a sales force through an agent gives the manufacturer a predetermined fixed sales cost.

➤ Distribution firms operate on incentive—no sales, no pay.

➤ Distribution firms provide local sales management.

➤ Manufacturers receive a trained sales force for no additional investment.

➤ It is possible to hire multiple firms for multiple lines so it is easier to grow faster.

➤ When you hire a manufacturers' agent, you not only hire the firm's manpower, you hire its connections and knowledge as well. There is minimal start-up time. This sales force already knows where to go to find your best customers.

FINDING A MANUFACTURERS' AGENT

There are literally thousands of sales agents around the country. Find a firm that offers products similar to yours—without competing directly. The easiest way to find a sales agent is to use the annual directory published by the Manufacturers' Agents National Association. To obtain your copy, contact them at (714) 859-4040.

DISTRIBUTION RESOURCES

MANA (Manufacturers' Agents National Association)
Box 3467 • Laguna Hills, CA 92654 • (714) 859-4040

MANA is the trade association for distribution firms and manufacturers' agents. It is a great resource for anyone considering hiring such a firm. MANA publishes a monthly magazine called Agency Sales, *a huge selection of research reports, and a series of special reports including "How to Work with Manufacturers' Agencies" and "Will Using Independent Sales Agents Meet Your (Clients') Sales Goals?" They have also recently put out a 3-volume series on business law with respect to the manufacturer-sales agent relationship.*

Sam Borofsky is a guerrilla salesman. His rep firm created the Nintendo video game craze almost singlehandedly. Borofsky's firm sells to Toys R Us, Woolworth's, and other mass merchandisers. By specializing in electronics, with a focus on video games, Borofsky has established a powerful niche at each store he sells to. At Toys R Us, where many salespeople struggle just to get a meeting, Sam spends more than three days in a row with the buyer, determining exactly which titles he ought to stock. His firm represents virtually every major video game company—if you were a video game company, would you rather have Sam selling for you or against you?

SPECIALIZED MARKETING TO ETHNIC & DEMOGRAPHIC GROUPS

Guerrillas take advantage of the natural target markets provided by ethnic and demographic groups.

In 1986, Norma and Hector Ortiz set out to fill what they perceived as a void in the advertising world. Now, seven years later, La Agencia de Orcí in Las Angeles specializes in developing advertising campaigns tailored to the Hispanic market. The agency is thriving, having billed over $27 million in 1993.

Ethnic marketing focuses on a natural target market, allowing you to stake out a position and establish affinity. Until recently this technique was often overlooked by the big guys. No more.

Goya Foods has become one of the fastest growing packaged food companies in the U.S. by focusing exclusively on Latin American foods. They offer black beans, achiote sauce, and Spanish rice to a growing middle-class market. As the market has expanded, they've continued to dominate it through targeted marketing to specific ethnic groups. While the black beans they sell are just like Progresso's and Campbell's and the Jolly Green Giant's black beans, they capture a large share of market by positioning their products specifically for these customers.

Guerrillas can and do count on word of mouth to spread their message with these groups. Properly positioned, the resulting sales can blossom when such groups express their appreciation with their purchasing dollars. While there are obvious markets like Blacks and Italians, the alert guerrilla is aware of small ethnic pockets (Paraguayans) or well-off cultural groups that are more demographic than ethnic (professional women or homosexuals). By clearly defining your product and using direct mail, direct response, and targeted marketing, you can quickly become the big fish in the smaller pond.

YOU CAN'T FAKE IT

Ethnic groups will resent a carpetbagging marketer attempting to exploit their market. So selling kosher foods to the Jewish market is more complicated than just adding a few words to your label. Hiring an African-American ad agency to sell to the African-American market is a smart first step, but you'll need to do more than that to be embraced by them. Each group has countless cultural particularities that need to be carefully thought through up front.

Be careful in the assumptions you make. Even if *you* are a member of the targeted group, it's easy to take some things for granted. For example, the African-American community was recently split over the use of light-skinned models in advertisements aimed at their community. Understanding these issues in advance helps you avoid getting burned. Our advice: Be genuine, do your homework (hire a consultant or ad agency if you need to), and go slowly.

SOURCES FOR DEMOGRAPHIC DATA

While you can count on increasing your sales if you successfully target an ethnic group, you'll need to know what sort of market size you're dealing with before you invest marketing dollars. Fortunately, the Bureau of the Census has a huge variety of demographic data on virtually every ethnic market, and most of it is available at no cost.

DEMOGRAPHIC RESOURCES

Aside from hiring a market research firm, there are a lot of places you can go to find census and demographic data. Here are just a few of them. The government is a good place to start. If you do decide to hire a firm, look in the Yellow Pages under "Market Research" to find one that matches your needs.

U.S. Department of Commerce
14th & Constitution Ave. • Washington, DC 20230 • (202) 377-2000

The Commerce Department houses the Bureau of the Census. Call them and speak to a Census Data Expert who can tell you what resources are available in the particular area you are researching.

American Demographics
P.O. Box 68 • Ithaca, NY 14851 • (800) 828-1133

monthly magazine

American Demographics Books
P.O. Box 68 • Ithaca, NY 14851 • (800) 828-1133

The book-publishing division of American Demographics *magazine. They put together a catalog of marketing books, many of which are geared toward market research.*

The Numbers News
P.O. Box 68 • Ithaca, NY 14851 • (800) 828-1133

Monthly newsletter published by American Demographics.

COMPANIES THAT SPECIALIZE IN MARKETING TO ETHNIC GROUPS

Below is a partial listing of companies that specialize in marketing to ethnic groups. The Standard Directory of Advertising Agencies, available in most business libraries, contains a more complete listing of agencies that specialize in reaching various ethnic markets.

MPI Coupon Distribution
1500 West El Camino Ave., suite 355 • Sacramento, CA 95833
(916) 441-7744

Specialize in black newspaper FSI networks (co-op FSI).

Businesses have embraced Kwanza, a holiday created in the mid-'60s to help black kids understand their heritage.

Offering kids an opportunity to create decorations, write essays, light candles, perform dances and rediscover their heritage is a great way to establish ties to a community. Put a display in your window, sponsor an event at the local school, or create a special brochure explaining the holiday for your customers.

Ethnic groups are not monolithic. At a top-level meeting, one marketer turned to a well-known black executive and said, "Maybe we can get Bill Cosby to endorse this. You know Bill, don't you?" [This is an honest-to-goodness true story.]

Understand that one of the strengths of ethnic marketing—the group's affinity for each other—can also be your Achilles heel. Don't be stupid and you'll do fine.

Segmented Marketing Services, Inc.
4265 Brownsboro Rd., Suite 225 • Winston-Salem, NC 27106
(919) 759-7477
Product sampling/field merchandising—African-American and Hispanic Church Family Gift Bag sampling.

Telemundo Group
1740 Broadway • New York, NY 10019 • (212) 492-5555
The largest Hispanic television network. Call telemundo and they'll send you a free video called Hispanic USA: The Marketing Niche of the 90s.

Asian Marketing Communication Research
1301 Shoreway Rd., Suite 100 • Belmont, CA 94002 • (415) 595-5028

Market Segment Research, Inc.
1320 S. Dixie Highway Suite 120 • Coral Gables, FL 33146
(305) 669-3900
Specialize in qualitative and quantitative research among Hispanics, African-Americans, Asians, and the general market.

Hispanic Market Connections, Inc.
5150 Camino Real, Suite D-11 • Los Altos, CA 94022 • (415) 965-3859
Specialize in market research geared toward the Hispanic market.

ETHNIC MARKETING BRAINSTORMS

List the products and services that you currently offer that would appeal to an ethnic group. Now brainstorm a dozen more.

_____

_____

_____

_____

_____

_____

_____

_____

_____

_____

LOGO

A visual shorthand that reminds people who you are and what you do.

Tops Appliance Warehouse has decided to use a giant nose as its logo. There isn't really a great reason to use a nose, but the sight of a 15-foot-high nose hanging on a billboard is quite extraordinary. Tops is able to build a brand identity by repeating the nose billboard. They repeat it so often that when a consumer needs to buy a refrigerator, he's got no choice but to at least consider the place with the big nose. This strategy has helped make them one of the fastest growing appliance retailers in the country.

Does a logo matter? Can a few carefully placed lines or a small picture really help stretch your ad budget, or is it folly to invest in a logo?

Think about the Jolly Green Giant, the rainbow-colored Apple, the bright yellow box of Kodak film, or the simple letters of The Gap. A logo helps position your company, giving your store or product an image and an easy-to-remember hook in the mind of your prospect. In today's society, where you often have only a few seconds to capture the customer's attention, a logo can make the crucial difference.

You have two basic choices when deciding on a logo:

➤ **The Specific logo**

If you have a vivid way of positioning your business, this type is the ideal marketing weapon. Betty Crocker is a great example—her wholesome old-fashioned look exactly positions the products. Apple Computer's logo is another great example. In a world filled with acronyms and technical jargon, the simplicity and universality of the Apple logo demonstrates the simplicity of their product.

Unfortunately, many guerrillas are unable to position themselves as precisely. An architect, for example, is probably unable to use one graphic icon to instantly demonstrate the quality, creativity, and cost-effectiveness of his business.

➤ **The Quality Logo**

The quality logo is ideal for many guerrillas. This logo, sometimes abstract but occasionally containing an icon, gives the prospect a solid, easily remembered image that will reinforce the positioning done in advertising, mailings, and brochures. The Jolly Green Giant, for example, has little or

nothing to do with asparagus—he's just memorable. Same with the Nike swoosh and the Olympic rings. Sometimes the logo includes the name of the company, but it doesn't have to.

These quality logos are great for businesses that advertise a lot. The icon or symbol can jump off the page and make impact, even if the prospect doesn't spend a lot of time reading the ad. Once well established, the logo alone creates complete recall of the entire position. Witness the Nike "swoosh." Just do it. Remember, though, that a quality logo means nothing when you start. It is a blank slate. If you don't have the marketing muscle to give it meaning, it will remain one.

When an icon isn't appropriate (for a bank or a supermarket, for instance), many businesses use an abstract logo. These can be silly when overdone, but new design software makes it easy and inexpensive to create a first-class logo for very little money.

An abstract logo can be just that—abstract. Don't worry too much about telling a complicated story about what each element means—If you have to describe it, then you're making it too cerebral. Tip: Always add the name of your business under the logo. A recent survey found that less than half of the top 100 brands had logos that were instantly recognizable without the name.

MISTAKES TO AVOID

➤ **Using the wrong logo.**

Don't use a cheap, common, or difficult-to-understand logo. Spend the time and money to do it right or don't do it all. When in doubt, hire a designer.

➤ **Not sticking with a logo.**

It takes years to build brand name recognition. Don't change your logo without a compelling reason.

LOGO RESOURCES

Logo SuperPower

Decathalon Corporation • 4100 Executive Park Drive, #16
Cincinnati, OH 45241 • (800) 648-5646

Logo Superpower is a graphic computer database of over 2,000 images that can be manipulated and combined to create professional-looking logos in a matter of minutes. The database can be purchased for use with the Macintosh or PC and should be used with a design software package that can customize the images. Logo SuperPower is available in four separate packages with prices ranging from $79 (400 images) to $279 (all 2,000 images).

GUERRILLA SUCCESS STORY

DeltaSonic Car Wash needed a new image and a new technique to boost sales. Car washing had traditionally been a man's duty, but as two-income/two-car families became more common, women were becoming a more critical market.

DeltaSonic adopted a new logo—a pair of red lips, puckered for a kiss. They invited you to have your car kissed by their brushless wash—an image that struck a chord with their market, especially with women.

In order to promote their washes, they turned to a vintage guerrilla technique—they paid their customers to advertise for them. Whenever you went in for a wash, they'd offer you a kissing lips bumper sticker, promoting the car wash. If the bumper sticker was on your car the next time you came for a wash, they gave you a small discount.

Within weeks, cars all over town were sporting the kiss bumper sticker. It became impossible to drive anywhere without being reminded that DeltaSonic was washing your neighbor's car. You either felt guilty for driving a dirty car, or reassured that bringing your beautiful old Corvette to them was a great idea.

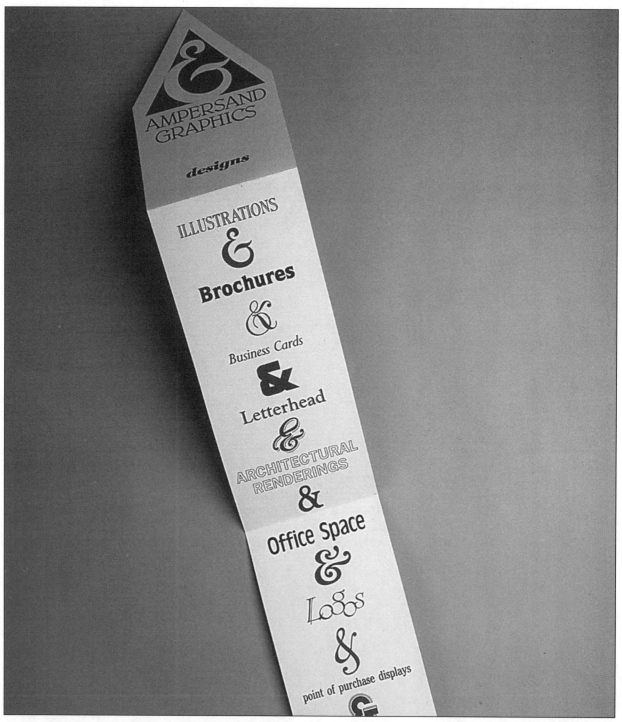

Logo and brochure for Ampersand Graphics. This is a great image for this graphic arts firm. The name goes with the logo and together they position the firm as a do-it-all, one-stop-shopping, graphic design firm.

Source: Ampersand Graphics • 7 Harbor Rd. • Morganville, NJ 07751 • (908) 591-9087

LOGO BRAINSTORMS

Sketch the logos for Nike, CBS, Apple, and Kodak. Now draw your company's. How does it compare?

AFFINITY MARKETING

Building relationships in the marketplace.

Tuxedo Junction is the largest supplier of tuxedos in the Buffalo area. They built their rental business around the lucrative prom season, and have created a clever affinity program to ingratiate themselves to the senior class.

Every year, the captain of the football team and the date of the head of the cheerleading squad are given a free tuxedo rental from Tuxedo Junction. As you can imagine, this endorsement makes it far easier for them to spread the word to the rest of the student body.

One reason that word of mouth is such an important guerrilla tool is that it builds trust. If your Aunt Mary recommends a house painter, then you can be sure that the painter is first rate. With just one sentence, Mary can turn the painter from anonymous businessman to trusted friend. Building trust is essential for all big-ticket sales. It may be established instantaneously by Aunt Mary, but will more likely be earned by the supplier through hard work.

The expensive way to build that trust is by running television and magazine ads. The less expensive method of building it by word of mouth takes too long for many marketers. But there's a powerful alternative: affinity marketing. Simply put, affinity marketing is the building and use of marketing partnerships.

Imagine a Christian bookstore selling Bibles and other inspirational books to a small but motivated local audience. The primary challenge is locating the prospects. The owner of the store could approach the local churches and make them an offer—refer your congregation to this store and in return receive 10% of all the sales that result.

This relationship helps all concerned. The congregation has found a convenient source for books and new income for their church. The pastor is pleased to generate income and help his congregation find inspirational material. And the owner of the store is delighted because she's able to generate significant sales with no up-front cost.

Clever affinity marketing relationships can be found in some unlikely places. Sears, for instance, uses the loyalty it has established with its core audience to help it sell home improvement and painting services. In each locality, it offers a local contractor the opportunity to use the Sears label for a fee. The contractor easily earns back the commission he must pay to Sears through the increased sales he generates. Contractors also find that once the trust is built (in this case, through the Sears name) it's easier to charge a higher price.

There are two kinds of affinity programs – the most common are the *authorized* affinity programs, which require the help of the group that controls your audience. In the cases above, both the church and Sears control an audience, and the guerrilla has to pay or somehow bargain for their active cooperation.

Unauthorized affinity programs are trickier. They involve grabbing an audience without the permission of the owner. We're pleased to note that unauthorized affinity programs have come to be called —by *BrandWeek* and others—guerrilla affinity programs (or sometimes, ambush marketing). But we'll stick to the term "unauthorized."

AUTHORIZED AFFINITY PROGRAMS

These programs can be difficult and time-consuming to set up, but once established they can generate incredible profits in the long run.

Ben & Jerry's took years to build a reputation before Jerry Garcia would permit them to name an ice cream flavor after him. The perseverance paid off—Cherry Garcia is among their best-selling flavors. Ben & Jerry's isn't the only beneficiary, of course. Jerry Garcia keeps his name in front of the public, and a generation of ice cream lovers will grow up believing he took his name from Ben & Jerry.

You'll find that the best authorized affinity partners are the ones that haven't previously participated in similar alliances. Finding a celebrity or an organization that has never been involved in co-marketing a product ensures that you'll maximize the trust that you generate and minimize the confusion of which product is associated with them. For example, putting Michael Jordan's name on a line of hats won't attract much new attention from his legions of fans—his name is already on dozens of products. On the other hand, if Jimmy Carter or Amnesty International or Rush Limbaugh endorse a product to their constituencies, sales will rocket.

The astute guerrilla will find an unaffiliated affinity partner that inhabits the same niche that his products do. A psychologist can team up with a family doctor to exchange referrals. A publisher of cookbooks can cross-promote with the maker of expensive cookware.

UNAUTHORIZED AFFINITY PROGRAMS

When Visa got the rights to be the exclusive credit card of the Olympic games, American Express decided to offer a donation to the U.S. Olympic Committee for every charge purchase made. Patriotic Americans felt good about giving money to American athletes, and much of Visa's huge investment was wasted.

Bars in every town run special *Monday Night Football* promotions. They use the huge marketing impact of the weekly game to encourage patrons to come to their taverns.

! *Understand the importance of opinion leaders.*
■ *Think about the last car, computer, or vacation you bought. Odds are, you asked someone you consider an expert for advice. When establishing affinities, pay attention to these experts. Once you've persuaded them to join your cause, their followers will soon join in.*

Until recently, *Monday Night Football* was not an active participant in these promotions. Rather than going through the expensive, time-consuming task of dealing with large organizations, many guerrillas associate themselves with an affinity group without participation or permission from the group itself. Of course, no guerrilla would "pretend" to be authorized without permission. You can't bill yourself as an "Official Sponsor of the Olympics" unless you really are, or unless you want to end up in trouble with the law.

There are countless good, legal examples. A bookstore runs a promotion offering a selection of baseball books, timed to coincide with opening day. A restaurant offers a discount to anyone who brings in a ticket stub from the nearby theater. A dentist gives a donation to the Democratic party for every person getting a cavity filled on Tuesdays.

There's nothing illegal about most ambush marketing programs. But you should be concerned about two issues: Never imply an endorsement from someone who hasn't actually given you one, and misusing a group's trademark and reputation will hurt your credibility and possibly cost you money. Don't alienate your customers. Supporting a political candidate with a sign in your window can cause you to lose customers who abhor her platform.

NON-COMMERCIAL AFFINITY PROGRAMS

Of course, not all interests are commercial ones. You couldn't be the official sponsor of world peace even if you wanted to, but you can grasp issues like peace and the environment and associate your business with such causes. Seventh Generation is a clothing and household supply catalog dedicated to selling renewable, nonpolluting products. They built their business by acquiring the names of members of environmental groups from mailing list houses. These people had a natural affinity for this sort of product, and the company had no problem making its original sales targets.

A company attempting to position itself as a supporter of the environment can pursue countless opportunities. They could give away a copy of Vice President Al Gore's book, *Earth in the Balance,* with every purchase, or offer refillable bottles, or set up a recycling booth. Origins Cosmetics uses recyclable containers and prints a message on the bottles that says "Please return to Origins for recycling." See *Community Involvement* for more ideas.

LEVERAGING YOURSELF

Entire businesses have been built around affinity marketing. There are newsletters for Star Trek fans, Fantasy Football leagues for NFL fans, licensed hats with NHL logos, and even Elvis Presley commemorative plates.

Some guerrillas have managed to create affinity marketing programs within their own organizations. Motivational speaker Zig Ziglar speaks before hundreds of thousands of people each year. His credibility is unmatched. Zig has created an entire line of books and audiotapes that sell to those who attend his lectures. This sideline has rapidly grown to become his major source of income. Now, the books and audiotapes help promote Zig's speeches, thus ensuring a complete circle. Of course, some marketers think of this as just line extension, but if you treat it in the same fashion you would an outside licenser, you'll be more careful with the way you leverage your audience.

Once you've established a reputation, the tables turn. Instead of leveraging the credibility and audience of other organizations, it is *your* credibility and audience that can be leveraged. This is a tremendous advantage to you—every time the person you endorse sells a good product, it provides free promotion for you.

In addition to the obvious step of finding companies that might be interested in leveraging your existing audience, you can tap the hundreds of companies that specialize in licensing well-known logos (from Budweiser to the New York Knicks) for use on everything from towels to cars. A complete list of licensers is available from EPM Communications. Call them at (718) 469-9330 and ask about the *EPM Licensing Letter Sourcebook* and the *Entertainment Marketing Sourcebook*.

SEVEN PLACES TO LOOK FOR AFFINITY PARTNERS

The secret of leveraging your business is to find an organization or individual with established relationships to a customer base. Pay that organization for access to the customers, and you both win.

For example, a database software maker could team up with the largest word processing software maker in Japan to sell his database software to Japanese company's clients. Or a long distance phone company could sell service to donors to the Leukemia Foundation. The possiblities are limitless. Here are seven places you can look for affinity partners:

One company that makes lighting switch-plates acquired a license to put the Teenage Mutant Ninja Turtles on its plates for $5,000. He sold $700,000 worth of switch-plates in the year after he began printing the Ninja Turtles on them.

1. Nonprofit organizations

2. Niche businesses with a similar audience

3. Niche celebrities

4. Sporting events and franchises

5. Service providers (doctors or consultants or lawyers...)

6. Retailers

7. Leading manufacturers in foreign markets

CELEBRITY BROKERS

These companies can help a guerrilla find the right celebrity to attach to an affinity marketing program. Aside from calling one of these firms, you can also look in Earl Blackwell's Celebrity Register, *available from Gale Research, or the* Celebrity Service International Contact Book, *available from Celebrity Service International. Call Gale Research at (800) 776-6265 or CSI at (212) 245-1460.*

Celebrity Service International
1780 Broadway, Suite 300 • New York, NY 10019 • (212) 245-1460

Washington Speakers Bureau
310 S. Henry St. • Alexandria, VA 22314 • (703) 684-0555

Ingels
7080 Hollywood Blvd., 11th floor • Hollywood, CA 90028
(213) 464-0800

AFFINITY MARKETING BRAINSTORMS

Make a list of non-competitive companies that have similar audiences that you might be able to work with to co-market your products.

_____

_____

_____

_____

_____

_____

_____

_____

_____

_____

COMMUNITY INVOLVEMENT

The way to your customer's heart is through a charitable cause.

Ben & Jerry's gives 7% of all its profits to charity. This outrageous statement of corporate involvement in the community has helped position their brand and make their ice cream incredibly profitable.

The old adage—you can do well by doing good—is definitely true for the guerrilla. Your business should be involved in the community because it's the right thing to do. It can also increase customer loyalty, sales, and profits.

Customers want to give their business to people who care about them. Even if you can't personally contact every prospect to let them know that you care about the local community, you can demonstrate it clearly through your company's actions.

Ben & Jerry's, The Body Shop, Reader's Digest, and dozens of other companies have established themselves as good corporate citizens. By publicly supporting ventures that help their target markets, they have broken through the clutter and attracted attention for their products and their good deeds. This is just a specialized kind of affinity marketing mentioned earlier in this section.

CHECKLIST OF THINGS THAT MAKE AN IMPACT AND GENERATE GOODWILL

➤ Sponsor a little league baseball team.

➤ Regularly donate food to a local homeless shelter and volunteer to help deliver and serve it.

➤ Sponsor a charity basketball game between your staff and the local police force. This works especially well for businesses with a lot of public contact, making it easier to sell a lot of tickets.

➤ Furnish your space with art by local artists. Some restaurants not only display the works, they sell them, giving all the money generated back to the artists. It spruces up your space and generates word of mouth.

➤ A hardware store trying to hold its own against a competitor like the local Home Depot could lend tools or donate supplies for a "fix up a senior citi-

BASICS

WHY COMMUNITY INVOLVEMENT?

The key to community involvement is finding a group that overlaps with your target market. Ideally, you want to provide a service to a group or organization that will also bring you, directly or indirectly, new customers or prospects. Join a community organization, help out a local charity, or give your services at a discount to a nonprofit group in your neighborhood. Not only will you generate goodwill and word of mouth, but you'll also have an outlet for showing your product or service to the rest of the community. If all goes well, you'll receive some free public relations and maybe some publicity as well.

zen's house" event. You could work with an organized social agency, or help organize a block event.

➤ Donate your parking lot for kids to set up a car wash to raise money for their school sports teams and organizations.

➤ Sponsor a road race to raise money for a local charity. If there isn't one in your community, consider starting one yourself.

➤ Sponsor a food drive for the homeless using your business as a drop-off point for canned foods.

➤ Donate space for the community to use as a base for a weekend SAFERIDES program. This program provides a place for kids who have been drinking to find a ride home.

➤ Support your local police department's DARE program. Donate giveaway items (like T-shirts with your logo and a DARE message) to students attending anti-drug presentations by the police.

➤ Offer the school a computer system or new playground equipment for every $50,000 in receipts from your store that they collect from parents and supporters.

➤ Set up a community fax machine that allows customers to receive brief faxes at your place of business for free.

➤ Offer a scholarship fund to your customers or the local high school—accept nominations and give cash to a selected graduate. The amount can be fairly small and still be welcome by the student and appreciated by the community.

➤ Place a drop-box in your store where your customers can make donations to a local charity. Offer to match a percentage of the donations with your own contribution.

➤ Sponsor a lecture series featuring subjects and personalities important to your customers. Hold the lectures and a series of roundtable discussions at your place of business. Perhaps you could turn it into a brown bag lunch series for local business people.

➤ Offer a discount coupon book and permit a local charity to sell it and keep the proceeds.

The owner of a dry cleaner in a small community in New York helps the homeless and draws traffic to her store at the same time. If you have old clothes that you want to get rid of, she will accept them at her store, clean them, and then donate them to the homeless. By advertising this service, she generates goodwill and word of mouth throughout the neighborhood. She has even received publicity from the local newspaper.

A new store donated $400 to the local high school drill team in exchange for their agreeing to rehearse in front of the store during the weekday rush hour or on Saturdays. Again, grand response and free PR.

COMMUNITY INVOLVEMENT RESOURCES

Doing Best by Doing Good

by Dr. Richard Steckel and Robin Simons • Published by Penguin Books

Things your business can do to create goodwill in the community and maybe earn some money along the way.

Profit and Philanthropy

Published by Calabria & Company

1605 Deerfield Dr. • Oshkosh, WI 54904 • (414) 235-0877

A bimonthly newsletter published by Calabria & Company, a consulting firm specializing in helping companies grow through community involvement.

Business Ethics Magazine

52 S. 10th St., Suite 110 • Minneapolis, MN 55403 • (612) 962-4700

This is a monthly magazine by the publishers of the Directory of Associations and Publications, *a leading source on ethical and socially responsible business.*

COMMUNITY INVOLVEMENT BRAINSTORMS

Make a list of charities in your market where your donations of cash, goods, or services can improve the quality of life for your customers.

_____

_____

_____

_____

_____

_____

_____

_____

_____

_____

TESTIMONIALS & ENDORSEMENTS

When your customers say good things about you, it has a lot more clout than when you say good things about yourself.

American Express has some of its most effective advertising campaigns built around trading out testimonials. Charles Lazarus, the owner of Toys-R-Us, appears in an American Express commercial that runs constantly. Pointing out that Toys-R-Us pampers its customers by accepting the American Express card, Lazarus is endorsing Amex and also building his own reputation. American Express obtains a great boost of confidence and Toys R Us receives terrific exposure.

Guerrillas realize that trust is an endangered species. It takes a lot of time and money to persuade a prospect to trust you enough to give you his business. That's why guerrillas are so quick to use testimonials. They're free, relatively easy to get, and flexible enough to add potency to almost any marketing weapon. Best of all, they're believed.

The primary reason that people don't buy from you is not price, not location, not service. It's usually trust. People are afraid of spending too much, of buying a lousy product, of not getting the service they need. Trust is the critical element in closing the sale.

If you're not a Fortune 500 company, how do you persuade a new prospect to buy from you? (Even if you *are* a Fortune 500 company, there's no guarantee that your business will be around tomorrow...) Consumers have become increasingly wary of scams, empty promises, and products that don't bring satisfaction. Unfortunately, they find that it's not always easy to distinguish a great product at a fair price from something that should be avoided.

The best way to generate trust is obvious but it isn't used very much. In our experience in teaching classes and running seminars, we've found that many guerrillas are hesitant to follow this technique because it frightens them.

Consider assembling a notebook with letters of recommendation from your clients. Do a first class job of presenting the letters—use plastic sleeves or, even better, laminate them. These testimonials, from real people, on real letterhead, are worth their weight in gold. Prospects know that you can't buy such praise for any amount of money, so the impact of one glowing letter after another will overwhelm their cynicism.

The frightening part is asking for the testimonials. Many entrepreneurs believe that asking for feedback (even from a loyal customer) is tantamount to asking the customer to complain. The insecure marketer is sure that the customer will suddenly realize he doesn't like your service very much and look elsewhere. Don't be afraid to ask for testimonials directly. You'll be pleasantly surprised at the results.

If you're still afraid to ask for a testimonial letter outright, try this: Send a survey to your customers. Ask them a few easy multiple choice questions about the quality of your product and the convenience of working with you. Then end the survey with this note:

"Like all of our interactions with you, we will keep all results of this survey confidential. But if you feel our service has been exceptional, we'd consider it a personal favor if you would enclose a letter that we could show to prospective customers to let them know your thoughts about doing business with us. Thanks."

When you show the first few letters to a new prospect, tell her, "Here's how our current customers feel. I hope that once we've done as good a job for you, you'll be willing to write a similar letter for us." As you acquire new customers, you'll be amazed how many respond with a positive letter. When someone realizes that he's writing for your testimonial book, he's likely to be particularly complimentary.

Encourage your customers to be as specific as possible. Testimonials that say "fine" and "good" aren't worthless, but they're not far from it. Instead, they should say, "We increased our profits 19% in 60 days, thanks to your unique service." Or, "My husband never compliments me on my cooking, but he hugged me after I served him your gorilla stew!"

Of course, the testimonials don't have to take the form of complete letters. They can also be short one-liners or brief paragraphs that articulate the essence of what's different about your business. If you're going to abridge a loyal customer's comments, be sure to check with her first.

Great testimonials clearly state the customer's problem, along with the real solution your company provided. We have trouble believing testimonials quoted in an ad signed by Mrs. T.P. Dallas. On the other hand, we have no difficulty believing complimentary comments made by Frank Delahanty, President, Davis Industries, 6808 Crandon Avenue, Chicago, Illinois.

MCI offered a testimonial in which prospects could call a toll free number and hear satisfied customers talking about their MCI service. The ad promoting the testimonials featured a photo of a satisfied executive. He was quoted as saying, "I love my MCI service. Call me and I'll tell you how they saved me money." It doesn't get more personal or more powerful than that.

Consider exchanging testimonials. Approach the businesses in your market and ask them for a testimonial that you can place in your advertising. Offer to give them one they can use in their advertising in exchange. A company that makes c compilers (a fancy software product) might approach the software makers who use their product in their business and ask them for endorse-

PAID TESTIMONIALS WITH IMPACT

Starting a designer jean company is tough. No one really needs designer jeans, so you need to create a fashion statement, then you need to make enough of a marketing impact that the fashionable people (and the stores they shop in) will hear about you.

No Excuses Jeans had a problem and saw an opportunity. They needed to break through the clutter and inexpensively reach their target audience of young women. Rather than spend their money on a limited and ultimately doomed ad campaign, they decided to spend it all on public relations.

During the scandal-ridden eighties, whenever a flashy young woman appeared in the news, it seemed like No Excuses was not far behind. Jessica Hahn, Marla Maples, and Fawn Hall were all featured as No Excuses spokespersons.

This led to an onslaught of publicity. These scorned women were parlaying their scandal into fame, and the press loved it. No Excuses received hundreds of millions of dollars of free publicity, and quickly positioned themselves as a slightly naughty alternative to Levis.

Their entire business was built on one guerrilla marketing technique.

One way to collect testimonials is to offer your customers something in return for their kind words. For example, if you own a car wash, offer a free month of washes to any customer who provides you with a testimonial you can use in your advertisements.

Or why not sponsor a contest offering a prize to a randomly drawn testimonial.

. . . .

Saturn has furthered its positioning as a different kind of car company by featuring unique customers with unique stories in its ads.

You'd be surprised at how much space they devote to the person rather than to the car. The best reason to use a testimonial is to enhance believability by using real people instead of a canned pitch. The people Saturn uses appear genuine and have a big impact on the viewer.

. . . .

ments. Featuring their users in the advertising for the compilers helps both parties: The compiler manufacturer gets a vote of confidence and the software maker receives added exposure.

Radius, a maker of expensive computer monitors, used this approach with *Wired* magazine. Radius gained the cachet of being associated with a hot new magazine, and *Wired* gained national exposure at no cost.

MAKING BEST USE OF YOUR TESTIMONIALS

➤ Print a booklet of your best testimonials (the thicker the better) and send them to your customers, to prospects, and to the media.

➤ Use testimonials in your print ads.

➤ Devote at least one panel in your brochure to testimonials from customers.

➤ Use voice testimonials in your radio advertising. Make sure you use the actual voices and not your own.

➤ Put testimonials on the walls of your conference or meeting area, or on a wall where your walk-in customers can see them.

➤ Include audio testimonials in the on-hold message people hear when they call your business.

CELEBRITY TESTIMONIALS

For a huge company like Nike that can afford superstars like Michael Jordan to endorse their product, celebrity testimonials are a way to cut through the clutter—millions of people respect Jordan's opinion, and even if we realize that he's being paid to endorse the product, it has an impact on our impression of it.

Guerrillas with smaller budgets can still find an affordable celebrity who fits their product or service. In fact, a minor celebrity with the perfect fit can have even more impact than a big name star. Omaha Steaks built their mail order business by using the famous chef James Beard's photo in their advertising for over fifteen years. Beard's distinctive appearance gave the steaks instant credibility and put them on the map.

Trizor Professional Cutlery used critic and cookbook author Craig Claiborne in their advertising. Claiborne's reputation as a journalist gave his endorse-

Chef's Choice built their reputation around Craig Claiborne's testimonial.

! *Careful when you edit endorsements and testimonials. If you offend the customer who gave you the endorsement, you'll do real damage to the relationship. To be safe, take a minute to run the edited testimonial by the satisfied customer. They'll generally give you an okay, and they'll be grateful for being consulted.*

....

Stew Leonard has made his wall of testimonials a tourist attraction. He puts photos of customers along with their testimonials on one wall of his store. People send postcards, photos, and testimonials in from all over the world just to be included on the wall.

....

ment tremendous impact and helped assuage fears that a $79 knife sharpener was just a gimmick.

The cost of using a celebrity for a niche marketing campaign is smaller than you might imagine. In fact, the best celebrity endorsements are free. Don't overlook local celebrities or experts, who often carry more weight than a movie star. For example, a local wine store could solicit an endorsement from the chef at the fanciest restaurant in town. The chef is known to many and, just as important, his customers perceive that he can't be bought—he has more credibility than your average Hollywood star.

After skipping over the 2,000 most famous stars from movies, TV, and sports, the availability of celebrities increases dramatically. Be unconventional in who you choose. It's so easy to always rely on the hot star of the moment (three years ago, everyone wanted Bill Cosby to endorse their products. Today it's Jerry Seinfeld). Instead, focus on minor celebrities who really add value to your product. Guy Kawasaki, former executive at Apple Computer, has endorsed several products directly to the Macintosh community—and helped them dramatically.

Herbie Hancock is well known for his work as a jazz musician. He's also an avid electronic musician and has endorsed several keyboards and music processors. Tom Peters endorses books and Carl Reiner endorses the Pritikin Longevity Spa. William F. Buckley liked his hand-held thesaurus so much he volunteered to endorse it—and tripled its sales.

THREE WAYS TO FIND NICHE ENDORSERS

➤ Take advantage of the "six degrees of separation." This popular theory states that everyone in America is six or less handshakes away from everyone else. Think about it. Your uncle went skiing with someone who's wife is related to...

Identify the person you'd like to endorse your product, then ask your friends and associates for ideas about how you might reach him. Send him an assortment of your products, along with some endorsements from your customers. Be straightforward—you're looking for a celebrity endorser and you're hoping that he loves your product enough to participate.

➤ Become opportunistic. Even celebrities need to buy things, and if you're delivering a quality product, sooner or later you're likely to attract well-known customers, even if it is only the mayor of your town. Have your employees keep their eyes and ears open for such valuable contacts.

➤ Identify and support a favorite charity. Doing good works is its own reward, but you'll also benefit if your chosen charity attracts celebrities that are recognized by your audience. For example, because the Boston Computer Museum attracts luminaries from all the leading hardware and software companies, supporting the museum will put a software company's product in front of the industry leaders, which can lead to testimonials and word of mouth.

Don't overestimate the value of a celebrity endorsement. Jimmy Connors made Nuprin's commercials memorable, but didn't help sales a bit. As consumers become increasingly jaded, a famous face (especially someone who isn't perceived as an expert) is worth less and less.

MAKING YOURSELF ACCESSIBLE

Set yourself apart from the competition by making it easier for your customers to do business with you.

Guerrilla Marketing Golden Rule: Your product or service must be as accessible to the customer as possible. Make it quick, easy, and hassle-free to do business with you.

There are all sorts of ways to make yourself more accessible than your competitors. According to a recent survey of customers of local service businesses, accessibility and convenience are often the factors that make people decide to go with one business over another.

"Do you accept credit cards?" If your answer is no, the lost sale dwarfs the few cents extra it costs your business to handle a card. For some businesses, honoring credit cards can increase business by up to 80%.

One retail store has a big sign in the front window that says "No Checks Accepted." The merchant would probably be better served by a sign that says "We Gladly Accept..." with a list of the methods of payment the customer *can* use.

ACCEPTING CREDIT CARDS MADE EASY

"Merchant status" refers to a business's right to accept and process credit cards. Small businesses often find it extremely difficult to obtain merchant status, but there are several companies that specialize in getting small businesses merchant accounts (at slightly higher cost than the local bank). If you've been stymied in the past, call the companies below for more information.

Charter Pacific Bank
30141 Agoura Rd. • Agoura Hills, CA 91301 • (800) 999-1484

Direct Marketing Guaranty Trust
141 Canal Street • Nashua, NH 03061 • (603) 882-9500

Litle & Co.
54 Stiles Road • Salem, NH 03079 • (603) 893-9333

Professional Marketing Associates
903 S. Hohokam Drive • Tempe, AZ 85281 • (602) 829-0131

EXPANDED BUSINESS HOURS AND OTHER CRUCIAL SERVICE ISSUES

Hours of operation is another area where you can separate yourself from your competition—especially if you're a bank! Who wrote the rule that banks can only be open from 9:00 A.M. to 3:00 P.M.? If we opened a bank called Guerrilla National Trust, we'd be open from noon to 6:00 P.M. and always on the weekends, when most people are free to do their banking.

What about 24-hour supermarkets? Kroger's grocery stores have built a reputation on this simple convenience. Going "Krogering" at 3:00 A.M. has become the chic thing to do in college towns all over the country.

Can parking really make a difference? How many stores have you driven by because it's just too much trouble to park? Here's one hint. Make sure your employees don't take up the parking spots right in front of the store. That's a big problem for a surprisingly large number of businesses. If you can't do anything about your existing parking situation, why not set up a valet parking system and offer to park your customers' cars for free!

If you're in a location where parking is tight, consider a co-marketing deal with a nearby parking garage. You send your customers there and validate their tickets, giving them a discount on parking. While some garages may require you to pay the full amount of the discount you offer your customers, others may welcome a chance to increase their business through your referals.

Delivery service is another way to set yourself apart. Pizza parlors were among the first to realize that delivery pays. Try adding delivery to a business that doesn't typically have it as a feature. If you own a bank, offer to visit people applying for a loan in their homes rather than making them come into the bank where they have to air their dirty laundry in front of everyone. A bank in Illinois used this technique to double their car loan business in just six months. Travel agents can deliver their tickets, and video rental stores might consider starting delivery services. There's even a Häagen Dazs in Manhattan that offers delivery!

Drop boxes are a must for businesses like video stores. They're even worth considering for dry cleaners, photofinishing shops, and shoemakers. When there are lots of competitors, anything you can do to keep a customer is worth considering.

A very successful national manufacturer of down comforters decided to expand its business by selling direct through mail order. All plans went on hold, though, because the new division couldn't qualify for merchant status with Visa or MasterCard. They would only be able to accept checks.

The first advertising campaign generated a huge response, but few callers ended up sending in their payment by check. Without credit cards, the venture was doomed.

Fortunately, the manufacturer found a bank that specialized in mail order businesses, got his status, and was able to turn a near-disaster into a profitable venture.

A Chinese restaurant in Harstdale, NY, offers commuters a great deal. They hand out menus in the morning as people get on the train to New York. The menu encourages the reader to call before getting on the train home—the food will be hot and ready when your train arrives.

This ingenious service costs the restaurant absolutely nothing (in fact, it helps them, since they know exactly when the customer will be coming in) and it has increased sales significantly.

Do your frequent buyers have to go through a hassle to buy from you? If you're a dry cleaner, do you make your best customers keep their yellow slips or do you store them? Does your video store require a lot of paperwork with each rental? Try to think about the entire process from your customer's point of view.

One final issue: Pennies! Most people look at pennies as a nuisance these days, but you can turn them into a blessing.

➤ Adjust your prices so that they always come out even and people who shop at your store don't have to use pennies. For example, if the sales tax in your area is 6%, charge $1.89 for an item instead of $1.99. The price with tax then comes out to an even $2.

➤ Better yet, let the prices come out uneven and give your cashiers the power to say "forget the pennies—it's on us." What a great gesture. Of course, you could raise your prices a nickel to compensate—people will remember the pennies long after they forget the price.

➤ At the very least, keep one of those penny cups by the register and allow people to take or leave pennies to make the exchange of money more convenient.

THE MYSTERY SHOPPER

Most business owners are too involved to objectively measure how easy it is to shop at their stores. So how can you eliminate the hassles? Hire a mystery shopper. Believe it or not, there are large national firms you can hire to shop in your stores and give you a written report about their experiences. More practically, you can retain friends or family members to do the same thing.

Have them call your store and try to order a product, claiming to hold only a Discover Card, or no credit card at all. Have them use a post office box, or a rural delivery address. See what happens to calls purporting to come from overseas. Have your mystery shoppers keep copious notes. If your business has strict policies that are costing you more in lost business than they're saving in overhead, it's time to reconsider them.

Have a shopper visit your store. How far away did he or she have to park? Are the signs clear? A grocery store near our house has an exit in the back but no entrance—you have to walk all the way around to the front to get in. Is your store accessible to the handicapped?

Call your business after hours. Do you get caught in voice mail limbo? There are dozens of large companies that will automatically put a caller on hold—essentially forever—if the call comes in after hours. Call during the day. How many rings before the phone is answered? Are you put on hold? At Federal Express, they are so fast they often answer *before* the first ring. This technological trick so spooked callers they had to slow down a bit—but they still answer on the first ring, giving callers confidence in their speed and efficiency.

To find the mystery shopping firm nearest you, look in the Business to Business Yellow Pages under "Shopping Services."

ACCESSIBILITY CHECKLIST

Use this list to give yourself an accessibility audit. Do you make the extra effort to make doing business with you easy, or do you need to change the way you handle a few of these elements?

➤ Hours

➤ Delivery on phone orders or in-store purchases
(Federal Express option, international shipments, local courier delivery, inexpensive delivery for those not in a hurry)

➤ Parking

➤ Credit cards and billing

➤ Checks accepted

➤ Billing
(With the advent of the credit card, many businesses have decided that billing is a bad risk. But for schools, businesses, and government agencies, this is often the *only* way to get the order.)

➤ COD

➤ Forms and ID required

➤ Delivery to post office boxes
(Many businesses avoid post office boxes because of credit card fraud. Work with your bank to determine the most cost-effective way to eliminate fraud—without alienating rural customers.)

➤ Handicapped accessibility (blind, deaf, physically disabled)

➤ Frequent buyer privileges
(A complicated, difficult program is worse than no program at all.)

A typesetter in New York uses his customers' phone numbers as their company IDs, Once he knows your number, his computer instantly tells him everything about your account—address, output preferred, method of delivery preferred, etc. Instead of forcing the consumer to memorize an account number or reiterate the same data each time, he makes it easy.

SPEED AND SERVICE

Speed and service can separate you from the competition and generate excellent word of mouth.

 If your business is based on speed and service, don't hide it—flaunt it. On every order you fill, put a sticker on the package advertising how quickly you serviced the account. Hewlett Packard recently sent us a package with a big green sticker announcing "Shipped in 6 Hours!"

. . . .

Most guerrillas don't think of speed and service as weapons, but they are, and quite powerful ones at that. When you realize that word of mouth is the most effective tool available to a guerrilla (see *Word of Mouth*), you start looking for things that build it. Speed and service are two of them.

Corporate Agents, based in Delaware, is devoted wholly to incorporating new companies. Traditionally, they've been used by lawyers, but they now market directly to entrepreneurs and small companies.

Call Corporate Agents on Tuesday afternoon, and by Thursday morning you'll receive a corporate seal, record book, stock certificates, and official papers. All for $250. Compare this with the tradtional method—paying a lawyer $1,000 and waiting a month.

What's the hurry? you may ask. After all, few businesses *need* to be incorporated in two days. The secret of Corporate Agents's success is that the speed, friendliness, and price together are so compelling that customers tell their friends and business associates about the astonishing service. Word of mouth is the key element in building their business.

Another speed example: Taco Clip Art is a small computer illustration company specializing in creating custom icons and drawings for newsletters and brochures. While illustrators traditionally take a week to a month to generate this sort of work, Taco's standard turnaround time is *90 minutes*.

They accomplish this by staffing up to prevent any backlog from accumulating, thereby permitting them to make every customer the first in line. As with Corporate Agents, the shock value of delivering a high quality product with astonishing speed generates word of mouth.

Service is another weapon that can accomplish the same thing. Ultimate Auto Body is an otherwise typical body shop. The auto owner doesn't care much about price, because his insurance company is paying. He doesn't care that much about quality either, because it's pretty hard to tell one bumper from another. But he does care about service.

When a customer arrives at Ultimate, they give him fresh perked coffee in a special ceramic mug that he can keep. Then they drive him back to his office, or he is welcome to sit and read Ultimate's wide collection of recent magazines.

When the car is fixed (right on time) the customer is amazed to discover that they've "detailed" it: cleaned it inside and out, meticulously washed and waxed it, made it spotless. No extra charge.

The detailing and the coffee mug may cost Ultimate $25 on every $1,000 job. A bargain when you consider the referral business it generates. There is even a testimonial letter from the mayor on the wall in the waiting room.

Speed and service can be the primary basis for creating an improved position for your business in relation to your competition. Try introducing speed into a business that is not traditionally associated with it. Take bookstores for example. Books are often used as gifts. Most people buy their books by going to the bookstore, taking the book home, wrapping it, bringing it to the post office, standing on line, and finally shipping it.

While many bookstores offer a shipping service, they rarely publicize this fact. A national bookstore that did nothing but ship gift books quickly and with no hassle could capture a new niche. Try calling 1-800-BOOKS123 and you'll be talking with a business that's done just that. Why didn't anybody think of this before?

Stand back and consider what services or speed improvements you can incorporate into your business to dazzle your customer. Here are some ideas to get you started:

HOW TO BE A LEADER IN CUSTOMER SERVICE

➤ Prepare a written document outlining the principles of your customer service. Hang it on your wall so customers know that your dedication to them is a primary objective.

➤ Even if you know how important customer service is to your business, your employees may not. Let them know exactly what is expected and reward them for delivering it.

➤ Make customer service your competitive edge. Do it better than anyone else in your industry. People will notice.

➤ Stay in touch with your customers by letter, postcard, newsletter, telephone, and trade shows. Ask your customers questions. Then listen carefully to their answers.

➤ Nurture the human bond as well as a business bond with your customers.

If you own a tire store and put snow tires on a customer's car, offer to store his regular tires for free. You are virtually guaranteed a fee later because the customer must return to have his regular tires replaced. More important, the customer leaves feeling you have provided him with a service he doesn't get anywhere else.

There's a full-service gas station in our area (a rarity in and of itself these days) that also checks the fan belt every time they check your oil. If you need a new belt, they offer you two: one that they install in your car, and one you keep in your trunk. Their suggestion to keep one in your trunk is a smart one, because if you break a fan belt, it's a cheap part to replace—unless of course you don't have one. Then you ruin your engine by driving the car to have the fan belt replaced. The station has done a great service by giving you good advice, and they've doubled their sales by selling you two fan belts.

Do them favors, educate them, offer gifts, play favorites, take them to the ballgame or the opera. Your customers deserve this treatment. If you won't do it, somebody else will.

➤ Throw parties for your customers and your employees. Bonds form faster and stronger at social gatherings.

➤ Invest in phone equipment (and personnel) that makes your business accessible, friendly, and professional.

➤ Act on the knowledge that customers value attention, dependability, promptness, and competence.

➤ Respond immediately to a dissatisfied customer. No business can satisfy everyone. Deal directly with the problem; be honest and do everything within reason to rectify the situation. Most customers will respect your effort; you may even be able to turn dissatisfaction into loyalty.

SOMETIMES YOU HAVE TO FIRE A CUSTOMER

There's a wonderful little inn in Northern Canada that has a secret "no" list. If you're on the list, you'll discover that every time you call for a reservation, the place is totally booked.

Virtually everything the guerrilla does is aimed at finding, romancing, and keeping customers. Why then, is it a good idea to get rid of some of your customers? Because of the 80/20 rule. In this case 20% of your customers account for 80% of your hassles.

Try as you might, there are some customers who just won't give you a fair chance. These are the people who buy a piece of furniture at Sears, keep it for ten years, then try to return it and get a new one for free by invoking Sears's Satisfaction Guaranteed policy. These are the customers who will sit down at your Sunday brunch buffet and eat $40 worth of caviar and lox. These are the customers who are consistently demanding, yet cross the street to buy from your competitor whenever he offers a discount.

Be careful! It's easy to lump a merely demanding customer with one who is a real problem. Businesses that are too quick to fire customers often find themselves in real trouble. Before you take the risky step of firing a customer and generating negative word of mouth, try this three-step approach for dealing with problem people:

➤ Talk to the customer and find out exactly what's bugging him.

➤ With the customer at your side, write down exactly what you can do to rectify the problem. Generally, you'll find that the actions he wants you to take aren't all that difficult. You may disagree about whose fault it is, but you *must* apologize and take responsibility. If you don't, don't even bother to try to fix the situation. You've already lost.

➤ Do what you promised. Work your way through the requests and keep the customer posted. When finished, ask him if he's satisfied.

A few customers will take your accommodation as a sign of weakness. They'll continue to whine and push and hassle you for even more. These are the customers you don't need. If your customer won't participate in this process in a constructive way, fire him. We recommend that you wait until a non-emotional moment in a conversation with the customer and say, "I'm sorry, Mr. X, but it seems as though our business isn't going to be able to satisfy you. I'd like to suggest that you consider doing business elsewhere. Some of the businesses who might be able to help you are: W, Y and Z (your competitors)." This is one case where sending business to your rivals is probably a good idea.

However, if you've taken these steps, you'll find that in 99% of the cases your customer will be delighted. He may never shop with you again, but at least he won't spread negative word of mouth.

Hewlett Packard sent us a product in this envelope. The sticker tells us they shipped it within six hours after it was ordered. Let customers know that doing things efficiently is important to you. It will impress them.

SPEED AND SERVICE BRAINSTORMS

Make a list of ten ways your company can dramatically increase the speed
of service and delivery.

_____

_____

_____

_____

_____

_____

_____

_____

_____

WORD OF MOUTH ADVERTISING

The most important element of any guerrilla marketing plan.

A car dealership that surveys buyers of their new models already knows who their most satisfied customers are. They should consider offering these customers a $300 certificate off the price of their next new car if they allow the dealership to give their name and phone number to twenty prospective buyers who could call and ask about their experience with the car and the dealership. There's no bribe here: The car owner gets $300 regardless of whether cars are sold, thus avoiding the appearance of impropriety. Is it worth $300 to generate positive word of mouth to twenty car buyers? It is if it helps close the sale.

Throughout this book, we've explained a multitude of ways to generate word of mouth. As customers grow more cynical and media gets ever more crowded, word of mouth advertising becomes even more important. Most businesses in this country survive *solely* on word of mouth, making it their only marketing tool.

Some people bristle at the connection of *word of mouth* to *advertising.* After all, conventional wisdom says you can't buy word of mouth the way you buy an ad. In fact, you *can* buy word of mouth advertising. The process isn't as direct as calling up your ad agency, but an investment of time and money will eventually pay off in increased word of mouth.

Understand that word of mouth is a critical tool, but realize that what appears to be word of mouth advertising is often the result of newspaper, magazine, radio, and direct mail advertising. Often, it's word of mouth that gets the credit, not the media. Don't delude yourself that you can hit it big with *no* media advertising.

Actually, word of mouth advertising is the ultimate result of years of careful planning, media spending, and quality service by a guerrilla. In order to generate a referral or a testimonial from a loyal customer, you've got to take the time to set the stage. You can do a hundred little things that make your business attractive to a customer, and the result will be a guerrilla's dream—a satisfied customer who sells for you.

Several sections of this book address specific techniques you can use to dramatically increase word of mouth. Pay close attention to *Speed and Service, Testimonials,* and *Community Involvement.*

ENCOURAGING WORD OF MOUTH

Here's a way to give your customers an incentive to sell for you. Give your best customers ten brochures, each coded with their names. The brochure gives a new customer a ten dollar discount, making it attractive for someone to give you a try. As a reward to the loyal customer who distributes the brochures to his friends, give him a special bonus for every customer who brings in a coupon with his name on it—maybe $5 off.

If you really want to be adventurous, offer the same deal to each of the new customers who comes in with a coupon. They too can give out ten more coupons, and so on, and so on....

HOW TO GENERATE WORD OF MOUTH

➤ **Business Cards Are a Great Word of Mouth Tool**

One accountant we know throws three into every piece of mail he sends out. He invariably gets several new clients every year from people who pass along his card.

➤ **Give Marketing Materials to Your New Customers**

Ad slicks, reviews, articles, and brochures remind them why they patronized you in the first place and spurs word of mouth endorsements.

➤ **Ask For It**

Nobody is better equipped to talk up your company than you—or perhaps your best customer. Tell all your customers: "If you're really satisfied with my service or products, I'd appreciate it if you'd tell your friends." By asking your customers to help you generate word of mouth, you remind them of how much they like your business, and tell them exactly how they can help you.

➤ **Follow the Lead of Subscription Magazines During the Christmas Season**

Most magazines will send out notice of a special gift-giving rate to induce subscribers to give the magazine as a holiday gift. The following year, they approach the recipient of the gift to renew the magazine on her own. The new customer probably wouldn't have subscribed without the recommendation of her friend who bought it for her in the first place—word of mouth.

➤ **Do an Extraordinary Job**

The single best way to generate word of mouth is to amaze your customers on a regular basis. We talk about this throughout the book because it is so often overlooked, but so powerful. By overdelivering on even the smallest request, you will consistently make such an impact that your customers will want to share you with their friends.

HOW TO OVERDELIVER

The secret of exceeding expectations is to find service areas of your business where a little extra attention from you will translate into great satisfaction for the customer. Here are examples:

New cars are usually delivered to customers with near empty gas tanks. This is a shortsighted way to start a relationship with a $20,000 customer. Mitsubishi dealerships deliver cars with full tanks of gas. This gesture probably costs

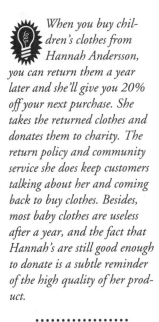

One T-shirt screen-printer sends out post-cards offering her customers a free T-shirt for every twelve ordered by someone they refer to the company. That's one way of hiring your customers to market your business for you. This particular T-shirt company doesn't even have to invest in postage. They just throw a postcard in with every order they ship out.

When you buy children's clothes from Hannah Andersson, you can return them a year later and she'll give you 20% off your next purchase. She takes the returned clothes and donates them to charity. The return policy and community service she does keep customers talking about her and coming back to buy clothes. Besides, most baby clothes are useless after a year, and the fact that Hannah's are still good enough to donate is a subtle reminder of the high quality of her product.

Restaurants rely on word of mouth for the bulk of their sales. Carmine's Restaurant in Manhattan developed several techniques guaranteed to increase word of mouth. First, they only accept reservations for parties of six or more. This requires their customers to find four friends to join them for dinner if they don't want to wait for a table. Second, they serve portions approximately double the normal size. This is guaranteed to generate enthusiastic discussions around the water cooler the next day at work. Finally, and with some brilliance, they load their food with an inordinate amount of garlic. The alliaceous affect of the garlic almost requires customers to tell their friends and family exactly how they acquired such an odor!

them about $16 a car, but it certainly generates a positive feeling—one that may translate into a personal recommendation.

Camp Arowhon sends each camper a birthday card annually. This gesture costs about fifty cents a kid, but the word of mouth it generates is worth far more.

Icons and Images, a typesetting firm in Connecticut, offers a standard turn-around of twenty-four hours on most jobs. But they often use a messenger to hand deliver a big job instead of relying on Federal Express. It only costs them a few extra dollars, and it gets the job to the client in a matter of hours. If they promised this extra service, it would be expected and probably less appreciated. But by delivering it as a free bonus, they win the loyalty of their demanding clients.

The Regent Beverly Wilshire (the hotel in the movie *Pretty Woman*) offers each guest a small snack. This snack consists of a silver bowl filled with perfect strawberries, another with whipped cream. While the hotel's location, interior, and service are terrific, people always seem to tell their friends about the strawberries.

MacConnection became the world's largest seller of Macintosh software by offering the fastest delivery in the industry. You can order software from them at midnight and have it delivered at no extra charge by the next day at noon. By focusing their business on speed, they raised the performance standard of the industry and generated significant word of mouth as well.

Guerrillas build their businesses by enlisting their customers to become salespeople.

WORD OF MOUTH BRAINSTORMS

Use this space to brainstorm a dozen ways your company can encourage existing customers to tell their friends about you.

_____

_____

_____

_____

_____

_____

_____

_____

_____

_____

CUSTOMER RESEARCH

The more you know about your customers the better you can serve them.

! BE CERTAIN TO RESPECT YOUR CUSTOMER'S ANONYMITY.
In the early 1970s, Business Week *magazine sent out a subscriber survey, asking all sorts of personal questions about income, investments, etc. In the survey, they promised to keep the results confidential, but an inspection of the survey under ultraviolet light indicated a hidden code number, making it easy for them to identify the respondent. This attempt to learn too much cost them the confidence and trust of that subscriber forever.*

So think twice before using any information on an individual, even in marketing that you do directly to that customer. Let the provider control what happens to that knowledge.

While customer research sounds a bit dull, it is one of the most powerful competitive weapons available to the guerrilla. It gives you insight into the desires and motives of your prospects. When properly executed, research may seem like cheating—it gives you the answers to the "will they buy" quiz before you spend a lot of money on marketing.

Never stop asking your customers questions. Customers are the best source of information about the most effective way to offer your product or service. In addition to generating valuable insight on how to run your business, your customers will be delighted you asked for their input.

Consider the countless times you've been kept standing in line at the airport, the doctor's office, or a restaurant, angrily thinking about how much better the service could be. Even a small business with one or two managers may have thousands of customers—all of whom can potentially give them free advice on what to sell and how to do it better.

You don't need to use a formal or expensive survey to get the process started. If you were interested in starting a meal delivery service, your first step would be to identify a group of potential customers. Once found, you'd need to determine what they'd like to buy and the best way to contact them (and others like them). To do so, you might create a survey like the one on the following page.

SAMPLE QUESTIONNAIRE

We're starting a new service that delivers dinners right to your home or apartment. You can order the meals from any of five restaurants on the menu we supply, then call us and we'll have the food to you within one hour. So that we can be of maximum service, we'd appreciate it if you would take a moment to answer these questions. Thank you!

How many people live in your home or apartment? _____

• What are their ages? _____

• Who usually prepares dinner where you live? _____

• How often do you eat out? _____

• What are the main benefits of having dinner delivered to your home?

1 _____

2 _____

3 _____

• How much would you pay for this service? _____

• What is your sex? M F

• What newspapers do you read? _____

• What radio stations do you listen to? _____

• What TV shows do you watch? _____

• Do you have cable TV?_____

• What magazines do you read? _____

• What type of work do you do? _____

• What are your favorite types of cuisine? _____

• Do you have any other comments or advice? Any restaurants you'd like to see included? Please use the back of this sheet to tell us your thoughts.

We're grateful for your time. If you give us your name and address, we'll send you a coupon good for free delivery of the first meal you order from us!

Name _____ Address _____

Even non-profit institutions can profit from surveys. The public library in Arlington, Massachusetts, knowing that it counted on community support for its funding, decided to survey its patrons. It put a ballot on the checkout counter, asking patrons whether the library should invest money in CDs, videotapes, or reference books.

The response was overwhelming and generated hundreds of suggestions on other topics as well. Naturally, when the library came up for funding at the next town council meeting, the newly empowered patrons were happy to support the additional funding.

Questionnaires need to be customer-friendly. It won't do you any good if nobody fills out and returns them. Avoid demographic questions about income or marital status. The easier (and more fun) you make the questions, the better your response. Keep the questionnaire short.

Try offering a coupon or a prize to anyone who returns the questionnaire. Donate a small amount to a local charity for each response. Let your customers know you value their opinions. Let them know that their feedback helps you provide them with better service.

Avoid leading questions (people will often tell you what you want to hear) but also avoid open-ended questions that people will balk at answering. The most effective questions allow YES or NO answers along with an explanation.

INFORMATION YOU CAN GATHER ON A QUESTIONNAIRE

➤ **Determine whether there is a need for your product. Do the people you are trying to reach already have your product or a good substitute.**

Do you own a home exercise machine?

When did you last buy a new car?

How often do you get a serious cold?

How often do you buy cold medication?

➤ **Find out more about your prospects.**

What is your occupation?

Where do your kids go to school?

How far do you commute to work?

How often do you exercise?

Do you enjoy the outdoors?

➤ **Find out the best way to reach your prospects.**

Do you read a daily newspaper. If so, which one?

Do you do most of your shopping in malls or in specialty shops?

How frequently do you buy something through a mail order catalog?

➤ **Who is the competition?**

What do you like most about the brand of soap you currently use?

How could your printer serve you better?

Which bank do you use?

Source: Target Marketing for the Small Business.

SUGGESTION BOXES

An ongoing way to survey your customers is to use a suggestion box. While this may seem quaint, it's a great way to get customer feedback *before* a small problem gets out of hand.

Stew Leonard's, the legendary supermarket, makes a big deal of its suggestion box. Every suggestion gets a response, and sometimes a coupon for a free ice cream cone. By carefully reading thousands of suggestions, management insures that they're not falling out of touch.

Be careful with your suggestion form. Remember that the average customer isn't going to spend much time with it. Better to get a large response to a few questions than to intimidate people with an overly long form. Offer a few multiple choice questions to get the survey started, then give them plenty of room to expand on their answers.

A top person should read and respond to every single suggestion (otherwise, what's the point?). No need to be defensive. The airlines are prime offenders here. One traveler we know was stuck in the smoking section on a Virgin Atlantic Airways flight from New York to London. He sent a letter to the airline, which responded by pointing out that they had a legal right to seat him there if there were no available seats. It's unclear how pointing this out was supposed to assuage his anger, but that was their answer. Virgin had a chance to turn a suggestion/complaint into a loyalty-building opportunity by offering a constructive solution and an apology, but instead let their ego get in the way and alienated the passenger.

Far better is the approach taken by Marriott. J.W. Marriott, Jr., the president of the company, personally reads and answers *every* letter to this huge company. In his letters, he usually takes personal responsibility for whatever occurred, and he ends by promising to try harder in the future. Marriott realizes that keeping customers is critical to their business, and J.W. Marriott demonstrates that by treating every incoming letter like the valuable customer survey that it is.

Hard Manufacturing was the leading producer of hospital cribs in the country, accounting for about 50% of the market. Sales growth was stalled until they did a survey.

Hard asked Pediatric Nurses, the professionals who actually use the cribs day in and day out, for advice on how to make a better crib. More than 40% of those surveyed responded— an astonishing number.

Ten years later, Hard is still profiting from the suggestions put forth by the nurses, many of which have been incorporated as patented improvements to Hard cribs. By producing exactly what its customers want, Hard has boosted its market share to more than 70%.

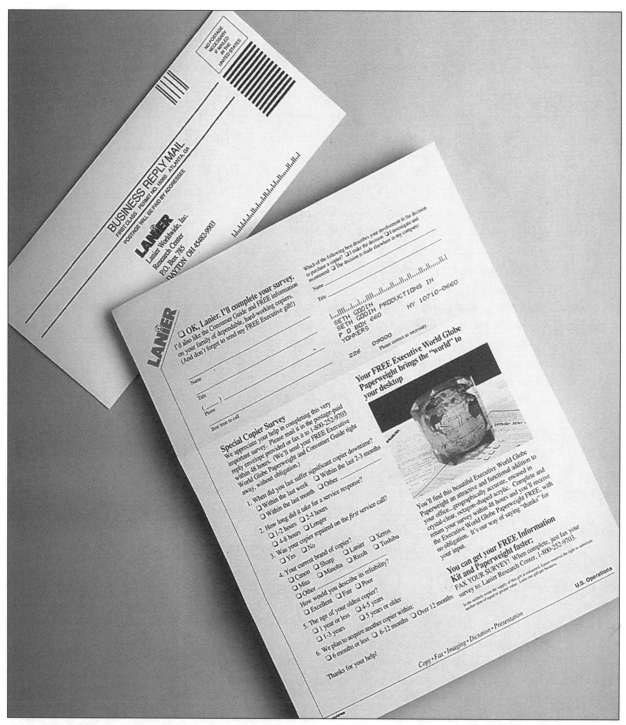

An actual customer survey used by Lanier Copiers. Notice that they offer something free to anyone who fills out the questionnaire, and they provide a business reply envelope so it's easy for people to send it back.

TELEPHONE SURVEYS

You'll be amazed at how much your customers are willing to tell you if you take the time to survey them over the phone. Consider using your incoming 800 line as an easy way to initiate a dialogue with your best customers. After a customer has called in and placed an order, have your operator ask, "Do you have a minute for me to ask you a few questions?" If the answer is yes, try to keep the session under a minute. While you need a script to make sure the questions are consistent from one customer to the next, try to keep the dialogue as unscripted as possible.

ORDERS ON ACCEPTANCE

Some businesses target markets that are hard to identify through a random survey. For example, you might decide to sell handmade brooches made out of obsolete computer chips. While this is conceivably a hot item, a general survey will make it difficult to find a target audience.

Mail order companies frequently run a test ad, soliciting orders for a product that does not yet exist. These dry tests are perfectly legal, as long as you follow a few simple steps:

➤ Make it clear in your ad that orders are subject to acceptance. You must inform recipients that there is the possibility that even though they have ordered the product, they might not receive it. In that instance, they'll just get their money back.

➤ Include your toll-free 800 phone number in the ad. When people call, take their order then survey them on the spot.

➤ Make it clear that you will only accept orders by phone. Don't cash any checks or deposit any payments that you receive by mail. Instead, send them back immediately, along with a note thanking them for their interest. Include a survey about future products you plan to sell and a small gift to apologize for any inconvenience you have caused.

The prospects you uncover during this initial stage may eventually become your best customers, so treat them well. They can spread word of mouth and give you product and sales advice.

GUERRILLA MARKET RESEARCH

In addition to direct research of your current customers, you can also profit by doing research on untapped markets you've decided to address. One way

NON-MEDIA

Guerrilla Success Story

Camp Arowhon is the oldest coed children's camp in North America. Located in Algonquin Park, Canada, several hours from Toronto, the camp is in the middle of nowhere.

Over the years, the camp attracted a loyal following, many of whom return for five, ten, or even fifteen summers. Some of them had parents or even grandparents who had attended the camp.

By 1985, shifting demographics and a stagnant Canadian economy had doomed many summer camps. Some shut down, others were losing money. Even Arowhon began feeling the pinch.

Joanne Kates, third generation director of Arowhon, decided to use guerrilla marketing to fill beds and increase market share. There were two straightforward elements to the campaign: Increase inquiries and turn those inquiries into sales.

The first step was to calculate a budget for the marketing campaign. Making use of an intensive customer survey, Joanne determined that her audience was not price sensitive. By raising prices 10% per year, she was able to generate additional money for marketing while positioning her camp as a premium product.

The camp generates inquiries by offering a free summer at camp as the prize in a sweepstakes. The actual cost of the

to obtain information at low cost is by employing the services of business students at a local college or university. The U.S. Small Business Administration sponsors the S.B.I. (Small Business Institute) Program that pairs businesses in need of market research with business schools throughout the country. This is also a great way for guerrillas to give something back to the educational system, offering students the opportunity to learn in real-life situations. The Small Business Administration gives the University $500 for each case the students complete. Call the Small Business Advancement National Center (501) 450-5377 for more information about the program, or write to the Office of Business Initiatives, Education and Training at the U.S Small Business Administration, 409 Third St. S.W., Mailcode 7110, Washington, DC 20416.

In addition to free research by business school students, you'll find enormous amounts of free market research in trade magazines. Most magazines do an annual industry update, in which they talk about gross sales, market leaders, major trends, etc. We're always amazed when we talk to fledgling entrepreneurs who have never bothered to subscribe to and read every single trade magazine covering their industry—these low-cost resources are invaluable.

Sometimes you need more specific and detailed market information than can be found though informal (and cheap) research. Two companies, Findex and Find SVP, specialize in selling expensive ($500 to $1,000) reports on specific industries. For example, for $900 Find SVP will sell you a 150-page report on the weight loss industry, complete with each major competitor, their estimated sales, projections on the future directions, etc. This may seem expensive, but it's often worth it, especially if the cost of launching your business is high.

KEEPING TRACK

You might think that you'll need sophisticated software to track your survey results. Actually, you can use virtually any computerized database, or even colored index cards.

The most important thing is consistency. If you want anything more than speculative focus group data (which is great as far as it goes) you'll need to be sure that you ask the same questions to a fairly large number of people. Try to design at least some of your questions to be easily quantified—yes or no questions are the easiest to answer and to track.

362

Once you've got hard data, it's much easier to make decisions. If you discover, for example, that 72% of your customers drink skim milk at home, the decision to stock it becomes pretty easy.

CUSTOMER RESEARCH RESOURCES

Marketing Research Association (MRA)
2189 Silas Dean Hwy., Ste. 5 • Rocky Hill, CT 06067 • (203) 257-4008

Target Marketing for the Small Business
by Linda Pinson and Jerry Jinnett
published by Upstart Publishing Company
12 Portland Street • Dover, NH 03820 • (800) 235-8866

Findex: The Worldwide Directory of Market Research, Reports, Studies and Surveys
7200 Wisconsin Ave. • Bethesda, MD 20814 • (800) 843-7751

prize is small, yet it was sufficient to double inquiries—each of which takes the form of a simple questionnaire.

To help turn inquiries into sales, Joanne invested funds in a brochure and a videotape that were signficantly better than the competition's.

Spending $15,000 more than her competition, Kates leapfrogged the other camps. By communicating quality and stability in every piece of communication sent to prospects, Camp Arowhon was able to increase market share.

There's been a waiting list for July slots at Arowhon for the last three years and August enrollments continue to climb.

APPENDIX

APPENDIX
FOR GUERRILLAS

When comparing advertising rates in different media, it is more important to look at CPM (cost per thousand) than straight ad prices. So, we've put together a random sampling of newspaper ad rates from across the country along with their CPMs. From this list, you can see that even though it costs more to buy a full page ad in the Fort Wayne (IN) Journal Gazette *than in the* Terre Haute Tribune Star, *the* Gazette *gives you a lot more bang for the buck.*

We've also included a random list of magazines to give you an idea of just how targeted you can get by advertising in them. Imagine you are in the business of selling classic cars. You probably couldn't advertise in a better publication than Special-Interest Autos.

APPENDIX

*Sample ad rates and
CPMs for newspapers
and magazines, radio
and television contacts,
and a list of the best
business books of all time.*

! *Most major newspapers
have different rates for
national and local adver-
tisers. So, if your company is
located in Alabama and you
want to place an ad in the*
Birmingham News, *make sure
you ask for the local ad rates,
which are lower than the
national rates.*

··················

NEWSPAPERS
··

*Here is a list of sample advertising rates and CPMs of several newspapers from each state.
The inch rates that we have quoted here are local rates.*

PAPER	TELEPHONE	AVG. DAILY CIRCULATION	AVG. DAILY INCH RATE	AVG. DAILY PAGE RATE	CPM
Alabama					
Birmingham News	(205) 325-2261	235,000	$54.08	$6,218.32	$26.46
Decatur Daily	(205) 353-4612	27,714	11.50	1,483.50	53.52
Jasper Mountain Eagle	(205) 221-2840	14,312	6.05	780.45	54.50
Alaska					
Anchorage Daily News	(907) 257-4200	76,488	39.95	5,153.55	67.38
Fairbanks Daily News Miner	(907) 456-6661	20,500	13.76	1,775.04	86.59
Juneau Empire	(907) 586-3740	21,000	13.76	1,733.76	82.56
Arizona					
The Arizona Republic	(602) 271-8000	485,000	154.18	12,154.38	25.06
Tribune Newspapers	(602) 898-6500	105,000	54.22	5,252.94	50.03
Daily News Sun	(602) 977-8351	17,000	10.50	1,354.50	79.68
Arkansas					
Arkansas Democrat-Gazette	(501) 378-3400	180,000	46.78	5,227.08	29.04
Jonesboro Sun	(501) 935-5525	30,000	11.45	1,477.05	49.23
Jacksonville Patriot	(501) 982-6506	16,000	6.50	955.50	59.72
California					
Los Angeles Times	(213) 237-5000	1,104,651	310.50	40,054.50	36.26
San Francisco Chronicle	(415) 777-1111	688,000	153.20	19,762.80	28.73
San Bernardino Sun	(909) 889-9666	94,000	38.36	3,947.58	42.00
Colorado					
Rocky Mountain News	(303) 892-5000	344,062	87.15	5,071.50	14.74
Co. Springs Gazette Telegraph	(719) 632-5511	102,000	37.50	4,837.50	47.43
Boulder Daily Camera	(303) 442-1202	34,633	16.19	1,931.13	55.76
Connecticut					
Hartford Courant	(203) 241-6200	231,922	138.00	10,672.17	46.02
Connecticut Post	(203) 333-0161	71,000	50.95	2,547.50	35.88
Norwich Bulletin	(203) 887-9211	33,359	20.00	2,257.50	67.67
Delaware					
News-Journal	(302) 324-2500	125,215	62.33	8,040.57	64.21
Delaware State News	(302) 674-3600	24,078	14.65	1,889.85	78.49
Washington, D.C.					
Washington Post	(202) 334-6000	832,000	176.00	17,556.00	21.10
Washington Times	(202) 636-3000	97,500	36.00	4,536.00	46.52
Florida					
Miami Herald	(305) 350-2111	405,779	134.50	18,157.50	44.75
Orlando Sentinel	(407) 420-5000	285,000	118.25	14,206.50	49.85
The News-Press	(813) 335-0200	116,477	55.90	7,211.10	61.91

PAPER	TELEPHONE	AVG. DAILY CIRCULATION	AVG. DAILY INCH RATE	AVG. DAILY PAGE RATE	CPM
Georgia					
Atlanta Constitution	(404) 526-5151	464,502	$131.88	$15,133.23	$32.58
Augusta Chronicle	(706) 724-0851	76,530	26.52	3,421.08	44.70
Marietta Daily Journal	(404) 428-9411	51,683	16.10	2,076.90	40.19
Hawaii					
Honolulu Advertiser	(808) 525-8000	192,000	65.45	8,065.13	42.01
Hawaii Tribune-Herald	(808) 935-6621	20,157	16.94	2,185.26	108.41
The Garden Island	(808) 245-3681	18,210	12.15	1,567.35	86.07
Idaho					
The Idaho Statesman	(208) 377-6400	64,238	28.94	2,878.92	44.82
Idaho Falls Post Register	(208) 522-1800	30,000	10.95	1,412.55	47.09
South Idaho Press	(208) 678-2201	14,000	10.10	1,302.90	93.06
Illinois					
Chicago Tribune	(312) 222-3232	600,000	42.00	4,539.00	7.57
The Daily Herald	(708) 870-3600	124,000	38.50	4,966.50	40.05
Daily Southtown Economist	(312) 586-8800	70,000	29.53	2,813.49	40.19
Indiana					
Indianapolis Star	(317) 633-1240	330,000	96.10	8,682.96	26.31
Fort Wayne Journal Gazette	(219) 461-8333	120,000	37.42	4,253.04	35.44
Terre Haute Tribune Star	(812) 231-4200	36,000	18.67	2,408.43	66.90
Iowa					
Cedar Rapids Gazette	(319) 398-8211	70,476	38.95	3,100.00	43.99
Sioux City Journal	(712) 279-5071	49,300	18.75	2,347.80	47.62
Telegraph Herald	(319) 588-5611	35,500	19.08	1,961.41	55.25
Kansas					
Wichita Eagle	(316) 268-6000	117,000	45.45	5,394.48	46.11
Hutchinson News	(316) 662-3311	38,100	11.92	1,525.76	40.05
Salina Journal	(913) 823-6363	31,000	11.40	1,453.50	46.89
Kentucky					
The Courier-Journal	(502) 582-4651	241,000	93.71	9,020.00	37.43
The Kentucky Post	(606) 292-7100	45,000	27.75	3,364.00	74.76
Mayfield Messenger	(502) 247-5223	7,600	6.70	774.00	101.84
Louisiana					
The Times Picayune	(504) 826-3279	280,000	104.38	12,622.50	45.08
The Advocate	(504) 383-1111	112,000	34.44	3,951.99	35.29
Lafayette Advertiser	(318) 235-8511	38,000	15.96	2,058.84	54.18
Maine					
Bangor Daily News	(207) 990-8000	73,330	30.00	3,870.00	52.78
Sun-Journal	(207) 784-5411	45,000	17.82	1,819.44	40.43

There are several companies throughout the United States that audit circulation data for various types of media, but the largest and most reputable is the Audit Bureau of Circulations. Located in Shaumburg, IL, the bureau audits circulations for newspapers and magazines. They provide printed releases called Publishers Statements *for anyone who subscribes to their service, and very often magazines and newspapers will include the statements in their media kits.*

Call the Audit Bureau of Circulations at (708) 605-0909.

PAPER	TELEPHONE	AVG. DAILY CIRCULATION	AVG. DAILY INCH RATE	AVG. DAILY PAGE RATE	CPM
Maryland					
Baltimore Sun	(410) 332-6000	406,000	$102.40	$9,009.00	$22.19
Frederick Post	(301) 662-1177	44,000	15.62	1,479.24	33.62
Hagerstown Daily Mail	(301) 733-5131	39,000	26.34	2,076.90	53.25
Massachusetts					
Boston Globe	(617) 929-2000	500,000	248.70	13,458.78	26.92
Boston Herald	(617) 426-3000	327,000	128.75	7,959.00	24.34
Springfield Union News	(413) 788-1200	113,498	33.74	4,352.46	38.35
Michigan					
Detroit Free Press	(313) 222-6400	1,200,000	263.00	34,321.50	28.60
Grand Rapids Press	(616) 459-1400	146,357	44.80	3,000.00	20.50
Lansing State Journal	(517) 377-1000	69,000	50.90	6,566.10	95.16
Minnesota					
Star Tribune	(612) 673-4000	413,603	184.60	10,936.62	26.44
St. Paul Pioneer Press	(612) 228-5427	211,000	61.10	6,384.42	30.26
Duluth News-Tribune	(218) 723-5281	65,000	29.16	2,431.80	37.41
Mississippi					
Jackson Clarion-Ledger	(601) 961-7000	110,000	53.13	3,956.40	35.97
Biloxi-Gulfport Sun Herald	(601) 896-2100	50,000	24.41	3,066.00	61.32
Natchez Democrat	(601) 442-9101	30,800	11.25	1,451.25	47.12
Missouri					
St. Louis Post Dispatch	(314) 340-8000	340,000	73.00	8,866.12	26.08
Kansas City Star	(816) 234-4141	291,299	103.01	12,041.70	41.34
Columbia Missourian	(314) 442-3161	40,000	8.60	1,109.40	27.74
Montana					
Billings Gazette	(406) 657-1200	57,000	28.00	2,672.97	46.89
Great Falls Tribune	(406) 761-6666	34,000	24.40	3,115.35	91.63
Havre Daily News	(406) 265-6796	5,000	5.99	638.55	127.71
Nebraska					
Omaha World-Herald	(402) 444-1000	224,000	47.30	4,423.41	19.75
Lincoln Star	(402) 475-4200	86,000	30.84	3,702.00	43.05
Beatrice Sun	(402) 223-5233	10,000	6.85	753.36	75.34
Nevada					
Las Vegas Review-Journal	(702) 383-0211	139,000	66.33	8,556.57	61.56
Reno Gazette Journal	(702) 788-6200	75,000	34.47	3,560.40	47.47
Elko Daily Free Press	(702) 738-3118	7,000	7.98	1,029.42	147.06
New Hampshire					
The Union Leader	(603) 668-4321	76,000	24.50	2,588.25	34.06
The Telegraph	(603) 882-2741	30,000	17.25	1,688.40	56.28
Berlin Reporter	(603) 752-1200	4,500	3.00	288.75	64.17
New Jersey					
The Star Ledger	(201) 877-4141	483,000	122.31	8,506.80	17.61
Asbury Park Press	(908) 922-6000	162,790	84.00	4,500.00	27.64
New Jersey Herald	(201) 383-1500	21,000	$14.67	$1,892.43	$90.12

PAPER	TELEPHONE	AVG. DAILY CIRCULATION	AVG. DAILY INCH RATE	AVG. DAILY PAGE RATE	CPM
New Mexico					
Albuquerque Journal	(505) 823-3800	151,936	66.25	8,385.00	55.19
New Mexican	(505) 983-3303	23,000	16.75	1,296.45	56.38
Los Alamos Monitor	(505) 662-4185	5,100	6.91	891.39	174.78
New York					
New York Times	(212) 556-1234	975,000	236.00	5,921.10	31.22
Long Island Newsday	(516) 454-2020	747,890	213.50	18,300.00	24.47
New York Daily Challenge	(718) 636-9500	77,000	45.90	5,921.10	76.90
North Carolina					
The Charlotte Observer	(704) 358-5000	232,294	59.71	6,593.40	28.38
Fayetteville Observer-Times	(910) 323-4848	45,000	25.10	3,237.90	71.95
Hickory Daily Record	(704) 322-4510	24,000	9.27	986.58	41.11
North Dakota					
The Forum	(701) 235-7311	65,500	28.00	3,500.00	53.44
The Bismark Tribune	(701) 223-2500	34,600	19.95	1,498.98	43.32
Ohio					
Cleveland Plain Dealer	(216) 344-4500	440,325	116.11	11,534.04	26.19
Columbus Dispatch	(614) 461-5000	265,773	77.90	8,290.80	31.20
Cincinnati Post	(513) 352-2000	104,863	53.98	6,963.42	66.40
Oklahoma					
The Daily Oklahoman	(405) 475-3311	255,000	73.36	12,055.05	47.27
Tulsa World	(918) 581-8300	186,271	53.49	5,585.70	29.99
Shawnee News-Star	(405) 273-4200	12,200	6.02	721.11	59.11
Oregon					
The Oregonian	(503) 221-8327	350,000	75.00	7,009.86	20.03
The Register-Guard	(503) 485-1234	77,900	25.89	2,594.34	33.30
Medford Mail Tribune	(503) 776-4411	27,576	13.10	1,344.18	48.74
Pennsylvania					
Philadelphia Inquirer	(215) 854-2000	500,000	185.71	17,188.00	34.38
Pittsburgh Post-Gazette	(412) 263-1100	252,000	85.00	9,638.00	38.25
Bucks County Courier Times	(215) 949-4000	72,000	33.92	3,125.67	43.41
Rhode Island					
The Evening Bulletin	(401) 277-7000	192,465	65.80	8,290.80	43.08
Woonsocket Call	(401) 762-3000	25,000	16.16	2,084.64	83.39
South Carolina					
The State	(803) 771-6161	150,000	40.00	5,040.00	33.60
Anderson Independent-Mail	(803) 224-4321	52,000	22.98	2,964.42	57.01
Greenville Piedmont	(803) 298-4100	128,000	42.30	4,636.80	36.23
South Dakota					
Argus Leader	(605) 331-2300	54,000	22.55	2,193.00	40.61
Rapid City Journal	(605) 394-8300	37,500	16.71	2,105.46	54.14
Brookings Register	(605) 692-6271	5,800	5.25	586.95	101.20

PAPER	TELEPHONE	AVG. DAILY CIRCULATION	AVG. DAILY INCH RATE	AVG. DAILY PAGE RATE	CPM
Tennessee					
Memphis Commercial Appeal	(901) 529-2211	200,000	$84.32	$9,702.30	$48.51
Knoxville News-Sentinel	(615) 523-3131	127,000	34.28	4,099.95	32.28
Jackson Sun	(901) 427-3333	38,000	23.75	3,063.75	80.63
Texas					
Houston Chronicle	(713) 220-7171	1,000,000	93.20	12,022.80	12.02
Austin American-Statesman	(512) 445-3500	174,000	41.65	4,663.26	26.80
Amarillo Daily News	(806) 376-4488	116,000	26.58	2,978.61	25.68
Utah					
The Salt Lake Tribune	(801) 237-2045	186,000	38.50	4,966.50	26.70
Deseret News	(801) 237-2100	65,000	38.50	4,966.50	76.41
Daily Spectrum	(801) 673-3511	23,000	9.86	868.00	37.74
Vermont					
Burlington Free Press	(802) 863-3441	54,000	35.95	3,000.00	55.56
Valley News	(603) 298-8711	19,000	9.05	1,126.73	59.30
Newport Daily Express	(802) 334-6568	5,500	5.63	708.64	128.84
Virginia					
Richmond Times-Dispatch	(804) 649-6000	211,000	49.32	6,153.84	29.17
The News & Advance	(804) 385-5555	41,000	24.31	3,135.99	76.49
Washington					
Seattle Times	(206) 464-2111	420,000	112.48	15,184.80	36.15
Spokesman-Review	(509) 459-5430	123,000	43.98	4,605.30	37.44
The Olympian	(206) 754-5420	36,000	22.95	2,282.01	63.39
West Virginia					
Charleston Gazette	(304) 348-5100	105,000	29.60	3,275.55	31.20
Wheeling News-Register	(304) 233-0100	48,000	16.12	1,644.72	34.27
Welch Daily News	(304) 436-3144	6,000	5.15	664.35	110.73
Wisconsin					
Milwaukee Journal	(414) 224-2000	230,000	61.98	7,995.42	34.76
Wisconsin State Journal	(608) 252-6100	118,000	36.55	4,714.95	39.96
The Journal Times	(414) 634-3322	38,000	21.50	1,994.34	52.48
Wyoming					
Casper Star-Tribune	(307) 266-0500	33,750	16.50	2,128.50	63.07
Wyoming State Tribune	(307) 634-3361	18,500	10.50	1,354.50	73.22
Rawlins Daily Times	(307) 324-3411	4,000	5.10	335.00	83.75

MAGAZINES

Here is a list of sample advertising rates and CPMs for a sampling of magazines (national, regional, and trade) published throughout the country.

MAGAZINE	TELEPHONE	AVG. PAID CIRCULATION	FULL PAGE AD RATE	1/3 PAGE AD RATE	CPM
The Advocate	(213) 871-1225	66,000	$2,950	$1,050	$44.70
Air Conditioning, Heating, & Refrigeration News	(313) 362-3700	35,724	7,311	2,600	204.65
Allure	(212) 880-8800	697,690	22,750	8,760	32.61
American Health	(212) 366-8900	800,000	21,040	8,750	26.30
The American Lawyer	(212) 973-2800	15,000	5,725	2,740*	381.67
Army Magazine	(703) 841-4300	105,396	3,890	1,520	36.91
The Atlantic	(212) 830-1900	450,000	12,110	4,720	26.91
Better Homes & Gardens	(212) 551-7068	7,600,000	127,750	50,075	16.81
Body, Mind & Spirit	(401) 351-4320	150,000	3,330	1,335	22.20
Business Ethics	(612) 962-4700	14,000	1,350	756	96.43
Business Week	(212) 512-3598	985,000	54,230	21,675	55.06
Car and Driver	(313) 649-1950	1,055,403	49,645	22,340	47.04
CD Review	(903) 924-7271	95,000	6,600	3,080	69.47
The Chemist	(301) 652-2447	5,000	560	230	112.00
Chocolatier	(212) 239-0855	150,000	5,108	2,178	34.05
Corvette Fever	(813) 644-7610	68,000	2,329	862	34.25
Cosmopolitan	(212) 649-3303	2,627,491	59,275	22,265	22.56
Country America	(212) 551-7036	1,000,000	32,300	13,000	32.30
Creativity Magazine	(212) 210-0100	25,725	6,093	1,863 *	236.85
Esquire	(212) 649-2000	737,134	29,555	11,825	40.09
Essence	(212) 642-0600	950,000	21,800	9,400	22.95
Family	(212) 532-0660	570,000	13,000	5,500	22.81
Family Circle	(212) 463-1000	5,000,000	95,520	37,810	19.10
Field & Stream	(212) 779-5450	2,000,000	48,460	18,010	24.23
Flower & Garden	(816) 531-5730	650,000	10,500	3,900	16.15
Forbes	(212) 620-2200	765,000	34,790	13,220	45.48
Fortune	(212) 586-1212	740,000	37,130	14,110	50.18
Game Informer Magazine	(612) 946-7245	200,000	4,103	NA	20.52
Harley Women	(708) 888-2645	20,000	948	378	47.40
Harper's Bazaar	(212) 903-5000	700,000	31,070	12,120	44.39
Inc.	(212) 326-2646	640,000	38,690	17,025	60.45
InfoWorld	(415) 572-7341	225,000	23,950	9,605	106.44
Ladies' Home Journal	(212) 953-7070	5,000,000	97,400	37,540	19.48
Law and Order	(708) 256-8555	31,778	2,175	865	68.44
Mac Home Journal	(415) 957-1911	82,000	5,200	2,200	63.41
MacWorld	(415) 243-0505	550,000	22,995	10,425	41.81
Mix	(510) 653-3307	44,745	3,035	1,345	67.83
Modern Bride	(212) 337-7000	351,712	24,150	8,950	68.66
Modern Maturity	(310) 496-2277	22,200,000	212,360	87,070	9.57
Mountain Bike	(719) 598-2272	120,000	3,685	1,695	30.71
Newsweek	(212) 445-4000	3,100,000	81,475	32,590	26.28

Before advertising in a magazine, call up and get them to send you a media kit. Not only will you get a sample issue of the magazine, but you'll get a whole packet of information about how to place your ad, deadlines, rates, special discounts if they exist, and special issues of the magazine that might be appropriate for your ad. Media kits are also full of demographic information about the market you'll be reaching with your ad, as well as statistical information from the Audit Bureau of Circulations.

MAGAZINE	TELEPHONE	AVG. PAID CIRCULATION	FULL PAGE AD RATE	1/3 PAGE AD RATE	CPM
The New Yorker	(212) 840-3800	700,000	$31,585	$11,725	$45.12
Ocean Navigator	(207) 772-2466	14,500	1,190	490	82.07
Omni	(910) 275-9809	700,000	21,730	9,995	31.04
Parents	(212) 878-8700	1,825,000	48,270	22,130	26.45
PC Techniques	(602) 483-0192	35,000	2,595	865	74.14
People	(212) 522-1212	3,150,000	83,000	35,500	26.35
Playboy	(312) 751-8000	3,400,000	48,860	21,680	14.37
Prevention	(212) 697-2040	3,150,000	42,220	17,315	13.40
Progressive Farmer	(205) 877-6000	640,000	29,273	11,709	45.74
Roads & Bridges	(708) 298-6622	65,000	5,255	2,365	80.85
Rolling Stone	(212) 484-1616	1,175,000	50,005	17,500*	42.56
Self	(212) 880-8800	1,314,315	33,410	12,730	25.42
Seventeen	(212) 407-9700	1,850,000	36,285	12,750	19.61
Shelter	(901) 853-7720	24,639	2,050	815	83.20
Shop Talk	(312) 978-6400	70,000	4,738	2,203	67.69
Shutterbug	(407) 268-5010	87,265	3,750	1,630	18.68
Sierra	(415) 923-5656	500,000	17,810	7,035	35.62
Soldier of Fortune	(303) 449-3750	105,000	2,200	880	20.95
Special-Interest Autos	(802) 442-3101	37,000	840	360	22.70
Sports Illustrated	(212) 522-1212	3,150,000	92,895	92,895	29.49
Spy	(212) 260-7210	165,000	6,120	2,720	37.09
Star	(212) 979-4810	3,375,000	39,500	17,550	11.70
Tennis	(203) 373-7000	800,000	30,720	12,030	38.40
Time	(212) 522-1212	4,000,000	101,000	40,400	25.25
TV Guide	(215) 293-8500	14,000,000	107,600	46,200	7.69
U.S. News & World Report	(202) 955-2000	2,150,000	56,300	22,585	26.19
US Magazine	(212) 484-1616	1,100,000	34,215	16,085	31.10
USA Weekend	(212) 715-2100	18,200,000	238,420	82,810	13.10
V.F.W. Magazine	(212) 532-0660	2,000,000	18,000	6,325	9.00
Video Business	(212) 887-8400	44,500	7,000	NA	157.30
Vogue	(212) 880-8405	1,100,000	38,600	14,660	35.09
Woman's Day	(212) 767-6000	4,600,000	92,895	36,710	20.19
Working Mother	(212) 551-9500	925,000	31,085	12,925	33.61

* 1/4 page ad rate.

RADIO NETWORK DIRECTORY

One of the strengths of radio is that it is such a local medium. There are fewer strong broadcasting networks than there are in television. This makes it easier and cheaper to buy local time, but it also presents challenges if you want to buy a nationwide (or even regional) ad slate without contacting each radio station individually.

A number of radio networks syndicate hour-long shows or news or feature bits. In exchange for the programming, the local station permits the network to include national advertising in the show. This advertising is often surprisingly inexpensive, and you can reach a huge, fairly targeted audience without much trouble. Here are the largest networks. Contact them for information about specific shows.

The American Sports Radio Network, Inc.
5025 Centennial Blvd. • Colorado Springs, CO 80919 • (719) 528-7040

American Urban Radio
463 7th Ave. • New York, NY 10018 • (212) 714-1000

Arbitron
142 West 57th St. • New York, NY 10019 • (212) 887-1300

ABC Radio Network
125 West End Ave. • New York, NY 10023 • (212) 456-5200

Banner Radio
125 West 55th St. • New York, NY 10019 • (212) 424-6160

CBS Radio Network
51 West 52nd St. • New York, NY 10019 • (212) 975-5354

CBS Spot Sales
51 W. 52nd St. • New York, NY 10019 • (212) 975-6769

CMN Radio Network
271 Madison Ave. • New York, NY 10016 • (212) 532-1900

Keystone Broadcasting
P.O. Box 1739 • Sharon, CT 06069 • (203) 364-2080

NBC Radio Networks/Westwood One
1700 Broadway • New York, NY 10019 • (212) 237-2500

Standard News Network
P.O. Box 64577 • Virginia Beach, VA 23467 • (804) 579-2369

USA Radio Network
2290 Spring Lake Rd. • Dallas, TX 75234 • (214) 484-3900

TELEVISION NETWORK DIRECTORY

Listed below are the phone numbers and addresses of the top broadcast and cable television stations throughout the country. They can give you national advertising rates and direct you to the right affiliates to find local and regional advertising information.

America's Disability Channel (ADC)
1777 Northeast Loop 410 • San Antonio, TX 78217 • (210) 824-7446

Arts & Entertainment Network (A&E)
235 E. 45th St. • New York, NY 10017 • (212) 661-4500

Black Entertainment TV (BET)
380 Madison Ave. • New York, NY 10017 • (212) 697-5500

Cable News Network (CNN)
Turner Broadcasting Network • 1 CNN Center • Box 105366
Atlanta, GA 30348 • (404) 827-1700

Capital Cities/ABC
77 W. 66th St. • New York, NY 10023 • (212) 456-7777

CBS Network Sales
51 W. 52nd St. • New York, NY 10019 • (212) 975-8058

Comedy Centeral (COM)
1775 Broadway • New York, NY 10019 • (212) 767-8600

Country Music Television (CMT)
685 3rd Ave., 20th floor • New York, NY 10017 • (212) 916-1000

Courtroom Television Network
600 3rd Ave. • New York, NY 10016 • (212) 973-2800

CNBC
2200 Fletcher Ave. • Fort Lee, NJ 07024 • (201) 585-2622

The Discovery Channel (DSC)
641 Lexington Ave., 8th floor • New York, NY 10022 • (212) 751-2120

The Family Channel (FAM)
977 Centerville Turnpike • Virginia Beach, VA 23467 • (804) 523-7301

Fox TV
205 E. 67th St. • New York, NY 10021 • (212) 452-5555

NBC Network
30 Rockefeller Plaza • New York, NY 10112 • (212) 664-4444

Turner Broadcasting Sales
420 Fifth Ave. • New York, NY 10018 • (212) 852-6600

OUR FAVORITE BUSINESS AND MARKETING BOOKS

Here is our list of recommended reading for all guerrillas. These books provide a solid foundation in sales, marketing, positioning, management, and copywriting techniques. If your local bookstore is out of stock and is unable to order a copy for you, try ordering through Harry W. Schwartz Bookshops, one of the leading business booksellers in the country. Their number is (800) 236-7323. **Of course, we also recommend the entire Guerrilla Marketing series!** *The titles are listed in the front of the book.*

MARKETING

Beyond 2000, the Future of Direct Marketing
by Jerry I. Reitman • Published by NTC Books

The greatest minds in direct marketing, including Herschell Gordon Lewis, Ron Bliwas, and Carol Nelson, contribute essays and advice on the future.

MaxiMarketing
by Stan Rapp & Thomas L. Collins • Published by Plume

Beyond MaxiMarketing
by Stan Rapp & Thomas L. Collins • Published by McGraw-Hill

Rapp and Collins have clearly articulated a new way of looking at markets and marketing. Their first book was remarkably prescient in predicting many of the changes that have occured in the last decade.

In Search of Excellence
by Tom Peters & Robert H. Waterman, Jr. • Published by Warner Books

Liberation Management
by Tom Peters • Published by Alfred A. Knopf, Inc.

Thriving on Chaos
by Tom Peters • Published by HarperPerennial

Along with Jay Levinson, Tom Peters is one of the inventors of modern marketing thought. In Search of Excellence *is the foundation of many of the concepts discussed in the other two books, and if you haven't read it, you should.*

The One to One Future
by Don Peppers & Martha Rogers, Ph.D
Published by Currency/Doubleday

The future of marketing is rapidly arriving. And the future is in database marketing. This book is the first to outline exactly what's involved in database marketing and points the way to the next generation of techniques and tools.

The Golden Mailbox
by Ted Nicholas • Published by Enterprise Dearborn

A very complete and readable look at the entire process of direct marketing. Ted Nicholas, one of the leading experts on the subject, covers everything from choosing your product to writing and designing your direct mail piece.

The Republic of Tea
by Mel Ziegler and Bill Rosenzweig • Published by Currency/Doubleday

A step-by-step look at the creation and marketing of a small business, complete with business plan. Inspirational.

POSITIONING

Positioning
by Al Ries & Jack Trout • Published by Warner Books

Bottom-Up Marketing
by Al Ries & Jack Trout • Published by Plume

Two classics of basic marketing thought from masters of the topic. If you are only going to read one marketing book (other than this one!), it should be Positioning.

ADVERTISING AND COPYWRITING

Direct Mail Copy that Sells
by Herschell Gordon Lewis • Published by Prentice-Hall

How to Make Your Advertising Twice as Effective at Half the Cost
by Herschell Gordon Lewis • Published by Bonus Books

Herschell Gordon Lewis used to write blood-and-guts slasher movies. Fortunately for us, he switched to copywriting and quickly became the master and guru of his craft. These books are required reading for anyone who writes brochures, ads, letters, or catalog copy.

Tested Advertising Methods
by John Caples • Published by Reward Books

How to Make Your Advertising Make Money
by John Caples • Published by Prentice Hall

John Caples invented the science of testing and measuring advertising. In more than fifty years of creating some of the most successful advertising ever, Caples kept careful track of what worked and what didn't. He shares it in these two classics.

SELLING

Ziglar on Selling
by Zig Ziglar • Published by Berkley

Secrets of Closing the Sale
by Zig Ziglar • Published by Berkley

The best book ever written about sales and selling. The companion cassette series is well worth the investment. Ziglar on Selling *is the long-awaited sequel, and a nice companion.*

See You at the Top
by Zig Ziglar • Published by Pelican

The road to becoming successful in guerrilla marketing is often filled with setbacks and frustrations. This book is the best one we've seen on how to set goals, motivate yourself and hang in there until you've reached the top.

Selling the Dream
by Guy Kawasaki • Published by HarperCollins

Guy Kawasaki was one of the small group of marketers responsible for the Macintosh's incredible success. His one-on-one, take-no-prisoners approach is detailed in this book. Great fun to read.

Customers for Life
by Carl Sewell & Paul B. Brown • Published by Pocket Books

Carl Sewell runs the most successful car dealership in the world, in large part because of the guerrilla techniques he uses. He describes every one of them in detail in this book. Inspirational.

Delivering Knock-Your-Socks-Off Service
by Kristin Anderson & Ron Zemke • Published by AMACOM

A more technical look at Carl Sewell's approach to marketing.

MANAGEMENT

The 90-Minute Hour
by Jay Conrad Levinson • Published by Plume

Jay's classic book on how to manage your time. It's your most important asset—don't waste it.

Swim with the Sharks without Being Eaten Alive
by Harvey Mackay • Published by William Morrow and Company

Harvey Mackay reveals his methods for outmanaging, outmotivating, and outnegotiating the competition.

Thinkertoys
by Michael Michalko • Published by Ten Speed Press

Being a good guerrilla demands creativity and the ability to think flexibly. In Thinkertoys, Michael Michalco teaches you how to harness your creative ability and apply it to your business endeavors.

Paradigms (formerly entitled Future Edge)
by Joel Arthur Barker • Published by HarperBusiness

Not so much a marketing book as a neat way of thinking about the future and how it will affect your life. If you ran a railroad in 1938 or a lamp company in 1988 this book would have saved your business.

Reengineering the Corporation
by Michael Hammer & James Champy • Published by HarperBusiness

The future of business management is in this book. A must-read for managers at every level.

Our thanks to the staff of Harry W. Schwartz Bookshops for helping us compile our list. Schwartz's has one of the best collections of business and marketing books in the country and can be contacted at (800) 236-7323.

THE GUERRILLA MARKETING NEWSLETTER

The Guerrilla Marketing Newsletter provides you with state-of-the-moment insights to maximize the profits you will obtain through marketing. The newsletter has been created to furnish you with the cream of the new guerrilla marketing information from around the world. It is filled with practical advice, the latest research, upcoming trends, and brand-new marketing techiques—all designed to pay off on your bottom line.

All subscribers to *The Guerrilla Marketing Newsletter* are given this unique and powerful guarantee: Examine your first issue for 30 days. If you aren't convinced that the newsletter will raise your profits, your subscription fee will be refunded—along with $2 just for trying it.

To subscribe, merely call or write:
Guerrilla Marketing International
260 Cascade Drive, Box 1336
Mill Valley, CA 94942
(800) 748-6444, in California (415) 381-8361

ABOUT THE AUTHORS

Jay Conrad Levinson is the author of the classic international bestseller, *Guerrilla Marketing*, plus $15\frac{1}{2}$ widely acclaimed books on business, careers, and time. His marketing books, now the most popular in the world, appear in 31 languages, embarrassing the author, who doesn't understand 30 editions of his books. They are now required reading in many university MBA programs around the globe.

Jay taught guerrilla marketing at the extension division of the University of California at Berkeley and has been a practitioner of it in the United States, where he was a senior vice president and creative director for J. Walter Thompson Advertising, as well as in Europe, where he served on the board of directors and was creative chief at Leo Burnett Advertising

He publishes *The Guerrilla Marketing Newsletter*, writes a monthly column for magazines, newspapers, telephone on-hold networks, and two Internet on-line services. He also conducts summer Guerrilla Marketing Workshops in Northern California and speaks throughout the world. Jay has won major marketing awards in all media in Europe and North America, but his greatest rewards come in the profits he wins for guerrilla-minded business people. He is married to Patsy, has one daughter, Amy, and lives north of San Francisco, where he works three days a week and wants the world to do the same.

Seth Godin is the president of Seth Godin Productions, a rapidly growing creator and packager of information. He has written or edited more than 75 books, including *The Information Please Business Almanac, Business Rules of Thumb, eMarketing, The Internet White Pages, Email Addresses of the Rich and Famous,* and *The Select Guide to Executive Recruiters.* His work has been featured in *Fortune, Business Week, Worth, Rolling Stone, The Wall Street Journal, The New York Times,* and other publications.

Godin started his first business at the age of 16, running a ski club for his high school. While in college, he co-founded Tufts Student Resources, which became the largest student-run business in the country. Since earning his MBA from Stanford, Godin has collected guerrilla marketing success stories. Send him yours: over the Internet at seth@sgp.com, or by fax at (914) 693-8132.

Jay Conrad Levinson's
Guerrilla Marketing International

With the success of the Guerrilla Marketing books sprang Jay Conrad Levinson's Guerrilla Marketing International (1986) - a company founded with the understanding that most businesses are not IBM's nor AT&T's and don't have huge marketing budgets with which to work - a company organized with the purpose of helping businesses learn to use the power of guerrilla marketing instead of the brute force of enormous marketing budgets.

To learn more about Guerrilla Marketing services or products contact Guerrilla Marketing International, PO Box 1336, Mill Valley, CA 94942. (415) 381-8361. http://www.gmarketing.com

Now You Can Continue
To Be a Guerrilla Marketer with
<u>The Guerrilla Marketing Newsletter</u>!

Now you can continue being an informed guerrilla marketer with The Guerrilla Marketing Newsletter. It provides you with state-of-the-moment marketing tips and insights to maximize your business profits.

To receive a free sample issue of The Guerrilla Marketing Newsletter, or to order, call 800-748-6444. Subscription rate is $59 yr. for 6 issues.